Health Policymaking
in the
United States

Third Edition

Health Policymaking in the United States

Third Edition

Beaufort B. Longest, Jr.

AUPHA
HAP

Your board, staff, or clients may also benefit from this book's insight. For more information on quantity discounts, contact the Health Administration Press Marketing Manager at (312) 424-9470.

This publication is intended to provide accurate and authoritative information in regard to the subject matter covered. It is sold, or otherwise provided, with the understanding that the publisher is not engaged in rendering professional services. If professional advice or other expert assistance is required, the services of a competent professional should be sought.

The statements and opinions contained in this book are strictly those of the author(s) and do not represent the official positions of the American College of Healthcare Executives, of the Foundation of the American College of Healthcare Executives, or of the Association of University Programs in Health Administration.

06 05 04   5 4 3 2

Library of Congress Cataloging-in-Publication Data

Longest, Beaufort B.
    Health policymaking in the United States / Beaufort B. Longest.— 3rd ed.
      p. ; cm.
    Includes bibliographical references and index.
    ISBN 1–56793-173-1 (alk. paper)
    1. Medical policy—United States—Decision making. 2. Health planning—
    United States. 3. Medical laws and legislation—United States. 4. Policy sciences—
    Methodology. I. Title.
    [DNLM: 1. Health Policy—United States. 2. Health Planning—legislation &
    jurisprudence—United States. 3. Policy Making—United States. WA 525 L852h
    2002]
    RA395.A3 L66 2002
    362.1'0973—dc21   2001051689

Acquisitions editor: Marcy McKay; Project manager: Joyce Sherman; Book and cover designer: Matt Avery.

Health Administration Press
A division of the Foundation
  of the American College
  of Healthcare Executives
1 North Franklin Street, Suite 1700
Chicago, IL 60606
(312) 424-2800

Association of University Programs
  in Health Administration
730 11th Street, NW
4th Floor
Washington, DC 20001
(202) 638-1448

For

BugHunter Boyardee & DJ Eviction

Their ages.   Their stages.

They *always* amazes.

CONTENTS

LIST OF ACRONYMS AND INITIALS

AAAC	Accreditation Association for Ambulatory Care
AAFP	American Academy of Family Physicians
AAHP	American Association of Health Plans
AAHSA	American Association of Homes and Services for the Aging
AAMC	Association of American Medical Colleges
AAP	American Academy of Pediatrics
AARP	American Association of Retired Persons
ACHE	American College of Healthcare Executives
ACP-ASIM	American College of Physicians–American Society of Internal Medicine
ACS	American Cancer Society
	American College of Surgeons
ADA	American Dental Association
	Americans with Disabilities Act
AFDC	Aid to Families with Dependent Children
AHA	American Heart Association
	American Hospital Association
AHCA	American Health Care Association
AHCPR	Agency for Health Care Policy and Research (Now Agency for Healthcare Research and Quality)
AHRQ	Agency for Healthcare Research and Quality (Formerly the Agency for Health Care Policy and Research)
AIDS	acquired immunodeficiency syndrome

AMA	American Medical Association
AMC	academic medical center
AMWA	American Medical Women's Association
ANA	American Nurses Association
APHIS	Animal and Plant Health Inspection Service
ARTCA	Antimicrobial Regulation Technical Corrections Act
AUPHA	Association of University Programs in Health Administration
BBA	Balanced Budget Act of 1997
BBRA	Balanced Budget Refinement Act of 1999
BCBSA	Blue Cross and Blue Shield Association
BIO	Biotechnology Industry Organization
BSR	Business for Social Responsibility
CARE	Ryan White Comprehensive AIDS Resources Emergency Act
CBA	cost-benefit analysis
CBO	Congressional Budget Office
CBSR	Canadian Business for Social Responsibility
CCD	Consortium for Citizens with Disabilities
CDC	Centers for Disease Control and Prevention
CDF	Children's Defense Fund
CEA	cost-effectiveness analysis
CERCLA	Comprehensive Environmental Response, Compensation and Liability Act
CFC	chlorofluorocarbon
CFR	*Code of Federal Regulations*
CHAMPUS	Civilian Health and Medical Program of the Uniformed Services
CHIP	Children's Health Insurance Program
CMS	Centers for Medicare & Medicaid Services (Formerly the Health Care Financing Administration)
CNN	Cable News Network
COBRA	Consolidated Omnibus Budget Reconciliation Act
COGR	Council on Governmental Relations
CON	certificate of need
COPD	chronic obstructive pulmonary disease
COTH	Council of Teaching Hospitals
CPSC	Consumer Product Safety Commission
CQI	continuous quality improvement
CRS	Congressional Research Service

CT	computed tomography
DEFRA	Deficit Reduction Act
DHEW	Department of Health, Education, and Welfare (Now Department of Health and Human Services)
DHHS	Department of Health and Human Services (Formerly Department of Health, Education, and Welfare)
DOJ	Department of Justice
DRG	diagnosis-related groups
DSH	disproportionate share hospital
EPA	Environmental Protection Agency
ERISA	Employee Retirement Income Security Act
ESRD	end-stage renal disease
FACCT	Foundation for Accountability
FAHS	Federation of American Hospitals
FDA	Food and Drug Administration
FEHBP	Federal Employees Health Benefits Program
FIFRA	Federal Insecticide, Fungicide, and Rodenticide Act
FR	*Federal Register*
FSIS	Food Safety and Inspection Service
GAO	General Accounting Office
GDP	gross domestic product
GME	graduate medical education
GPO	Government Printing Office
HCFA	Health Care Financing Administration (Now Centers for Medicare & Medicaid Services)
HEDIS	Health Plan Employer Data and Information Set
HHA	home health agency
HHS	Health and Human Services
HIAA	Health Insurance Association of America
HIV	human immunodeficiency virus
HMO	health maintenance organization
HRSA	Health Resources and Services Administration
HSA	Health Systems Agency
ICF	intermediate care facility
IOM	Institute of Medicine

JCAHO	Joint Commission on Accreditation of Healthcare Organizations
MAACS	maximum allowable actual charges
MedPAC	Medicare Payment Advisory Commission
MPSMS	Medicare Patient Safety Monitoring System
MRI	magnetic resonance imaging
NAACP	National Association for the Advancement of Colored People
NACH	National Association of Children's Hospitals
NCHSR	National Center for Health Services Research and Technology Assessment
NCI	National Cancer Institute
NCQA	National Committee for Quality Assurance
NEDSS	National Electronic Disease Surveillance System
NHSC	National Health Service Corps
NIA	National Institute on Aging
NIBIB	National Institute of Biomedical Imaging and Bioengineering
NIH	National Institutes of Health
NMA	National Medical Association
NOW	National Organization for Women
NPA	National Policy Association
NPRM	notice of proposed rulemaking
NSF	National Science Foundation
OAR	Office of Aids Research (National Institutes of Health)
OBRA	Omnibus Budget Reconciliation Act
ODA	Orphan Drug Act
OMB	Office of Management and Budget
OSHA	Occupational Safety and Health Administration
PAC	political action committee
PhRMA	Pharmaceutical Research and Manufacturers of America
POS	point of service
PPO	preferred provider organization
PPRC	Physician Payment Review Commission
PPS	prospective payment system
PRO	Peer Review Organization

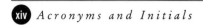

ProPAC	Prospective Payment Assessment Commission
PSRO	Professional Standards Review Organization
QuIC	Quality Interagency Coordination (task force)
RBRVS	resource-based relative value scales
RN	registered nurse
ROE	return on equity
SCHIP	State Children's Health Insurance Program
SHCC	State Health Coordinating Council
SHPDA	State Health Planning and Development Agency
SNF	skilled nursing facility
SSI	Supplemental Security Income
TANF	Temporary Assistance to Needy Families
TEFRA	Tax Equity and Fiscal Responsibility Act
TQM	total quality management
TSCA	Toxic Substances Control Act
UPMCHS	University of Pittsburgh Medical Center Health System
USDA	United States Department of Agriculture
USPHS	United States Public Health Service
VA	Veterans Affairs
WBGH	Washington Business Group on Health
WHO	World Health Organization
WISMedPAC	Wisconsin Medical Society Political Action Committee

LIST OF WEB SITES IN TEXT

Academy for Health Services Research and Health Policy	www.ahsrhp.org
Agency for Healthcare Research and Quality (Formerly the Agency for Health Care Policy and Research)	www.ahcpr.gov
Alcoa	www.alcoa.com
Alliance for Retired Americans (Formerly the National Council of Senior Citizens)	www.retiredamericans.org
American Academy of Family Physicians	www.aafp.org
American Academy of Pediatrics	www.aap.org
American Association of Health Plans	www.aahp.org
American Association of Homes and Services for the Aging	www.aahsa.org
American Association of Retired Persons	www.aarp.org
American Cancer Society	www.cancer.org
American College of Healthcare Executives	www.ache.org

American College of   www.acponline.org
  Physicians–American Society
  of Internal Medicine
American College of Surgeons   www.facs.org
American Dental Association   www.ada.org
American Health Care   www.ahca.org
  Association
American Heart Association   www.americanheart.org
American Hospital   www.aha.org/index.asp
  Association
American Medical Association   www.ama-assn.org
American Medical Women's   www.amwa-doc.org
  Association
American Nurses Association   www.ana.org
Association of American   www.aamc.org
  Medical Colleges
Association of University   www.aupha.org
  Programs in Health
  Administration

Baxter International Inc.   www.baxter.com
Biotechnology Industry   www.bio.org
  Organization
Blue Cross and Blue Shield   www.bluecares.com
  Association
Business for Social   http://www.bsr.org
  Responsibility

Cable News Network   www.cnn.com
Canadian Business for Social   http://www.cbsr.bc.ca
  Responsibility
Census Bureau   www.census.gov
Centers for Disease Control   www.cdc.gov
  and Prevention
Centers for Medicare and   www.cms.gov
  Medicaid Services
    (Formerly Health Care
    Financing Administration)
Cone, Inc.   www.coneinc.com
Conference Board   www.conference-board.org
Congressional Budget Office   www.cbo.gov

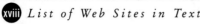

PREFACE

THE DECISIONS that constitute health policy occupy an increasingly important place in American life. Not only does health remain an important personal goal of most people, but also its pursuit is of increasing significance to the nation's economy and to its system of social justice. Thus, it should surprise no one that health policy receives a great deal of attention from government.

Health policy is defined in this textbook as the set of authoritative decisions made within government that pertain to health and to the pursuit of health. The phrase *authoritative decisions* is crucial in the definition and refers to decisions that are made anywhere within the three branches of government—at any level of government—that are within the legitimate purview (i.e., within the official roles, responsibilities, and authorities) of those making the decisions.

Through a long history of incremental and rather modest steps, an extensive array of health policies has evolved in the United States. Although this history has been punctuated occasionally by dramatic developments in health policy, especially the emergence of Medicare and Medicaid in 1965, it is a story of slow but persistent evolution and modification.

Health policy's role in the pursuit of health is played out across many fronts because health is determined by many variables: the physical environment in which people live and work, their biology and behavior, social factors, and access to health services. The effects of health policies are seen in each of these determinants of health.

Whether at the federal, state, or local level, governments formulate, implement, and constantly modify health policies within an intricately choreographed policymaking process. The central and unifying purpose of this book is to provide a comprehensive model of this process for those who have an interest in or a curiosity about health policy and the policymaking process. An understanding of this process is essential to political competence. For typical health professionals, political competence is at most a secondary interest. However, a degree of political competence sufficient to permit one to effectively analyze the public policy environment that affects them and their work, and to exert influence in that environment, is an increasingly important attribute for those whose professional lives are devoted to the pursuit of better health.

The model of the health policymaking process presented in this book was first developed and refined for the benefit of my students. The fact that the model proved useful as a framework for their understanding of the extraordinarily complicated process of health policymaking stimulated me to present it to a broader audience through the first edition of this book. The second edition was, and now this third edition is, driven by the fact that the book has been utilized in courses in health policy as a means to provide students with an overview of the policymaking process. The model offers a useful framework for putting the various aspects of policymaking in perspective and serves as a foundation on which students can build their more detailed knowledge of the process.

The structure of this textbook largely reflects the model of the policymaking process. Following definitions of health and of health policy in chapter 1, a new chapter 2 emphasizes the ways policy affects health determinants. An overview of the context (the political marketplace) and the process of policymaking are presented in chapter 3. The various components of the process are presented in detail in chapters 4–7. Chapter 8, another new chapter, addresses the concept and elements of political competence, defined as the dual ability to analyze the public policy environment of a health-related organization, system, or interest group and to exert influence in this environment. Information to strengthen both abilities is also presented.

The book includes an appendix that lists chronologically the most important federal laws pertaining to health enacted in the United States. In addition to providing synopses of these laws, the chronology illustrates several important characteristics of the nation's health policy. The list clearly shows, for example, that the vast majority of health policies are but modifications of or amendments to previously enacted laws. Incrementalism has indeed prevailed in the development of American health policy. The list also shows that health policy mirrors the various determinants of health. There are policies to address the environments in which people live, their lifestyles, and their genetics, as well as numerous policies related to the provision and payment for health services.

In this edition, a feature called The Real World of Health Policy has been added. Scattered throughout the text, the reader will find excerpts from Congressional testimony, examples of rules or proposed rules issued by implementing agencies, reprints of illustrative news stories, executive orders, and other documents that illustrate how the policymaking process unfolds. The intent is to enliven the text and to illustrate key aspects of health policy with these examples drawn from the real world.

ACKNOWLEDGMENTS

I wish to acknowledge the contributions made by several people to this revised book and to thank them for their help. Denise Warfield provided secretarial support. Linda Kalcevic provided superb editorial assistance throughout the revision. Mark Nordenberg, Arthur Levine, Herbert Rosenkranz, and Bernard Goldstein provided a professional environment conducive to and supportive of scholarship. I thank Marcy McKay and Joyce Sherman at Health Administration Press for their professional competence in bringing this book to fruition. Most of all, however, I want to thank Carolyn Longest. Sharing life with her continues to make many things possible for me and doing them seem worthwhile.

HEALTH AND HEALTH POLICY

HEALTH AND its pursuit are tightly interwoven into the social and economic fabric of all industrialized nations. Health plays a direct and very important role not only in the physical and psychological well-being of people, but in a nation's economic circumstances as well. Thus, it should be to no one's surprise that in the United States health and the activities associated with its pursuit receive considerable attention from all levels of government. This book is about the intricate process public policymakers use as one means through which to influence the pursuit of health—public policymaking. Attention is focused primarily on the policymaking process at the federal level, although much of what is covered applies to policymaking at the state and local levels.

In this chapter, the basic and underpinning definitions of health and health policy—and their relationship to each other—are discussed. In chapter 2 the impact of policy on health and its pursuit is considered more fully. In chapter 3 a model of the public policymaking process is outlined and described; this model is specifically applied to health policymaking. The various interconnected parts of the model are then covered in detail in subsequent chapters.

Health Defined

Although health is a universally important concept, its definition is far from universally agreed upon. Health can be considered in negative or positive terms and narrowly or broadly. Thought of negatively, health is viewed as the minimization, if not the absence, of some variable, as in the absence of infection or the shrinking of a tumor. At the extreme negative end of the conceptualization of health, it is thought of as the complete absence of disease or dysfunction.

In contrast, considered positively, health can be viewed as a state in which variables are maximized. For example, viewing health positively and broadly, the World Health Organization (WHO) (www.who.int) defines health as the "state of complete physical, mental, and social well-being, and not merely the absence of disease or infirmity" (WHO 1948). One contemporary version of this definition offered by economists Santerre and Neun (2000) considers health to be the condition in which a person is of sound body and mind and free of any disease or physical pain. Another contemporary definition of health, incorporating a positive and broad perspective, views health as a state in which the biological and clinical indicators of organ function are maximized and in which physical, mental, and role functioning in everyday life are also maximized (Brook and McGlynn 1991).

The way in which health is conceptualized or defined in any society is important because it reflects the society's values regarding health and how far the society might be willing to go in aiding or supporting the pursuit of health among its members. A society that defines health in negative and narrow terms might choose to intervene in the pursuit of health only in life-threatening traumas and illnesses. Conversely, a society in which health is defined broadly and in positive terms might obligate itself to pursue a variety of significant interventions in its efforts to help its members attain desired levels of health. Generally, negative and narrow conceptualizations of health lead to interventions that focus on correcting or reducing an undesirable state. Positive and broad conceptualizations of health, on the other hand, stimulate proactive interventions aimed at many variables in the quest for health.

Health Determinants

The enormous range of possible targets for intervention in the pursuit of health in any society is illustrated by the fact that health in human beings is a function of many variables, or health determinants as they are often called. Health determinants include, for individuals or for a population of individuals, the physical environments in which people live and work; their behaviors; their biology (genetic makeup, family history, and physical and mental health problems acquired during life); a host of social factors that include economic circumstances, socioeconomic position in society, and income distribution; discrimination based on factors such as race/ethnicity, gender, or sexual orientation, and the availability of social networks or social support; and the health services to which they have access (Blum 1983; Evans, Barer, and Marmor 1994; Berkman and Kawachi 2000).

The Real World of Health Policy

Healthy People 2010: Understanding and Improving Health

Healthy People 2010 *is a comprehensive, nationwide health promotion and disease prevention agenda. It is designed to serve as a roadmap for improving the health of all people in the United States during the first decade of the 21st century. Its overarching goals are (1) to help individuals of all ages increase life expectancy and improve their quality of life; and (2) to eliminate health disparities among different segments of the population in the United States. It identifies a set of determinants of health—individual biology and behavior, physical and social environments, policies and interventions, and access to quality healthcare (see Exhibit 1)—and notes that they have a profound effect on the health of individuals, communities, and the nation. Health determinants are identified and described as follows in* Healthy People 2010:

Biology refers to the individual's genetic makeup (those factors with which he or she is born), family history (which may suggest risk for disease), and the physical and mental health problems acquired during life. Aging, diet, physical activity, smoking, stress, alcohol or illicit drug abuse, injury or violence, or an infectious or toxic agent may result in illness or disability and can produce a "new" biology for the individual.

Behaviors are individual responses or reactions to internal stimuli and external conditions. Behaviors can have a reciprocal relationship to biology; in other words, each can react to the other. For example, smoking (behavior) can alter the cells in the lung and result in shortness of breath, emphysema, or cancer (biology) that then may lead an individual to stop smoking (behavior). Similarly, a family history that includes heart disease (biology) may motivate an individual to develop good eating habits, avoid tobacco, and maintain an active lifestyle (behaviors), which may prevent his or her own development of heart disease (biology).

Personal choices and the social and physical environments surrounding individuals can shape behaviors. The social and physical environments include all factors that affect the life of individuals, positively or negatively, many of which may not be under their immediate or direct control.

Exhibit 1

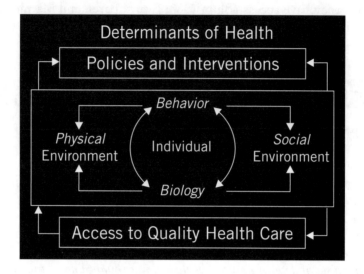

Social environment includes interactions with family, friends, co-workers, and others in the community. It also encompasses social institutions, such as law enforcement, the workplace, places of worship, and schools. Housing, public transportation, and the presence or absence of violence in the community are among other components of the social environment. The social environment has a profound effect on individual health, as well as on the health of the larger community, and is unique because of cultural customs; language; and personal, religious, or spiritual beliefs. At the same time, individuals and their behaviors contribute to the quality of the social environment.

Physical environment can be thought of as that which can be seen, touched, heard, smelled, and tasted. However, the physical environment also contains less tangible elements, such as radiation and ozone. The physical environment can harm individual and community health, especially when individuals and communities are exposed to toxic substances; irritants; infectious agents; and physical hazards in homes, schools, and worksites. The physical environment also can promote good health, for example, by providing clean and safe places for people to work, exercise, and play.

Policies and interventions can have a powerful and positive effect on the health of individuals and the community. Examples include health promotion campaigns to prevent smoking; policies mandating child restraints and safety belt use in automobiles; disease prevention services, such as immunization of children, adolescents, and adults; and clinical services, such as enhanced mental health care. Policies and interventions that promote individual and community health may be implemented by a variety of agencies, such as transportation, education, energy, housing, labor, justice, and other venues, or through places of worship, community-based organizations, civic groups, and businesses.

The health of individuals and communities also depends greatly on *access to quality health care*. Expanding access to quality health care is important to eliminate health disparities and to increase the quality and years of healthy life for all people living in the United States. Health care in the broadest sense not only includes services received through health care providers but also health information and services received through other venues in the community.

Source: Excerpted from U.S. Department of Health and Human Services. November 2000. *Healthy People 2010: Understanding and Improving Health.* 2nd ed. Washington, DC: U.S. Government Printing Office. This report can also be read on the Internet at www.health.gov/healthypeople.

In considering health in regard to individuals or populations, it is important to remember that people vary along many dimensions, including their health and their health-related needs. The citizenry of the United States is a remarkably diverse montage. Although not capturing the full richness of their diversity, nor all of the variation in their health and health-related needs, two demographic variables bear significantly on the health of the American people: the changing age structure of the population and its racial and ethnic diversity.

As Census 2000 revealed, about 35 million Americans were over the age of 65, and about 17 million of those were over 75 years of age (www.census.gov). By 2020, these numbers will increase to about 53 million and 21 million, respectively (Burner, Waldo, and McKusick 1992). These demographic changes are important in thinking about health and its pursuit because older people consume relatively more health services, and their health-related needs differ in significant ways from those of younger people. Older people are more likely to consume long-term-care services and community-based services intended to help them cope with various limitations in the activities of daily living.

Advancing age can mean increased fragility and susceptibility to acute health problems, such as injuries resulting from falls or infections and to chronic health problems such as emphysema or cirrhosis. Cardiovascular disease, cancer, diabetes, and osteoarthritis remain serious health problems for many elderly people. Especially devastating can be the combination of acute and chronic health problems with cognitive impairments such as Alzheimer's disease that occur with advancing age.

Although the view of the United States as a great melting pot of people and cultures was always more myth than reality, two groups now challenge this view in fundamental ways. African Americans and, especially, Latinos represent growing parts of the population. In Census 2000, approximately 35 million African Americans and 35 million Latinos were included in the United States population total of 281.4 million. Each group represented more than 12 percent of the total population. Both groups are presently disproportionately underserved for health services and are underrepresented in all of the health professions. Both groups suffer discrimination that significantly affects their health (Krieger 2000).

African Americans have long faced fewer opportunities for education, employment, health services, and long and healthy lives compared to the numerically predominant European Americans (Hacker 1992; Ayanian 1993). Gaps in health between these two groups continue (Williams 1999). For some of the same reasons, and for a variety of others, including language, geographic concentration, and cultural preferences, many Latinos are also unlikely to become well integrated into the nation's dominant culture.

Compelling evidence shows continuing disparities in the burden of illness and death experienced by African Americans, Latinos, and other racial and ethnic minorities including American Indians and Alaska Natives, compared to the United States population as a whole. Significant details about these disparities can be found on the Internet at www.statehealthfacts.kff.org, a web site maintained by the Kaiser Family Foundation. This resource offers comprehensive recent information for all 50 states, the District of Columbia, and U.S. territories on a broad range of health policy–related topics including managed care, health insurance coverage and the uninsured, Medicaid, Medicare, women's health, minority health, and HIV/AIDS.

The importance of addressing disparities in health status is magnified because the very groups currently experiencing poorer health status are expected to grow as a proportion of the total population. This has led the U.S. Department of Health and Human Services (DHHS) (www.dhhs.gov) to establish The Initiative to Eliminate Racial and Ethnic Disparities in Health (www.raceandhealth.hhs.gov). In implementing this initiative DHHS has identified six focus areas in which racial and ethnic minorities experience serious disparities in health access and outcomes: (1) infant mortality, (2) cancer screening and management, (3) cardiovascular disease, (4) diabetes, (5) HIV infection/AIDS, and (6) immunizations. These six health areas were selected for emphasis because disparities in them are known to affect multiple racial and ethnic minority groups and to do so at all life stages.

The continued existence of health disparities—and the injustices that underlay them—led the federal government to establish as one of the nation's highest health goals the elimination of these disparities. *Healthy People 2010* contains two overarching goals (see the Real World of Health Policy above). The first goal is increasing life expectancy and improving quality of life. The second goal is eliminating health disparities among different segments of the population, including differences that occur by gender, race or ethnicity, education or income, disability, geographic location, or sexual orientation (U.S. DHHS 2000).

Although the nation's population is diverse, with differences in health-related needs and with disparities in health status and in access to the benefits of the services of the healthcare system, the dominant culture does reflect a rather homogeneous set of values that directly affects the basic approach to health in the United States. To a very great extent, American society places a high value on individual autonomy, self-determination, and personal privacy and maintains a widespread, although not universal, commitment to justice for all members of the society. Other characteristics of the core society that significantly influence the pursuit of health include a deep-seated faith in the potential of technological rescue and, although it may be beginning to change, a long-standing obsession with prolonging life with scant regard for the costs of doing so. These values help shape the private and public sectors' efforts related to health, including the elaboration of public policies germane to health and its pursuit.

The Real World of Health Policy

Rules to Redesign and Improve Care

The Institute of Medicine (IOM) (www.iom.edu) is a private, nonprofit institution that provides health policy advice under a congressional charter granted to the National Academy of Sciences. In a recent report, Crossing the Quality Chasm: A New Health System for the 21st Century, *the IOM (2001) notes that healthcare today routinely fails to deliver its potential benefits and too frequently actually harms those it seeks to serve. The report describes a chasm between the healthcare the nation receives and the care it could receive. The report recommends a sweeping redesign of the American healthcare system and provides overarching principles for specific direction for policymakers, healthcare leaders, clinicians, regulators, purchasers, and others. The following is excerpted from the report itself and from a news release about the report.*

The nation's health care industry has foundered in its ability to provide safe, high-quality care consistently to all Americans, says a new report from the Institute of Medicine of the National Academies. Reorganization and reform are urgently needed to fix what is now a disjointed and inefficient system.

To spur an overhaul, Congress should create an "innovation fund" of $1 billion for use during the next three to five years to help subsidize promising projects and communicate the need for rapid and significant change throughout the health system, the report adds. Just as a solid commitment of public funds and other resources supported the ultimately successful mapping of the human genome, a similar commitment is needed to redesign the health care delivery system so all Americans can benefit.

* * *

To initiate across-the-board reform, the federal Agency for Healthcare Research and Quality [AHRQ] should identify 15 or more common health conditions, most of them chronic, the report says. Then, health care professionals, hospitals, health plans, and purchasers should develop strategies and action plans to improve care for each of these priority conditions over a five-year period.

To stay aware of the big picture, the U.S. Department of Health and Human Services (HHS) should monitor and track quality improvements in six key areas: safety, effectiveness, responsiveness to patients, timeliness, efficiency, and equity. And the secretary of HHS should report annually to Congress and the president on progress made in those areas, the report says.

In addition, public and private purchasers should develop payment policies that reward quality. Current methods provide little financial reward for improvements in the quality of health care delivery and may even inadvertently pose barriers to innovation. With input from relevant private and public interests, the federal government should identify, test, and evaluate various payment options that more closely align compensation methods with quality-improvement goals.

The committee also offers 10 new rules intended to make the health system more responsive to patients' needs and preferences and to encourage their participation in decision-making. These rules also are intended to promote the development of systems that are consciously and carefully designed to be safe, anticipate patient needs, promote cooperation among clinicians, use resources wisely, and make available information on quality and safety performance.

New Rules To Redesign And Improve Care

Private and public purchasers, health care organizations, clinicians, and patients should work together to redesign health care processes in accordance with the following rules:

1. *Care based on continuous healing relationships.* Patients should receive care whenever they need it and in many forms, not just face-to-face visits. This rule implies that the health care system should be responsive at all times (24 hours a day, every day) and that access to care should be provided over the Internet, by telephone, and by other means in addition to face-to-face visits.

2. *Customization based on patient needs and values.* The system of care should be designed to meet the most common types of needs, but have the capability to respond to individual patient choices and preferences.

3. *The patient as the source of control.* Patients should be given the necessary information and the opportunity to exercise the degree of control they choose over health care decisions that affect them. The health system should be able to accommodate differences in patient preferences and encourage shared decision-making.

4. *Shared knowledge and the free flow of information.* Patients should have unfettered access to their own medical information and to clinical knowledge. Clinicians and patients should communicate effectively and share information.

5. *Evidence-based decision-making.* Patients should receive care based on the best available scientific knowledge. Care should not vary illogically from clinician to clinician or from place to place.

6. *Safety as a system property.* Patients should be safe from injury caused by the care system. Reducing risk and ensuring safety require greater attention to systems that help prevent and mitigate errors.

7. *The need for transparency.* The health care system should make information available to patients and their families that allows them to make informed decisions when selecting a health plan, hospital, or clinical practice, or when choosing among alternative treatments. This should include information describing the system's performance on safety, evidence-based practice, and patient satisfaction.

8. *Anticipation of needs.* The health system should anticipate patient needs, rather than simply reacting to events.

9. *Continuous decrease in waste.* The health system should not waste resources or patient time.

10. *Cooperation among clinicians.* Clinicians and institutions should actively collaborate and communicate to ensure an appropriate exchange of information and coordination of care.

Source: Excerpted with permission of National Academy Press from Committee on Quality of Health Care in America, Institute of Medicine. 2001. *Crossing the Quality Chasm: A New Health System for the 21st Century.* Washington, DC: National Academy Press.

Health Policy Defined

In view of the obvious desirability of health to individuals as well as to the larger society and of the important role that the quest for health plays in the nation's economy—the United States spent more than $1.3 trillion in pursuit of health in 2000, and this could rise to more than $2.6 trillion by 2010 (see Figure 1.1)—it is not surprising that government at all levels is keenly interested in health and in how it is pursued. This interest is reflected vividly in the diverse activities that occur within the expansive forum of public policymaking and in the resulting public policies that relate to health.

Figure 1.1   Growth in National Health Expenditures

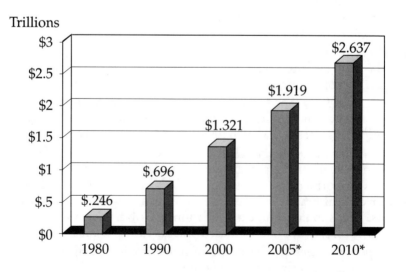

Trillions

Source: Health Care Financing Administration, Office of the Actuary, 2001.
*Projections.

There are many definitions of public policy, and no universal agreement on them. For example, Peters (1999) defines public policy as the "sum of government activities, whether acting directly or through agents, as it has an influence on the life of citizens." Birkland (2001, 132) defines public policy as "a statement by government of what it intends to do or not to do, such as a law, regulation, ruling, decision, or order, or a combination of these." Cochran and Malone (1995) define public policy as "political decisions for implementing programs to achieve societal goals." Drawing on these and many other definitions, in this book I define public policy as *authoritative decisions made in the legislative, executive, or judicial branches of government that are intended to direct or influence the actions, behaviors, or decisions of others.*

The phrase *authoritative decisions* is crucial in the definition of public policy. It specifically refers to decisions that are made anywhere within the three branches of government—at any level of government—that are within the legitimate purview (i.e., within the official roles, responsibilities, and authorities) of those making the decisions. The decision makers can be legislators, executives of government, or judges. Part of playing these decision-making roles is the legitimate right—indeed, the responsibility—to make certain decisions. For example, legislators are entitled to decide on laws, executives to decide on rules to implement laws, and judges to review and interpret decisions made by others. These relationships are illustrated in Figure 1.2. A useful web site for information about all three branches of the federal government, as well as information about state and local governments, is www.firstgov.gov. FirstGov is an official United States government web site.

In the United States, public policies, whether they pertain to health or to other policy domains such as defense, education, transportation, or commerce, are made through a dynamic *public policymaking process.* This process, which is modeled in chapter 3, involves many interactive participants in several interconnected phases of activities.

When public policies or authoritative decisions pertain to health or influence the pursuit of health, they are *health policies.* Health policies are established at federal, state, and local levels of government, although usually for different purposes. Generally, health policies affect or influence groups or classes of individuals (such as physicians, the poor, the elderly, or children) or types or categories of organizations (such as medical schools, managed care organizations, integrated healthcare systems, medical technology producers, or employers).

At any given time, the entire set of health-related policies, or authoritative decisions that pertain to health, made at any level of government can be said to constitute that level's *health policy.* Thus, health policy

Figure 1.2   Roles of Three Branches of Government in Making Policies

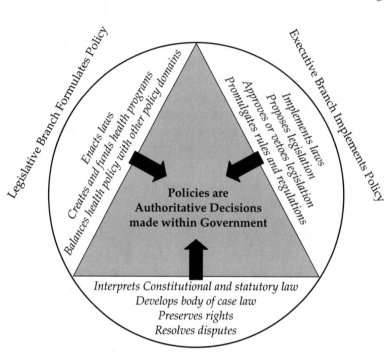

Judicial Branch Interprets Policy

is a very large set of decisions reached through the public policymaking process. It is useful to think of health policy as a set of numerous decisions rather than one large decision. Some countries, Canada and Great Britain most notably, have developed expansive, well-integrated policies to help shape their societies' pursuit of health in fundamental ways. These broad and expansive polices can be thought of as macro—health policies intended to govern their approaches to the pursuit of health almost entirely. The United States, in contrast, has a few large health-related policies, such as its Medicare program or its regulation of pharmaceuticals, but the U.S. government chooses a more incremental or piecemeal approach to health policy. The net result is a very large number of policies, but few of them dealing with the pursuit of health in any broad, comprehensive, or integrated way.

Policies made through the *public* policymaking process are distinguished from policies established in the *private* sector. Although it is beyond the scope of this book to discuss private-sector health policies in any depth, authoritative decisions made in the private sector by such decision makers as executives of healthcare organizations about such issues as their product lines, pricing, and marketing strategies, for example, are policies. Similarly, authoritative decisions made within such organizations as the Joint Commission on Accreditation of Healthcare Organizations (JCAHO) (www.jcaho.org), a private accrediting body for health-related organizations, or by the National Committee for Quality Assurance (NCQA) (www.ncqa.org), a private organization involved in assessing and reporting on the quality of managed care plans about what criteria to use in their reviews of healthcare organizations and managed care plans, are also private-sector health policies.

The Real World of Health Policy

Retiree Health Benefits

The General Accounting Office (GAO) (www.gao.gov) is the investigative arm of Congress. GAO exists to support the Congress in meeting its Constitutional responsibilities and to help improve the performance and accountability of the federal government for the American people. GAO examines the use of public funds, evaluates federal programs and activities, and provides analyses, options, recommendations, and other assistance to help Congress make effective oversight, policy, and funding decisions.

GAO's primary products are reports, often called "blue books," and testimony before Congress. GAO also issues correspondence (letters), which are narrower in scope, of more limited interest, and without recommendations. With virtually the entire federal government subject to its review, the agency issues a steady stream of products. The following material is excerpted from a correspondence report to the Chairman of the Committee on Health, Education, Labor, and Pensions of the U.S. Senate from Kathryn G. Allen, Director, Health Care—Medicaid and Private Insurance Issues.

May 1, 2001

The Honorable James M. Jeffords
Chairman, Committee on Health, Education, Labor, and Pensions
United States Senate

Dear Mr. Chairman:
In 1999, about 10 million retired people aged 55 and over relied on employer-sponsored health insurance as either their primary source of

coverage or a supplement to their Medicare coverage.[1] For some of these individuals, however, concerns exist that the continued availability of employer-sponsored coverage may be uncertain. As we reported in 1998, the percentage of employers offering retiree coverage to early retirees—those aged 55 to 64—had dropped from about 70 percent in the 1980s to about 40 percent in 1997.[2]

Concerned about declining employer-sponsored health coverage for early retirees and Medicare-eligible (age 65 and over) retirees, you asked us to examine if this trend is continuing. In particular, you asked that we examine

- changes employers have made to the availability and terms of their health insurance plans with respect to retiree coverage;
- how factors such as economic conditions, Medicare changes, and demographic trends may influence employers' future provision of retiree health benefits; and
- the ability of retirees without employer-sponsored coverage to obtain alternative coverage.

To answer these questions, we reviewed available employer survey data; analyzed the March supplements of the 1995 to 2000 Current Population Survey; reviewed applicable laws and court decisions pertaining to changes in employer-sponsored coverage; obtained individual insurance market premiums from insurers and health plans; and interviewed employee benefits consulting firms and several large employers. Appendix I (*not included in this excerpt*) provides additional information on our methodology. We conducted our work from June 2000 through February 2001 in accordance with generally accepted government auditing standards.

Results in Brief

Despite a sustained strong economy and several years of relatively low rates of increase in health insurance premiums, the decline in the availability of employer-sponsored retiree health benefits has not reversed since 1997—the last year for which we had reported previously—and several indicators suggest that there may be further erosion in these benefits. Employer benefit consultants we contacted generally indicated that retiree health benefits were continuing to decline. Two widely cited employer

---

1 In this report, "employer-sponsored" is used to refer to any employment-based group health coverage, including health plans offered under collectively bargained agreements and multiple employer associations.

2 *Private Health Insurance: Declining Employer Coverage May Affect Access for 55- to 64-Year-Olds* (GAO/HEHS-98-133, June 1, 1998). A list of related GAO products is included at the end of this report (*not included in this excerpt*).

benefit surveys, however, provide conflicting data as to whether the proportion of employers sponsoring retiree health insurance remained stable or declined slightly from 1997 through 2000. In some cases, employers provide retiree health benefits to current retirees or long-term employees, but newly hired employees are not eligible. To date, however, the percentage of retirees with employer-sponsored coverage has remained relatively stable over the past several years, with about 37 percent of early retirees and 26 percent of Medicare-eligible retirees receiving retiree health coverage from a former employer. This stability may also be linked to employers' tendency to reduce coverage for future rather than current retirees. In some cases, employers that continue to offer retiree health benefits have reduced the terms of these benefits by increasing the share of premiums that retirees pay for health benefits, increasing copayments and deductibles, or capping the employers' expenditures for coverage.

Several current and developing market, legal, and demographic factors may contribute to a further decline in employer-sponsored retiree health benefits. These factors include

- a resumption of health insurance premiums rising at a rate faster than general inflation;
- a slowdown in economic growth and potential softening of the labor market;
- proposed changes in Medicare coverage, such as adding a new prescription drug benefit, that could affect the costs and design of employers' supplemental health benefits for Medicare-eligible retirees;
- a recent circuit court ruling allowing claims of violations of federal age discrimination law when employers make distinctions in health benefits they offer retirees on the basis of Medicare eligibility; and
- the movement of the baby boom generation into retirement age, leading some employers to have a growing number of retirees relative to active workers.

Retirees whose former employers reduce or eliminate health benefits often face limited or unaffordable alternatives to obtaining coverage. Retirees may purchase coverage on their own—either individual insurance policies for those under 65 or Medicare supplemental plans for those 65 or older. However, despite federal laws that guarantee access to some individual insurance policies to certain individuals who lose group coverage, retirees' ages and often poorer health status combine to make individually purchased health insurance expensive. For example, the majority of states do not restrict the price of premiums carriers may charge individuals who purchase individual insurance policies. Thus, carriers in these states may charge 60-year-old males a monthly premium close to 4 times higher than what they charge 30-year-old males, and there may be an even bigger difference if the older individual is not healthy. Similarly, the number of Medicare supplemental plans that federal law guarantees to retirees over 65 whose employers eliminate coverage is limited, and they do not include coverage for benefits such as prescription drugs. Thus, retirees seeking alternative coverage could receive less comprehensive coverage and pay more for it than they had previously.

* * *

Sincerely yours,

Kathryn G. Allen
Director, Health Care—Medicaid and Private Insurance Issues

Source: Excerpted from United States General Accounting Office. May 2001. *Retiree Health Benefits: Employer-Sponsored Benefits May Be Vulnerable to Further Erosion.* Washington, DC: GAO, Report number GAO-01-374, a Correspondence Report to the Chairman, Committee on Health, Education, Labor, and Pensions, U.S. Senate.

This book focuses on the public policymaking process and on the public-sector health policies that result from this process. Private-sector health policies also play a vitally important role in the ways society pursues health. The rich and complex blend of public policies and private-sector policies and actions that shape the American pursuit of health is a reflection of the fact that Americans have been extraordinarily reluctant to yield control of the healthcare system to government. In part, this reflects a unique feature of the American psyche that Morone (1990, 1) captures eloquently when he says:

> At the heart of American politics lies a dread and a yearning. The dread is notorious. Americans fear public power as a threat to liberty. Their government is weak and fragmented, designed to prevent action more easily than to produce it. The yearning is an alternative faith in direct, communal democracy. Even after the loose collection of agrarian colonies had evolved into a dense industrial society, the urge remained: the people would, somehow, put aside their government and rule themselves directly.

In no aspect of American life is this "dread and yearning" more visible or relevant than in regard to health and to health policy. Despite a substantive role for government in health policy, which is more fully explored in subsequent chapters, and a role as a provider of health services in government facilities, most of the resources utilized in the pursuit of health in the United States are under the control of the private sector. Even when government is involved in health affairs, it often seeks ways to ensure broader access to health services that are provided predominantly through the private sector. As will be discussed extensively in this book, the Medicare and Medicaid programs are prime examples of this approach. [See Note 1; additional information can be found at the Centers for Medicare & Medicaid Services' web site (www.cms.gov). CMS was formerly the Health Care Financing Administration (HCFA).]

Forms of Health Policies

Health policies take one of several basic forms. Some policies are the decisions made by legislators that are codified in the statutory language of specific pieces of enacted legislation. These are laws. Other policies are the rules and regulations established in order to implement laws or to operate government and its various programs. Still others are the judicial branch's decisions related to health. Examples of health policies include:

- the 1965 federal public law (P. L. 89-97)[2] that established the Medicare and Medicaid programs;
- an executive order regarding operation of federally-funded health centers;
- a court's ruling that an integrated delivery system's acquisition of yet another hospital violates federal antitrust laws;
- a state government's procedures for licensing physicians;
- a county health department's procedures for inspecting restaurants; and
- a city government's ordinance banning smoking in public places within the city.

Thus, health policies may take any of several specific forms. The various forms in common represent a particular type of authoritative decision made within government.

Laws

Laws enacted at any level of government are policies. A federal law that is a health policy, for example, is the 1983 Amendments to the Social Security Act (P.L. 98-21) that authorized the prospective payment system (PPS) for reimbursing hospitals for Medicare beneficiaries. Another example is the Breast and Cervical Cancer Prevention and Treatment Act of 2000 (P.L. 106-354) that created an optional Medicaid category for low-income women diagnosed with cancer through the Centers for Disease Control and Prevention's (www.cdc.gov) breast and cervical cancer early detection screening program. State examples include state laws that govern the licensure of health-related practitioners and institutions. Laws, when they are "more or less freestanding legislative enactments aimed to achieve specific objectives" (Brown 1992, 21), are sometimes called programs. The Medicare program is a federal-level example. The Medicaid program, although actually financed jointly by federal and state governments, is a state-level example of a program.

The Real World of Health Policy

National Institute of Biomedical Imaging and Bioengineering Establishment Act

Public Law 106-580
106th Congress

An Act

To amend the Public Health Service Act to establish the National Institute of Biomedical Imaging and Bioengineering.

Be it enacted by the Senate and House of Representatives of the United States of America in Congress assembled,

SECTION 1. SHORT TITLE.

This Act may be cited as the "National Institute of Biomedical Imaging and Bioengineering Establishment Act".

SEC. 2. FINDINGS.

The Congress makes the following findings:

(1) Basic research in imaging, bioengineering, computer science, informatics, and related fields is critical to improving health care but is fundamentally different from the research in molecular biology on which the current national research institutes at the National Institutes of Health ("NIH") are based. To ensure the development of new techniques and technologies for the 21st century, these disciplines therefore require an identity and research home at the NIH that is independent of the existing institute structure.

(2) Advances based on medical research promise new, more effective treatments for a wide variety of diseases, but the development of new, noninvasive imaging techniques for earlier detection and diagnosis of

disease is essential to take full advantage of such new treatments and to promote the general improvement of health care.

(3) The development of advanced genetic and molecular imaging techniques is necessary to continue the current rapid pace of discovery in molecular biology.

(4) Advances in telemedicine, and teleradiology in particular, are increasingly important in the delivery of high quality, reliable medical care to rural citizens and other underserved populations. To fulfill the promise of telemedicine and related technologies fully, a structure is needed at the NIH to support basic research focused on the acquisition, transmission, processing, and optimal display of images.

(5) A number of Federal departments and agencies support imaging and engineering research with potential medical applications, but a central coordinating body, preferably housed at the NIH, is needed to coordinate these disparate efforts and facilitate the transfer of technologies with medical applications.

(6) Several breakthrough imaging technologies, including magnetic resonance imaging ("MRI") and computed tomography ("CT"), have been developed primarily abroad, in large part because of the absence of a home at the NIH for basic research in imaging and related fields. The establishment of a central focus for imaging and bioengineering research at the NIH would promote both scientific advance and United States economic development.

(7) At a time when a consensus exists to add significant resources to the NIH in coming years, it is appropriate to modernize the structure of the NIH to ensure that research dollars are expended more effectively and efficiently and that the fields of medical science that have contributed the most to the detection, diagnosis, and treatment of disease in recent years receive appropriate emphasis.

(8) The establishment of a National Institute of Biomedical Imaging and Bioengineering at the NIH would accelerate the development of new technologies with clinical and research applications, improve coordination and efficiency at the NIH and throughout the Federal Government, reduce duplication and waste, lay the foundation for a new medical information age, promote economic development, and provide a structure to train the young researchers who will make the pathbreaking discoveries of the next century.

SEC. 3. ESTABLISHMENT OF NATIONAL INSTITUTE OF BIOMEDICAL IMAGING AND BIOENGINEERING.

(a) In General.—Part C of title IV of the Public Health Service Act (42 U.S.C. 285 et seq.) is amended by adding at the end the following subpart:

Subpart 18—National Institute of Biomedical Imaging and Bioengineering

PURPOSE OF THE INSTITUTE

Sec. 464z. (a) The general purpose of the National Institute of Biomedical Imaging and Bioengineering (in this section referred to as the 'Institute') is the conduct and support of research, training, the dissemination of health information, and other programs with respect to biomedical imaging, biomedical engineering, and associated technologies and modalities with biomedical applications (in this section referred to as 'biomedical imaging and bioengineering').

(b)(1) The Director of the Institute, with the advice of the Institute's advisory council, shall establish a National Biomedical Imaging and Bioengineering Program (in this section referred to as the 'Program').

(2) Activities under the Program shall include the following with respect to biomedical imaging and bioengineering:

(A) Research into the development of new techniques and devices.

(B) Related research in physics, engineering, mathematics, computer science, and other disciplines.

(C) Technology assessments and outcomes studies to evaluate the effectiveness of biologics, materials, processes, devices, procedures, and informatics.

(D) Research in screening for diseases and disorders.

(E) The advancement of existing imaging and bioengineering modalities, including imaging, biomaterials, and informatics.

(F) The development of target-specific agents to enhance images and to identify and delineate disease.

(G) The development of advanced engineering and imaging technologies and techniques for research from the molecular and genetic to the whole organ and body levels.

(H) The development of new techniques and devices for more effective interventional procedures (such as image-guided interventions).

(3)(A) With respect to the Program, the Director of the Institute shall prepare and transmit to the Secretary and the Director of NIH a plan to initiate, expand, intensify, and coordinate activities of the Institute with respect to biomedical imaging and bioengineering. The plan shall include such comments and recommendations as the Director of the Institute determines appropriate. The Director of the Institute shall periodically review and revise the plan and shall transmit any revisions of the plan to the Secretary and the Director of NIH.

(B) The plan under subparagraph (A) shall include the recommendations of the Director of the Institute with respect to the following:

(i) Where appropriate, the consolidation of programs of the National Institutes of Health for the express purpose of enhancing support of activities regarding basic biomedical imaging and bioengineering research.

(ii) The coordination of the activities of the Institute with related activities of the other agencies of the National Institutes of Health and with related activities of other Federal agencies.

(c) The establishment under section 406 of an advisory council for the Institute is subject to the following:

(1) The number of members appointed by the Secretary shall be 12.

(2) Of such members—

(A) six members shall be scientists, engineers, physicians, and other health professionals who represent disciplines in biomedical imaging and bioengineering and who are not officers or employees of the United States; and

(B) six members shall be scientists, engineers, physicians, and other health professionals who represent other disciplines and are knowledgeable about the applications of biomedical imaging and bioengineering in medicine, and who are not officers or employees of the United States.

(3) In addition to the ex officio members specified in section 406(b)(2), the ex officio members of the advisory council shall include the Director of the Centers for Disease Control and Prevention, the Director of the National Science Foundation, and the Director of the National Institute of Standards and Technology (or the designees of such officers).

(d)(1) Subject to paragraph (2), for the purpose of carrying out this section:

(A) For fiscal year 2001, there is authorized to be appropriated an amount equal to the amount obligated by the National Institutes of Health during fiscal year 2000 for biomedical imaging and bioengineering, except that such amount shall be adjusted to offset any inflation occurring after October 1, 1999.

(B) For each of the fiscal years 2002 and 2003, there is authorized to be appropriated an amount equal to the amount appropriated under subparagraph (A) for fiscal year 2001, except that such amount shall be adjusted for the fiscal year involved to offset any inflation occurring after October 1, 2000.

(2) The authorization of appropriations for a fiscal year under paragraph (1) is hereby reduced by the amount of any appropriation made for such year for the conduct or support by any other national research

institute of any program with respect to biomedical imaging and bioengineering.

(b) USE OF EXISTING RESOURCES.—In providing for the establishment of the National Institute of Biomedical Imaging and Bioengineering pursuant to the amendment made by subsection (a), the Director of the National Institutes of Health (referred to in this subsection as "NIH")—

(1) may transfer to the National Institute of Biomedical Imaging and Bioengineering such personnel of NIH as the Director determines to be appropriate;

(2) may, for quarters for such Institute, utilize such facilities of NIH as the Director determines to be appropriate; and

(3) may obtain administrative support for the Institute from the other agencies of NIH, including the other national research institutes.

(c) CONSTRUCTION OF FACILITIES.—None of the provisions of this Act or the amendments made by the Act may be construed as authorizing the construction of facilities, or the acquisition of land, for purposes of the establishment or operation of the National Institute of Biomedical Imaging and Bioengineering.

(d) DATE CERTAIN FOR ESTABLISHMENT OF ADVISORY COUNCIL.—Not later than 90 days after the effective date of this Act under section 4, the Secretary of Health and Human Services shall complete the establishment of an advisory council for the National Institute of Biomedical Imaging and Bioengineering in accordance with section 406 of the Public Health Service Act and in accordance with section 464z of such Act (as added by subsection (a) of this section).

(e) CONFORMING AMENDMENT.—Section 401(b)(1) of the Public Health Service Act (42 U.S.C. 281(b)(1)) is amended by adding at the end the following subparagraph:

(R) The National Institute of Biomedical Imaging and Bioengineering.

SEC. 4. EFFECTIVE DATE.

This Act takes effect October 1, 2000, or upon the date of the enactment of this Act, whichever occurs later.

Approved December 29, 2000.

Rules or Regulations

The rules or regulations (the terms are used interchangeably in the policy context) established to guide the implementation of laws are another form of policies. Such rules, made in the executive branch of government by the organizations and agencies responsible for implementing laws are also policies. The rules associated with the implementation of complex laws routinely fill hundreds and sometimes thousands of pages. Rulemaking is an important and highly proscribed activity in the larger policymaking process and is discussed in detail in Chapter 4.

The Real World of Health Policy

A Food and Drug Administration (FDA) Rule Permitting Use of Ozone as an Antimicrobial Agent on Food, Including Meat and Poultry

Federal Register: June 26, 2001 (Volume 66, Number 123)
Rules and Regulations
Page 33829–33830

DEPARTMENT OF HEALTH AND HUMAN SERVICES
Food and Drug Administration

21 CFR Part 173
[Docket No. 00F-1482]

Secondary Direct Food Additives Permitted in Food for Human Consumption

AGENCY: Food and Drug Administration, HHS.

ACTION: Final rule.

SUMMARY: The Food and Drug Administration (FDA) is amending the food additive regulations to provide for the safe use of ozone in gaseous and aqueous phases as an antimicrobial agent on food, including meat and poultry. This action is in response to a petition filed by the Electric Power Research Institute, Agriculture and Food Technology Alliance.

DATES: This rule is effective June 26, 2001. Submit written objections and requests for a hearing by July 26, 2001. The Director of the Office of the Federal Register approves the incorporation by reference in accordance with 5 U.S.C. 552(a) and 1 CFR part 51 of a certain publication listed in Sec. 173.368(c), effective as of June 26, 2001.

ADDRESSES: Submit written objections to the Dockets Management Branch (HFA-305), Food and Drug Administration, 5630 Fishers Lane, rm. 1061, Rockville, MD 20852.

FOR FURTHER INFORMATION CONTACT: Robert L. Martin, Center for Food Safety and Applied Nutrition (HFS-215), Food and Drug Administration, 200 C St. SW., Washington, DC 20204-0001, 202-418-3074.

SUPPLEMENTARY INFORMATION: In a notice published in the *Federal Register* of September 13, 2000 (65 FR 55264), FDA announced that a food additive petition (FAP 0A4721) had been filed by the Electric Power Research Institute, Agriculture and Food Technology Alliance, 2747 Hutchinson Ct., Walnut Creek, CA 94598. The petition proposed to amend the food additive regulations in part 173 (21 CFR part 173) to provide for the safe use of ozone in gaseous and aqueous phases as an antimicrobial agent for the treatment, storage, and processing of foods.

The proposed use would include the use of this additive on raw agricultural commodities (RACs) in the preparing, packing, or holding of such commodities for commercial purposes, consistent with section 201(q)(1)(B)(i) of the Federal Food, Drug, and Cosmetic Act (the act) (21 U.S.C. 321(q)(1)(B)(i)), as amended by the Antimicrobial Regulation Technical Corrections Act of 1998 (ARTCA) (Public Law 105-324). The petitioner is not proposing that the additive be intended for use for any application under section 201(q)(1)(B)(i)(I), (q)(1)(B)(i)(II), or (q)(1)(B)(i)(III) of the act, which use would be subject to regulation by the Environmental Protection Agency (EPA) as a pesticide chemical. The proposed use of the additive includes the use to reduce the microbial contamination on RACs. Under ARTCA, the use of ozone as an antimicrobial agent on RACs in the preparing, packing, or holding of such RACs for commercial purposes, consistent with section 201(q)(1)(B)(i) of the act, and not otherwise included within the definition of "pesticide chemical" under section 201(q)(1)(B)(i)(I), (q)(1)(B)(i)(II), or (q)(1)(B)(i)(III) is subject to regulation by FDA as a food additive.

Although this use of ozone as an antimicrobial agent on RACs is regulated under section 409 of the act (21 U.S.C. 348) as a food additive, the intended use may nevertheless be subject to regulation as a pesticide under the Federal Insecticide, Fungicide, and Rodenticide Act (FIFRA). Therefore, manufacturers intending to market ozone for such use should contact the EPA to determine whether this use requires a pesticide registration under FIFRA.

FDA has evaluated data in the petition and other relevant material. Based on this information, the agency concludes that the proposed use of the additive is safe, that the additive will achieve its intended technical effect, and therefore, that the regulation in part 173 should be amended as set forth below.

In accordance with Sec. 171.1(h) (21 CFR 171.1(h)), the petition and the documents that FDA considered and relied upon in reaching its decision to approve the petition are available for inspection at the Center for Food Safety and Applied Nutrition by appointment with the information contact person listed above. As provided in Sec. 171.1(h), the agency will delete from the documents any materials that are not available for public disclosure before making the documents available for inspection.

The agency has carefully considered the potential environmental effects of this rule as announced in the notice of filing for FAP 0A4721. No new information or comments have been received that would affect the agency's previous determination that there is no significant impact on the human environment and that an environmental impact statement is not required.

This final rule contains no collection of information. Therefore, clearance by the Office of Management and Budget under the Paperwork Reduction Act of 1995 is not required.

Any person who will be adversely affected by this regulation may at any time file with the Dockets Management Branch (address above) written objections by July 26, 2001. Each objection shall be separately numbered, and each numbered objection shall specify with particularity the provisions of the regulation to which objection is made and the grounds for the objection. Each numbered objection on which a hearing is requested shall specifically so state. Failure to request a hearing for any particular objection shall constitute a waiver of the right to a hearing on that objection. Each numbered objection for which a hearing is requested shall include a detailed description and analysis of the specific factual information intended to be presented in support of the objection in the event that a hearing is held. Failure to include such a description and analysis for any particular objection shall constitute a waiver of the right to a hearing on the objection. Three copies of all documents are to be submitted and are to be identified with the docket number found in brackets in the heading of this document. Any objections received in response to the regulation may be seen in the Dockets Management Branch between 9 a.m. and 4 p.m., Monday through Friday.

List of Subjects in 21 CFR Part 173

Food additives, Incorporation by reference.

Therefore, under the Federal Food, Drug, and Cosmetic Act and under authority delegated to the Commissioner of Food and Drugs and redelegated to the Director, Center for Food Safety and Applied Nutrition, 21 CFR part 173 is amended as follows:

PART 173—SECONDARY DIRECT FOOD ADDITIVES PERMITTED IN FOOD FOR HUMAN CONSUMPTION

1. The authority citation for 21 CFR part 173 continues to read as follows:

Authority: 21 U.S.C. 321, 342, 348.

2. Section 173.368 is added to subpart D to read as follows:

Sec. 173.368 Ozone.

Ozone (CAS Reg. No. 10028-15-6) may be safely used in the treatment, storage, and processing of foods, including meat and poultry (unless such use is precluded by standards of identity in 9 CFR part 319), in accordance with the following prescribed conditions:

(a) The additive is an unstable, colorless gas with a pungent, characteristic odor, which occurs freely in nature. It is produced commercially by passing electrical discharges or ionizing radiation through air or oxygen.

(b) The additive is used as an antimicrobial agent as defined in Sec. 170.3(o)(2) of this chapter.

(c) The additive meets the specifications for ozone in the Food Chemicals Codex, 4th ed. (1996), p. 277, which is incorporated by reference. The Director of the Office of the Federal Register approves this incorporation by reference in accordance with 5 U.S.C. 552(a) and 1 CFR part 51. Copies are available from the National Academy Press, 2101 Constitution Ave. NW., Washington, DC 20055, or may be examined at the Office of Premarket Approval (HFS-200), Center for Food Safety and Applied Nutrition, Food and Drug Administration, 200 C St. SW., Washington, DC, and the Office of the Federal Register, 800 North Capitol St. NW., suite 700, Washington, DC.

(d) The additive is used in contact with food, including meat and poultry (unless such use is precluded by standards of identity in 9 CFR part 319), in the gaseous or aqueous phase in accordance with current industry standards of good manufacturing practice.

(e) When used on raw agricultural commodities, the use is consistent with section 201(q)(1)(B)(i) of the Federal Food, Drug, and Cosmetic Act (the act) and not applied for use under section 201(q)(1)(B)(i)(I), (q)(1)(B)(i)(II), or (q)(1)(B)(i)(III) of the act.

Dated: June 15, 2001.
L. Robert Lake,
Director of Regulations and Policy, Center for Food Safety and Applied Nutrition.

Operational Decisions

When organizations or agencies in the executive branch of a government, regardless of level, implement laws, they invariably must make many operational decisions as implementation proceeds. These decisions, which are different from the formal rules that also influence implementation, are also policies. For example, in implementing the Water Quality Improvement Act (P.L. 91-224) the several federal agencies with implementation responsibilities establish operational protocols and procedures that help them deal with those affected by the provisions of this law. These protocols and procedures, because they are authoritative decisions, are a form of policies.

The Real World of Health Policy

Expanding Access to Prescription Drugs for Safety-Net Patients

HHS News Release
June 18, 2001

A new initiative announced today by HHS Secretary Tommy G. Thompson will help community health centers and other safety-net providers develop new ways to expand their ability to buy drugs and improve access to prescription drugs for patients.

"Through this initiative, organizations will be able to stretch scarce resources and buy more of the drugs their patients need," Secretary Thompson said. "The initiative responds to proposals from local safety-net providers and it exemplifies our commitment to support grassroots efforts that improve primary care services for uninsured and underserved Americans."

Through demonstration projects, the new initiative will allow organizations that participate in the 340B drug discount program to take actions to reduce administrative costs and make buying drugs easier for patients. Entities approved for the demonstrations will be able to:

- participate in single purchasing and dispensing systems that serve covered entity networks;
- contract with multiple pharmacy services providers; and
- use contracted pharmacy services to supplement in-house pharmacy services.

By being able to undertake these activities, community health center networks and other covered entities will improve their economies of scale, allowing individual centers to purchase more drugs without increasing total expenditures. Contracting with multiple pharmacy service providers and supplementing in-house pharmacy services will improve patients' access to prescription drugs by increasing the number of pharmacy sites where these drugs can be obtained. This is an important improvement because patients of safety-net providers often cannot afford to travel from their neighborhoods to a distant pharmacy to have prescriptions filled.

Currently, organizations eligible to participate in the drug discount program—established by Section 340B of the Public Health Service Act—cannot take these cost-saving steps.

The 340B discount program requires drug manufacturers to sell drugs to specified safety-net health care providers at a discount rate determined by a formula in the legislation that created the program. Discounts average 25 percent to 40 percent on most drugs.

Approved demonstration projects will be time limited and will be evaluated on benefits provided as well as on compliance with requirements of the 340B law. If the demonstrations are successful, the new methods of accessing discounted drugs will be incorporated into the 340B program's published guidelines. Eligible organizations should submit proposals to the Health Resources and Services Administration's Office of Pharmacy Affairs. HRSA is the lead HHS agency for improving access to health care for individuals and families nationwide.

Source: www.hhs.gov/news, the web site of *HHS News.*

Judicial Decisions

Judicial decisions are another form of policies. An example is the United States Supreme Court's ruling in 2000 (by a 5–4 vote) that the Food and Drug Administration (FDA) (www.fda.gov) cannot regulate tobacco. Another is the United States Supreme Court's reversal in 1988 of the earlier decision of the United States Court of Appeals for the Ninth Circuit in the *Patrick v. Burget* case. The decision in this case, which involved the relationship between peer review of professional activities and antitrust liability, is a policy because the reversal is an authoritative decision that has the effect of directing or influencing the actions, behaviors, or decisions of others. As is often the case with judicial decisions, this one disrupted an established pattern of prior decisions and behaviors. Similarly, an opinion issued in 1992 by a DHHS administrative law judge stating that a hospital was in violation of the Rehabilitation Act Amendments of 1974 (P.L. 93-516) when it prohibited an HIV-positive staff pharmacist from preparing intravenous solutions is also a policy (Lumsdon 1992).

The Real World of Health Policy

Supreme Court of the United States
National Labor Relations Board v. Kentucky River Community Care, Inc., et al.
Certiorari to the United States Court of Appeals for the Sixth Circuit
No. 99-11815 Argued February 21, 2001—Decided May 29, 2001
When co-respondent labor union petitioned the National Labor Relations Board [NLRB] to represent a unit of employees at respondent's residential care facility, respondent objected to the inclusion of its registered nurses in the unit, arguing that they were "supervisors" under §2(11) of the National Labor Relations Act (ACT), 15 U.S.C. §152(11), and hence excluded from the Act's protections.

⁂

This passage from the syllabus released in connection with the Supreme Court's Slip Opinion for the case (which can be read in its entirety on the web site of the Supreme Court of the United States (www.supremecourtus.gov), describes one of the ways courts are involved in policymaking: interpretation of application of public laws. The importance of this role is reflected in the two news stories that appeared about the case in the American Hospital Association's newsletter, AHA News.

Supreme Court Case Focuses on NLRB Interpretation of Nurse Supervisor
The U.S. Supreme Court heard oral arguments February 21, 2001 in an appeal of a ruling by the 6th Circuit Court of Appeals involving the legal question of which nurses qualify as supervisors, exempting them from collective bargaining under the National Labor Relations Act.

In *National Labor Relations Board v. Kentucky River Community Care* (KRCC), the NLRB has asked the Supreme Court to resolve conflicts among the courts of appeal concerning interpretation of the term "independent judgment" in the act's definition of "supervisor."

The act defines a supervisor as "any individual having authority, in the interest of the employer, to hire, transfer, suspend, lay off, recall, promote, discharge, assign, reward, or discipline other employees, or responsibly to direct them, or to adjust their grievances, or effectively to recommend such action, if in connection with the foregoing the exercise of such authority is not of a merely routine or clerical nature, but requires the use of independent judgment."

In the 6th Circuit ruling, the appeals court rejected the NLRB's interpretation that nurses electing to join an AFL-CIO affiliate at KRCC, an operator of non-profit mental health facilities in Kentucky, were not supervisors.

Lane Dennard, a partner at King & Spalding in Atlanta who has argued a similar NLRB case for a health care employer, said employers hope the Supreme Court will provide additional instruction in interpreting independent judgment so they can clearly identify supervisors and train them in the act's provisions.

Michael Hawkins, a partner in Dinsmore & Shoal in Cincinnati who is representing KRCC before the Supreme Court, said the justices probed witnesses about NLRB's interpretation of independent judgment and the KRCC RNs' authority and duties.

A decision is likely by late April or May, he said.

Source: Reprinted from *AHA News*, Vol. 37, No. 8, by permission, February 26, 2001. Copyright 2001, by Health Forum, Inc.

* * *

Supreme Court Decision Seen Limiting Unions' Ability to Organize Nurses

In a 5–4 decision May 29, 2001, the U.S. Supreme Court ruled that registered nurses who use independent judgement in directing employees are supervisors, upholding a lower court ruling and thereby making it harder for unions to organize nurses into collective bargaining units.

In the case of *National Labor Relations Board (NLRB) vs. Kentucky River Community Care Inc.,* Justices William Rehnquist, Sandra Day O'Connor, Anthony Kennedy, Clarence Thomas and Antonin Scalia found that under the National Labor Relations Act (NLRA), the health care facility was accurate in its definition of the RNs as supervisors due to the nature of their duties, supporting an earlier decision by the 6th Circuit Court of Appeals.

Justices John Stevens, David Souter, Ruth Bader Ginsburg and Stephen Breyer dissented.

In his majority opinion, Scalia wrote that the NLRA deems employees to be supervisors if they practice one of 12 functions: authority to hire, transfer, suspend, lay off, recall, promote, discharge, assign, reward, discipline or direct other employees, or to adjust their grievances, if in connection with the foregoing the exercise of such authority is not of a merely routine or clerical nature. All of these functions require the use of independent judgment, the act states.

Scalia pointed to an earlier case of *NLRB vs. Health Care & Retirement Corp. of America,* in which the board argued that nurses did not exercise their authority in the interest of the employer when their independent judgment was exercised incidental to professional or technical judgment and, thus, were not supervisors.

But the court ruled in that case that an employee who uses independent judgment to engage in one of the 12 listed activities, including responsible direction of other employees, is a supervisor.

The court found that the board's test for determining supervisory status in the Kentucky case was inconsistent with the NLRA because the board rejected the facility's proof of supervisory status on grounds that employees do not use "independent judgment" when they exercise "ordinary professional or technical judgment in directing less-skilled employees to deliver services in accordance with employer-specified standards."

Stevens said in his dissenting opinion, "The National Labor Relations Board correctly found that [Kentucky River] failed to prove that the six registered nurses employed at its facility in Pippa Passes, KY, are "supervisors within the meaning of the National Labor Relations Act."

Stevens added that the court's willingness to treat the RNs as supervisors even if they have no subordinates is ironic when compared to the board's undisturbed decision to deny supervisory status to another group of professionals employed by the facility.

A spokesperson for AHA said the ruling will provide hospitals with more flexibility and will allow hospitals to use more fully the talents and knowledge of their nursing staffs as part to their supervisory teams.

The American Nurses Association (ANA) said the decision will have a chilling effect on the ability of nurses to form unions and gain workplace protections as employers try to claim that many more RNs are supervisors, because they direct the work of others such as nurses' aides and licensed practical nurses.

"By limiting the number of nurses who may be a part of a collective bargaining unit, this Supreme Court decision amounts to a partial gag order on nurses who want to protect patients from harmful management practices that routinely lead registered nurses to organize," said ANA President Mary Foley, R.N. "Without guaranteed workplace protections, nurses who continue to speak out on patient safety issues run the risk of losing their livelihoods."

Source: Reprinted from *AHA News,* Vol. 37, No. 22, by permission, June 4, 2001. Copyright 2001, by Health Forum, Inc.

Another way to consider health policies is to recognize that any type of policy, whether law, rule or regulation, operational decision, or judicial decision, fits into one of several broad categories of policies. The categories are typically divided into distributive, redistributive, and regulatory (Birkland 2001). Sometimes the distributive and redistributive categories are combined into an allocative category. Sometimes, the regulatory category is subdivided into competitive regulatory and protective regulatory categories (Ripley and Franklin 1991). For our purposes, as is discussed in the next section, all the various forms of health policies fit into one of two basic categories—allocative or regulatory.

Categories of Health Policies

In capitalist economies, such as that of the United States, the presumption is that private markets best determine the production and consumption of goods and services, including health services. In such economies, government generally intrudes with policies only when private markets fail to achieve desired public objectives. The most credible arguments for policy intervention in the nation's domestic activities begin with the identification of situations in which markets are not functioning properly.

The health sector is especially prone to situations in which markets do not function very well. Theoretically perfect (i.e., freely competitive) markets, which do not exist in reality but which provide a standard against which real markets can be assessed, require that:

- buyers and sellers have sufficient information to make informed decisions;
- a large number of buyers and sellers participate;
- additional sellers can easily enter the market;
- each seller's products or services are satisfactory substitutes for those of their competitors; and
- the quantity of products or services available in the market does not swing the balance of power toward either buyers or sellers.

The markets for health services in the United States violate these underpinnings of competitive markets in a number of ways. Complexity of health services reduces the ability of consumers to make informed decisions without guidance from the sellers or from other advisors. Entry of sellers in the markets for health services is heavily regulated, and widespread insurance coverage affects the decisions of both buyers and sellers in these markets. These and other factors mean that the markets for health services frequently do not function competitively, thus quite literally inviting policy intervention.

Furthermore, the potential for private markets, on their own, to fail to meet public objectives related to health and its pursuit in the society is not limited to the production and consumption of health services. For example, markets, on their own, might not stimulate the conduct of enough socially desirable medical research or the education of enough physicians or nurses without the stimulus of policies that subsidize certain costs associated with these ends. These and many similar situations in which markets do not lead to desired outcomes provide the underlying philosophical basis for the establishment of public policies to correct market-related problems or shortcomings.

The nature of the problems or shortcomings of the market that health policies are intended to overcome or ameliorate helps shape the policies in a direct way. Based on their basic purposes, health policies fit broadly into allocative or regulatory categories, although the potential for overlap between the two categories is considerable.

Allocative Policies

Allocative policies are designed to provide net benefits to some distinct group or class of individuals or organizations, at the expense of others, to ensure that public objectives are met. Such policies are in essence subsidies through which policymakers seek to alter demand for or supplies of particular products and services or to guarantee access to products and services for certain people. For example, on the basis that without subsidies to medical schools markets would undersupply the preparation of physicians, government has heavily subsidized the medical education system. Similarly, on the basis that markets would undersupply hospitals in sparsely populated regions or low-income areas, government subsidized the construction of hospitals for many years.

Other subsidies have been used to ensure that certain people have access to health services. The most important examples of such policies, based on the magnitude of expenditures, are the Medicare and Medicaid programs. Medicare expenditures exceeded $227 billion in 2000 and could reach $441 billion by 2010. Medicaid expenditures exceeded $201 billion in 2000 and could reach $446 billion by 2010 (HCFA 2001). In addition, federal funding to support access to health services for Native Americans, veterans, and migrant farm workers, and state funding for mental institutions are other examples of allocative policies that are intended to assist individuals in gaining access to needed services. Some think of subsidies as reserved for people on the basis of their impoverishment. However, subsidies such as those inherent in much of the financial support for medical education, the Medicare program, the benefits of which are not based primarily on the financial need of the recipients, and the exclusion from taxable income of employer-provided health insurance benefits illustrate that poverty is not a necessary condition for the receipt of the subsidies available through the allocative category of health policies.

Regulatory Policies

Policies designed to influence the actions, behaviors, and decisions of others by directive are regulatory policies. In a variety of ways, all levels of government establish regulatory policies. As with allocative policies, government establishes such policies to ensure that public objectives are met. The five basic categories of regulatory health policies are:

- market-entry restrictions;
- rate- or price-setting controls on health service providers;
- quality controls on the provision of health services;
- market-preserving controls; and
- social regulation.

The first four of these are variations of economic regulation; the fifth seeks to achieve such socially desired ends as safe workplaces, nondiscriminatory provision of health services, and reduction in the negative externalities (side effects) that can be associated with the production or consumption of products and services.

Market-entry-restricting regulations include those through which health-related practitioners and organizations are licensed. Planning programs, through which approval for new capital projects by health services providers must be obtained from the state before the projects can proceed, are also market-entry-restricting regulations.

Although price-setting regulation is out of favor, an example is government's control of the retail prices charged by natural gas or electric public utilities. Some aspects of the pursuit of health are also subject to price regulations. The federal government's control of the rates at which it reimburses hospitals for care provided to Medicare patients under the prospective payment system (PPS) and its establishment of a fee schedule for reimbursing physicians who care for Medicare patients are examples of price regulation with enormous impact.

A third class of regulations are those intended to ensure that health services providers adhere to acceptable levels of quality in the services they provide and that producers of health-related products such as imaging equipment and pharmaceuticals meet safety and efficacy standards. For example, the FDA is charged to ensure that new pharmaceuticals meet these standards. In addition, the Medical Devices Amendments (P.L. 94-295) to the Food, Drug and Cosmetic Act (P.L. 75-717) placed all medical devices under a comprehensive regulatory framework administered by the FDA.

Because the markets for health services do not behave in truly competitive ways, government intervenes in these markets by establishing and enforcing rules of conduct for market participants. These rules of conduct form a fourth class of regulation, market-preserving controls. Antitrust laws, such as the Sherman Antitrust Act, the Clayton Act, and the Robinson-Patman Act, which are intended to maintain conditions that permit markets to work well and fairly, are good examples of this type of regulation.

The four classes of regulations outlined above are all variations of economic regulation. The primary purpose of social regulation, the fifth class of regulation, is to achieve such socially desirable outcomes as workplace safety and fair employment practices and to reduce such socially undesirable outcomes as environmental pollution or the spread of sexually transmitted diseases. Social regulation usually has economic impact, but the impact is secondary to the primary purposes of the regulations. Federal and state laws pertaining to environmental protection, disposal of medical wastes, childhood immunization requirements, and the mandatory reporting of communicable diseases are but a few obvious examples of social regulations at work in the pursuit of health.

Whether public policies take the form of laws, rules or regulations, judicial decisions, or macro-policies, they are always established within the context of a complex public policymaking process. Both allocative and regulatory policies are made within the process, and the activities and mechanisms used to create both categories of policies are essentially identical. A comprehensive model of this process, which applies to any level of government, is presented in chapter 3. Before examining the model, however, it will be useful to consider the ways that health policies affect health and its pursuit. A direct and crucially important connection between health policies and health, which makes an understanding of the health policymaking process all the more important to everyone involved in the pursuit of health, is described briefly in the next section and more extensively in chapter 2.

The Connection Between Health Policies and Health

From government's perspective, the central purpose of health policy is to enhance health or to facilitate its pursuit by the citizenry. Of course, it is possible for other purposes to be served through specific health policies, including providing economic advantages to certain individuals and organizations. But the defining purpose of health policy, so far as

Figure 1.3 The Impact of Policy on Health Determinants and on Health

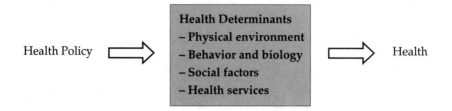

government is concerned, is to support the people in their quest for health.

Health policies have their impact on health through an intervening set of variables, health determinants. The health determinants, in turn, directly affect health. Thus, when examining the ways in which health policy can affect health, consider the role of health policy in the following health determinants:

- the physical environments in which people live and work;
- the behavioral choices that people make and the role that biology plays in their health;
- the social factors that affect people's health, including their economic circumstances; their socioeconomic position in society; income distribution within the society; discrimination based on factors such as race/ethnicity, gender, or sexual orientation; and the availability of social networks/social support; and
- the health services available to people and their access to these services.

Health policies have effects on each of these determinants of health, and thus on health, as shown in Figure 1.3. The nature of these effects is explored more fully in chapter 2.

The Real World of Health Policy

State Health Policy

An unsettled debate over the appropriate distribution between a strong central federal government and the states regarding health policy responsibilities dates from the nation's founding. Over the years, the balance has shifted from time to time, with the federal government playing an especially dominant role in health policy for most of the period since the mid-1960s. In recent years, however, stimulated by changes in states' responsibilities for operating the Medicaid program and the failure in the early 1990s of federally led attempts at comprehensive reform of the healthcare system, the traditional health policy roles of the states have been reinforced and, in some states, new broader roles in health policy have been undertaken.

Traditionally, the states have played substantial roles in several areas of health policy. Lipson (1997) identifies three in particular: (1) financing or paying for health services for several categories of people; (2) ensuring the public's health; and (3) regulating health-related professionals and organizations, including health insurance organizations and plans. In recent years, in some states, a fourth role has been added: experimenting with comprehensive health reform strategies.

In their roles as payers, states assume significant responsibility for funding their Medicaid programs. Although the costs of these programs are shared with the federal government, this program typically consumes 15 percent or more of state budgets. Medicaid is among the highest policy priorities—let alone, health policy priorities—for the states. In addition to their funding roles in the Medicaid program, the states also typically pay the costs of providing health insurance benefits for state employees and their dependents and, in many states, for other public-sector workers such as teachers. Some states have also developed programs to pay for health services for their uninsured citizens who are not covered by Medicaid (Gold 1997). It is highly likely that states will continue to play increasingly important funding roles as part of their health policy responsibilities.

States also have major health policy responsibilities in protecting the public's health, their oldest and most fundamental responsibility in the pursuit of health. States were granted constitutional authority to establish laws that protect the public's health and welfare. This responsibility engages states in protecting the environment (the federal government delegates to the states responsibility for monitoring the environment and ensuring that environmental standards are met within their boundaries); in ensuring safe practices in workplaces and food service establishments; in mounting programs to prevent injuries and promote healthy behaviors; and in providing health services such as public health nursing and communicable disease control, family planning and prenatal care, and nutritional counseling.

In their roles as regulators of health-related professionals and organizations, states rely on their legal authority to regulate almost every aspect of the healthcare system and many other aspects of the overall pursuit of health. The states license and regulate the various health professions through the provisions of their practice acts, and they license and monitor health-related organizations. States establish and monitor compliance with environmental quality standards.

A particularly important aspect of the role of states in health-related regulation is their responsibility for the health insurance industry as it operates within their boundaries. States control the content, marketing, and price of health insurance products and health plans because the 1945 McCarran-Ferguson Act (P.L. 79-15) left most insurance regulation to the states. However, some more recent changes in federal law illustrate both the current status of the tenuous line between federal and state regulation of this important aspect of the nation's pursuit of health and how fuzzy the line is now and may increasingly be in the future.

For example, the 1974 Employee Retirement Income Security Act (P.L. 93-406), commonly known as ERISA, preempts the states' regulation of pensions and self-insured employer health plans. The 1985 Consolidated Omnibus Budget Reconciliation Act (P.L. 99-272), also known as COBRA 1985, gives people leaving a job in any state the right to retain their existing employer-provided health insurance for up to 18 months by paying the premiums, plus a small surcharge, directly. The 1996 Health Insurance Portability and Accountability Act (P.L. 104-191) provides employees who work for companies that offer health insurance benefits guaranteed access to health insurance if and when they change jobs or become unemployed. The legislation also guarantees renewability of health insurance coverage so long as premiums are paid.

The coexistence of federal and state regulation of health insurance holds some difficult challenges for future policymaking, "as Congress and the states wrestle with such issues as how to mandate standards for managed care; whether to regulate physician-operated health networks as insurance companies; and how to insure children from families too rich to be eligible for Medicaid and too poor to afford private insurance" (Kuttner 1997, 67).

In recent years, a fourth health policy role has gained momentum and importance in many states; the states are expressing willingness to experiment with comprehensive approaches to healthcare reform. The states have long been viewed as "laboratories" for public policymaking (Sparer and Brown 1996). In the states, this view holds, combinations of problems and potential solutions can be addressed through policies. In so doing, the results in one state can demonstrate the possible usefulness of these solutions for other states and in some instances for federal policymakers.

In reality, to date, the role of states as laboratories for health policy has not been played particularly well. As Davidson (1997, 894) notes, in speaking of the states' efforts at comprehensive reform of their healthcare systems, "On the one hand, we have fifty individual political markets which, implicitly, act or fail to act for their own reasons; on the other hand, we have the phenomenon of many, if not most, states taking up the same thorny topic in the same period." He means that a variety of states, each pursuing solutions to the same problem in idiosyncratic ways under unique sets of reasons in the same time frames, are unlikely to treat each other as laboratories or to benefit much from the other's experiences. This view is supported by Oliver and Paul-Shaheen (1997, 721) who conclude from their study of six states that enacted major health reform legislation in recent years that the wide variation among their approaches to reform "casts doubt on the proposition that states can invent plans and programs for other states and the federal government to adopt for themselves."

However, whether or not the states are particularly good laboratories for other states or for the federal government, they are increasingly playing larger roles in health policy innovation. In the absence of federal solutions, they must find solutions to their own problems. States are increasingly struggling with a number of health policy issues and they will continue to face them well into the future (Peterson 1997). Their efforts to find solutions to the health-related problems facing their citizens, coupled with continuing expansion of their traditional roles in health policy, mean that states will have significant and growing roles in future health policy.

The Objectives of Health Policy

Some relationships in an increasingly complex world are so simple that they tend to be overlooked in the effort to understand more baffling challenges. One such relationship is the direct and powerful correlation between policy objectives and policies. Policies are *always* developed to achieve someone's policy objectives. This relationship, in and of itself, makes no assumptions about either the appropriateness or the attainability of objectives; it merely recognizes the innate relationship between objectives and the policies that are intended to achieve them.

The best starting place in understanding policies is the objectives to which they are directed. The relationship, per se, between objectives and policies makes no assumptions about whose objectives are being pursued, or in what mix the objectives of various individuals, organizations, and interest groups are being pursued, although this is obviously quite instrumental in determining the types of policies that are developed.

Simple though it may be, the relationship between policy objectives and policies is extremely important. The objectives toward which health policies are directed, perhaps more than anything else, shape policies. The set of objectives to which past health policies have been directed offer some insight into what may prevail in the future.

Because health in human beings is a function of a number of interrelated environmental, behavioral and biological, and social determinants, health policies have emerged to meet specific objectives related to each type of variable. As a result, the nation now has a multitude of health policy objectives—very large in number and unranked in relation to each other—in a variety of areas. Under the expansive rubric of the nation's health policy can be found an intermingled set of objectives pertaining to:

- adding years and quality to life;
- eliminating disparities in health and in access to health services among segments of the population;
- improving access to, reducing the costs of, and increasing the quality of health services;
- removing from the environment substances and conditions that have a negative impact on health;
- advancing the scientific and technological base of the pursuit of health;
- improving the housing and living conditions of the nation's citizens;
- improving the economic circumstances of the nation's citizens;
- making people more safety conscious on highways and in other potentially dangerous places;
- improving nutrition of the nation's citizens;
- moderating consumption of food, drink, and chemicals; and
- modifying unsafe sexual behaviors and practices.

This pattern is very likely to continue.

Coupled with persistent concern about how to pay for achieving any and all of these objectives, this plethora has stimulated a vast montage of poorly integrated—sometimes even conflicting—policies.

Objectives for numerous and varied policies—even if each in and of itself is clear-cut and rational—should not be mistaken for a comprehensive and integrated set of health policy objectives for the nation. This larger, more difficult, and much more important challenge still awaits the attention of health policymakers, who show few signs of taking it on and who work within a policymaking process that neither encourages nor facilitates the necessary broad thinking or actions. Meeting this challenge will require extraordinarily broad thinking. Such thinking, typically a difficult task in any situation, is made more so in regard to health policy by the splintering effect of the diversity of individuals, organizations, and interest groups who seek to influence policymakers' thinking and actions so that they reflect the idiosyncratic interests and preferences of those who have the power to exert influence.

Broad, coordinated thinking about health policy objectives by policymakers is also made more difficult by other structural characteristics of the American policymaking process. The process has a number of features that work to splinter thinking and isolate decisions rather than to stimulate comprehensive visions of where policies should lead the nation and ideas on how to orchestrate the integrated set of decisions needed to realize the vision. The constitution-based separation of powers, important though it is in maintaining the integrity of the democratic form of government, nevertheless permits good policies formulated in one branch to be poorly implemented in another. Perhaps as often, splendid ideas generated by those with implementation roles fall on deaf ears of legislators unwilling to entertain or consider them.

The unsuccessful effort at broad-scale health reform initiated by the Clinton administration in the early 1990s, despite varying opinions of the specific details of the plan outlined in the President's Health Security proposal, was a laudable attempt toward broader thinking regarding health policy (Hacker 1997). But it should escape no one that the focus of that plan was singularly on reforming the way the nation's health services were organized and financed. These services play a vital part in society's larger pursuit of health, but only a part. Truly expansive health policy thinking must also incorporate attention to the physical and social environments in which people live and work and must give more attention to their behaviors and biology as important determinants of their health. Continued myopia may prevail, in large measure because of the nature of the political arena in which health policy is forged. This arena is more fully described in chapter 3.

The Role and Importance of Political Competence in the Pursuit of Health

Because there is a powerful connection between health policy and health, anyone professionally involved in the pursuit of health through any of the determinants shown in Figure 1.3 has a vested interest in understanding the health policymaking process. An understanding of this process is the first step in developing a higher degree of *political competence*. Much more is said about political competence in chapter 8, and in many ways this book is about enhancing political competence. Suffice it to say in this chapter that it is composed of the dual abilities to assess the impact of public policies on one's domain of interest or responsibility on the one hand, and to exert influence in the public policymaking process on the other hand.

The single most important factor in political competence—whether the ability to assess impact of public policies or to exert influence in the policymaking process—is to understand the public policymaking process as a *decision-making* process. Public policies, including health policies, are decisions, albeit decisions made in a particular way by particular people—policymakers. Viewed in this way, it becomes as important to consider developing an understanding of policymaking as developing an understanding of a particular type of decision making: its context, participants, and processes.

As will be discussed throughout the book, the decision-making process through which public policies are made includes three tightly interwoven and interdependent phases: formulation, implementation, and modification. The phases do not unfold in neat sequence. Instead, they blend together in a gestalt of actors, actions, and, sometimes, inactions that yield policies. Figure 1.4 illustrates the closely intertwined nature of the relationships among the phases of policymaking.

This figure of the policymaking process emphasizes the continuous interrelationships and flows among the phases of the policymaking process. It also illustrates the cyclical character of public policymaking and shows it as an ongoing phenomenon, one without definitive beginnings or endings. In this view of public policymaking, policy formulation (making the decisions that are policies) is inextricably connected to policy implementation (taking actions and making additional decisions, which are themselves policies, necessary to implement policies). Neither phase is complete without the other. Because neither formulation nor implementation achieves perfection or exists in a static world, policy modification is a vitally necessary and complementary third component in the process. Modifications in previously formulated and implemented policies can range across a gamut from minor alterations in implementation, to new rules and regulations used in implementation, to modest amendments to existing legislation, to fundamental policy changes reflected in new public laws. Chapter 3 describes this process in more detail.

Increasingly, political competence is important to those who wish to be effectively involved in the pursuit of health. Within the context of the political marketplace, where public policymaking occurs, many participants seek to further their objectives by influencing the outcomes

Figure 1.4   The Intertwined Relationships Among Policy Formulation, Implementation, and Modification

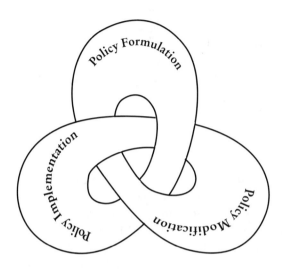

of this process. Political competence is an imperative ingredient for success in this arena. This competence entails knowing how and where to exert influence. Knowing where to seek to exert influence is also based on a thorough knowledge of the complex process through which public policies are formulated, implemented, and modified.

Armed with an understanding of the policymaking process, politically competent people understand that they can become involved in the process at many points. For example, they might become involved in setting the policy agenda by helping define the problems that policies might address, by participating in the development of possible solutions to the problems; or by helping to create the political circumstances necessary to turn the ideas for solving problems into actual policies (Kingdon 1995). Politically competent people also know how to effectively participate in the actual drafting of legislative proposals or in providing testimony in the hearings in which legislation is developed and refined. They also know that they can influence health policy by focusing on the rulemaking that helps guide the implementation of legislation enacted into laws. Such involvement routinely includes providing formal comment on proposed rules or providing ideas and comments to task forces and commissions established by rulemaking agencies as a means to obtain advice on their work.

The point is that an adequate degree of political competence is a necessary condition for effectively participating in the policymaking process. Through effective participation one can exert influence on future health policies and, thus, on the determinants of health and ultimately on health itself. This competence is built on a base of understanding of the public policymaking process, which is modeled in chapter 3 and discussed in depth in subsequent chapters. First, however, in chapter 2 fuller consideration is given to the critical relationship between public policy and the pursuit of health.

Summary

Health can be usefully conceptualized as the maximization of the biological and clinical indicators of organ function and the maximization of physical, mental, and role functioning in everyday life (Brook and McGlynn 1991). Thinking of health in this way emphasizes the need to address many variables, or health determinants, if health is to be affected: the physical environments in which people live and work; their behaviors and genetics; social factors, including economic circumstances, socioeconomic position in society, income distribution, discrimination based on factors such as race/ethnicity, gender, or sexual orientation, and the availability of social networks/social support; and the type, quality, and timing of health services that people receive.

Health policies are defined as authoritative decisions made within government that are intended to direct or influence the actions, behaviors, or decisions of others pertaining to health and its determinants. These policies are the principal means through which government in a developed society helps shape the pursuit of health by its members. These decisions can take the form of laws, rules and operational decisions made in the context of implementing laws, and judicial decisions. Health policies, like other public policies, can be allocative or regulatory in nature.

Notes

1. *Medicare*, the principal social health insurance program in the United States, was enacted into law as Title XVIII of the Social Security Act (P.L. 89-97) on 30 July 1965. Medicare is a federally administered program and is the nation's single largest health insurer, covering about 40 million Americans. It insures one of every seven Americans for a variety of hospital, physician, and other health services at an annual cost in 2000 of approximately $222 billion. Program beneficiaries include virtually all

of those over the age of 65 as well as disabled individuals who are entitled to Social Security benefits and people with end-stage renal disease.

The Medicare program has traditionally included two parts, A and B. Part A covers inpatient hospital care, very limited nursing home services, and home health services. Part A is paid for through a payroll tax of 2.9 percent that is split evenly between employees and their employers. Part B covers physician services, physician-ordered supplies and equipment, and certain ambulatory services such as hospital outpatient visits. Part B is voluntary, although about 97 percent of Part A beneficiaries choose to enroll in Part B, and is paid for by a combination of enrollee monthly premiums ($45.50 in 2000) and by general tax revenues. A third part of Medicare, the Medicare+Choice program, which is sometimes known as Part C, was established by the Balanced Budget Act of 1997 (BBA, P.L. 105-33) and expanded beneficiaries' options for participation in private-sector healthcare plans.

Because Medicare does not cover all of the health expenses of the elderly, most of them also have private supplemental, or Medigap, health insurance plans. In recent years, some of the Medicare population has moved into managed care programs, especially into health maintenance organizations (HMOs). Only about 16 percent of Medicare beneficiaries are currently enrolled in managed care plans.

Medicaid, enacted along with Medicare, as Title XIX of the Social Security Act (P.L. 89-97), is an important part of the federal-state social welfare structure. It provides health insurance coverage for preventive, acute, and long-term care for some of the nation's poorer citizens. Long-term care is an important provision of Medicaid that will be increasingly utilized as the nation's population ages. The Medicaid program has paid for almost 45 percent of the total cost of care for persons using nursing facility or home health services in recent years. This program covers about 41 million people, at an annual cost in 2000 of about $200 billion. Medicaid expenditures are among the fastest-growing components of most state budgets. As a result, states have shifted many of their Medicaid program beneficiaries into managed care plans in an attempt to slow the rate of growth in program expenditures.

The Medicaid program's costs are covered by a combination of federal subsidies to the states depending on the per capita income in each state and state funds. In return for the subsidy, the states administer their Medicaid programs, but do so under broad federal guidelines regarding the scope of services to be covered, the level of payments to healthcare services providers, and eligibility requirements for coverage under the program.

Title XXI of the Social Security Act, known as the State Children's Health Insurance Program (SCHIP), is a new program established by BBA. In addition to allowing states to craft or expand an existing state insurance program, SCHIP provides more federal funds for states to expand Medicaid eligibility to include a greater number of children who are currently uninsured. With certain exceptions, these are low-income children who would not qualify for Medicaid based on the plan that was in effect on April 15, 1997.

2. Federal public laws are given a number that designates both the enacting Congress and the sequence in which the law was enacted. P.L. 89-97, for example, means that this law was enacted by the 89th Congress and was the 97th law passed by that Congress. A briefly annotated chronological list of important federal laws pertaining to health can be found in the Appendix.

Discussion Questions

1. Discuss the ways in which health can be conceptualized by a society. What are the determinants of health in humans? What is the connection between how a society defines health and how it pursues health?
2. Define *public policies* and *health policies*.
3. What forms do health policies take? Give an example of each.
4. Compare and contrast the two basic categories of health policies.
5. Discuss the connection between health policies, health determinants, and health.
6. Discuss the role of states in health policy.
7. What is political competence? Why is it important to anyone who is interested in being involved in the pursuit of health?

References

Ayanian, J. Z. 1993. "Heart Disease in Black and White." *New England Journal of Medicine* 329 (9): 656–58.

Berkman, L. F., and I. Kawachi (eds.). 2000. *Social Epidemiology*. New York: Oxford University Press.

Birkland, T. A. 2001. *An Introduction to the Policy Process: Theories, Concepts, and Models of Public Policy Making*. Armonk, NY: M.E. Sharpe.

Blum, H. K. 1983. *Expanding Health Care Horizons: From a General Systems Concept of Health to a National Health Policy*, 2nd ed. Oakland, CA: Third Party Publishing Company.

Brook, R. H., and E. A. McGlynn. 1991. "Maintaining Quality of Care." In *Health Services Research: Key to Health Policy*, edited by E. Ginzberg, 784–817. Cambridge, MA: Harvard University Press.

Brown, L. D. 1992. "Political Evolution of Federal Health Care Regulation." *Health Affairs* 11 (4): 17–37.

Burner, S. T., D. R. Waldo, and D. R. McKusick. 1992. "National Health Expenditures Projections Through 2030." *Health Care Financing Review* 14 (1): 1–29.

Cochran, C. L., and E. F. Malone. 1995. *Public Policy: Perspectives and Choices*. New York: McGraw Hill.

Davidson, S. M. 1997. "Politics Matters! Health Care Policy and the Federal System." *Journal of Health Politics, Policy and Law* 22 (3): 879–96.

Evans, R. G., M. L. Barer, and T. R. Marmor. 1994. *Why Are Some People Healthy and Others Not? The Determinants of Health of Populations*. New York: Aldine De Gruyter.

Gold, M. 1997. "Markets and Public Programs: Insights from Oregon and Tennessee." *Journal of Health Politics, Policy and Law* 22 (2): 633–66.

Hacker, A. 1992. *Two Nations: Black and White, Separate, Hostile, Unequal*. New York: Macmillan.

Hacker, J. S. 1997. *The Road to Nowhere*. Princeton, NJ: Princeton University Press.

Health Care Financing Administration. 2001. *National Health Expenditure Projections, 2000–2010*. Washington, DC: Health Care Financing Administration.

Kingdon, J. W. 1995. *Agendas, Alternatives, and Public Policies*, 2nd ed. New York: HarperCollins College Publishers.

Krieger, N. 2000. "Discrimination and Health." In *Social Epidemiology*, edited by L. F. Berkman and I. Kawachi, 36–75. New York: Oxford University Press.

Kuttner, R. 1997. "The Kassebaum-Kennedy Bill—The Limits of Incrementalism." *New England Journal of Medicine* 337 (2): 64–67.

Lipson, D. J. 1997. "State Roles in Health Care Policy: Past as Prologue?" In *Health Politics and Policy*, 3rd ed., edited by T. J. Litman and L. S. Robins, 176–97. Albany, NY: Delmar Publishers.

Lumsdon, K. 1992. "HIV-Positive Health Care Workers Pose Legal, Safety Challenges for Hospitals." *Hospitals* 66 (18): 24–32.

Morone, J. A. 1990. *The Democratic Wish: Popular Participation and the Limits of American Government*. New York: Basic Books.

Oliver, T. R., and P. Paul-Shaheen. 1997. "Translating Ideas into Actions: Entrepreneurial Leadership in State Health Care Reforms." *Journal of Health Politics, Policy and Law* 22 (3): 721–88.

Peters, G. B. 1999. *American Public Policy: Promise and Performance*. Chappaqua, NY: Chatham House/Seven Rivers.

Peterson, M. A. 1997. "States: The Policy Crucible." *Journal of Health Politics, Policy and Law* 22 (3): 687–89.

Ripley, R., and G. Franklin. 1991. *Congress, Bureaucracy, and Public Policy*, 5th ed. Pacific Grove, CA: Brooks-Cole.

Santerre, R. E., and Neun, S. P. 2000. *Health Economics: Theories, Insights, and Industry Studies*. Fort Worth, TX: Harcourt College Publishers.

Sparer, M. S., and L. D. Brown. 1996. "The Limits and Lessons of the Laboratory of Federalism." In *Health Policy, Federalism, and the American States*, edited by R. E. Rich and W. D. White. Washington, DC: Urban Institute Press.

Williams, D. R. 1999. "Race, Socioeconomic Status, and Health: The Added Effects of Racism and Discrimination." In *Socioeconomic Status and Health in Industrial Nations: Social, Psychological, and Biological Pathways*, Vol. 896, edited by N. E. Adler, M. Marmot, B. S. McEwen, and J. Stewart. New York: Annals of the New York Academy of Sciences.

World Health Organization. 1948. Preamble to the Constitution of the World Health Organization as adopted by the International Health Conference, New York, June 19–22, 1946; signed on July 22, 1946 by the representatives of 61 States (Official Records of the World Health Organization, no. 2, p. 100) and entered into force on April 7, 1948. "Constitution of the World Health Organization, 1948." In *Basic Documents*, 15th ed. Geneva, Switzerland: World Health Organization, 1948.

IMPACT OF HEALTH POLICY

AS WAS discussed briefly in chapter 1, health policies affect health through their effects on health determinants. These effects and the impact of health policies on individuals, organizations, and interest groups are explored in more detail in this chapter. It is important to understand the effects and impacts of health policies—both on health determinants and, ultimately, on individuals, organizations and systems, and interest groups—in order to fully appreciate the important role health policy plays in the nation's pursuit of health.

Health Policy and Health Determinants

Recall that health in individuals and populations is determined by:

- the physical environments in which people live and work;
- the behavioral choices that people make and the role that biology plays in their health;
- the social factors that affect people's health, including their economic circumstances, their socioeconomic position in society, income distribution within the society; discrimination based on factors such as race/ethnicity, gender, or sexual orientation, and the availability of social networks/social support; and
- the health services available to people and their access to these services.

The nature of the impact of health policy on these health determinants is explored in the following sections.

Health Policies and the Physical Environment

When people are asked about what they think contributes to their health, they respond that the quality of their health services is a very important contributor. But, they also list clean air, safe neighborhoods, and well-paying jobs (Louis Harris and Associates 1996). People think their physical environments contribute to their health status, and they are right. When people are exposed to harmful agents such as asbestos, excessive noise, ionizing radiation, or toxic chemicals their health is directly affected.

Dangerous exposure possibilities pervade the physical environments of many people. Some of the exposure is through such agents as synthetic compounds that are introduced into the environment as by-products of technological growth and development. Some exposure is through wastes that result from the manufacture, use, and disposal of a vast range of products. And some of the exposure is through naturally occurring agents such as carcinogenic ultraviolet radiation from the sun or naturally occurring radon gas in the soil.

Often, the hazardous effects of naturally occurring agents are exacerbated by combination with agents introduced by human activities. For example, before its ban, the widespread use of Freon in air conditioning systems and of chloroflourocarbons (CFCs) in aerosolized products reduced the protective ozone layer in earth's upper atmosphere, allowing an increased level of ultraviolet radiation from the sun to strike the planet's inhabitants. Similarly, exposure to naturally occurring radon gas appears to act synergistically with cigarette smoke as a carcinogenic hazard.

The health effects of exposure to hazardous agents, whether they are introduced into the environment or occur naturally, are well understood. Air, polluted by a number of agents, has a direct, measurable effect on such diseases as asthma, emphysema, lung cancer, and on the aggravation of cardiovascular disease. Asbestos, which can still be found in buildings constructed prior to its ban, causes pulmonary disease. Lead-based paint, when ingested, causes permanent neurological defects in infants and young children. This paint is still found in older buildings and is especially concentrated in poorer urban communities.

Government, over many decades, has been involved in a variety of efforts to exorcize environmental health hazards through public policies. Examples of such federal policies include the Clean Air Act (P.L. 88-206), the Flammable Fabrics Act (P.L. 90-189), the Occupational Safety and Health Act (P.L. 91-596), the Consumer Product Safety Act (P.L. 92-573), the Noise Control Act (P.L. 92-574), and the Safe Drinking Water Act (P.L. 93-523).

Health policies that mitigate the negative influences of the physical environments in which people live and work or that take advantage of positive potential for environmental conditions to affect health are important aspects of any society's ability to help its members achieve higher levels of health. But there are other determinants of health as well. They provide additional avenues to improved health.

Health Policies and Human Behavior and Biology

As Rene Dubos observed decades ago, "To ward off disease or recover health, men [as well as women and children] as a rule find it easier to depend on the healers than to attempt the more difficult task of living wisely" (1959, 110). The price of this attitude is partially reflected in the causes of death in the United States. Ranked from highest to lowest by the Centers for Disease Control and Prevention (CDC) (www.cdc.gov), the ten leading causes are heart disease, cancer, stroke, chronic obstructive pulmonary disease (COPD), accidents, pneumonia/influenza, diabetes, suicide, nephritis/nephritic syndrome/nephrosis, and chronic liver diseases/cirrhosis.

Underlying these causes of death are a set of behaviors—including choices about the use of tobacco and alcohol, diet and exercise, illicit drug use, sexual behavior, and violence—as well as genetic predispositions that help explain the pattern. Furthermore, underlying the behavioral factors and choices are such root factors as stress, depression, anger, hopelessness, and emptiness, which are exacerbated by economic and social conditions. Behaviors are heavily reflected in the diseases that kill and debilitate Americans.

Science has shown that changes in behaviors can change the pattern of causes of death. The death rate from heart disease, for example, has declined dramatically in recent decades. Although aggressive early treatment has played a role in reducing this death rate, better control of several behavioral risk factors, including cigarette smoking, elevated blood pressure, elevated levels of cholesterol, diet and exercise, and stress reduction, explain much of this improvement. Even with this impressive improvement, however, heart disease remains the most common cause of death and will continue to be an important cause for the foreseeable future. Cancer death rates continue to grow, with much of the increase attributable to lung cancer, a type of cancer that is strongly correlated with behavior. Deaths from accidents and suicides are also obviously affected by behaviors, as are those from liver cirrhosis.

Even in the face of the direct relationships between particular behaviors and certain deadly diseases, policymakers have been reluctant to impose penalties for behaviors that lead to illness and death or to provide overt rewards for the avoidance or modification of such behaviors. Instead, health policy interventions in diseases that are behaviorally caused or exacerbated have favored increased funding for research into the behaviors or increased efforts to influence behavior through education. Venturing into the domains of individual choice and liberty rights has been carefully avoided. It is clear, however, that the impacts of human behavior and genetics on health are potentially productive avenues for increased and perhaps different policy interventions in the future.

Health Policies and Social Factors

In addition to their physical environments, behaviors, and genetics, a number of social factors, many of them interconnected, also play roles in the health of people. Chronic unemployment, the absence of a supportive family structure, poverty, homelessness, discrimination, and numerous other social factors affect the health of people as surely and often as dramatically as harmful viruses or carcinogens.

People who live in poverty experience measurably worse health status (i.e., more frequent and more severe health problems) than people who are more affluent. African Americans, Latinos, and Native Americans, who are disproportionately represented below the poverty line, experience worse health status than the white majority (Klerman 1992).

The poor also obtain their health services in a different manner than the more affluent. Instead of receiving care that is coordinated, continuing, and comprehensive, the poor are far more likely to receive a patchwork of services, often provided by public hospitals, clinics, and local health departments. In addition, poor people are more often treated episodically, with one provider intervening in one episode of illness and another provider handling the next episode.

The impact of economic conditions on the health of children is especially dramatic. Impoverished children have double the rates of low birth weight and more than double the rates of conditions that limit school activity compared to other children (Starfield 1992). These children are more likely to become ill and to have more serious illnesses than other children because of their increased exposure to harmful environments, inadequate preventive services, and limited access to health services.

Economic circumstances are only part of a larger set of social factors that unevenly affect people in their quests for health. Living in an inner city or rural setting often increases the challenge of finding health services because the availability of providers is not adequate in many of these locations. Lack of adequate information about health and about health services is a significant disadvantage, one compounded by language barriers, functional illiteracy, or marginal mental retardation. Even cultural backgrounds and ties, especially among many Native Americans, Latinos, and Asian immigrants, for all the support they can provide, sometimes also create a formidable barrier between people and the mainline healthcare system.

A good example of health policy intended to address social factors is a policy designed to expand health insurance coverage for uninsured, low-income children. P.L. 105-33, the Balanced Budget Act of 1997, contains provisions for expanding health insurance coverage of children by establishing the State Children's Health Insurance Program (SCHIP). This policy, as well as many others, has partially addressed some of the social factors that affect health. However, a great deal remains to be done in addressing the social factors that help determine health. An agenda in this area has been proposed by the leaders of the National Policy Association (www.npa1.org) and the Academy for Health Services Research and Health Policy (www.ahsrhp.org). Based on the relationships established by research between health and social factors, these two organizations have urged that health policy be developed to address social factors in five specific areas (Auerbach, Krimgold, and Lefkowitz 2000, 15–16):

- Investing in young children through policies that explicitly recognize the importance throughout the lifespan of early development. Examples include improved parenting programs, comprehensive preschool programs, family support, and education.
- Providing services and opportunities for the neediest through policies that seek to confer the benefits of higher socioeconomic status on those at the lower end of the scale, to prevent discrimination and to foster a civil society. Examples are improvements in housing, education, nutrition, job training, disease prevention, and access to healthcare.
- Improving the work environment including appropriate involvement of employees in decision making, more employee control over work, a greater variety of work, opportunities for development, appropriate compensation and rewards, increased job security, improved leave policies, and worker protections.
- Strengthening support at the community level through policies that build social networks, encourage economic development and empowerment, increase civic participation and trust, and reduce or mitigate the effects of economic and racial segregation.
- Creating a more equal economic environment through tax, transfer, and employment policies. Examples include increases in the Earned Income Tax Credit, minimum wage, unemployment compensation,

and welfare payments in states where they are low. Other examples include managing the economy to continue to buffer business cycle extremes and keep unemployment low.

Health Policies and Health Services

Another important determinant of health is the availability of and access to health services, which are any of a host of "specific activities undertaken to maintain or improve health or to prevent decrements of health" (Longest, Rakich, Darr 2000, 5). Health services can be preventive (e.g., behavior modification, blood pressure screening, mammography); acute (e.g., surgical procedures, antibiotics to fight infection); chronic (e.g., control of diabetes or hypertension); restorative (e.g., physical rehabilitation of a stroke or trauma patient); or palliative (e.g., pain management or comfort measures in terminal stages of disease) in nature.

The production and distribution of health services require a vast set of resources, including money, human resources, and technology, that are heavily influenced by health policies. Health services are provided through the healthcare system, which comprises the organizations and systems or networks of organizations that transform these resources into health services and distribute them to consumers. The system itself is also influenced by health policies. Similar to their impact on the other determinants of health, health policies have major bearing on the nature of the health services available to people through their impact on the resources required to produce the services, as well as on the healthcare system through which the services are organized, delivered, and paid for. How policies affect resources used to provide health services and the healthcare system are examined in the next sections, beginning with monetary resources.

Money

As shown in Figure 1.2 in the previous chapter, national health expenditures have grown steadily over the decades and are expected to continue to do so. They may exceed $2.6 trillion by 2010. These expenditures represented 13.1 percent of the gross domestic product (GDP) in 2000, and could rise to 15.9 percent of GDP by 2010 (www.cms.gov/stats/ nheproj/). The United States spends more on health than does any other country (Organization for Economic Cooperation and Development 2000; Anderson and Hussey 2001), in large part because of some significant variations in the policies that affect health services in various countries. For example, other countries have been far more likely to adopt policies such as global budgets for their healthcare systems, or to impose restrictive limitations on the supplies of health services than has the United States.

The implications of the level of health expenditures and the rate of increase in these expenditures over the past several decades, as well as projections of future increases, are significant. The increasing health expenditures, in part, reflect higher prices. These higher prices have reduced access to health services by making it more difficult for many people to purchase either the services or the insurance needed to cover those services. For many workers, the increases in health expenditures have absorbed much of the growth of their real compensation, meaning lower wages as employers spend more to provide health insurance benefits. Some employers have dropped health insurance altogether. The number of people without health insurance in the United States grew during the 1990s, from about 35.6 million in 1990 to more than 42 million by the end of the decade (Fronstin 2000).

Because federal and state governments now pay for so much health-care, rising health expenditures have put substantial pressures on their budgets. As health expenditures consume a growing portion of government resources, it becomes more difficult for government to support other priorities such as education, other social programs, or tax relief.

The Real World of Health Policy

Budget Options

The Congressional Budget Office (CBO) (www.cbo.gov) produces an annual report to the House and Senate Committees on the budget that is intended to help inform policymakers about options for the federal budget. These reports present a broad range of possibilities, typically focusing on options to cut spending or to increase it, and options to cut taxes or to increase revenues.

The policy options addressed in these reports come from many sources. In keeping with CBO's mandate to provide objective and impartial analysis, the discussion of each proposal or option presents the cases for and against it. The inclusion or exclusion of a particular idea does not represent an endorsement or rejection by CBO. As a nonpartisan Congressional agency, CBO does not make recommendations about policy.

The report released in February 2001, as is typical of these reports in recent years, begins with an introduction that discusses how the emergence of large surpluses has transformed the budget debate, presents rationales for the budget options presented, and explains how to use this volume. Part one (chapter 1) looks at the costs and benefits of paying down federal debt held by the public. Part two (chapters 2 through 5) examines options for spending. Chapter 2 is a broad discussion of proposals that would expand federal programs for retirement, health, and education. Chapter 3, in similar fashion, discusses proposals that would increase spending for physical capital and information. Chapter 4 provides an overview of defense spending and presents specific options to increase or decrease it. Chapter 5 includes numerous options to cut nondefense spending, organized by the functional categories of the budget—agriculture; health; international affairs; general science, space, and technology; social security, and so on. Each function is given a specific number: health is function number 550, for example. In the report, each functional category is introduced by a page of background information about recent spending trends in that function. Part three (chapters 6 and 7) looks at revenue options. Chapter 6 presents a broad discussion of significant proposals for cutting taxes. Chapter 7 contains specific options for increasing revenues, which follow the one-page format used in chapter 5.

In the February 2001 report, chapter 5, Functional Category 550, Health, contains the following background information:

Budget function 550 includes federal spending for health care services, disease prevention, consumer and occupational safety, health-related research, and similar activities. (Medicare has its own budget category, Function 570.) The largest component of spending is the federal/state Medicaid program, which pays for health services for some low-income women, children, and elderly people as well as people with disabilities. Mandatory outlays for Medicaid increased by over 10 percent per year in the early 1990s and have risen significantly again in the past few years. CBO estimates that in 2001, the federal government will spend $130 billion on Medicaid and a total of $173 billion on function 550. Discretionary outlays make up only about $34 billion of that total, but they have more than doubled since 1990. Those outlays have grown every year of the past decade.

In chapter 5, Options to Cut Nondefense Spending, the following option is included along with 10 other options:

Reduce the Enhanced Federal Matching Rates for Certain Administrative Functions in Medicaid

Under current law, the federal government pays part of the costs that states incur in administering their Medicaid programs. For most administrative activities, the federal matching rate is 50 percent, but that rate is higher for certain activities. For example, the federal government pays 75 percent of the costs of skilled medical professionals who are employed in Medicaid administration, 75 percent of the costs of utilization review, 90 percent of the development costs of systems for claims processing and information management, and 75 percent of the costs of operating such systems.

The purpose of enhanced matching rates is to give states incentives to develop and support particular administrative activities that the federal government considers important for the Medicaid program. But once the administrative systems are operational, there may be less reason to continue to pay higher rates. If the federal share of all Medicaid administrative costs was 50 percent, savings would be $880 million in 2002 and $14.9 billion over the 2002–2011 period (see Exhibit 1).

Without the higher matching rates, states might be inclined to cut back on some activities, with adverse consequences for the quality of care and for program management. States might, for example, hire fewer nurses to conduct utilization review and oversee care in nursing homes, or they might undertake fewer improvements to their management information systems. However, if the Congress wished to protect particular administrative functions, it could maintain the higher matching rates for them while it reduced the matching rates for others.

Exhibit 1

	Outlay Savings (Millions of dollars)
2002	880
2003	1,110
2004	1,200
2005	1,290
2006	1,400
2002–2006	5,880
2002–2011	14,860

Source: Excerpted from Congressional Budget Office. February 2001. *Budget Options.* Washington, DC: CBO.

Human Resources

The talents and abilities of a large and diverse workforce comprise another of the basic resources used to provide health services. These human resources are directly affected by health policies. More than 11.6 million health-related workers in the United States today represent about 8.7 percent of the civilian workforce. There are about 723,000 physicians;

2.1 million registered nurses (RNs); 185,000 pharmacists; 159,000 dentists; and more than 3 million allied health workers in over 200 distinct disciplinary groups such as clinical laboratory technology, dental hygiene, dietetics, medical records administration, occupational therapy, physical therapy, radiologic technology, respiratory therapy, and speech-language pathology/audiology to name but a few (National Center for Health Statistics 2000).

The nature of the significant impact of health policies on health-related human resources can be seen in the fact that the number of physicians was doubled over the span of mid-1960s to mid-1990s, to a considerable extent in response to federal policies intended to increase their supply. The Health Professions Educational Assistance Act of 1963 (P.L. 88-129) and its amendments of 1965, 1968, and 1971 helped to double the capacity of the medical schools in the United States by the early 1990s. Now, however, the attention of policymakers is turned to concerns about the perceived oversupply of physicians and about the inadequate proportion practicing in the primary care specialties of general practice, family practice, general internal medicine, and general pediatrics.

Technology

A third type of resources used in providing health services, and on which health policies have significant impact, is health-related technology. Broadly defined, technology is the application of science to the pursuit of health. Technological advances result in better drugs, devices, and procedures used in providing health services. A major influence on the pursuit of health in the United States, technology has eradicated many diseases and greatly improved diagnoses and treatment for others. In fact, diseases that once were not even diagnosed are now routinely and effectively treated. Advancing technology has brought medical science to the early stages of understanding disease at the molecular level and intervening in diseases at the genetic level.

The United States produces and consumes more, and spends far more, than any other nation for health-related technology; it has provided technology with a uniquely favorable economic and political environment. As a result, health-related technology is widely and readily available to the citizens of the United States.

Funding for the research and development (R&D) that leads to new technology is an important way in which health policy affects the pursuit of health, although the private sector also pays for a great deal of the R&D that leads to new health-related technology. This nation has a long history of support for the development of health-related technology through policies that directly support biomedical research and that encourage private investment in such research. From a total of about $300 in 1887, the National Institutes of Health (NIH) budget grew to $20.3 *billion* in 2001 (www.nih.gov). In addition, encouraged by policies that permit firms to recoup their investments in research and development, private industry also spends heavily on biomedical R&D. In fact, the Pharmaceutical Research and Manufacturers of America (PhRMA) (www.phrma.org) reports that its member companies spent $26.4 billion on research in 2001.

Another way in which health policy affects technology is through the application of regulatory policies, such as those promulgated by the FDA as a means of ensuring technology's safety and efficacy. FDA's mission is to promote and protect the public health by permitting safe and effective medical products to reach the market in a timely way, and monitoring products for continued safety after they are in use.

As technology has advanced, the costs of health services have risen as the new technology is utilized and paid for. One paradox of advancing health-related technology is that, even as people live longer because of these advances, they then may need and utilize additional health services. The net effect drives up health expenditures both for the new technology and for other services made possible by extended life. The costs associated with use of technology generate policy issues of their own.

The Real World of Health Policy

Overview of New Hospital Technologies for Fiscal Year 2002

The Medicare Payment Advisory Commission (MedPAC) (www.medpac. gov) is an independent federal body established by the Balanced Budget Act of 1997 (P.L. 105-33) to advise the United States Congress on issues affecting the Medicare program. One of the important aspects of MedPAC's advice involves updating the levels at which hospitals are reimbursed by the Medicare program for taking care of Medicare beneficiaries. Reimbursement levels are set at a base level, but provisions are made for an allowance to cover scientific and technological advances (S&TAs). In establishing the magnitude of the allowance, MedPAC considers only those new technologies that have progressed beyond the initial experimental stage of development but are not fully diffused in the inpatient hospital setting. Payment for fully diffused technology is included in the base level of reimbursement to hospitals. The following information about new technologies illustrates the pace and extent of new technological advances in healthcare, and their impact on costs and on reimbursement policy in the Medicare program. It was considered by MedPAC in determining the allowance for 2002.

To encourage hospitals to adopt new technologies that enhance quality of care for Medicare beneficiaries but increase costs, MedPAC includes an allowance for scientific and technological advances in its hospital update framework. In determining the magnitude of the allowance, we consider only those new technologies that have progressed beyond the initial experimental stage of development but are not fully diffused in the inpatient hospital setting. Payment for fully diffused technology is subsumed in the base.

Current Approach

The allowance for scientific and technological advances (S&TAs) represents MedPAC's best estimate of the incremental increase in costs for a given fiscal year that will result from hospitals adopting new technologies or new applications of existing technologies beyond that automatically reflected in the payments hospitals receive. To derive the fiscal year 2002 allowance, we are using a qualitative method similar to our approach for fiscal years 2000 and 2001. First, we reviewed the technologies included in fiscal year 2000 and 2001 updates that continue to diffuse and estimated changes in their overall use and costs predicted for fiscal year 2002 (MedPAC 1999, 2000). Next, we attempted to identify new technological advances for this year's update by reviewing select medical literature, trade journals and popular press; approvals of drugs, devices, and biologics by the Food and Drug Administration (FDA); and information from other federal and private organizations. As in prior analyses, we did not attempt to identify all cost-increasing technologies, but focused on the most significant medical and scientific advances from a cost and potential diffusion perspective. Finally, we included only those quality-enhancing technologies that met the following criteria as best as we could determine:

- The technology was approved by the FDA as appropriate.
- At least an estimated 5 percent but no more than 75 percent of relevant Medicare beneficiaries (patients whose medical condition warrants use of the technology) would receive the technology.
- Substantially higher net treatment costs would result from use of the new technology.

We divided new technologies into five broad categories that we believe encompass virtually all of the advances expected to contribute significantly to increased costs:

- information systems;
- drugs and biologics;
- devices and diagnostics;
- imaging technology; and
- surgical/procedural techniques and other technological advances.

These categories are similar to those we used for the 2000 and 2001 allowance except that we have grouped drugs with biologics and devices with diagnostics and have added a category for surgical and procedural techniques. While advances in cardiology continue to increase costs significantly, we have generalized the categories of drugs and biologics and devices and diagnostics to include advances in all specialties.

In some cases, the new technology would replace a less expensive older technology. In addition, the cost of new technologies may be partially offset by productivity increases. For the purpose of determining the S&TA adjustment, we attempt to estimate the net of the new and old technology costs. In calculating the adjustment, it is also important to keep in mind that the use of these new technologies is limited to a fraction of patients in certain diagnosis related groups. Thus, while the list of S&TAs appears impressive in scope, the S&TA contribution to total hospital costs remains relatively minor.

The following sections contain categorical listings of FDA-approved scientific advances since our last review of this topic in June 2000 as well as recently developed technologies which were identified in our two previous reviews of S&TAs (MedPAC 1999, 2000) but which continue to diffuse.

Information Systems

Coordination of health care across different providers is critical to ensuring quality of care, and delivery of coordinated health care is dependent on the availability of integrated information systems. In light of the trend for more coordinated care delivery by hospitals, information systems will probably continue to account for a significant proportion of increased costs in fiscal year 2002. This will encompass multisite, integrated information systems that capture, store and tabulate financial, pharmacy, radiology, patient care, and laboratory data. In particular, recent emphasis on reduction and elimination of systematic medical errors will prompt hospitals to invest further in information systems that can detect medication errors and diagnostic inaccuracies (Institute of Medicine 2000). As hospitals continue to develop clinical and financial data repositories and electronic medical records, technology to standardize, aggregate, integrate, and transfer information through secure channels across multiple providers within a network as well as to parties outside a health care system, including Medicare, becomes a high priority expense.

The Balanced Budget Act of 1997 (BBA) required Medicare to cover interactive telemedicine consultations in areas designated as health professional shortage areas. Telemedicine—the electronic delivery of health care information and services—continues to diffuse into underserved areas. Rural hospitals continue to expand existing and implement new uses of telemedicine, which will increase access to care for Medicare beneficiaries but will require continued investment in this technology.

Video-conferencing, which uses the internet and web-based diagnostic software, may enable physicians to care more efficiently for patients, especially in the intensive care unit (ICU). Using this technology, nurses will be more effective in communicating with and transmitting data to intensivists and other physicians who are not physically present in the ICU.

Drugs and Biologics

MedPAC believes that continued diffusion of new drugs and biologics will have at least a modest impact on total costs for hospitals in fiscal year 2002. Stunning advances in molecular and genetic medicine have yielded innovative yet costly approaches to treating certain diseases. For example, drugs and biologics recently approved by the FDA include:

- platelet aggregation inhibitors to treat acute coronary syndrome (GP IIb/IIIa inhibitors);
- new antiarrhythmics;
- protease inhibitors to reduce perioperative blood loss in patients undergoing cardiopulmonary bypass;
- a quinolone derivative to treat intermittent claudication;
- an agent to treat acute deep-vein thrombosis;
- fibrin sealants that prevent or reduce bleeding from small blood vessels during and after surgery;
- an injectable sustained-release formulation to treat lymphomatous meningitis;
- a retinoid and a fusion protein to treat certain lymphomas;
- a genetically engineered protein that reduces symptoms of rheumatoid arthritis;
- a recombinant thrombin inhibitor to reverse anticoagulation associated with heparin-induced thrombocytopenia;
- a synthetic plasma expander to treat hypovolemia;
- a skin construct to treat venous leg ulcers;
- anti-infectives to treat certain bacterial infections, including those caused by gram-negative organisms and resistant strains;
- new cyclooxygenase-2 (cox-2) inhibitors for osteoarthritis and rheumatoid arthritis;
- an anticoagulant to prevent clot formation after surgery;
- antineoplastics for certain cancers;
- agents to reduce the side effects of some cancer therapies;
- new agents for surgical anesthesia and sedation;

- mitoxantrone, an approved cancer drug, for treatment of advanced or chronic multiple sclerosis; and
- verteporfin (injection) followed by laser treatment for age-related macular degeneration.

Devices and Diagnostics

New devices and diagnostics are a perpetual source of increased costs for hospitals. MedPAC believes that continued diffusion of advances in this category will have a small impact on total hospital costs for fiscal year 2002. Some recent advancements include:

- biventricular pacing devices with implantable defibrillators for congestive heart failure;
- catheter-based devices that remove blood clots from occluded coronary arteries or bypass grafts;
- stents (liver, biliary, and lung);
- endovascular devices that reinforce aortic aneurysms;
- intravascular brachytherapy systems that administer radiation energy for treatment of in-stent restenosis;
- an electronic device to treat postoperative nausea;
- abdominal implant for treatment of chronic, intractable (drug-refractory) nausea and vomiting secondary to gastroparesis;
- biological sensors (continuous glucose monitoring system);
- drug delivery implants with and without biosensors that monitor drug or chemical concentrations in body fluids:
- a brain stem implant device for patients who experience total hearing loss when the removal of a tumor damages their cranial hearing nerves;
- robotics for minimally invasive surgery (robotic-enhanced endoscopic systems for arterial revascularizaton, three-dimensional video and robot-assisted port-access mitral valve operation, and robotic-enhanced laparoscopic surgery for gall bladder and reflux disease);
- microchip devices for various indications; for example, for restoring vision in patients with diseases of the retina;
- a fully automated blood testing system;
- immunoblot assay for hepatitis C Virus;
- an ultrasonic scalpel or ultrasonically activated shears;
- handheld radio-guided probes or detection devices to assist in certain surgeries; and
- a laser to treat pain caused by herniated or ruptured spinal discs.

Imaging Technology

Over the past several decades, tremendous quality-of-care enhancements have been achieved in the fields of radiology, imaging and nuclear medicine. In the next year, new imaging technology and additional applications of existing technologies including magnetic resonance imaging, positron emission tomography, ultrasound and computed tomography, will continue to increase costs for hospitals. MedPAC believes that diffusion of advances in these areas will have a small impact on total hospital costs in fiscal year 2002. Some recent advancements include:

- digital mammography and breast imaging devices (T-scan) to clarify ambiguous mammograms;
- mini-magnetic resonance devices to view internal body structures;
- handheld ultrasound devices;
- expanded uses for endoscopic ultrasonography;
- electron-beam computed tomography to detect blockages in arteries;
- functional anatomic mapping systems;
- positron emission tomography to diagnose certain cancers;
- radiosurgery devices that direct radiation to treat certain solid tumors; and
- new imaging agents to detect certain lung tumors and certain brain and spinal lesions.

Surgical/procedural Techniques and Other Technological Advances

MedPAC anticipates that new surgical or procedural techniques will collectively result in a small increase in total hospital costs for fiscal year 2002. Some examples include:

- transmyocardial revascularization, a laser treatment that opens tiny channels in the heart muscle, increasing cardiac blood flow in patients with severe angina;
- laser angioplasty;
- minimally invasive and off-pump coronary artery bypass surgery;
- new and expanded transplantation procedures and techniques;
- intraclot recombinant tissue plasminogen activator for deep venous thrombosis of the extremities;
- photodynamic therapy for treatment of various tumors;
- hand-assisted laparoscopic surgery;
- radio frequency ablation of unresectable hepatic malignancies;
- extra corporeal life support for cardiac and pulmonary failure;
- extracorporeal perfusion for the treatment of acute liver failure; and
- permanent sacral nerve stimulation for fecal incontinence.

Source: Excerpted from MedPAC. March 2000. *Report To The Congress: Medicare Payment Policy,* Appendix A, pages 163–66. Washington, DC: Medicare Payment Advisory Commission.

Health Policy and Individuals, Organizations and Systems, and Interest Groups

Health policies were defined in chapter 1 as authoritative decisions made within government; however, they are more than decisions. Policies have important consequences in the lives of individuals, organizations and systems, and interest groups. The important question—who do health policies affect?—is addressed in the following sections. At the most basic level, the answer to this question, of course, is everyone. Health is a state that exists in everyone and health policy affects the pursuit of this state by and for everyone. No one escapes the impact of health policies. No one avoids the consequences of health policies, although individuals experience these consequences in different ways, under different circumstances, to different degrees, at different times, and, therefore, with varying levels of interest. Beyond this generality, however, lies the fact that health policy is of consequence to some people for reasons apart from its effect on their health.

Many organizations and systems actively participate in the nation's pursuit of health. People who are employed in these organizations and systems, who govern them, or independently practice their professions within them, have an intense interest in health policies that affect these organizations and systems. The missions and purposes of the organizations or systems are directly affected by health policies, as are day-to-day operations. In addition to those who work in health organizations and systems, many individuals view the successful pursuit of health for the entire population as a noble societal goal and become involved in health policy for this reason.

Individuals, organizations, and systems having the greatest or most concentrated interest in the policymaking process are more likely to become involved with interest groups as a means of more effectively addressing their interests. Because interest groups are explored more fully in other chapters, suffice it to say here that they are groups of people with similar policy goals who band together to pursue those goals. Thus, it is useful to consider the impact of health policies on individuals, on organizations and systems that participate in the pursuit of health, and on health-related interest groups to which individuals, as well as organizations and systems, can belong.

Health Policies and Individuals

The impact of health policy at the level of individuals is very real and very important, and the consequences of health policies for individuals can be enormous. Government engages in health policymaking primarily to support the nation's citizens in their quest for health, although secondary purposes, such as the economic interests of certain participants involved in the activities related to the pursuit of health, may also be served. As discussed in a previous section, the mechanism of governmental support for the pursuit of health is the impact that health policy has on the determinants of human health: the physical and social environments in which people live and work; their behaviors and biology; and the type, quality, and timing of the health services they receive. Each of these determinants, in terms of their effects on individuals, is important to them—extremely so for some individuals. But the relationship between health policy and the hundreds of millions of individuals who are affected is highly idiosyncratic.

The clearer, or at least simpler, way to visualize the relationship between policies and those affected by them is to examine the relationship between policies and collectives or groups of individuals; that is, between policies and organizations and interest groups. But, eventually, all health policy affects individuals. People breathe cleaner or dirtier air, eat more or less healthful food, have more open or restricted access to health services, and benefit from more or fewer technological advances as a direct result of health policies.

Health Policies and Health-Related Organizations and Systems

The existence and accomplishments of many organizations and systems are affected by health policies. Certainly, the missions, objectives, and internal structures and resources, including the quality of their leadership, greatly influence the accomplishments of health-related organizations and systems. However, the performance levels achieved by these organizations and systems—whether measured in terms of contribution to health outcomes for customers, financial strength, reputation, growth, competitive position, scope of services provided, or some other parameter—are also heavily influenced by the nature of the opportunities and threats imposed on them from their external environments.

The external environments faced by health-related organizations and systems include biological, cultural, demographic, ecological, economic, ethical, legal, policy, psychological, social, and technological dimensions. Policies that affect an organization or system are only part of its external environment, although they may constitute a critically important part. As Figure 2.1 illustrates, policies, along with the other variables in the external environment of an organization or system, provide it with a set of opportunities and threats to which it can—indeed, must—respond.

Figure 2.1 The Relationship Between an Organization or System's External Environment and Its Performance

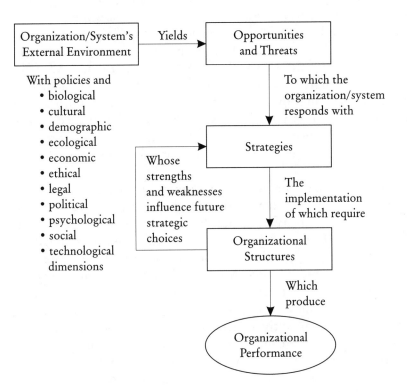

The organization or system responds to these threats and opportunities with strategies and organizational structures created to carry out the strategies. The quality of the strategies and structures, in terms of their ability to make appropriate responses to the relevant threats and opportunities, result in organizational performance. But, very importantly, the series of events that culminate in organizational performance are triggered by the opportunities and threats the organization or system faces. And these opportunities and threats are the direct result of conditions in the organization or system's external environment, including the public policies that affect it. Thus, it is useful to consider the specific nature of health policy concerns and the interests of some of the organizations and systems in the health sector.

A rich variety of organizations and systems populate the health sector; their diversity defies easy categorization, although a common thread among them is that they are all affected by and have interests in health policies. Hospitals, state or county health departments, health maintenance organizations (HMOs), hospices, and nursing homes are examples of health services providers. Although there are no guarantees for the future, there is abundant evidence that, for the most part, the organizations and systems that provide health services in the United States have developed under extraordinarily favorable public policies. For example, enactment in 1946 of the Hospital Survey and Construction Act (P.L. 79-725) placed Congress squarely in support of expanded availability of health services and improved facilities. This legislation, known as the Hill-Burton Act after its authors, provided funds for hospital construction and marked the beginning of a decades-long program of extensive federal developmental subsidies aimed at increasing the availability of health services.

Another important aspect of the development of health-related organizations and healthcare systems, also supported and facilitated by public policy, has been the expansion of health insurance coverage. Beginning during World War II, when wages were frozen, health insurance and other benefits in lieu of wages became attractive features of the American workplace. Encouraged by policies that excluded these fringe benefits from income or Social Security taxes and by a United States Supreme Court ruling that employee benefits, including health insurance, could be legitimately included in the collective bargaining process, employer-provided health insurance benefits grew rapidly in the middle decades of the twentieth century (Health Insurance Association of America 1992).

Beyond private-sector growth in health insurance coverage came the passage in 1965 of the Medicare and Medicaid legislation, providing more access to mainstream health services through publicly subsidized health insurance for the aged and many of the poor. With enactment of these programs, fully 85 percent of the American population had some form of health insurance.

Although public policies have been extremely important factors in the development of health-related organizations and systems, the vast majority of them have emerged in the context of a market economy. Thus, much about the healthcare system in the United States has been shaped by the market forces of supply and demand, and by the related decisions and actions of the buyers and sellers in this marketplace. The combination of market forces and public policies has shaped a complex and dynamic healthcare system.

In the healthcare system, health services are provided through a large and diverse variety of organizations and systems. One way to envision the diversity of these health services organizations and systems is to consider a continuum of health services that people might use over the course of their lives and to think of the organizational settings that provide them (Longest, Rakich, and Darr 2000). Pre-birth, the continuum could begin with organizations (or programs) that minimize negative environmental impact on human fetuses or that provide genetic counseling, family planning services, prenatal counseling, prenatal ambulatory care services, and birthing services. This would be followed early in life by pediatric ambulatory services; pediatric inpatient hospital services, including neonatal intensive care units (NICUs) and pediatric ICUs (intensive care units); and both ambulatory and inpatient psychiatric services for children.

For adults, the most relevant health services organizations are those providing adult ambulatory services, including ambulatory surgery centers and emergency and trauma services; adult inpatient hospital services, including routine medical, surgical, and obstetrical services, as well as specialized cardiac care units (CCUs), medical intensive care units (MICUs), surgical intensive care units (SICUs), and monitored units; stand-alone cancer units, with radiotherapy capability and short-stay recovery beds; ambulatory and inpatient rehabilitation services, including specific subprograms for orthopedic, neurological, cardiac, arthritis, speech, otologic, and other services; ambulatory and inpatient psychiatric services, including specific subprograms for psychotics, day programs, counseling services, and detoxification; and home health care services.

In their later years, people might add to the list of relevant health services organizations those providing skilled and intermediate nursing services; adult day care services; respite services for caregivers of homebound patients, including services such as providing meals, visiting nurse and home health aides, electronic emergency call capability, cleaning, and simple home maintenance; and hospice care and associated family services, including bereavement, legal, and financial counseling.

The health services produced in the healthcare system have traditionally been provided by autonomous or independent health services organizations, with little attention to coordination of the continuum of services. Reflecting strongly held preferences for independence and autonomy among the leaders of most of these organizations—Ummel (1997; 13) characterizes this phenomenon as a "deeply rooted fixation on autonomy"—the organizations remained essentially independent of each other except for their arms'-length transactions and economic exchanges.

More recently, however, many health services organizations have significantly changed how they relate to each other (Zelman 1996; Shortell et al. 2000). Mergers, consolidations, acquisitions, and affiliations between and among previously independent organizations are now commonplace. At the extreme end of this activity is vertical integration, in which many organizations join into unified organizational arrangements or systems of organizations. The development of vertically integrated systems capable of providing a largely seamless continuum of health services including primary, acute, rehabilitation, long-term, and hospice care increasingly characterize healthcare. This phenomenon began in the 1970s and is traced in Figure 2.2.

Technically, vertical integration links organizations that are at different stages of the production process of delivering health services. For example, acute hospital services can be linked with home health care agencies, group practices of physicians, and rehabilitative services organizations. Vertical integration can move forward or backward. A large health services delivery system, for example, can integrate backward by linking to a medical supply company from which it will obtain inputs at favorable prices. In forward integration, the same large delivery system can move forward toward the customer by integrating with a physician group practice to link the flow of the practice's patients to the system.

Driven largely by the emergence of managed care and its demands for more and better coordination of patient care along the health services continuum, vertical integration is best understood in the context of what it replaces: a fragmented, compartmentalized state in which health services organizations are predominantly independent of each other or are formally linked only to groups of similar organizations through horizontal integration.

In addition to managed care, a combination of several other market and policy pressures is driving this shift in the healthcare system. They include continuing pressure to contain healthcare costs, growing pressure for higher levels of quality and safety in healthcare, more cohesion among employers regarding their interests in and sense of urgency about reducing their health-benefit expenditures, and the prevalence and continuing growth of managed care for both privately insured and publicly sponsored consumers. These forces show no signs of abatement, and will very likely continue to exert pressure for more integration among organizations within the healthcare system into the foreseeable future. Although there is still extreme diversity in the forms of integration and wide geographic differences in the pace and extent of integration, the shift is markedly toward more integration among health services organizations.

Of course, not all health services organizations are part of integrated systems. Furthermore, a number of people question the rationale for vertical integration and its potential growth (Goldsmith 1994; Slomski 1995). Although the question of how far health services organizations will integrate remains unanswered, eventually the unfolding pattern of

Figure 2.2 The Changing Structure of American Healthcare: Fragmentation to Integration

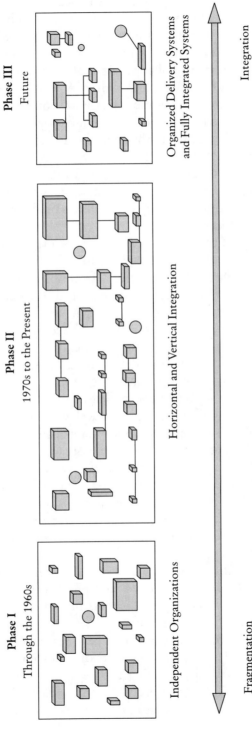

integration may lead to an overall American healthcare system that is composed largely of sets of vertically integrated delivery systems.

Health services in the future may in fact be organized and delivered through even more extensively integrated systems and networks in which providers, spanning the full continuum of health services, are integrated with health plans or insurers and perhaps with suppliers to form entities that tie together many categories of organizations involved in the pursuit of health. Although limited in number and scope, some more fully integrated systems have already formed. The jury is still out on integrating insurers and health plans with delivery systems, but these more fully integrated systems or networks of organizations can provide an extensive and coordinated continuum of health services to enrolled populations and may be the future of the nation's decreasingly fragmented approach to its pursuit of health.

The policy interests of service provider organizations and systems may differ somewhat, but certain generic policy interests are widely shared among them. The attention of those in charge of provider organizations and systems tends to be sharply focused, for example, on policies that might affect access to their services, the costs of those services, or their revenues from them. These individuals also typically tend to be very concerned about policies that relate to the structure of the healthcare system, including antitrust issues involved in mergers and consolidations, policies that relate to meeting the needs of special populations that they may serve, policies pertaining to quality assurance, and a number of ethical and legal issues that arise in providing access to affordable health services of an appropriate quality to all who need them.

Related to, but different from, the organizations and systems that provide health services directly are a variety of health-related organizations that produce resources for the service providers to use in conducting their work or in facilitating this work in some way. This category of organizations can be called *secondary provider organizations*. It includes educational institutions that help produce the healthcare system's work force; insurance companies and health plans that organize and facilitate payment for health services, at least those insurers and plans that are not integrated into provider systems; and pharmaceutical, medical supply, and biomedical technology companies, among others, whose products are used in providing health services.

Secondary provider organizations have health policy interests of their own. For example, the policy interests of educational organizations and programs involved in producing the health workforce include certain traditional ones. They are especially interested in policies that affect the resources used in their educational missions, such as faculty, buildings, and equipment. Interest is also keen in policies that relate to licensure and practice guidelines as well as in those that may influence the demand for their programs' graduates, including policies that affect the number of people covered under public insurance programs and the extent of this coverage.

Beyond these long-standing and continuing educational policy interests are some newer ones. For example, given the crucial role that health-related practitioners play in the nation's pursuit of health, increasing attention is being given to their necessary competencies if they are to make a maximum contribution to health. In one extensive analysis, Shugars, O'Neil, and Bader (1991, 18–20) concluded that future health-related practitioners in general should be prepared to:

- *Care for the community's health.* Practitioners should have a broad understanding of the determinants of health such as environment, socioeconomic conditions, behavior, medical care, and genetics and be able to work with others in the community to integrate a range of services and activities that promote, protect, and improve health.
- *Expand access to effective care.* Practitioners should participate in efforts to ensure access to healthcare for individuals, families, and communities and to improve the public's health.
- *Provide contemporary clinical care.* Practitioners should possess up-to-date clinical skills to meet the public's healthcare needs.
- *Emphasize primary care.* Practitioners should be willing and able to function in new healthcare settings and interdisciplinary team arrangements designed to meet the primary healthcare needs of the public.
- *Participate in coordinated care.* Practitioners should be able to work effectively as team members in organized settings that emphasize high-quality cost-effective integrated services.
- *Ensure cost-effective and appropriate care.* Practitioners should incorporate and balance cost and quality in the decision-making process.
- *Practice prevention.* Practitioners should emphasize primary and secondary preventive strategies for all people. (*Primary* prevention is prevention of the disease or injury itself through such means as requiring motorcycle helmets be worn, education programs concerning smoking and substance abuse, and measles immunization. *Secondary* prevention blocks progression of an injury or disease through such means as using Papanicolaou smears to look for early cellular changes that are thought to be precursors of cancer [Pickett and Hanlon 1998].)
- *Involve patients and families in the decision-making process.* Practitioners should expect patients and their families to participate actively

both in decisions regarding their personal healthcare and in evaluating its quality and acceptability.

- *Promote healthy lifestyles.* Practitioners should help individuals, families, and communities maintain and promote healthy behavior.
- *Assess and use technology appropriately.* Practitioners should understand and apply increasingly complex and often costly technology and use it appropriately.
- *Improve the healthcare system.* Practitioners should understand the determinants and operations of the health system from a broad political, economic, social and legal (and ethical) perspective to continuously improve the operations and accountability of that system.
- *Manage information.* Practitioners should manage and use large volumes of scientific, technological, and patient information.
- *Understand the role of the physical environment.* Practitioners should be prepared to assess, prevent, and mitigate the impact of environmental hazards on the health of the population.
- *Provide counseling on ethical issues.* Practitioners should provide counseling for patients in situations where ethical issues arise, as well as participate in discussions of ethical issues in healthcare as they affect communities, society, and the health professions.
- *Accommodate expanded accountability.* Practitioners should be responsive to increasing levels of public, governmental, and third-party participation in and scrutiny of the shape and direction of the healthcare system.
- *Participate in a racially and culturally diverse society.* Practitioners should appreciate the growing diversity of the population and the need to understand health status and healthcare through differing cultural values.
- *Continue to learn.* Practitioners should anticipate changes in healthcare and respond by redefining and maintaining professional competency throughout practice life.

The education and deployment of a workforce whose members possess these competencies will be affected not only by policies, many of them state policies, that affect a broad range of issues related specifically to the education of this workforce, but also by policies that relate more generally to the costs of operating the healthcare system, providing access to its services, and ensuring the quality of those services. The leaders of health-related educational organizations can be expected to maintain their traditional health policy interests and to add these newer ones to the list.

Health plans and insurance organizations are vitally interested in policies that affect their operations and decisions. Because insurers and health plans are licensed by the states, they have interests in both federal and state health policies that affect their markets and operations. Similarly, pharmaceutical and biotechnology firms and companies in the medical supply business have wide-ranging health policy interests, including specific interests in policies that affect their markets, products, and profits.

Indeed, all service provider organizations, as well as the secondary providers that supply them with needed resources, are interested in health policy, if only because policy affects their performance levels. Mesch (1984) constructed a set of questions that people in senior-level management positions can use to determine the relative interest they might have in the impact of public policies on their organizations or systems. The questions, in an adapted form, are:

- Do public policies influence your organization or system's capital allocation decisions or its strategic plans for services and markets?
- Have previous strategic plans been scrapped or substantially altered because of changes in public policy?
- Is your organization or system's industry becoming more competitive? More marketing oriented? More technology dependent?
- Does the interplay between public policies and the other variables in your organization or system's external environment seem to be influencing strategic decisions?
- Are you and other senior-level managers in your organization or system displeased with the results of past strategic planning because of surprises resulting from changes in public policies that affected your organization or system's performance?

If the managers of a health-related organization or system, whether a service provider or a secondary provider of resources, can answer yes to even one of these questions, then they are likely to be very interested in the public policymaking process and in relevant policies. If the answer to most or all of the questions is "yes," as is typically the case for contemporary health-related organizations and systems, they will consider interest in their organization or system's public policy environment to be absolutely imperative and will make strong operational commitments to understanding and effectively responding to the threats and opportunities presented to their organization or system by public policy (Longest 1997).

Health Policies and Health-Related Interest Groups

Health services and secondary provider organizations, as discussed in the previous section, are not the only entities with health policy concerns and interests. A wide variety of health-related interest groups, including some that are consumer-based or that are organized around individual health practitioner memberships, exist because of the collective interests of their individual or organizational members in health policymaking and the resulting health policies.

As will be discussed more fully in chapter 3, one of the most significant features of the policymaking process and its political environment in the United States, as much so in health as in any other domain, is the presence of a large number of interest groups whose purpose is to serve the collective interests of their members. These groups seek to analyze the policymaking process to discern policy changes that might affect their members and inform them about such changes. They also seek to influence the process to provide the group's members with some advantage. The interests of their constituent members define the health policy interests of these groups.

Some of the health-related interest groups have service provider organizations and systems for their members. Hospitals can join the American Hospital Association (AHA) (www.aha.org); long-term care organizations can join the American Health Care Association (AHCA) (www.ahca.org) or the American Association of Homes and Services for the Aging (AAHSA) (www.aahsa.org); and HMOs, preferred provider organizations (PPOs), and other network-based health plans can join the American Association of Health Plans (AAHP) (www.aahp.org).

Other interest groups represent individual health practitioners. Physicians can join the American Medical Association (AMA) (www. ama-assn.org). African-American physicians may also choose to join the National Medical Association (NMA) (www.natmed.org), and women physicians may also choose to join the American Medical Women's Association (AMWA) (www.amwa-doc.org). In addition, physicians have the opportunity to affiliate with groups, usually termed "colleges" or "academies," where membership is based on medical specialty. Prominent examples are the American College of Surgeons (ACS) (www.facs. org) and the American Academy of Pediatrics (AAP) (www.aap.org). Other personal membership groups include the American College of Healthcare Executives (ACHE) (www.ache.org), American Nurses Association (ANA) (www.ana.org), and the American Dental Association (ADA) (www.ada.org), to name only some.

Often, in addition to national interest groups, service provider organizations as well as individual health practitioners can join state and local groups, usually affiliates of national groups, that also represent their interests. For example, states have state hospital associations and state medical societies. Many urban centers and densely populated areas even have groups at the regional, county, or city level.

The secondary provider organizations also have their own interest groups. Examples include:

- American Association of Health Plans (which was also listed above as an interest group whose members are service provider organizations) (AAHP);
- Association of American Medical Colleges (AAMC) (www.aamc.org);
- Association of University Programs in Health Administration (AUPHA) (www.aupha.org);
- Biotechnology Industry Organization (BIO) (www.bio.org);
- Blue Cross and Blue Shield Association (www.bluecares.com);
- Health Insurance Association of America (HIAA) (www.hiaa.org); and
- Pharmaceutical Research and Manufacturers of America (PhRMA) (www.phrma.org).

Like groups whose members are service providers, these groups whose members are secondary providers also place particular focus on policies that affect their members directly.

In addition to interest groups of service and secondary providers, there are a number of interest groups to which individuals, as individuals or consumers rather than as executives or health practitioners, can belong. Reflecting the diversity of the population from which their members are drawn, groups with individual member constituencies are quite varied. In forming what Buchholz (1994) calls "solidarity groups," some of these groups are based at least in part on feelings of common identity based on a shared characteristic such as race, gender, age, or connection to a specific disease or condition. Examples include:

- American Association of Retired Persons (AARP) (www.aarp.org);
- American Heart Association (AHA) (www.americanheart.org);
- National Association for the Advancement of Colored People (NAACP) (www.naacp.org);
- National Organization for Women (NOW) (www.now.org).

Interest groups such as NAACP and NOW serve the health interests of their members as part of much broader agendas focused generically on racial and gender equality. Although the Fourteenth Amendment to the U.S. Constitution guarantees equal protection under the law, American history clearly shows how difficult this equality has been to achieve. Interest groups, such as the NAACP and NOW, have made their central public policy goal equality at the polls; in the workplace; and in education, housing, health services, and other facets of life in America.

The specific health policy interests of groups representing African Americans encompass adequately addressing this population segment's unique health problems—widespread disparities in health status and access to health services, higher infant mortality, higher exposure to violence among adolescents, higher levels of substance abuse among adults, and, compared to other segments of the population, earlier deaths from cardiovascular disease and many other causes. Similarly, groups representing the interests of women seek to address their unique health problems. In particular, they focus on such health-related interests of their members as breast cancer, childbearing, osteoporosis, family health, and funding for biomedical research on women's health problems.

A growing proportion of the American population is over the age of 65; the elderly have specific health interests related to their stage of life. As people age, they consume relatively more healthcare services and their healthcare needs differ from those of younger people. They also become more likely to consume long-term-care services and community-based services intended to help them cope with various limitations in the activities of daily living. In addition to their unique health needs, older citizens have a special health policy history and, therefore, a unique set of expectations and preferences regarding the nation's health policy. The Medicare program, in particular, includes extensive provisions for health benefits in the context of the nation's social insurance support for its older citizens and is a key feature of this history. Building on the specific interests of older people and their preferences to preserve and extend their healthcare benefits through public policies, organizations such as AARP and the National Council of Senior Citizens (www.ncscinc.org) have become important organizations for serving the health policy interests of their members.

Other interest groups with individual constituencies reflect member interests based primarily on specific diseases or conditions such as the American Cancer Society (ACS) (www.cancer.org) or the Consortium for Citizens with Disabilities (CCD) (www.c-c-d.org). The American Heart Association (AHA), for example, has more than 4.2 million volunteer members. Its overall goal is the reduction of disability and death from cardiovascular diseases and stroke, the leading causes of death in the United States.

AHA pursues its goal through a number of avenues, including direct funding of research, public and professional education programs, and community programs designed to prevent heart disease. It also seeks to serve its members' interests through influencing public policy related to heart disease. As the AHA notes on its web page, in pursuing its central goal the association "plans, coordinates and implements a national legislative and regulatory program in conjunction with its 15 affiliates, including maintaining and expanding contact with members of Congress, the Executive Branch, selected health coalitions and other national organizations."

The Real World of Health Policy

American Heart Association
Federal Public Policy Agenda
107th Congress

Research

Basic/Clinical Research—To reduce disability and death from cardiovascular diseases and stroke, the AHA seeks to double in five years federal funding for the National Institutes of Health, and achieve significant real growth in federal funding at the National Heart, Lung, and Blood Institute and the National Institute of Neurological Disorders and Stroke.

Health Promotion and Disease Prevention

Tobacco—To discourage tobacco use—a major modifiable risk factor for cardiovascular diseases and stroke—the AHA supports a broad set of public policy measures including but not limited to significant price increases on tobacco products; full FDA authority over the manufacture, sale, distribution, labeling and promotion of tobacco products; significant funding for tobacco control programs; and the elimination of smoking in public places.

Physical Activity—The AHA has determined that both sedentary lifestyles and obesity are major risk factors for cardiovascular diseases. To promote physical activity and to assist populations to maintain a healthy weight, the AHA supports public policy measures to ensure the incorporation of physical activity as a major component of appropriate disease prevention and health promotion efforts.

Nutrition—To give consumers the information they need to follow a prudent diet, the AHA supports public policy priorities to ensure improvements in the Nutrition Labeling and Education Act, and to expand and support the federal government role in nutrition education and adherence to U.S. dietary guidelines.

Quality and Availability of Care

Access to Health Care—The AHA supports public policy priorities to prompt access to appropriate quality medical care, including appropriate preventive care, risk modification programs and heart and stroke rehabilitative programs.

Emergency Cardiovascular and Stroke Care—The AHA strongly supports regulatory and legislative measures to ensure prompt access to appropriate quality medical care, including the implementation of an effective heart and stroke chain of survival and the passage of appropriate public access defibrillation laws.

Cardiovascular and Stroke Drugs and Devices—The AHA supports equal access to the most appropriate cardiovascular and stroke drugs, treatments and medical devices.

Charitable Organizations

Non-Profit Advocacy—The AHA supports legislative and regulatory measures to ensure the AHA's ability to advocate its views before Congress and the regulatory agencies.

Tax Policy—In order to preserve and enhance the important contributions of the non-profit sector, the AHA will be vigilant in ensuring that legislative and administrative actions support the continued vitality of the sector, including the preservation of the charitable deduction.

Source: Reprinted with permission from the American Heart Association. The association's advocacy agenda can be read at www.americanheart.org/Support/Advocacy.

Summary

Health policies have direct and often dramatic impact on the determinants of health. These determinants include the physical environments in which people live and work; their behaviors and biology; social factors such as their economic circumstances, their socioeconomic position in society, income distribution within the society; discrimination based on factors such as race/ethnicity, gender, or sexual orientation, and the availability of social networks/social support; and their access to appropriate health services.

In addition to their impact on health determinants, and through this impact, their relationship to the health of individuals and populations, health policies also affect the lives of individuals in other ways. Policies also have important effects on health-related organizations and systems, and on interest groups. Health policy is of consequence to some people, organizations and systems, and interest groups for reasons quite apart from its effect on the health of individuals. The ability of health-related organizations and systems to fulfill their missions is heavily influenced by the relative generosity or parsimony of reimbursement policies for example. Interest groups exist to serve the interests of their members, and these interests often involve a role in exerting influence in the development of health policy.

Discussion Questions

1. For whom does health policy have consequences?
2. Discuss the impact of health policies on the physical environment.
3. Discuss the impact of health policies on human behavior and biology.
4. Discuss the impact of health policies on the social factors that help determine health.
5. Discuss the impact of health policies on health services in terms of the money, human resources, and technology used to produce these services.
6. Discuss the consequences of health policy for individuals, for health-related organizations and systems, and for interest groups.

References

Anderson, G., and P. S. Hussey. 2001. "Comparing Health System Performance in OECD Countries." *Health Affairs* 20 (3): 219–32.

Auerbach, J. A., B. K. Krimgold, and B. Lefkowitz. 2000. *Improving Health: It Doesn't Take A Revolution.* Washington, DC: National Policy Association and Academy for Health Services Research and Health Policy.

Buchholz, R. A. 1994. Business Environment and Public Policy: Implications for Management, 5th ed. Upper Saddle River, NJ: Prentice-Hall.

Dubos, R. 1959. *The Mirage of Health.* New York: Harper.

Fronstin, P. 2000. *Sources of Health Insurance and Characteristics of the Uninsured: Analysis of the March 2000 Current Population Survey.* EBRI Issue Brief No. 228. Washington, DC: Employee Benefit Research Institute.

Goldsmith, J. 1994. "The Illusive Logic of Integration." *Healthcare Forum Journal* 35 (5): 26–31.

Health Insurance Association of America. 1992. *Source Book of Health Insurance Data.* Washington, DC: The Association.

Institute of Medicine. 2000. *To Err Is Human. Building a Safer Health System.* Washington, DC: National Academy Press.

Klerman, L. V. 1992. "Nonfinancial Barriers to the Receipt of Medical Care." *The Future of Children* 2 (2): 171–85.

Longest, B. B., Jr. 1997. *Seeking Strategic Advantage Through Health Policy Analysis.* Chicago: Health Administration Press.

Longest, B. B., Jr., J. S. Rakich, and K. Darr. 2000. *Managing Health Services Organizations and Systems*, 4th ed. Baltimore: Health Professions Press.

Louis Harris & Associates. 1996. *Getting Involved Survey*. New York: Louis Harris and Associates.

Medicare Payment Advisory Commission. March 1999. *Report to the Congress. Medicare Payment Policy*. Washington, DC: MedPAC.

————. June 2000. *Report to the Congress. Selected Medicare Issues*. Washington, DC: MedPAC.

Mesch, A. H. 1984. "Developing an Effective Environmental Assessment Function." *Managerial Planning* 32 (1): 17–22.

National Center for Health Statistics. 2000. *Health, United States, 2000*. Washington, DC: National Center for Health Statistics.

Organization for Economic Cooperation and Development. 2000. *OECD Health Data 2000*. Paris: OECD.

Pickett, G. E., and J. J. Hanlon. 1998. *Public Health Administration and Practice*. St. Louis, MO: Mosby, Inc.

Shortell, S. M., R. R. Gillies, D. A. Anderson, K. M. Erickson, and J. B. Mitchell. 2000. *Remaking Health Care in America: The Evolution of Organized Delivery Systems*, 2nd ed. San Francisco: Jossey-Bass Publishers.

Shugars, D. A., E. H. O'Neil, and J. D. Bader (eds.). 1991. *Healthy America: Practitioners for 2005, An Agenda for Action for U.S. Health Professional Schools*. Durham, NC: Pew Health Professions Commission.

Slomski, A. J. 1995. "Maybe Bigger Isn't Better After All." *Medical Economics* 72 (4): 55–60.

Starfield, B. 1992. "Child and Adolescent Health Status Measures." *The Future of Children* 2 (2): 25–39.

Ummel, S. L. 1997. "Pursuing the Elusive Integrated Delivery Network." *Healthcare Forum Journal* 40 (2): 13–19.

Zelman, W. A. 1996. *The Changing Health Care Marketplace: Private Ventures, Public Interests*. San Francisco: Jossey-Bass Publishers.

3

THE CONTEXT AND PROCESS OF HEALTH POLICYMAKING

WHETHER HEALTH policies take the form of laws, rules or regulations, operational decisions, or judicial decisions, as described in chapter 1, they are all decisions, and they are made through a well-established, although very complex, decision-making process. Policies in both the allocative and regulatory categories are made through this process. With certain variations, policies at the federal, state, and local levels of government are made through very similar processes. Furthermore, the structure of the decision-making process is the same for all policy domains, whether the domain is health, education, defense, taxes, welfare, or other domains. Although health policy is the focus, all public policy is made through a decision-making process called policymaking.

The domain of health policy is very broad because health is a function of several determinants: the physical environment within which people live and work; their behaviors and biology; social factors; and the health services to which they have access. Not only is the health policy domain broad, there are numerous overlaps and blurred lines between the health domain and other policy domains. For example, it is impossible, as a practical matter, to consider health policy aside from its relationship to tax policy. Health policy cannot be separated from the fact that government must finance, essentially through taxes, the services or programs established by health policy, whether in the form of health services for the beneficiaries of the Medicare program, research in biomedical laboratories, or other services. At a minimum, any dollars spent as a result of health policies always have alternative uses in other domains to which the money could be directed by policymakers.

Another example of how policy domains overlap is the 1996 Personal Responsibility and Work Opportunity Reconciliation Act (P.L. 104-193), also known as the Welfare Reform Act, which had significant health implications. In addition to the obvious impact of changes in the nation's welfare policy on such health determinants as the social and economic environments faced by affected people, this law affects eligibility for the Medicaid program in a fundamental way. Since the establishment of the Medicaid program in 1965, eligibility for a key welfare benefit, Aid to Families with Dependent Children (AFDC), and eligibility for Medicaid benefits have been linked. Families receiving AFDC have been automatically eligible for Medicaid and enrolled in the Medicaid program. The Welfare Reform Act, however, replaced AFDC with the Temporary Assistance to Needy Families (TANF) block grant. Under the provisions of the TANF block grant, states are given broad flexibility to design income support and work programs for low-income families with children and are required to impose federally mandated restrictions, such as time limits, on federally funded assistance.

The Welfare Reform Act does provide that children and parents who would have qualified for Medicaid based on their eligibility for AFDC continue to be eligible for Medicaid, but, in the absence of AFDC, states find it necessary to use different mechanisms to identify and enroll former AFDC recipients in their Medicaid programs. This example of the overlap between the policy domains of health and welfare is typical of the ways in which policy in one domain relates to policy in other domains.

The purpose of this chapter is to present both a model of the public policymaking process and a description of the political context within which the policymaking process takes place. The political context—or political marketplace, as it is often called—is discussed first.

The Context of Health Policymaking: The Political Marketplace

A useful conceptualization of the political marketplace for health policies can be based on the operation of traditional economic markets because economic markets and political markets share a number of characteristics. Many different kinds of products and services, including those used in the pursuit of health, are bought and sold in the context of economic markets. In these markets, willing buyers and sellers enter into economic exchanges involving something of value to both parties. One party demands and the other supplies. By dealing with each other through market transactions, individuals and organizations buy needed resources and sell their outputs. These relationships can be summarized as follows:

Sellers   Economic Exchanges in Market Transactions   Buyers
(Suppliers) ◄─────────────────────────────────► **(Demanders)**

Because people are calculative regarding the relative rewards and costs incurred in the exchanges they make in markets, they negotiate these exchanges. Negotiation (or bargaining) involves two or more parties attempting to settle what each shall give and take (or perform and receive) in an economic transaction between them. The next section shows a parallel between this feature of economic markets and the operation of political markets. In the interactions of negotiation that take place in an economic market, the parties attempt to agree on a mutually acceptable outcome in a situation where their preferences for outcomes are usually negatively related. Indeed, if the preferences for outcomes are positively related, an agreement or contract can be reached almost automatically.

More typically, among parties to a negotiation, at least two types of issues must be resolved through the negotiations. One type of issue involves the division of resources, the so-called "tangibles" of the negotiation, such as who will receive how much money and what products or services in the exchange. Another type of issue centers on the resolution of the psychological dynamics and the satisfaction of personal motivations of the parties in the negotiations. These issues are the so-called "intangibles" of the negotiation and can include such things as appearing to win or lose, to compete effectively, or to cooperate fairly.

Negotiations in economic exchange situations usually follow one of two strategic approaches: cooperative (win/win) or competitive (win/lose) strategies. The choice of the negotiating strategy best used in any particular situation is a function of the interaction of several variables. Greenberger et al. (1988) contrast the optimal conditions for the use of cooperative negotiating strategies with the optimal conditions for competitive strategies. Cooperative negotiating strategies work best when

- The tangible goal of both negotiators is to attain a specific settlement that is fair and reasonable.
- Sufficient resources are available in the environment for both negotiators to attain their tangible goal, more resources can be attained, or the situation can be redefined so that both negotiators can "win."
- Each negotiator thinks it is possible for both of them to attain their goals through the negotiation process.
- The intangible goals of both negotiators are to establish a cooperative

relationship and to work together toward a settlement that maximizes their joint outcomes.

Competitive negotiating strategies work best when

- The tangible goal of both negotiators is to attain a specific settlement or to get as much as they possibly can.
- Resources available are not sufficient for both negotiators to attain their goals, or their desires to get as much as possible makes it impossible for one or both to actually attain their goals.
- Both negotiators think it is impossible for both of them to attain their goals simultaneously.
- The intangible goal of both negotiators is to beat the other.

The Operation of Political Markets

Much about the operation of economic markets applies to the way political markets operate. Health policies, indeed, all public policies, are made within the context of political markets, which in many ways operate like traditional economic markets. There are, however, some notable differences between economic and political marketplaces. The most fundamental difference is that in economic markets buyers or demanders express their preferences by spending their own money. That is, in economic markets buyers reap the benefits of their choices, and they also directly bear the costs of their choices. In political markets, on the other hand, the linkage between who receives benefits and who bears costs is not so direct. Feldstein (1996), for example, observes that public policies are routinely established that impose costs on future generations. The nature of the political marketplace dictates that many of the decisions of contemporary policymakers are influenced by the preferences of current voters, perhaps to the detriment of future generations. This phenomenon can be seen in policies related to decisions about such allocative policies as Social Security and Medicare.

The Real World of Health Policy

Changing Demographics Are Driving the Need for Changes in Social Security

The main reason for Social Security's long-range financing problem is demographics. We're living longer and healthier lives . . . and this is good news. When the Social Security program was created in 1935, a 65-year-old had an average life expectancy of 12½ more years; today, it's 17½ years—and rising. In addition, 76 million baby boomers will begin retiring in about 2010, and in about 30 years, there will be nearly twice as many older Americans as there are today. At the same time, the number of workers paying into Social Security per beneficiary will drop from 3.4 to 2.1. These changes will strain our retirement system.

Social Security Is an Economic Compact Among Generations

Many people think that their Social Security tax contributions are held in interest-bearing accounts earmarked for their own future retirement needs. Social Security is actually an intergenerational compact—the Social Security taxes paid by today's workers and their employers go mostly to fund benefit payments for today's retirees.

Social Security is now taking in more in taxes than is paid out in benefits, and the excess funds are credited to Social Security's trust funds. There is now about $900 billion in the trust funds, and they are projected to grow to more than $6 trillion in the next 25 years. But benefit payments will begin to exceed taxes paid in 2015, and the trust funds will be exhausted in 2037. At that time, Social Security will be able to pay only about 72 percent of benefits owed . . . if no changes are made.

Choices Lie Ahead

There are a variety of ways to ensure the long-term stability of Social Security. But each option involves difficult trade-offs that need to be discussed.

For example, on the benefit side, some people propose that the retirement age for full Social Security benefits should be raised further. They say that Americans are living longer and healthier lives than ever before. Also, people are spending an increasing number of years in retirement. This strains the system. Critics say most Americans now choose to retire early, and that it would be hard for some people to find good jobs or to work beyond the current retirement age because of their health or the nature of their jobs.

On the revenue side, some people believe that Social Security taxes should be paid on all income. They say that the current earnings limit of $76,200 in 2000 allows wealthier Americans to avoid paying Social Security taxes on some of their income. Critics say that Social Security is supposed to be a foundation for retirement planning. If wealthier people contributed more to Social Security, they would have to receive more in benefit—and in some cases much more.

On the investment side, some people support creating individual savings accounts for all workers to supplement or replace part of Social Security benefits. They say that workers would have the potential for more money in retirement than if they rely only on Social Security, and that they could have the freedom to choose how to invest their savings. Critics say that you can get higher returns on investments only by taking higher risks. And they say that if the accounts were a supplement to Social Security, a way to fund them would have to be created. If the accounts were to replace part of Social Security, a lower level of guaranteed Social Security benefits would have to be established.

Some people think the government and not individuals should invest Social Security reserves in the stock market. They say the government is better able to risk a market downturn than are individual workers. Critics say that the government could end up owning a sizable share of private companies.

There are many other options and suggestions being discussed.

Source: Excerpted from Social Security Administration. August 2000. *The Future Of Social Security.* Washington, DC: Social Security Administration, Publication No. 05-10055.

Feldstein (1996) also points out that decision makers in political markets use different decision criteria than those used in traditional economic markets. In both markets, wise decision makers take into account both the benefits and the costs of their decisions. In political markets, however, decision makers may use different time frames. Because legislators stand for periodic reelection, they typically favor policies that provide immediate benefits to their constituencies and they tend to weigh only, or certainly more highly, immediate costs. Unlike most decision makers in economic markets, where the costs and benefits of decisions are taken into account over the long run, in political markets decision makers are more likely to base decisions on whether immediate benefits exceed immediate costs. An obvious consequence of this is that policies with *immediate* benefits, but with burdensome *future* costs, occur.

The differences between the operations of economic and political markets notwithstanding, both those who "supply" policies and those individuals or groups who "demand" policies recognize the innate value of policies. In political markets, both suppliers and demanders stand to reap benefits or incur costs because of policies. Policies are valued commodities in the political marketplace. These relationships are shown in Figure 3.1.

Given that demanders and suppliers in political markets will enter into exchanges involving policies, it is important to know who the demanders and suppliers are and what motivates their decisions and actions in these markets.

Figure 3.1 The Operation of Political Markets

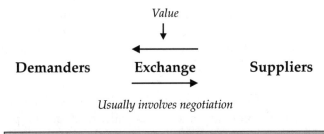

> Structurally and operationally, a political
> market is very much like an economic market.

Demanders and Suppliers of Health Policies

Thinking of political markets as operating similarly to economic markets—that is, as markets in which something of value is exchanged between suppliers and demanders—permits public policies to be viewed as valued commodities, as a means of satisfying certain demanders' wants and needs in much the same way that products and services produced and sold in the private sector's economic markets serve to satisfy demanders (usually called consumers). In private markets, demanders seek products and services that satisfy them. In political markets, demanders seek public policies that satisfy their preferences. Policymakers are in positions to supply the public policies that demanders seek.

The Demanders of Health Policies

Broadly, the demanders of health policies can include anyone who considers such policies to be relevant to the pursuit of health for themselves or others about whom they care, or who considers such policies to be a means to some other desired end, such as economic advantage. It is these desired ends of enhanced health or other advantages that motivate the participation of demanders in political markets, just as desired ends motivate participation in economic markets.

For individuals, however, effective participation in the political marketplace, as individuals, presents certain problems and limitations. For example, if they are to participate effectively, individuals must acquire substantial amounts of policy-relevant information. This usually involves time and money, often in considerable amounts. Beyond this, individual participants or demanders often must be prepared to expend additional resources, again money and time, in support of achieving desired policies.

This expense problem is exacerbated by the fact that any particular health policy might have significant, or even noticeable, benefits for only a relatively small number of individuals. Consequently, demanders participate as individuals to a very limited degree in the political markets for policies.

Organizations, with their pooled resources, have a significant advantage over individuals in the political marketplace. They may have the necessary resources both to garner needed policy-relevant information and to support their efforts to achieve desired policies. Their pooled resources are not their only advantage over individuals in the political marketplace. The health policy interests of organizations may be very concentrated. A change in Medicare policy that results in an increased deductible of $100 per year for certain individuals is one thing. A policy change that results in several million dollars of revenue for a health services organization is quite another. Organizations tend to be more effective demanders of health policy than individuals, in part because the stakes for them tend to be higher.

The most effective demanders of policies, however, are the well-organized interest groups. (More is said about interest groups and their role in influencing the public policymaking process in subsequent chapters.) Interest groups are groups of people or organizations with similar policy goals who enter the political process to try to achieve their goals. By combining and concentrating the resources of their members, interest groups can have a much greater impact in political markets than either individuals or organizations.

In effect, interest groups provide their members, whether individuals or organizations, with greater opportunities to participate effectively in the political marketplace. This is what the American Medical Association (AMA) (www.ama-assn.org) does for individual physicians; what the American Association for Retired Persons (AARP) (www.aarp.org) does for older individuals; what the American Association of Health Plans (AAHP) (www.aahp.org) does for its member organizations; and what the Pharmaceutical Research and Manufacturers of America (PhRMA) (www.phrma.org) does for its member companies. Because of their powerful roles in political markets, interest groups, as demanders of health policy, are described more fully below.

Interest Groups in the Political Marketplace

Interest groups arise in democratic societies from the existence of groups of people interested in particular benefits to be derived or outcomes to be achieved through their collective action within the political marketplace, specifically through influencing the public policymaking process. They are ubiquitous in the United States, as much so in the health domain as in any other. The right to organize such groups, as well as to participate in them, is granted by and protected by the U.S. Constitution. The First Amendment to the Constitution guarantees the American people the right "peaceably to assemble, and to petition the Government for a redress of grievances." However, constitutional guarantees notwithstanding, from the nation's beginning to the present day, political theorists have disagreed about whether interest groups play essentially positive or negative roles in American political life (Olson 1965; Wilson 1973; Ornstein and Elder 1978; Moe 1980; Truman 1993; Peters 1999; Edwards, Wattenberg, and Lineberry 2001).

James Madison, writing in several of *The Federalist Papers* in 1788, discussed the relationship of groups, which he called "factions," to democratic government. In *Federalist* Number 10, he defined a faction as "a number of citizens, whether amounting to a majority or a minority of the whole, who are united and actuated by some common impulse of passion, or of interest, adverse to the rights of citizens, or to the permanent and aggregate interests of the community." As can be seen in the last part of his definition, Madison felt strongly that factions, or interest groups, were inherently bad. He also believed, however, that the formation of such groups was a natural outgrowth of human nature (he wrote in *Federalist* Number 10 that "the latent causes of faction are sown into the nature of man") and that government should not seek to check this activity.

In his wisdom, Madison felt that what he called the "mischiefs of faction" could and should be contained by setting the "ambition" of one faction against the selfish preferences and behaviors of other factions or groups. So began an enduring history of uncertainty about and ambiguity toward the role of interest groups in public policymaking in the United States. One point about which there is neither uncertainty nor ambiguity, however, is that interest groups play an active role in the public policymaking process. Reflecting widely divergent views on the manner in which interest groups play their role in this process, two very distinct perspectives on ways in which groups influence policymaking have emerged: the pluralist and the elitist models.

The Pluralist Perspective. People who hold the pluralist perspective on the role of interest groups in policymaking believe that because so many interest groups are operating, everyone's interests can be represented by one or more of them. Adherents to the pluralist model usually maintain that interest groups play an essentially positive role in public policymaking. The pluralists argue that a very large variety of interest groups compete with and counterbalance each other in the political marketplace where public policymaking occurs. Adherents to the pluralist perspective do not question that some groups are stronger than others. However, pluralists argue that as they seek their preferred outcomes power is widely dispersed among competing groups, with groups winning some of the time and losing some of the time.

Pluralist theory about how the policymaking process works includes several interconnected arguments that, when taken together, constitute what has come to be called a group theory of politics (Truman 1993). The central tenets of the group theory of how the public policymaking process works, at all levels of government, include the following:

- Interest groups provide essential linkages between people and their government.
- Interest groups compete among themselves for outcomes of the policymaking process, with the interests of some groups counterbalanced by the interests of others.
- No group is likely to become too dominant in the competition; as groups become powerful, other countervailing interests organize or existing groups intensify their efforts. An important mechanism for maintaining balance among the competing groups is their ability to rely on various sources of power. Groups representing concentrated economic interests may have money, but consumer groups may have larger numbers of members.
- The competition among interest groups is basically fair. Although there are exceptions, groups typically play by the rules of the game.

In the face of a large and growing number of interest groups, some observers have concluded that the pluralist approach of encouraging and facilitating the formation of interest groups is out of control. Indeed, a very large number of groups have emerged to play parts in the American policymaking process. More than 22,000 interest groups today, with national memberships in such domains as business, education, religion, science, and health, are actively pursuing a variety of policy interests on behalf of their members (*Encyclopedia of Associations* 1987). The problem, according to the critics of pluralism, is not merely the large number of groups, but the fact that government seems to consider the demands and preferences of all interest groups to be legitimate.

There is little argument that government does attempt to satisfy the preferences of many interests, sometimes in conflicting ways. Lowi (1979) coined the phrase "interest group liberalism" to refer to his view of the federal government's excessive deference to interest groups. Others call the phenomenon hyperpluralism (Edwards, Wattenberg, and Lineberry 2001).

Whether they call it interest group liberalism or hyperpluralism, critics of the pluralist approach to the role of interest groups in the public policymaking process strongly agree on two points:

- Interest groups have become too influential in the policymaking process. Satisfying their multiple and often conflicting demands seems to drive government rather than government being driven by a desire to base policy decisions on considerations of what is best for the nation as a whole—that is, on the public interest.
- Seeking to satisfy the multiple and often conflicting demands of various interest groups leads to confusion, contradiction, and even paralysis in the policymaking process. Rather than making a difficult choice between satisfying X or Y, government seems frequently to pretend there is no need to make the choice and seeks to satisfy both X and Y.

In addition to those who criticize the pluralist approach as dysfunctional and out of control are those who believe that the perspective itself is misguided, even wrong. Instead of everyone having a chance to participate in influencing the policymaking process through one group or another, some people believe that such influence actually resides only in the hands of an elite few.

The Elitist Perspective.   Whereas pluralists point with pride to the remarkable number of organized interest groups actively and aggressively participating in the American process of public policymaking, people holding the elitist perspective point out how relatively powerless and ineffectual most groups are. The elitist perspective on the role of interest groups, which is the opposite of the pluralist viewpoint, grows out of a power elite model of American society.

This model is based on the idea that real political power in the United States is concentrated in the hands of the very small proportion of the population that controls the nation's key institutions and organizations and much of its wealth. In the elitist perspective, these so-called "big interests" look out for themselves in part by disproportionately influencing, if not controlling, the public policymaking process. Whether this model accurately reflects the nature of the American political marketplace is debatable, but the model does represent the opinions of a growing majority of Americans concerning which members of the society have the most influence in the political marketplace.

The elitist theory holds that a power elite, often referred to as "the establishment," acts as a gatekeeper to the public policymaking process. That is, unless the power elite considers an issue to be important the issue does not even get on the policy agenda. Furthermore, the theory holds, once an issue is on the agenda, public policies made in response to triggering problems mostly reflect the values, ideologies, and preferences of this governing elite (Buchholz 1994). Thus, the power elite dominates public policymaking through its superior position in society. It shapes the formulation of policies and controls their implementation through taking powerful roles in the nation's economic and social systems. It has been argued that the nation's social and economic systems in fact depend upon elite consensus on behalf of the fundamental values of the system, and the only policy alternatives that will be given serious consideration are those that fall within the shared consensus (Dye 2001).

The central tenets of the power elite theory relating to how the public policymaking process works in regard to the role of interest groups stand in stark contrast to the pluralist perspective. These tenets are:

- Real political power resides in a very small number of groups; the large number of interest groups is practically meaningless because the power differentials among them are so great. Other groups may win minor policy victories, but the power elite always prevails on the significant policy issues.
- Members of the power elite share a consensus or near consensus on the basic values that should guide public policymaking: private property rights, the preeminence of markets and private enterprise as the best way to organize the economy, limited government, and the importance of both individual liberty and individualism.
- Members of the power elite have a strong preference for incremental changes in public policies. Incrementalism in policymaking permits time for the economic and social systems to adjust to changes without feeling threatened, with a minimum of economic dislocation or disruption, and with minimal alteration in the social system's status quo.
- Elites take care in protecting their power bases. Some limited movement of non-elites into elite positions is permitted to maintain social stability, but only after non-elites clearly accept the elites' consensus values. (Dye and Zeigler 1993; Edwards, Wattenberg, and Lineberry 2001)

Which Perspective Is Correct? Those who hold the power elitist perspective challenge those who hold the pluralist perspective by pointing to the highly concentrated and interlocked power centers in American society. Studies of the concentration of political power do find that about one-third of the top leadership positions in the United States—corporate, foundation, and university governing boards, for example—are held by people who occupy more than one such position (Dye 1994).

Those who prefer the pluralist perspective, however, are equally quick to cite numerous examples in which those who traditionally have been grossly underrepresented in the inner circles of the power elite have succeeded in their collective efforts to influence significantly the public policymaking process in the United States. African Americans, women, and consumers in general provide powerful examples of the ability of the disenfranchised or of people who have long been ignored by policymakers to organize as effective interest groups and thus to redirect the course of the public policymaking process in dramatic ways.

Neither the pluralist nor the elitist perspective alone fully explains how the interests of individuals or of organizations, acting through interest groups, relate to the public policymaking process. The results of the policymaking process affect to varying degrees the interests of all individuals and all organizations. Many with interests, if not all, can influence the policymaking process, although, again, not to equal degrees. Both the elitist and the pluralist approach have something of value to contribute to efforts at understanding the roles that interest groups play in the marketplace for public policies. Whether such groups play their roles proactively by seeking to stimulate new policies that serve the interests of their members or reactively by seeking to block policy changes that they do not believe serve their members' best interests, they are intrinsic to the public policymaking process. Interest groups provide their members a way to link their policy preferences into a more powerful, collective voice that greatly increases the likelihood of a significant influence on policymaking.

The Suppliers of Health Policies

Because policies are made in the executive, legislative, and judicial branches of government, the list of potential suppliers of health policies—the policymakers—is lengthy. Members of each branch of government play roles as suppliers of policies in the political market, although the roles are played in very different ways.

Legislators as Suppliers

One group of public policy suppliers is elected legislators, whether members of the U.S. Congress, state legislatures, or city councils. Few aspects of the political marketplace are as interesting, or as widely observed and studied, as the question of motivation behind the policymaking decisions and actions of elected legislators. To a large extent, this intense interest in the motivations of policy suppliers reflects the desire by policy demanders for some effective means to pursue their desired policies by exerting influence over the suppliers.

Although neither extreme fully reflects the motivations of legislators, the end points on a continuum of behaviors policymakers might exhibit can be represented by those who seek to maximize the public interest on one end, and by those who seek to maximize self-interest on the other end. A legislator at the public interest extreme would always seek policies that maximize the public interest, although the true public interest might not always be easy to identify. A legislator whose motivations lie at the self-interest extreme would always behave in a manner that maximizes self-interest, whether that interest is reelection, money, prestige, power, or whatever appeals to the self-serving person.

In the political marketplace, legislators can be found all along the continuum between extreme public- and extreme self-interest motivations. Although some people incorrectly ascribe dominant self-interest motives to all legislators, the actions and decisions of most legislators, most of the time, are more likely to reflect a complex mixture of the two motivations, with exclusively self-interested or public-interested motives only rarely dominating decisions.

Motives aside, legislators at all levels of government are key suppliers of policies, especially of policies in the form of laws. In political markets, legislators constantly calculate the benefits and costs of their policymaking decisions, and consider who will reap these benefits and bear these costs. Factoring in the interests they choose to serve, they make their decisions accordingly. Their calculations become complicated when the costs and benefits of a particular decision affect many different people in different ways, as most policies do.

In effect, policies typically create winners and losers. The gains enjoyed by some people come at the financial expense of others, or at least at the expense of having someone's problems ignored or someone's preferred solutions postponed. Without overgeneralization, it is fair to say that most of the time most legislators seek to maximize their own net political gains through their policy-related decisions because reelection is an abiding objective.

In view of the reality of winners and losers being created by most policies, legislators may find that their best strategy is to permit the winners their victory, but not by a huge margin, and in so doing to cushion the impact on the losers. For example, suppose a legislator is considering a policy that would increase health services for an underserved population but at the expense of higher taxes on others. Options include various policies with the following outcomes: (1) few services at relatively low cost; (2) more services at higher costs; and (3) many services at very high costs. Facing such a decision, and applying the concept of net political gain, policymakers might opt for the provision of a meaningful level of services, but one far below what could have been provided and at a cost below what would have been required for a higher level of services. The "winners" receive more services, but the expense for the "losers" who have to pay for the new services is not as great as it might have been. Through such "political calculus," legislators routinely seek to maximize their net political gains.

Executives and Bureaucrats as Suppliers

At all levels of government, members of the executive branch play an important role as suppliers of policies, although their role differs from that of legislators. Presidents, governors, mayors, and other senior public-sector executives offer policies in the form of legislative proposals and seek to have legislators enact their preferred policies. Chief executives, as well as those in charge of government departments and agencies, also make policies directly in the form of rules or regulations used to guide the implementation of laws, and in the operational protocols and procedures they use to operationalize the policies they are responsible for implementing. Career bureaucrats who also participate in these activities and thus become suppliers of policies in the political marketplace join elected and appointed executives and managers in their rulemaking and operational duties.

Elected and politically appointed officials of the executive branch often are affected by the same self-interest/public-interest dichotomy that affects legislators; reelection concerns in particular often directly influence their decisions. Like legislators, elected and politically appointed members of executive branches are apt to calculate the net political gains available through their policy-related decisions and actions. As a result, their motivations and behaviors are often quite similar to those of legislators as they participate in the political marketplace. However, there are some important differences between the motivations and behaviors of elected and appointed members of the executive branch of a government and the elected members of its legislative branch.

The most fundamental difference derives from the fact that the executive branch generally bears greater responsibility than does the legislative branch for the state of the economy and is widely perceived to bear even more responsibility than it actually does. Presidents, governors, and mayors, along with their top appointees, are held accountable much more explicitly for economic conditions than the Congress, state legislatures, or city councils. Although legislators do not escape this responsibility altogether, the public typically lays most of the responsibility for the economy at the feet of the executive branch. Even when people do blame the legislative branch, they tend, at least in part, to hold the entire Congress or the state or city legislature collectively responsible rather than to blame individual legislators.

The concentration of responsibility for the condition of the economy in the executive branch heavily influences the decision making that takes place there. Because of the close connection between government's budget and the state of the economy, the budget implications of every policy decision will be very carefully weighed in the executive branch. Not infrequently, positions on health policies will differ between the legislative and executive branches because members in the two branches attach different degrees of importance to the budget implications of the policies they are considering.

Career bureaucrats, or civil servants, in the executive branch, whose participation in rulemaking and operations makes them suppliers of policies, also participate in policymaking in the legislative branch as well. When they collect, analyze, and transmit information about policy options and initiate policy proposals in their areas of expertise, they are important participants in policymaking within the legislative branch. However, the motivations and behaviors of career bureaucrats tend to differ both from those of legislators and those of elected or appointed members of executive branches.

The behaviors and motivations of career bureaucrats in the public sector are often analogous to those of employees in the private sector. Workers in both settings typically seek to satisfy certain of their personal needs and desires through their work. This can obviously be categorized as serving their self-interests in both cases. But government employees are no more likely to be totally motivated by self-interests than are private-sector workers. Most workers in both sectors are motivated by similar blends of self-interest and interest in what is good for the larger society.

However, it is also fair to point out that most career bureaucrats watch a constantly changing mix of elected and senior government officials—with an equally dynamic set of policy preferences—parade past them, while they remain as the most permanent human feature of government. It should surprise no one that career bureaucrats develop strong senses of identification with their home departments or agencies or that they develop attitudes of protectiveness toward them. This protectiveness is most visible in the relationships between government agencies or departments and those with legislative oversight over them, including authorization, appropriation, and performance review responsibilities. Many career bureaucrats equate the well-being of their agencies, in terms of their size, budgets, and prestige, with the public interest. This obviously is not necessarily the case.

The Judiciary as Supplier

The judicial branch of government also is a supplier of policies. For example, whenever a court interprets an ambiguous law, establishes judicial procedure, or interprets the U.S. Constitution, it makes policies. These activities are not conceptually different from those involved when legislators enact public laws or when members of the executive branch establish rules and regulations to guide implementation of laws or make operational decisions regarding their implementation. All these activities represent policymaking because they lead to authoritative decisions made within government for the purpose of influencing or directing the actions, behaviors, and decisions of others.

Policymaking in the judicial branch, however, does differ in certain ways from that in the legislative and executive branches, not only in focus but in operation as well. The responsibilities of courts require them to focus narrowly on the issues involved in specific cases or situations. This stands in stark contrast to the wide-open, if not chaotic, political arena in which most other public policymaking occurs.

The courts are involved in numerous and diverse aspects of health policy, reflecting the entire range of determinants of health (i.e., physical environment, behavior and genetics, social factors, and health services). The courts, for example, are routinely involved in policymaking in a wide range of areas such as termination of treatment, environmental protection, approval of new drugs, and genetics. In the past decade, the courts have been especially active in health policy regarding the organization and delivery of health services in four specific areas (Anderson 1992; Potter and Longest 1994):

- the coverage decisions made by insurers in both the private and public sectors;
- the Medicaid program's payment rates to hospitals and nursing homes;
- the antitrust issues involved in hospital mergers; and
- issues related to the charitable mission and tax-exempt status of nonprofit hospitals.

The heart of the judiciary's ability to supply policies lies in its role in interpreting the law. This power includes the power to declare federal and state laws unconstitutional—that is, to declare laws enacted by the legislative branch to be null and void. The judiciary also interprets the meaning of laws, an important role because many public laws contain vague language. A particularly important element in their role as suppliers of policies rests on the fact that the courts can exercise the powers of nullification, interpretation, and application to the rules and regulations established by the executive branch in carrying out its implementation responsibilities.

An example of the interpretative role of the courts in health policymaking is the ruling by the U.S. Supreme Court in April 1995 that the federal Employee Retirement Income Security Act (ERISA) (P.L. 93-406) does not preclude states from setting hospital rates. The case that resulted in this ruling arose out of New York's practice of adding a surcharge to certain hospital bills to raise money to help pay for health services for some of the state's low-income citizens. The state's practice was challenged by a group of commercial insurers and HMOs and by New York City (Green 1995). A number of health-related interest groups filed a joint *amicus curiae* ("friend of the court") brief in the case in which they asserted that Congress, in enacting ERISA, never intended for it to be used to challenge state health reform plans and initiatives. The Supreme Court's ruling is seen generally as supportive of state efforts to broaden access to health services for their poorer residents through various reforms and initiatives.

Health policymaking within the judicial branch of government is far more prevalent in state courts and lower federal courts than in the U.S. Supreme Court. A state-level example of courts making important health policy can be seen in Pennsylvania courts in cases involving the tax-exempt status of healthcare organizations. In one 1995 case, for example, the Indiana County, Pennsylvania, Court of Common Pleas rebuffed the leaders of Indiana Hospital in their appeal to have the hospital's tax-exempt status restored after the exemption had been revoked by the county in 1993. In making its ruling, the court held that the hospital failed to meet adequately one of the state's tests through which an organization qualifies for tax exemption. Among other things, at the time of this case the state required a tax-exempt organization "to donate or render gratuitously a substantial portion of its services."

In making its ruling, the Indiana County Court took note of the fact that Indiana Hospital's uncompensated charity care in fiscal year 1994 had amounted to approximately 2 percent of its total expected compensation, and contrasted this with an earlier case resulting from the revocation of the tax-exempt status of a nursing home in the state. The state Supreme Court decision in the St. Margaret Seneca Place nursing home case (*St. Margaret Seneca Place v. Board of Property Assessment Appeals and Review, County of Allegheny, PA*) had been that the nursing home did meet the state's test because it demonstrated that it bore more than one-third of the cost of care for half of its patients.

The variation in these and several other Pennsylvania cases in the courts' interpretation of the state's partial test for tax-exempt status (i.e., the requirement that a tax-exempt organization is "to donate or render gratuitously a substantial portion of its services") led to enactment in 1997 of clarifying legislation on this and other points regarding the determination of tax-exempt status. Late in that year, the Governor of Pennsylvania signed into law House Bill 55, known as the Institutions of Purely Public Charity Act, or Act 55. This act permits an institution to meet the charitable purpose test and qualify for tax exemption if it has a charitable mission, is free of private profit motive, is designated a 501 (c)(3) by the federal government and is organized for any of the following reasons:

- relief of poverty;
- advancement and provision of education including secondary education;
- advancement of religion;
- prevention and treatment of disease or injury, including mental retardation and mental illness;
- government or municipal purposes; or
- accomplishment of a purpose that is recognized as important and beneficial to the public and that advances social, moral, or physical objectives.

The act specifically clarified, quite liberally, how an institution could meet the requirement for donating or rendering gratuitously a substantial portion of its services. Act 55 established 3 percent of an institution's total operating expenses as the necessary contribution of charitable goods or services. In this instance, court decisions were not only policies themselves, but the impact of the decisions eventually led to a significant change in Pennsylvania's public laws.

It is generally acknowledged that, because the pursuit of health in the United States is so heavily influenced by laws and regulations, the courts are a major factor in the development and implementation of health policies (Christoffel 1991). The courts include not only the federal court system, but the systems of the 50 states and the territories. Each of these systems has developed in idiosyncratic ways. Each court system has a constitution to guide it, specific legislation to contend with, and its own history of judicial decisions.

Although the federal and state courts play significant roles as suppliers of policies, their behaviors and motivations as well as their roles differ significantly from those of participants in the legislative and executive branches. In their wisdom, the drafters of the U.S. Constitution created the three branches and ensured under Article III the judicial branch's independence, at least largely so, from the other branches.

An independent judiciary facilitates adherence to the rules of the game by which all participants in the policymaking process must play. Federal judges are appointed rather than elected, and the appointments are for life. Consequently, federal judges, once they occupy these roles, are not subject to the same self-interest concerns related to reelection that many other policymakers must face. This enhances their ability to act in the public interest, although judges, like all policymakers, vary in their personal commitments to this objective.

The Real World of Health Policy

Court Rejects Drug Discounts for Vermonters

Montpelier, VT, June 9, 2001—An appeals court has barred Vermont from offering reduced drug prices under a state program, saying a federal agency acted improperly when it approved the program.

Under the program, the state offered enrollees discounts of up to 30 percent, then required pharmaceutical companies to make up the difference. The Vermont plan had been approved by the federal Health and Human Services Department.

The program, which has been copied by several other states, was challenged in federal court by a trade group representing the pharmaceutical industry.

A three-judge panel of the United States Court of Appeals for the District of Columbia Circuit ruled on Friday that Vermont lacked the authority to offer the same prescription rebates and discounts offered under federal Medicaid insurance.

Congress imposed those rebate requirements to reduce the cost of Medicaid, the court said, but because Vermont's program resulted in no Medicaid savings, the federal health agency acted improperly in approving it, the judges said.

"It's a big win for the pharmacy companies and a big loss for Vermont's seniors who need medication," Gov. Howard Dean said after the ruling on Friday.

In a statement, the Pharmaceutical Research and Manufacturers of America, the trade group representing the industry, said it was pleased with the ruling. "Vermont's plan would have put the Medicaid program—the nation's safety net for the poor and disabled—in jeopardy," the statement said.

A spokeswoman for Health and Human Services said the decision was being reviewed.

Vermont, New Hampshire and Maine have put together another program, a regional buying pool, that also will offer discounts. But it is not due to begin until Nov. 1.

Source: Reprinted by permission of The Associated Press.

Interplay Among Demanders and Suppliers in the Political Marketplace

Within the context of the political marketplace, many participants—both demanders and suppliers of policies—seek to further their objectives. The various objectives can be self-interest objectives involving some health or economic advantage, or public-interest objectives based on views about what is best for the public, or at least some specific subset of society such as the elderly, poor, or medically underserved. In both cases, the outcome depends greatly on the relative abilities of some participants in the exchanges within the marketplace to influence actions, behaviors, and decisions of other participants.

It is important for anyone interested in the political marketplace to realize that not all participants have equal footing. This is true because participants have different amounts of power and influence for use in this market, just as they do in economic markets.

Power and Influence in Political Markets

Influence in political markets, just as in private economic markets, is "simply the process by which people successfully persuade others to follow their advice, suggestion, or order" (Keys and Case 1990, 38). But to have influence one must also have power. *Power*, in the context of market relationships and exchanges, whether in economic or political markets, is the potential to exert influence. More power means more potential to influence others. Therefore, an understanding of influence requires an understanding of power.

Those who wish to exert influence in the political marketplace must first acquire power, using the various sources of such power that might be available to them (Alexander and Morlock 1997). The classic scheme for categorizing the sources or bases of interpersonal power includes legitimate, reward, coercive, expert, and referent power (French and Raven 1959). Several of these bases of interpersonal power have direct application to the issue of the power of individuals, organizations, and interest groups in political markets.

Legitimate power, for example, derives from relative position in a social system or in an organization or group; this form of power is also called *formal power* or authority. It exists because it is advantageous to assign or ascribe certain powers to individuals, organizations, or groups for them to be able to fulfill their duties or to perform their work effectively. Thus, elected officials, appointed executives, and judges, as well as health professionals, corporation executives, union leaders, and many other individual participants in the political marketplace possess certain legitimate power that accompanies their social or organizational positions. Similarly, certain organizations and interest groups, including both suppliers and demanders of policies, possess legitimate or formal power. That is, they can exert influence in the policymaking process because they are recognized as legitimate in the process.

Reward power is based on the ability to reward compliance with the behaviors that are sought in others. Reward power stems in part from the legitimate power a person, organization, or group holds. Reward power comes in many forms. Within organizations it includes the obvious: pay increases, promotions, work and vacation schedules, recognition of accomplishments, and such status symbols or perks as club memberships and office size and location. In economic markets, reward power lies in the hands of consumers by virtue of their buying power. In political markets, reward power is more likely to come in the form of such political capital as favors that can be provided or exchanged, specific influence with particular individuals or groups, and whatever influence can be stored for later use. *Coercive power* is the opposite of reward power and is based on the capacity to withhold or to prevent someone from obtaining desired rewards.

The Real World of Health Policy

Lobbyist's Medical School Ploy Made Law

TALLAHASSEE, June 20, 2001—Gov. Jeb Bush signed a health care bill Tuesday that contains a provision sought by a single influential lobbyist, loosening admission standards at Florida's medical schools to guarantee slots to military academy graduates.

But the battle rages on over a last-minute maneuver so linked in the public mind to a sole beneficiary that lawmakers and medical experts simply call it the "Spinelli amendment."

The governor will ask the courts to rule whether he can veto broad language on the same subject, tied to an appropriation to the University of Florida, in the $48-billion state budget he signed last Friday.

The amendment was the inspiration of Michael Spinelli, an Orlando-area lobbyist and campaign fund-raiser who is friendly with some Central Florida lawmakers, including state Sen. Dan Webster, R-Winter Garden.

Spinelli's son, Joseph, is a U.S. Naval Academy midshipman whose application to UF's medical school was rejected. The lobbyist could not be reached Tuesday, but he said of his work on the bill last month: "I helped out a little bit."

In what is widely seen as a textbook case of the Legislature tilting to the interests of the well-connected, Webster's amendment was adopted on an unrecorded voice vote and became embedded in a huge bill with dozens of provisions important to state agencies and health professions. A few lawmakers raised questions, but Webster fended them off.

The amendment surfaced on the Senate floor on the last night of the session during hurried discussion of a 318-page health care "train." The bill deals with myriad of health care issues from licensing fees for doctors to the relocation of the state Board of Nursing from Jacksonville to Tallahassee.

"It's a train, I guess, because it is large and had many different items," Bush said Tuesday. "But they were all health-related and they all went through a process, so we did sign it into law."

The broader provision, which Bush said "compromises the integrity of the legislative process," required medical schools at UF, the University of South Florida and Florida State University to guarantee space to all students or graduates of the four military academies. The bill Bush signed Tuesday requires two slots in each medical school be set aside each year for military school applicants.

Bush first became aware of the Spinelli amendment when he read about it in the St. Petersburg Times last month. Flying on a state aircraft to Miami, the governor shook his head as he read the story, remarking to fellow passengers, "Did you see this? He failed the test."

Dr. Robert Watson, a top UF official, said the provision gives military-school graduates an unfair advantage and demeans those Annapolis or West Point grads who have met the school's rigorous admissions standards.

"If you have a quota for any group and they have lesser qualifications than others, it means you will be denying spots to medical school for those who deserve them based on merit. There are no quotas for admission to this medical school," said Watson, senior associate dean for educational affairs at UF's College of Medicine. "Next, we'll have two set-asides for the children of legislators."

For lawmakers to carve out a "quota" for a select few "doesn't sound very Republican to me," Watson said.

Webster, the amendment's sponsor, referred questions to legislative aide Kathy Mears, who described his role as brokering a compromise on the session's next-to-last day by tailoring a narrower admissions policy for military academy graduates than the unlimited one already in the budget that, as a conference committee report, could not be changed.

Mears described Spinelli as a constituent, saying "Michael is in our district." She said the two-slots-per-med-school provision won't help Joseph Spinelli directly because he will go to medical school out of state.

"It wasn't for Joseph, but it was as a result of that experience that Sen. Webster learned that military academy graduates are not being accepted at any Florida schools."

UF's Watson said that was "absolutely, completely, totally false." He said five military school graduates are members of the current 100-or-so medical school class.

Source: Reprinted with permission from the *St. Petersburg Times*, June 20, 2001. Steve Bousquet; Staff Writer Alisa Ulferts contributed to this report. (Copyright *St. Petersburg Times* 2001.)

Expert power, which tends to reside in individuals more so than the other sources of power, but which can also reside in a group or organization, derives from possessing expertise valued within the political marketplace, such as expertise in solving problems or performing crucial tasks. People with expert power often occupy formal positions of authority in organizations or groups, which transfers some of the expert power to the organization or group. People with expert power that can be exercised in the policymaking arena may also simply be trusted advisers or associates of other participants in the political marketplace.

Referent power derives from the fact that some people, organizations, and interest groups engender admiration, loyalty, and emulation from others to such an extent that they gain power to exert influence as a result. In the marketplace for policies, this form of power, when it pertains to individuals, is called *charismatic power*. Charismatic power usually belongs to a select few people, who typically have very strong convictions about the correctness of their preferences and great self-confidence in their own abilities, and who are widely perceived to be legitimate agents of change. It is rare for a person, organization, or interest group to be able to gain sufficient power to heavily influence policymaking simply from referent or charismatic power, even in political markets where charisma is highly valued. But it can certainly give the other sources of power in the political marketplace a boost.

Importantly, for the use and for understanding the impact of power, these bases of power in the political marketplace are interdependent. They can and do at times complement or conflict with each other. For example, people, organizations, or groups that are in a position to use reward power, and who do so wisely, can strengthen their referent power. Conversely, those who abuse coercive power might quickly weaken or lose their referent power. Effective participants in the marketplace for policies—those individuals, organizations, and groups that succeed at translating their power into influence—tend to be fully aware of the sources of their power and to act accordingly. They seem to understand intuitively the costs and benefits associated with using each kind of power they possess and can draw on them appropriately in different situations and with various people they wish to influence.

Power and Influence of Interest Groups

Some interest groups, including several in the health domain, have been extraordinarily powerful and influential participants in the political marketplace. These groups are very effective demanders of public policies. To fully appreciate the extent of their power and the influence it permits, it is necessary to understand *iron triangles*, a model of the relationships that sometimes exist among participating individuals, organizations, and groups in the political marketplace.

Any policy domain, whether it is health or another domain, such as defense or education, attracts a set of participating individuals, organizations, and groups, each of which has some stake in the policies affecting the domain and thus seeks to play a role in policymaking in the domain. Some of the participants, or stakeholders, in a domain demand policies; others supply policies. These stakeholders form a *policy community*, whose members share an interest in a particular policy domain.

Traditionally, the membership in the policy community formed around a particular policy domain such as health has included any legislative committees with jurisdiction in the domain, the executive branch agencies responsible for implementing public laws in the domain, and the private-sector interest groups involved in the domain. The first two categories are suppliers of the policies demanded by the third category. This triad of organized interests has been called an iron triangle because its three sides provide stability and the ability to withstand attempts to make undesired changes in the status quo, at least when all three sides of the triangle are in accord on the appropriate policies in the domain.

A policy community that could be appropriately characterized as a very strong and stable iron triangle dominated the health policy domain until the early 1960s when battle lines began to be drawn over the eventual shape of Medicare policy. This triangle featured a small number of powerful interest groups with concordant views that, for the most part, had sympathetic partners in the legislative committees and in the relevant implementing agencies of government.

During this period, the private-sector interest group members of the iron triangle that dominated health policy, notably the American Medical Association (AMA) (www.ama-assn.org) and the American Hospital Association (AHA) (www.aha.org), joined later by the American College of Physicians (ACP) (www.acponline.org) and the American College of Surgeons (ACS) (www.facs.org), generally held a consistent view of the appropriate policies in this domain. Their shared view of optimal health policy was that government should protect the interests of health services providers and not intervene in the financing or delivery of health services (Starr 1982; Wilsford 1991; Peterson 1993). Under the conditions and expectations extant in these rather straightforward relationships, it was relatively simple for the suppliers and demanders of policies to satisfy each other. This triangle was unbreakable into the second half of the twentieth century.

Beginning with the policy battles over Medicare, and with the addition of Medicaid to the debate, however, things began to change dramatically. Fundamental differences emerged among the participants in the health policy community in terms of their views of optimal health policy. No longer did a solid block of concordant private-sector interests drive health policy decisions. The differences over questions of optimal policy shattered the theretofore homogeneous position on health policy that had existed between the AMA and AHA. Even more damaging, a process of splintering within the memberships of these groups began.

Today the medical profession no longer speaks through the single voice of the AMA; organizations such as the ACP, which has now joined with the American Society of Internal Medicine to form ACP-ASIM, and the American Academy of Family Physicians (AAFP) (www.aafp.org) can and sometimes do support different policy choices. Similarly, the AHA now is joined in policy debates by the diverse preferences of organizations representing the specific interests of teaching hospitals, public hospitals, for-profit hospitals, or some other subset of hospitals. These changes among the private-sector interest groups eroded the previous solidarity between their concordant interests and the public-sector members of the health policy community.

Rather than as an iron triangle, the contemporary health policy community is more accurately described as "heterogeneous and loosely structured, creating a network whose broad boundaries are defined by the shared attentiveness of participants to the same issues in the policy domain" (Peterson 1993, 409). There is an important difference, however, between shared attentiveness to health policy issues and agreed-upon positions on optimal health policy or on issues related to it. The loss of concordance among the members of the old iron triangle in health policy has diminished somewhat the power of certain interest groups. Nevertheless, they remain highly influential, and other interest groups have been able to assume influential roles in health policymaking as well. On balance, interest groups remain extraordinarily powerful influences in health policymaking.

Ethics in the Political Marketplace

A fundamental fact about political markets, as places where individuals, organizations, and groups seek to further their policy objectives, is that humans control them. Thus, various mixes of altruism and egoism influence what takes place in political markets. Human control of the public policymaking process means that its operation as well as its outcomes and consequences are directly affected by the ethics of those who participate in the process.

Ethics play an important part in the operation of political markets and in the public policymaking processes that unfold within them. Ethical considerations help shape and guide the development of new policies by contributing to ways in which problems are defined and their policy solutions are structured. Ethical behavior, for any and all participants in the political markets where policymaking occurs, is guided by four philosophical principles: respect for the autonomy of other people, justice, beneficence, and nonmaleficence.

The ethical principle of *respect for autonomy* is based on the concept that individuals have the right to their own beliefs and values and to the decisions and choices that further these beliefs and values. This ethical principle undergirds much of the formal system of government the nation's founders envisioned. Beauchamp and Childress (2001) have pointed out that no fundamental inconsistency or incompatibility exists between the autonomy of individuals and the authority of government so long as government's authority does not exceed the limits set by those who are governed. In this context, autonomy pertains to the rights of citizenship in the United States. Specifically, autonomy relates to the rights of individuals to independent self-determination regarding how they live their lives and to their rights regarding the integrity of their bodies and minds. Respect for autonomy in health policymaking influences issues that pertain to privacy and individual choice, including behavioral or lifestyle choices.

Public policymaking that reflects a respect for the principle of autonomy can sometimes be better understood in contrast to its opposite—paternalism. Paternalism implies that someone knows what is best for other people. Policies guided by a preference for autonomy limit paternalism. One of the most vivid examples of the influence of the principle of autonomy in health policymaking is the 1990 Patient Self-Determination Act (P.L. 101-508). This policy is designed to give individuals the right to make decisions concerning their medical care, including the right to accept or refuse treatment and the right to formulate advance directives regarding their care. These directives allow competent individuals to give instructions about their healthcare, to be implemented at some later date should they then lack the capacity to make medical decisions. In concept, this policy gives people the right to exercise their autonomy in advance of a time when they might no longer be able to exercise that right actively.

The principle of respect for autonomy includes several other elements that are especially important in guiding ethical behavior in policymaking. One of these is telling the truth. Respect for people as autonomous beings implies honesty in relationships. Closely related to honesty is the element of confidentiality. Confidences broken in the policymaking process can impair the process. A third element of the autonomy principle that is important to the policymaking process is fidelity. This means doing one's duty and keeping one's word. Fidelity is often equated with keeping promises. When participants in the policymaking process tell the truth, honor confidences, and keep promises, the process is more ethically sound than if these things are not done.

A second ethical principle of significant importance to public policymaking is the principle of *justice*. The degree of adherence to this principle directly affects the policymaking process and policies themselves. In Rawls' (1971, 5) words, "One may think of a public conception of justice as constituting the fundamental charter of a well-ordered human association." Much of its impact on policies and on policymaking hinges on defining justice as fairness (Rawls 1971). The principle of justice also includes the concept of just deserts, which holds that justice is done when a person receives that which he or she deserves (Beauchamp and Childress 2001).

The practical implications for health policymaking of the principle of justice are felt mostly in terms of distributive justice—that is, in terms of fairness in the distribution of health-related benefits and burdens in society. It has been argued that

> Public health policy is just (fair) where, to the extent possible, it provides services to those in need and imposes burdens and costs on those who endanger the public health. Services provided to those without need are wasteful and, given scarce resources, may deny benefits to those with genuine need. Regulation aimed at persons or businesses where there is no danger imposes costs and burdens without a corresponding public benefit. Ideally, services should be allocated on the basis of need and burdens should be imposed only where necessary to prevent a serious health risk (Gostin 2000, 104–05).

The most difficult policy question deriving from application of the ethical principle of justice is, of course, "What is fair?" The various participants in political markets and in the health policymaking process hold varying opinions on the issue of what is fair distribution of the benefits and burdens involved in the pursuit of health in American society. Useful insight into the range of possible views on fairness in this matter can be gained from considering the three most prominent perspectives on justice.

The *egalitarian* perspective of justice holds that everyone should have equal access to both the benefits and burdens arising from the pursuit of health and that fairness requires recognition of different levels of need. The influence of the egalitarian view of justice can be seen in a number of health policies. Policies intended to remove discrimination in the provision of health services reflect the preference for equality. Policies intended to provide more resources to those who need them most (e.g., Medicare for the elderly or Medicaid for the poor) are also based on an egalitarian view of fairness.

The *libertarian* perspective of fairness requires a maximum of social and economic liberty for individuals. Policies that favor unfettered markets as the means of distributing the benefits and burdens associated with the pursuit of health reflect the libertarian theory of justice.

The third perspective, the *utilitarian* view of fairness, is best served when public utility is maximized. This is sometimes expressed as the greatest good for the greatest number. Many health policies, including those pertaining to restricting pollution, ensuring safe workplaces, and controlling the spread of communicable diseases, have been heavily influenced by a utilitarian view of what is just in the distribution of the benefits and burdens arising from the American pursuit of health.

The principle of justice provides much of the underpinning for all health policies, whether they are in the allocative or regulatory categories. Allocative policies that adhere closely to the principle of justice allocate benefits and burdens according to the provisions of a morally defensible system rather than through arbitrary or capricious decisions. Regulatory policies that are guided by the principle of justice have a fair and equitable impact on those to whom the regulations are targeted. The nation's legal system exists in part to help ensure that the principle of justice is respected in the formulation and implementation of public policies and to serve as an appeals mechanism for those who believe that the process has not adequately honored this principle.

Two other ethical principles have direct relevance to public policy-making: beneficence and nonmaleficence. *Beneficence* in policymaking means that participants in the process act with charity and kindness; that is, they overtly seek to do good. This principle is widely reflected in policies through which benefits in some tangible form are provided. Thus, application of the principle of beneficence characterizes such allocative policies as the Medicare and Medicaid programs. But beneficence includes the complex concept of balancing benefits and burdens. Participants in the political marketplace who seek policies that benefit them or their interests exclusively while burdening others violate the principle of beneficence. Policymakers who are guided by the principle of beneficence make decisions that maximize the net benefits to society as a whole and balance fairly the benefits and burdens of their decisions.

Nonmaleficence, a principle with deep roots in medical ethics, is exemplified in the dictum *primum non nocere*—first, do no harm. Policymakers who are guided by the principle of nonmaleficence make decisions that minimize harm. The principles of beneficence (do good) and nonmaleficence (do no harm) are clearly reflected in health policies that seek to ensure the quality of health services and products. Such policies as the Clinical Laboratory Improvement Amendments 1988 (P.L. 100-578) and the policies that the FDA uses to ensure the safety of pharmaceuticals are examples. Policies that support the conduct and use of outcome studies of clinical care, such as those that established and maintain the Agency for Healthcare Research and Quality (AHRQ) (www.ahcpr.gov), are also examples of policies that reflect the principles of beneficence and nonmaleficence.

The Real World of Health Policy

Quality Standards for Clinical Laboratories

Congress passed the Clinical Laboratory Improvement Amendments (CLIA) in 1988 establishing quality standards for all laboratory testing to ensure the accuracy, reliability and timeliness of patient test results regardless of where the test was performed. A laboratory is defined as any facility which performs laboratory testing on specimens derived from humans for the purpose of providing information for the diagnosis, prevention, treatment of disease, or impairment of, or assessment of health. CLIA is user fee funded; therefore, all costs of administering the program must be covered by the regulated facilities.

The final CLIA regulations were published on February 28, 1992 and are based on the complexity of the test method; thus, the more complicated the test, the more stringent the requirements. Three categories of tests have been established: waived complexity, moderate complexity, including the subcategory of provider performed microscopy (PPM), and high complexity. CLIA specifies quality standards for proficiency testing (PT), patient test management, quality control, personnel qualifications and quality assurance, as applicable. Because problems in cytology laboratories were the impetus for CLIA, there are also specific cytology requirements.

The Health Care Financing Administration (HCFA) is charged with the implementation of CLIA, including laboratory registration, fee collection, surveys, surveyor guidelines and training, enforcement, approvals of PT providers, accrediting organizations and exempt states. The Centers for Disease Control and Prevention(CDC) is responsible for test categorization and the CLIA studies.

To enroll in the CLIA program, laboratories must first register by completing an application, pay fees, be surveyed, if applicable and become certified. CLIA fees are based on the certificate requested by the laboratory (that is, waived, PPM, accreditation, or compliance) and the annual volume and types of testing performed. Waived and PPM laboratories may apply directly for their certificate as they aren't subject to routine inspections. Those laboratories, which must be surveyed routinely; i.e., those performing moderate and/or high complexity testing, can choose whether they wish to be surveyed by HCFA or by a private accrediting organization. The HCFA survey process is outcome oriented and utilizes a quality assurance focus and an educational approach to assess compliance.

Data indicates that CLIA has helped to improve the quality of testing in the United States. The total number of quality deficiencies has decreased approximately 40% from the first laboratory survey to their second. Similar findings were demonstrated in the review of PT data. The educational value of PT in laboratories was known before CLIA existed. Initial PT failures are also addressed with an educational, rather than punitive, approach by CLIA.

Work is currently in progress with the CDC and HCFA to develop a final CLIA rule which will reflect all comments received and new technologies.

Source: This material is excerpted from the Centers for Medicare & Medicaid Services' (formerly the Health Care Financing Administration's) web site, www.cms.gov.

Having considered the context within which health policies are made, especially the structure and operations of the political markets for policies, and having identified the demanders and suppliers who interact in these markets as well as some of the important operational and ethical aspects of these interactions, it is now possible to consider the intricate process through which public policies are made. The consideration begins in this chapter at the conceptual level; an applied discussion of the policymaking process follows in subsequent chapters.

A Conceptual Model of the Public Policymaking Process

The most useful way to conceptualize a process as complex and intricate as the one through which public policies are made is through a schematic model of the process. Although such models, like the one used here, tend to be oversimplifications of real processes, they nevertheless can accurately reflect the component parts of the process as well as their interrelationships. Figure 3.2 is a model of the public policymaking process in the United States.

Key Features of the Policymaking Process

A brief overview of several key features of the policymaking model is presented in this section. These features are important to understanding the policymaking process. The component parts of the model serve to structure much more detailed discussions in chapters 4, 5, 6, and 7.

Figure 3.2   A Model of the Public Policymaking Process in the United States

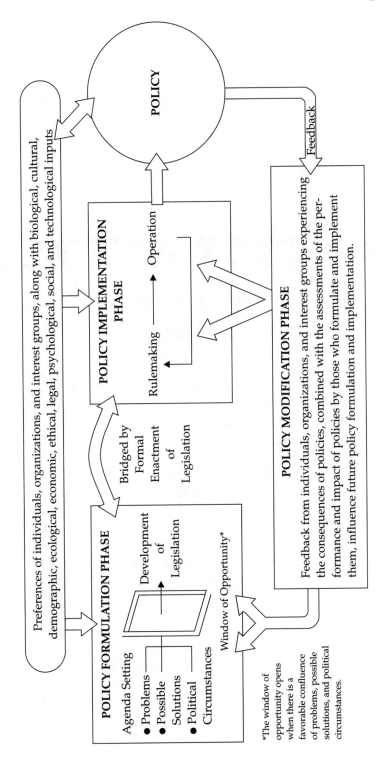

Preferences of individuals, organizations, and interest groups, along with biological, cultural, demographic, ecological, economic, ethical, legal, psychological, social, and technological inputs

POLICY

POLICY FORMULATION PHASE

Agenda Setting
● Problems
● Possible Solutions
● Political Circumstances

Development of Legislation

Window of Opportunity*

Bridged by Formal Enactment of Legislation

POLICY IMPLEMENTATION PHASE

Rulemaking ⟶ Operation

POLICY MODIFICATION PHASE

Feedback from individuals, organizations, and interest groups experiencing the consequences of policies, combined with the assessments of the performance and impact of policies by those who formulate and implement them, influence future policy formulation and implementation.

Feedback

*The window of opportunity opens when there is a favorable confluence of problems, possible solutions, and political circumstances.

Cyclical Process

As the model in Figure 3.2 clearly illustrates, the policymaking process is distinctly cyclical. The circular flow of the relationships among the various components of the model reflects one of the most important features of public policymaking. The process is a continual cycle in which all decisions are subject to subsequent modification. Public policymaking, including that in the health domain, is a process within which numerous decisions are reached but then revisited as circumstances change. This cyclical nature of health policymaking in which decisions are made and then revisited is routinely visible regarding Medicare policy.

The Real World of Health Policy

Changing Medicare Policy

When it was enacted, the Balanced Budget Act of 1997 (BBA) was expected to produce $112 billion in Medicare savings in the first five years (federal fiscal years 1998 through 2002), reducing the projected annual growth rate in program spending from the 8.8 percent baseline estimate to 5.6 percent (Congressional Budget Office 1997). In fact, Medicare spending has grown much more slowly than anticipated: by March 1999, estimated spending for that five-year period was $84 billion less than was expected when the BBA was enacted, and the annual rate of increase was down to 3.9 percent (Congressional Budget Office 1999). There was particular concern about declines in payments for hospital inpatient, skilled nursing facility (SNF), and home health agency (HHA) services, as well as disruptions in the new Medicare+Choice program that was intended to offer expanded private plan options to Medicare beneficiaries (Medicare Payment Advisory Commission 1999).

In response to this concern, the Congress passed the Balanced Budget Refinement Act of 1999 (BBRA), which modified some of the provisions in the BBA that affected payments to providers and plans, adding an estimated $11 billion to Medicare spending in fiscal years 2000 through 2002. Despite this legislation, the latest estimate of program spending in the first five post-BBA years has fallen another $28 billion; estimated Medicare spending for this period is therefore a total of $224 billion (18.2 percent) below the original baseline projection (Congressional Budget Office 2000). This has raised questions about the impact of reduced Medicare payments on the continued viability of the providers and plans that serve the program's beneficiaries.

Comparing trends in estimated Medicare payments with a budget baseline, however, does not necessarily indicate the real impact of the policy changes that have taken place since the BBA. First, "savings" do not necessarily indicate actual reductions in payment levels, although they frequently are misinterpreted that way; they only indicate that spending will be lower than if current law were unchanged. Second, the baseline projection—which is based on the assumption that current law and regulations will continue indefinitely—frequently is an artifact of the budget process. Current law often includes provisions that never were intended to take effect, but were included in previous legislation to inflate future spending estimates and provide easy "savings" in subsequent legislation.

Third, the impact of any change in Medicare provider payments can be meaningfully evaluated only by examining the corresponding costs incurred by those providers. (Of course, not only the actual but also the appropriate level of costs must be considered.) Finally, Medicare does not function in isolation, but as part of an intricate pattern of cross-subsidization among payers, providers, patients, and services. As this pattern shifts over time, the effects of individual policy changes may also vary, and assessing their implications may be more complex than first appears.

How the (Medicare) World Looked in 1997

Over the years, one of the most effective forces driving changes in Medicare payment policy has been the imminent insolvency of the Medicare Hospital Insurance (HI) Trust Fund. The HI Trust Fund, which is used to pay for hospital inpatient services, is financed through payroll taxes at a fixed percentage of earnings. By contrast, the Medicare Supplementary Medical Insurance (SMI) Trust Fund, which is used to pay for physician and other ambulatory services, is financed by a combination of enrollee premiums and general tax revenues, set each year to meet the next year's expected costs. Unlike the SMI Trust Fund, then, the HI Trust Fund's annual revenues and expenses generally do not coincide, and it could run out of money, raising the question of whether and how the corresponding services would be paid for.

Each year, the Social Security and Medicare Trustees report on the recent and projected performance of the Trust Funds under their purview. Several times in the past two decades, these projections have indicated imminent insolvency for the HI Trust Fund, and each time the Congress took major action (Aaron and Reischauer 1995). In the early 1980s, insolvency was projected before the end of that decade, and the Congress responded first with the Tax Equity and Fiscal Responsibility Act of 1982 (TEFRA) and then with the Social Security Amendments of 1983.

TEFRA tightened the limits on payments for acute care hospital inpatient operating costs and called for the development of a PPS to cover those costs; the Social Security Amendments of 1983 enacted that PPS. These actions strengthened the HI Trust Fund, but by the early 1990s, it was again faced with insolvency before the end of the decade. The Omnibus Budget Reconciliation Act (OBRA) of 1993 again tightened hospital payments, but the Trust Fund's prospects remained bleak. A balanced budget bill passed by the Congress in 1995 contained major changes in the Medicare program, but agreement could not be reached between the legislative and executive branches and the bill was vetoed.

By the Spring of 1997, the HI Trust Fund was projected to become insolvent during fiscal year 2000—which was only four years away (see Exhibit 1). Moreover, this deficit was expected to accelerate: by fiscal year 2006—in less than a decade—the obligations of the Trust Fund would exceed its assets by well over $400 billion, with the surge in baby boomer retirees not yet having begun.

Exhibit 1   Actual and Projected Balances in Medicare Hospital Insurance Trust Fund, 1995–2006 (as of April 1997)

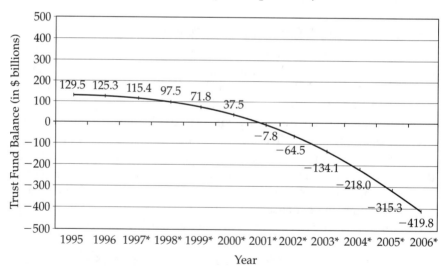

Source: Excerpted and adapted with permission from Stuart Guterman, *Putting Medicare in Context: How Does the Balanced Budget Act Affect Hospitals?* July 2000. Washington, DC: The Urban Institute, pp. 2–5.

Influenced by External Factors

Another important feature of the public policymaking process shown in Figure 3.2 is that the entire process is influenced by factors external to the process itself. This makes the policymaking process an *open system,* one in which the process interacts with and is affected by events and circumstances in its external environment. This important phenomenon is shown in the model by the impact of the preferences of the individuals, organizations, and interest groups who are affected by policies, along with biological, cultural, demographic, ecological, economic, ethical, legal, psychological, social, and technological inputs, on the policymaking process. Two examples of these inputs are discussed below: technological and legal inputs.

As was discussed in chapter 2, the role of technology in the pursuit of health is dramatic. The United States is the world's major producer and consumer of health-related technology. As the policymaking model shows, technological inputs flow into the policymaking process. Among other impacts, the costs of new technologies must be factored into public, as well as private, insurance programs. Figure 3.2 also shows that technology is affected by the policies produced by the process. Funding for the NIH is a good example of such impacts.

The Real World of Health Policy

The Impact of Medical Technology on Future Health Care Costs

The following is excerpted from a study conducted by the Center for Health Affairs of Project HOPE for the Health Insurance Association of America (HIAA) (www.hiaa.org) and Blue Cross and Blue Shield Association (BCBA) (www.bluecares.com). The passage is the Conclusion section of the study.

Historically, new medical advances have exerted an upward impact on health care costs. We expect this to continue in the coming five years, at perhaps a slightly higher pace than the average trend for the 1990s. Increased pressure to buy new medical technology will result as consumers and providers resist efforts on the part of public and private payers to control costs in the near term. Policy changes on the horizon, such as a Medicare drug benefit, may accelerate technology's influence toward the latter half of our forecast period.

Any discussion of the costs of new medical technologies raises a crucial question about the benefit side of the equation. The key question from a societal perspective is not how much technology costs, but whether investments in medical technology are worth the health gains produced. A growing body of research suggests that Americans strongly support medical innovation and are willing to pay for technology. Among many new technologies, there is evidence that they may be cost effective if used in appropriately selected individuals.

The challenge to policymakers and the insurance community is to put in place the incentives for more appropriate use of technology. The challenge for the research community is to enable policymakers and users to better understand the circumstances in which a new technology adds value.

Source: Excerpted with permission from P. E. Mohr, et al. February 28, 2001. *The Impact of Medical Technology on Future Health Care Costs.* Bethesda, MD: Project HOPE.

Legal inputs include decisions made in the courts that affect health and its pursuit. As noted earlier, such decisions are themselves policies. In addition, decisions made within the legal system are important influences on the other decisions made within the policymaking process. Legal inputs help shape all other policy decisions, including reversing them on occasion when they are not consistent with the constitution.

Components Are Interactive and Interdependent

A third important feature of the policymaking model is that it emphasizes the various distinct component parts or phases of the policymaking process, but also shows that they are highly interactive and interdependent. The conceptualization of the public policymaking process as a set of interrelated phases has been used by a number of authors, although there is considerable variation in what the phases of activities are called in these models as well as in their comprehensiveness. Brewer and de Leon (1983) provide a good generic example; Paul-Shaheen (1990) applies such a model specifically to health policymaking.

The public policymaking process includes three interconnected phases:

- policy formulation, which incorporates activities associated with setting the policy agenda and, subsequently, with the development of legislation;

- policy implementation, which incorporates activities associated with rulemaking that help guide the implementation of policies and the actual operationalization of policies; and
- policy modification, which allows for all prior decisions made within the process to be revisited and perhaps changed.

The formulation phase (making the decisions that lead to public laws) and the implementation phase (taking actions and making additional decisions necessary to implement public laws) are bridged by the formal enactment of legislation, which shifts the cycle from its formulation to implementation phase. Once enacted as laws, policies remain to be implemented.

Implementation responsibility rests mostly with the executive branch, which includes many departments that have significant health policy implementation responsibilities—for example, the Department of Health and Human Services (DHHS) (www.dhhs.gov) and the Department of Justice (DOJ) (www.usdoj.gov), and independent federal agencies, such as the Environmental Protection Agency (EPA) (www.epa.gov) and the Consumer Product Safety Commission (CPSC) (www.cpsc.gov). These and many other departments and agencies in the executive branch of government exist primarily to implement the policies formulated in the legislative branch.

The Real World of Health Policy

Children First

Bipartisan consensus is a concept rarely associated with the current U.S. Congress. One policy issue, however, has drawn support from both sides of the aisle in recent years: addressing the plight of the nation's 10 million uninsured children. After all, children are the segment of the population least able to control whether or not they are insured. They are also the least expensive to cover. Unsurprisingly, in the aftermath of the 1994 debacle, the most significant investment the federal government has made in health care is the creation of the Children's Health Insurance Program (CHIP). There are now two government programs available to lower-income, uninsured children: Medicaid, which serves our most destitute children, and CHIP, which is targeted toward kids in working-class families.

Gregg Haifley of the Children's Defense Fund (CDF) estimates that two-thirds of uninsured children qualify for Medicaid or CHIP. Yet these children continue to go without insurance—and not because their parents have some aversion to government-provided coverage. According to a survey from the Kaiser Commission on Medicaid and the Uninsured, 93 percent of parents whose uninsured children were eligible for Medicaid said they would be willing to enroll their kids in the program; 91 percent believe that having health coverage for their children is important. Statistics show that this belief is well founded: Families USA says that uninsured children are six times more likely than children with private insurance to go without needed medical care.

The failure of Medicaid and CHIP to provide health coverage to all needy children can be traced to the fact that these programs were never conceived to be available to every American under the age of 18. Here a comparison to Medicare, the health care program for the elderly, is instructive. Medicare is a universal program: Once Americans hit the age of 65, they are automatically enrolled. (For that reason, 98.7 percent of elderly Americans have health insurance, according to the U.S. Census Bureau.) Medicaid and CHIP, in contrast, are means-tested programs. Administrators must identify families that might be eligible for help, determine whether these families do in fact qualify, and then constantly reevaluate children's eligibility to remain in the program. Unfortunately, many states aren't quite up to this yeoman's task.

In fact, for years many state governments were more interested in keeping children out of Medicaid than in encouraging families to sign up for assistance. California's application form, for example, was anything but user-friendly; it was 40 pages long. As Gregg Haifley of CDF puts it, stock-owning citizens' tax returns weren't that lengthy. In some parts of the country, Medicaid applicants had to provide ample documentation of families' economic holdings—right down to the value of their car. And even after the federal government separated Medicaid from welfare in 1989, some states insisted that applicants go to welfare offices for a face-to-face interview, which was neither convenient for working parents nor (given the comportment of some welfare caseworkers) particularly pleasant.

After the passage of CHIP three years ago, however, most state legislatures began making much more of an effort to reach out to eligible kids. This newfound enthusiasm was partially the result of a big public relations push from the White House and health care activist groups, which were eager to spread the word about the new program. In addition, CHIP provided states with more money and flexibility than Medicaid. Armed with their CHIP funds, many states unfurled glossy ad campaigns, brought state employees up to speed on the fine print of government regulations, and truncated applications (the aforementioned 40-page California form is now only four pages).

Despite these efforts, it's been difficult to make a significant dent in the numbers of uninsured children. Some working families without insurance simply assume that they are ineligible for assistance because at least one parent holds a job. And states with large immigrant populations, like New York and California, have found that illegal residents are hesitant to enroll their children in CHIP or Medicaid, even when their sons or daughters are U.S. citizens, for fear that noncitizen family members could be targeted for deportation or might jeopardize their opportunity to become legal U.S. residents. According to Families USA, 21 percent of uninsured children come from mixed-citizenship families. Unless program administrators can communicate to these parents that their families will not be penalized for enrolling their citizen children in government health programs, this fear could be a significant obstacle to paring down the number of children without health insurance.

Unfortunately, the numbers of uninsured children could increase in the future. According to benefits consultant group William M. Mercer, health care costs will rise significantly. If this happens, more employers will drop coverage for low-wage workers and their dependents. The CHIP program, meanwhile, has not been designed to expand automatically if more children lose their health coverage and qualify for government assistance. CHIP is a bloc-grant program; that is, Uncle Sam gives participating states a parcel of money, and state governments can define benefits and cap enrollment in the program as they see fit. In an economic downturn, some states may decide to get their budgets under control by skimping on CHIP.

If we are really serious about ensuring that all American children have health coverage, we should create a program for them that is roughly analogous to Medicare. Senator John D. Rockefeller IV of West Virginia and Congressman Pete Stark of California, both Democrats, have offered a proposal to enroll all children into a "MediKids" program at birth. Parents would be charged a premium on their annual income tax returns for each month during the year when no other form of health insurance was available to their children. Enrollees would maintain their eligibility until age 23. As Rockefeller explained when he introduced the legislation, a major boon of this approach is that it would largely eliminate "challenging outreach, paperwork, or re-determination hoops to jump through." Under our current system, an enormous amount of effort goes into tracking down eligible children, sorting out whether they qualify for Medicaid or CHIP, and determining whether they maintain their eligibility as their parents' salaries fluctuate and employment status changes. By enrolling all children in a national health program, we would go a long way toward ensuring that every child has access to quality health care—a guarantee that children in virtually every other industrial country can already count on.

Source: Excerpted with permission from Alexandra Starr, January 1, 2001–January 15, 2001."Children First," *The American Prospect* 12 (1).

It is important to remember that some of the decisions made within the implementing entities, as they implement policies, become policies themselves. For example, rules and regulations promulgated to implement a law and operational protocols and procedures developed to support a law's implementation are just as much policies as is the law itself. Similarly, judicial decisions regarding the applicability of laws to specific situations or regarding the appropriateness of the actions of implementing organizations are decisions that are themselves public policies. Policies are established within both the policy formulation and the policy implementation phases of the overall process.

The policy modification phase exists because perfection cannot be achieved in the other phases and because policies are established and exist in a dynamic world. Suitable policies made today may become inadequate with future biological, cultural, demographic, ecological, economic, ethical, legal, psychological, social, and technological changes. Pressure to change established policies may come from new priorities or perceived needs by the individuals, organizations, and interest groups that are affected by the policies.

Policy modification, which is shown as a feedback loop in Figure 3.2, may entail nothing more than minor adjustments made in the implementation phase, or modest amendments to existing public laws. In some instances, however, the consequences of implementing certain policies can feed back all the way to the agenda-setting stage of the process. For example, formulating policies to contain the costs of providing health services—a key challenge facing policymakers today—is, to a large extent, an outgrowth of the success of previous policies that expanded access and subsidized an increased supply of human resources and advanced technologies to be used in providing health services.

A Highly Political Process

One feature of the public policymaking process that the model presented in Figure 3.2 cannot adequately show—but one that is crucial to understanding the policymaking process—is the *political* nature of the process in operation. While there is a belief among many people—and a naive hope among still others—that public policymaking is a predominantly rational decision-making process, this is not the case.

The process would no doubt be simpler and better if it were driven exclusively by fully informed consideration of the best ways for policy to support the nation's pursuit of health, by open and comprehensive debate about such policies, and by the rational selection from among policy choices strictly on the basis of ability to contribute to the pursuit of health. Those who are familiar with the policymaking process, however, know that it is not driven exclusively by these considerations. A wide range of other factors and considerations influence the process. The preferences and influence of interest groups, political bargaining and vote trading, and ideological biases are among the most important of these other factors. This is not to say that rationality plays no part in health policymaking. On a good day, it will gain a place among the flurry of political considerations, but "It must be a very good and rare day indeed when policymakers take their cues mainly from scientific knowledge about the state of the world they hope to change or protect" (Brown 1991, 20).

The highly political nature of the policymaking process in the United States accounts for very different and competing theories about how this process plays out. At the opposite ends of a continuum sit what can be characterized as strictly public-interest and strictly self-interest theories of how policymakers behave. Policies made entirely in the public interest would be those that result when all participants act according to what they believe to be the public's interest. Alternatively, policies made entirely through a process driven by self-interests would reflect an intricate calculus of the interplay of the various self-interests of the diverse participants. Policies resulting from these two hypothetical extremes of the way people might behave in the policymaking process would indeed be very different.

In reality, however, health policies always reflect various mixes of public-interest and self-interest influences. The balance between the public and self-interests being served are quite important to the ultimate shape of health policies. For example, the present coexistence of the extremes of excess (e.g., exorbitant incomes of some physicians and health plan managers, esoteric technologies, and various overcapacities in the healthcare system) alongside true deprivation (e.g., lack of insurance for millions of people and inadequate access to basic health services for millions more) resulting from or permitted by some of the nation's existing health policies suggests that the balance has been tipped too often toward the service of self-interests.

This aside, public policymaking in the health domain in the United States is a remarkably complex and interesting process, although, as in all domains, clearly an imperfect process. The intricacies of the process are explored more thoroughly in the following chapters, where each of its interconnected phases is examined in more detail. One should keep in mind, as the separate components of the public policymaking process are examined individually and in greater detail, that policymaking, in general, is a highly political process; that it is continual and cyclical in its operation; that it is heavily influenced by factors external to the process; and that the component phases and the activities within the phases of the process are highly interactive and interdependent.

Summary

Health policies, like those in other domains, are made within the context of the political marketplace, where demanders for and suppliers of policies interact. The demanders of policies include all of those who view public policies as a mechanism through which to meet some of their health-related objectives or other objectives, such as economic advantage. Although individuals alone can demand public policies, the far more effective demand emanates from organizations and especially from organized interest groups. The suppliers of health policy include elected and appointed members of all three branches of government as well as the civil servants who staff the government.

The interests of the various and diverse demanders and suppliers in this market cannot be completely coincident—often they are in open conflict—and the decisions and activities of any participants always affect and are affected by the activities of other participants. Thus, public policymaking in the health domain, as well as in other domains, is very much a human process, a fact with great significance for the outcomes and consequences of the process.

The policymaking process itself is a highly complex, interactive, and cyclical process that incorporates formulation, implementation, and modification phases. These phases are discussed in turn in chapters 4, 5, 6, and 7.

Discussion Questions

1. Compare and contrast the operation of traditional economic markets with political markets.
2. Who are demanders and suppliers of health policies? What motivates each in the political marketplace?
3. Compare and contrast the pluralist and elitist perspectives on interest groups in the political marketplace.

4. Define power and influence. What are the sources of power in political markets?
5. What role does the application of ethical principles play in political markets?
6. Draw a schematic model of the public policymaking process.
7. Describe the general features of the model drawn in Question 6.

References

Aaron, H. J., and R. D. Reischauer. 1995. "The Medicare Reform Debate: What Is the Next Step?" *Health Affairs* 14 (4): 8–30.

Alexander, J. A., and L. L. Morlock. 1997. "Power and Politics in Health Services Organizations." In *Essentials of Health Care Management*, edited by S. M. Shortell and A. D. Kaluzny, 256–85. Albany, NY: Delmar Publishers, Inc.

Anderson, G. F. 1992. "The Courts and Health Policy: Strengths and Limitations." *Health Affairs* 11 (4): 95–110.

Beauchamp, T. L., and J. F. Childress. 2001. *Principles of Biomedical Ethics*, 5th ed. New York: Oxford University Press.

Brewer, G. D., and P. de Leon. 1983. *The Foundations of Policy Making*. Homewood, IL: Dorsey.

Brown, L. D. 1991. "Knowledge and Power: Health Services Research as a Political Resource." In *Health Services Research: Key to Health Policy*, edited by E. Ginzberg, 20–45. Cambridge, MA: Harvard University Press.

Buchholz, R. A. 1994. *Business Environment and Public Policy: Implications for Management*, 5th ed. Upper Saddle River, NJ: Prentice Hall.

Christoffel, T. 1991. "The Role of Law in Health Policy." In *Health Politics and Policy*, 2nd ed., edited by T. J. Litman and L. S. Robins, 135–47. Albany, NY: Delmar Publishers, Inc.

Congressional Budget Office. December 1997. *Budgetary Implications of the Balanced Budget Act of 1997*. Washington, DC: CBO.

———. 1999. *March 1999 Baseline: Medicare*. Washington, DC: CBO.

———. 2000. *March 2000 Baseline: Medicare*. Washington, DC: CBO.

Dye, T. R. 1994. *Who's Running America? The Clinton Years*, 6th ed. Upper Saddle River, NJ: Prentice-Hall.

———. 2001. *Understanding Public Policy*, Upper Saddle River, NJ: Prentice-Hall.

Dye, T. R., and H. Zeigler. 1993. *The Irony of Democracy: An Uncommon Introduction to American Politics*, 9th ed. San Diego, CA: Harcourt Brace & Company.

Edwards. G. C., M. P. Wattenberg, and R. L. Lineberry. 2001. *Government in America: People, Politics, and Policy*. White Plains, NY: Longman Publishing Group.

Encyclopedia of Associations. 1987. Farmington Hills, MI: The Gale Group.

Feldstein, P. J. 1996. *The Politics of Health Legislation: An Economic Perspective*, 2nd ed. Chicago: Health Administration Press.

French, J. R. P., and B. H. Raven. 1959. "The Basis of Social Power." In *Studies of Social Power*, edited by D. Cartwright, 150–67. Ann Arbor, MI: Institute for Social Research.

Gostin, L. O. 2000. *Public Health Law: Power, Duty, Restraint.* Berkeley, CA: University of California Press.

Green, J. 1995. "High-Court Ruling Protects Hospital-Bill Surcharges." *AHA News* 31 (18): 1.

Greenberger, D., S. Strasser, R. J. Lewicki, and T. S. Bateman. 1988. "Perception, Motivation, and Negotiation." In *Health Care Management: A Text in Organization Theory and Behavior*, 2nd ed., edited by S. M. Shortell and A. D. Kaluzny, 81–141. New York: John Wiley & Sons.

Keys, B., and T. Case. 1990. "How to Become an Influential Manager." *The Executive* 4 (4): 38–51.

Lowi, T. J. 1979. *The End of Liberalism*, 2nd ed. New York: Norton.

Medicare Payment Advisory Commission. March 1999. *Report to the Congress: Medicare Payment Policy.* Washington, DC: MedPAC.

Moe, T. 1980. *The Organization of Interests.* Chicago: University of Chicago Press.

Olson, M. 1965. *The Logic of Collective Action.* Cambridge, MA: Harvard University Press.

Ornstein, N. J., and S. Elder. 1978. *Interest Groups, Lobbying and Policymaking.* Washington, DC: Congressional Quarterly Press.

Paul-Shaheen, P. A. 1990. "Overlooked Connections: Policy Development and Implementation in State-Local Relations." *Journal of Health Policy, Politics and Law* 15 (4): 133–56.

Peters, B. G. 1999. *American Public Policy: Promise and Performance*, 3rd ed. Chatham, NJ: Chatham House.

Peterson, M. A. 1993. "Political Influence in the 1990s: From Iron Triangles to Policy Networks." *Journal of Health Politics, Policy and Law* 18 (2): 395–438.

Potter, M. A., and B. B. Longest, Jr. 1994. "The Divergence of Federal and State Policies on the Charitable Tax Exemption of Nonprofit Hospitals." *Journal of Health Politics, Policy and Law* 19 (2): 393–419.

Rawls, J. 1971. *A Theory of Justice.* Cambridge, MA: The Belknap Press of Harvard University Press.

Starr, P. 1982. *The Social Transformation of American Medicine.* New York: Basic Books, Inc.

Truman, D. B. 1993. *The Governmental Process*, 2nd ed. reprinted. Berkeley, CA: University of California, Institute of Governmental Studies.

Wilsford, D. 1991. *Doctors and the State: The Politics of Health in France and the United States.* Durham, NC: Duke University Press.

Wilson, J. Q. 1973. *Political Organizations.* New York: Basic Books, Inc.

4

POLICY FORMULATION: AGENDA SETTING

I N THIS chapter, as well as in chapters 5, 6, and 7, the three distinct phases of the overall health policymaking process modeled in the previous chapter are examined in detail. This chapter focuses on the agenda setting that occurs in the policy formulation phase of the policymaking process. Chapter 5 focuses on the development of legislation that also occurs in the policy formulation phase. Chapter 6 describes the policy implementation phase and chapter 7, the policy modification phase. These four chapters address the model's application to health policymaking almost exclusively at the national level of government. However, much that is said about the actual process of public policymaking applies to the process as it plays out at state or local levels of government as well. The contexts, participants, and specific mechanisms and procedures used in policymaking obviously differ among the three levels of government, but the core process of policymaking is very similar (Figure 4.1).

Overview of the Policy Formulation Phase

The formulation phase of health policymaking includes two distinct and sequentially related parts: agenda setting and legislation development (see the shaded portion of Figure 4.1). Each of these parts entail complex sets of activities in which policymakers and those who would influence their decisions and actions engage.

The result of the formulation phase of policymaking is policy in the form of new public laws or amendments to existing laws. The public laws or amendments pertaining to health that eventually emerge from the

Figure 4.1 A Model of the Public Policymaking Process in the United States: Agenda Setting in the Policy Formulation Phase

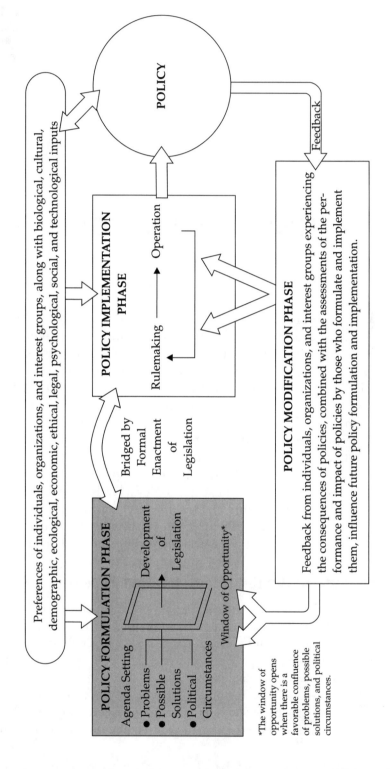

formulation phase are initiated by the interactions of a diverse array of health-related problems, possible solutions to the problems, and dynamic political circumstances that relate both to the problems and to their potential solutions. Before anything else can happen in the sequential policymaking process, some mechanism must initiate the emergence and subsequent movement of certain problem/solution combinations through the process in which public laws are developed as potential policy solutions to the problems.

A useful way to think about how this aspect of the policymaking process unfolds is to consider that, at any particular time, there are a great many problems or issues related to health. Many of them have possible solutions that are apparent to policymakers. Often these problems have alternative solutions, each of which has its supporters and detractors. Diverse political interests that pertain to the problems and to their potential solutions overlay the existence of problems and potential solutions. *Agenda setting*, a crucial initial step in the policymaking process, describes the ways in which particular problems emerge and advance to the next stage.

Once a problem that might be addressed through public policy rises to a prominent place on the political agenda—through the confluence of the problem's identification, the existence of possible policy solutions to the problem, and the political circumstances surrounding both the problem and its potential solutions—it can, but does not necessarily, proceed to the next point in the policy formulation phase, development of legislation. Kingdon (1995) equates the movement of certain problems, along with their associated potential solutions, to the point at which legislation might be developed to address the problems with their passing through a window of opportunity (see Figure 4.1).

At this second point in policy formulation, policymakers put forth specific legislative proposals: one can think of these as hypothetical or unproved potential solutions to the problems they are intended to address. These proposals then go through a process involving carefully prescribed steps that can, but do not always, lead to policies in the form of new public laws or, more likely, in the form of amendments to previously enacted laws.

Only a small fraction of the potential universe of problems that might be addressed through public policy ever emerge from agenda setting with sufficient impetus to advance them to the point of having specific legislative proposals developed as a means of addressing them. And, even when they do, only some of the attempts to enact legislation are successful. The path of legislation—that is, of policy in the form of public laws—can be long and arduous (Hacker 1997). The details of this path that pertain to agenda setting are described in this chapter and, in regard to the development of legislation, in Chapter 5.

Agenda Setting

Kingdon (1995) describes agenda setting in public policymaking as a function of the confluence of three "streams" of activities: problems, possible solutions to the problems, and political circumstances. Some people prefer the term "issue" to Kingdon's choice of "problem" to refer to something that might trigger policymaking (Lowi 1964; Gormley and Boccuti 2001). It really does not matter which term is used; we will use problem to be consistent with Kingdon's terminology. In his conceptualization, when problems/possible solutions/political circumstances flow together in a favorable alignment, a "policy window" (Kingdon 1995, 166) opens. When this happens, a problem/potential solution combination that might lead to a new public law or an amendment to an existing one emerges from the set of competing problem/possible solution combinations and moves along in the policymaking process (see Figure 4.2).

Current health policies in the form of public laws, such as those pertaining to environmental protection, licensure of health-related practitioners and organizations, funding for AIDS research or for women's health, and regulation of managed care plans, exist because these problems or issues emerged from agenda setting and triggered changes in policy in the form of changes in public law. However, the mere existence of problems in these areas was not sufficient to trigger the development of legislation intended to address them.

The existence of health-related problems, even very serious ones such as millions of people without adequate health insurance coverage or the continuing widespread use of tobacco products, does not invariably lead to the establishment of policies intended to solve or ameliorate these problems. There must also be potential solutions to the problems as

Figure 4.2 Agenda Setting as the Confluence of Problems, Possible Solutions, and Political Circumstances

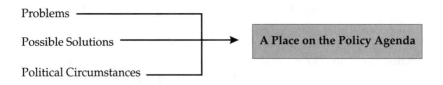

well as the political will to enact specific legislation intended to solve or ameliorate the problems. Obviously, agenda setting is crucial to the nature of the nation's health policies. Agenda setting is best understood in the context of its three key variables: problems, possible solutions, and political circumstances.

Problems

The breadth of this initiating variable in agenda setting can be seen in the range of possible public policies that have the potential to affect the pursuit of health. Remember, chapters 1 and 2 discussed health as a function of several determinants: the physical environments in which people live and work; their behaviors and biology; social factors; and the type, quality, and timing of health services that they receive.

Beyond this, as shown overarching Figure 4.1, the preferences of individuals, organizations, and interest groups as well as the biological, cultural, demographic, ecological, economic, ethical, legal, psychological, social, and technological aspects of American life also affect the policy-making process—as much at the point of agenda setting as anywhere in the process. These inputs join with the consequences of the policies produced through the ongoing policymaking cycle (see the feedback loop from the policies that result from the process shown in Figure 4.1) to continually supply those responsible for setting the nation's policy agenda with a massive pool of contenders for a place on that agenda. But, from among the contenders, how do certain problems find a place on the agenda while others do not?

Problems That Drive Policy Formulation

Only some problems or issues trigger policy formulation. Generally, the problems that eventually lead to the development of legislation are those broadly identified by policymakers as important and urgent. Problems that do not meet these criteria tend to languish at the bottom of the agenda or never find a place on the agenda at all. Price (1978) argues that whether a problem receives aggressive congressional intervention in the form of policymaking depends on its public salience and the degree of group conflict surrounding it. He defined a publicly salient problem or issue as one with a high actual or potential level of public interest. He defined conflictive problems or issues as those that stimulate intense disagreements between or among interest groups, or those that pit the interests of groups against the larger public interest. Price contends that the incentives for legislators to intervene in problems or issues are highest when salience is high and conflict is low. Conversely, incentives are lowest when salience is low and conflict is high.

Whether or not a problem is considered important changes with circumstances. A problem with a low priority among policymakers is unlikely to lead to policy formulation. If, however, policymakers give the problem a higher priority, a policy developed in response to the problem is much more likely. The long-running "on—again, off-again" debate in the U.S. Congress of patients' rights legislation illustrates this point.

The Real World of Health Policy

Patients' Rights Legislation

Over the last few years, patients' rights has emerged as one of the most hotly debated health policy issues before the Congress. While a number of different versions of patients' rights legislation have emerged, most of these proposals generally seek to require health insurance plans to give consumers more information, greater access to care in emergency rooms and with medical specialists, and new mechanisms to appeal health plan denials. One of the most controversial issues in the debate is the extent to which consumers should also be given expanded rights to sue their health plans if they are denied coverage for a service and harmed as a result. Another point of contention is whether federal legislation should provide a uniform set of minimum protections for everyone and override existing state laws, or instead provide greater flexibility for states to fashion their own rules.

The patients' rights debate has been fueled by a dramatic increase in recent years in managed care—92% of all insured workers were in some type of managed care plan in 2000, up from 54% in 1993. Public opinion surveys show that Americans express generally negative views about managed care, with majorities saying that managed care plans decreased the amount of time doctors spend with patients, made it harder for the sick to see medical specialists, and decreased the quality of health care for the sick. Most Americans say they support patients' rights legislation, but support declines when potential cost consequences are raised.

Source: This information was excerpted with the permission of the Henry J. Kaiser Family Foundation of Menlo Park, California. The Kaiser Family Foundation is an independent health care philanthropy and is not

associated with Kaiser Permanente or Kaiser Industries
(www.kaisernetwork.org/adwatch/_patient_rights.cfm#Background).

Problems that lead to attempted policy solutions in the form of changes in public law find their place on the agenda along any of several paths. Some problems emerge because the trends in certain variables eventually reach unacceptable levels—at least, levels unacceptable to some policymakers. Growth in the number of people with AIDS, the number who are uninsured, and costs in the Medicare program are examples of trends that eventually reached levels at which policymakers felt compelled to address the underlying problems through legislation.

An example of a problem that emerged in this way, one that led to specific legislation, was the growing recognition that large numbers of people feel locked into their jobs because they fear that they might not be able to obtain health insurance if they change jobs. Preexisting health problems or conditions could be cited as a basis for rejecting their applications for insurance benefits in the new job. In response to this problem, the Health Insurance Portability and Accountability Act of 1996 (HIPPA) (P.L. 104-191) significantly limits the use of preexisting condition exclusions and enhances the portability of health insurance coverage when people change jobs. Other provisions in this law guarantee availability and renewability of health insurance coverage for certain employees and individuals and an increase in the tax deduction for health insurance purchased by the self-employed.

Another problem that is emerging on the policy agenda is patient safety in health services organizations. Policymakers are still attempting to better define and understand the causes of this problem. Their interest in the problem and attention to it was spurred by evidence compiled by the Institute of Medicine (IOM) (www.iom.org) and reported in *To Err Is Human: Building a Safer Health System* (Committee on Quality of Health Care in America, Institute of Medicine 1999), and in a follow-up report, *Crossing the Quality Chasm: A New Health System for the 21st Century* (Committee on Quality of Health Care in America, Institute of Medicine 2001). These reports highlight in compelling detail the fact that almost 100,000 people die per year as a result of medical mistakes. In a typical response to emerging problems such as the one identified by the information in the IOM reports, legislators sought to better understand the problem and to begin to consider their role in addressing the problem through hearings on the subject. In this instance, hearings were organized and held by the Health, Education, Labor, and Pensions Committee of the United States Senate.

The Real World of Health Policy

Agenda
Committee on Health, Education, Labor, and Pensions
Hearings on
Patient Safety: What Is the Role for Congress?
May 24, 2001

Witnesses

Panel 1

> The Honorable Paul H. O'Neill
> Secretary, U.S. Department of the Treasury

> The Honorable Tommy G. Thompson
> Secretary, U.S. Department of Health and Human Services

Panel 2

> Lucian Leape, M.D.
> Adjunct Professor of Health Policy, Harvard School of Public Health

> Donald M. Berwick, M.D., M.P.P.
> President and CEO, Institute for Healthcare Improvement

> James P. Bagian, M.D., P.E.
> Director, National Center for Patient Safety, Department of Veterans Affairs

> John R. Brumstead, M.D.
> Chief Medical Officer, Fletcher Allen Health Care

Secretary Thompson's testimony at this hearing is reprinted below.

Testimony
Tommy G. Thompson
Secretary, Department of Health and Human Services
Before the
Senate Health, Education, Labor, and Pensions Committee
May 24, 2001

Good morning, Mr. Chairman and members of the Committee. I am honored to appear before you today to discuss the important issue of reducing medical errors and improving the safety of the health care services that Americans receive.

I would like to commend you, Mr. Chairman, and your colleagues for the role that you have played in helping to focus attention on this issue and for your commitment to finding solutions to what is by any estimate one of the leading public health challenges that we face today. Your leadership in this area has constituted a vital service to the Nation and will be critical as we move forward in this endeavor.

For the most part, the findings described in the Institute of Medicine's (IOM) landmark November 1999 report, *To Err Is Human: Building a Safer Health System*, are no longer front-page news. But the findings are no less serious, and they present no less of a challenge for all of us who care deeply about the quality of our Nation's health care system and the lives of the people who are affected when mistakes occur.

Another report released by the IOM in March 2001, *Crossing the Quality Chasm: A New Health System for the 21st Century*, has served as a reminder of what the 1999 errors report made clear. A wide gap exists in the quality of care people receive and the quality of care that we as a Nation are capable of providing. And, most troubling of all, too many people in the United States are harmed or lose their lives as a result of the health care services that they receive.

While the statistics are familiar, they bear repeating: according to the IOM report, between 44,000 and 98,000 Americans die each year as a result of medical errors, making them the 8th leading cause of death in the United States. More people die from medical errors than from automobile accidents, breast cancer, or AIDS. Further, the report suggests that medical errors result in approximately $29 billion in excess health care expenditures and lost productivity each year.

While there has been some debate about the numbers in the errors report, I think we can all agree that no matter whether it is 44,000, or 98,000, or some other number—it is too many. I think we would also agree that these errors are not solely the fault of individual doctors, nurses, and other clinicians. I believe that our health care workforce is comprised of the most talented and dedicated professionals in the world. Rather, these errors are the result of systems of care that are not adequately designed to prevent errors and their consequences.

As a result, this is not an issue that individual doctors, nurses, and other clinicians can fix by themselves. In fact, it is not an issue that any one group alone can fix—whether it is the Congress, the Administration, the States, oversight organizations, health professional groups, large purchasers of health care services, or patients themselves. We will only arrive at a solution if all of us who have a stake in the system agree to tackle medical errors together.

I want to assure you, Mr. Chairman and members of the Committee, that this Administration stands ready to do its part and is committed to continue working with you and others to address this issue. The IOM errors report provided a number of important recommendations that we have taken into consideration in deciding what the Administration and the Department of Health and Human Services, in particular, should be doing in this area.

Those recommendations addressed what can be done to improve safety at the clinical level, where care is provided, and they also addressed what we who are responsible for setting the policies and regulations governing the health care system can do to improve health care safety. In particular, the report highlighted the need to establish a national focus to create leadership, research, and tools to enhance the knowledge base about safety; to identify and learn from medical errors through mandatory and voluntary reporting systems; to raise standards and expectations for improvements in safety through the actions of oversight bodies, group purchasers, and professional organizations; and to implement safe practices at the delivery level.

Since the IOM errors report was issued, there have been broad discussions about what steps need to be taken, and policy makers and industry leaders have agreed that more research is needed to help us expand our understanding about when and how errors occur. We need to evaluate what is most effective in reporting about errors and specific interventions to improve patient safety, as well as what kinds of activities will best support these interventions. It is also essential that there be close collaboration among all of the interested public- and private-sector groups, the States, and the many Federal agencies involved in patient safety activities.

Effective solutions will be the ones that are based on changes in systems not just individuals. I believe that the first step is to facilitate the collection and analysis of information that will help providers and others learn from the safety problems identified so that they are not repeated. As noted in the IOM errors report, the second step is ensuring that the members of the public receive the information they need about the safety of the health care system, and that those organizations with oversight responsibilities receive the information that they can use to carry out their designated functions.

Further, it is critically important to find ways to encourage the implementation of what we know from research will improve patient safety practices in hospitals, clinics, nursing homes, doctors' offices, and other settings. To achieve this goal, it is critical for all of these organizations to develop their own internal processes and activities for addressing their particular safety problems. Only organizations in which providers and staff are freely able to review, analyze, and discuss the specific factors that prevent patients from getting the safest and best possible care in their institutions will be able to identify opportunities to change their system to remedy the problems.

Reducing medical errors and improving patient safety is not simply about what doctors, nurses, and other clinicians do or don't do when they treat patients. Reducing medical errors and improving patient safety is about all of us who have a role to play exercising commitment and leadership in this area, and in the case of patients, helping them to take an active role, too.

There are many current HHS programs to achieve these aims and the President's budget request of $72 million for HHS for medical errors and patient safety—an increase of $15 million over FY 2001—will strengthen these current activities.

What are our current activities? To build the research base about when and how errors occur, the Agency for Healthcare Research and Quality (AHRQ) is presently investing its FY 2001 appropriation of $50 million for new patient safety research. This research will support large demonstrations in states, health care systems, and networks to test reporting strategies and patient safety interventions; help develop and test the use of appropriate technologies to reduce medical errors, such as hand-held electronic medication systems; and increase our understanding of how the environment of care affects the ability of providers to improve safety.

The Centers for Disease Control and Prevention (CDC) is pursuing a number of patient safety initiatives, including the National Electronic Disease Surveillance System (NEDSS). NEDSS will electronically link data collected by private-sector health care organizations and public health departments. It can serve as a model for how to increase efficiency, volume, accuracy, completeness and timeliness of reporting and exchanging information. In FY 2000, CDC provided funding for 14 States to develop NEDSS systems. CDC has also provided funding for 32 States and three large metropolitan areas to assess their current health information systems and to determine how they can implement NEDSS specifications and standards. The FY 2002 Budget includes an increase of $2 million for CDC to collect more information on hospital acquired infections.

The Food and Drug Administration (FDA) also has several initiatives underway to improve patient safety. For example, the FY 2002 Budget includes an increase of $10 million for the FDA to improve and respond to data collected on adverse events. FDA is working to improve labeling and packaging standards to reduce the chances of clinicians confusing drugs with similar names, making dosage errors, and in causing adverse interactions between drugs. In addition, the FDA is requiring all registered blood establishments to report any event associated with biologics, including blood, blood components and source plasma that represents a deviation in manufacturing. FDA has also been piloting a program to educate and encourage hospital personnel to accurately identify and report injuries, deaths and close calls associated with medical products.

Further, as you are aware, the Health Care Financing Administration (HCFA) already contracts with the Peer Review Organizations (PROs) in each State to improve the quality of care and reduce errors through the collegial dissemination of best practices. However, HCFA is also developing the Medicare Patient Safety Monitoring System (MPSMS) to assure the public that rates of hospital adverse events are being scrutinized.

There are also a number of activities underway to help foster greater collaboration between Federal agencies, and between the Federal government and the public- and private-sectors. Several weeks ago, I announced the formation of a new Patient Safety Task Force within HHS. The Task Force, which is comprised of AHRQ, CDC, the FDA, and HCFA, will coordinate an effort to improve existing HHS systems to collect data on patient safety. Working closely with the States and private-sector partners, the Task Force will identify how these existing systems can be more user-friendly, and reduce the burden of data reporting on providers and others, and improve the value of the information that is collected.

I also want to note that HHS spearheads the existing Quality Interagency Coordination (QuIC) Task Force. As you know, QuIC is coordinating the overall Federal response to the IOM's report on medical errors. In particular, within the last year, the QuIC has held a national summit to set the agenda on patient safety research; initiated a breakthrough series with the Institute for Healthcare Improvement to foster improvements in high-risk settings in health care facilities that the Federal government manages; and helped produce materials for dissemination to the public on steps that people can take to prevent medical errors from happening to them.

The Department has also established a number of partnerships with the private sector. AHRQ and HCFA are both involved in working with the National Forum for Healthcare Quality Measurement and Reporting (Quality Forum), which has broad participation from all parts of the health care system, including national, State, regional, and local groups representing public and private purchasers, employers, health care professionals, and others. We are partnering with the Quality Forum and its members to identify where the research most strongly supports specific evidence-based interventions that will improve patient safety. Also, HCFA is collaborating with the Leapfrog Group, an alliance of large employers concerned with improving health care quality, to develop initiatives to improve safety through the use of these large employers' leverage as health care purchasers.

As I mentioned, the President has requested $72 million for HHS for medical errors and patient safety in the budget he has sent to Congress. With these additional resources, we can expand on the work already stated and enhance our health infrastructure to improve patient safety.

In particular, the Budget includes an increase of $3 million, or six percent, for AHRQ to strengthen the current systems. I believe the improved data collection system that the HHS Patient Safety Task Force is pursuing is vital. These systems for learning must be distinguished from systems for public accountability. We clearly need both. Just as the health care industry needs to know what changes will best prevent medical mistakes, the public expects and has a right to receive information demonstrating that the health care delivery system is as safe as possible. The system under development by the Patient Safety Task Force is a system for learning. It will be based on data collected from existing reporting requirements, to be used by health care providers and leaders of the health care facilities to change the way that care is provided.

We will operate this new data collection system on the basis of a number of key goals and priorities—ones that the Patient Safety Task Force has identified. We believe that it is critically important to encourage reporting of errors. For instance, we do not believe that information on error rates by hospital or by individual physician would encourage these providers to come forward. In fact, doing so would actually prevent the collection of fair and reliable information, and we believe that making this information public would actually discourage reporting.

Providers should be encouraged to come forward with information about their medical mistakes, problems, and "near misses" that they have encountered, as part of the Department's efforts and of organizational and local efforts to increase patient safety. The Department's goal, and the goal of safety initiatives more generally, should be to reduce medical mistakes, not punish people for what has happened in the past. For that reason, confidentiality of the data collected is essential.

We do think that information from this system should to be made available to the public, but only after a thorough analysis of the data. Information should be available about what types of errors occur most frequently; what specific actions providers are taking to reduce those errors; what types of programs are associated with lower rates of injury for patients; what individuals and family members can do to reduce their risk of harm; and what public agencies or oversight bodies can do to assist.

Second, we believe that we must ensure that reporting to our database does not increase the potential for liability or disciplinary action. This does not mean that patients will have less access to the information currently available about their condition or the care that they received. However, it does mean that strong confidentiality and peer review protections should be extended to cover those people who come forward to submit reports about patient safety problems. These protections should cover not only information submitted to our database, but should also extend to data, analyses, and reports developed as part of organizational and local programs and initiatives to improve patient safety and quality. These initiatives by individual organizations and collaborative groups will play an important role in determining whether the Department's findings will actually affect the care provided at specific institutions, which have very diverse circumstances and opportunities for improving safety. In addition, these protections should be applied to the Federal agencies taking part in the systems and the contractors and others involved. While HHS has some peer review protections in place as a result of agencies' authorizing legislation, only you, Mr. Chairman, and your colleagues on the Committee and in Congress can create the kind of peer review protections that are needed—protections that can stretch across all of the States and health care systems involved.

We are also committed to reducing the burden on providers, the States, and others that must now submit data to multiple agencies, in many different formats on each individual event that occurs. Simply put, systems need to make it easy for front-line doctors, nurses, managers, and others to help us capture the data we all need to improve patient safety. We owe it to those people who provide health care services each and every day—many of them life-saving interventions—to lessen their paperwork and administrative tasks.

As important as peer review protections are, we think it is equally important to protect patients' privacy. All patients can be sure that the privacy of their information would be maintained. Current laws that govern the use of data by our agencies require that this information remain confidential.

Lastly, we believe that our new patient safety data collection system should facilitate quick, short-turnaround analyses, as well as longer-term research. We have a critical need to know how we can improve safety now, as well as a need for evaluation research that examines the effectiveness of various approaches to reducing errors over time. Our new data collection system will make it possible to do both. We have to ensure that the data collected is converted into information that providers can and will use. Our goal is not to collect data for the sake of collecting data.

In addition to using data to improve safety, we will use the data collected in these systems to put together the National Quality Report that AHRQ was charged with producing when its reauthorization legislation was passed in December 1999. This report will provide a clear, easily understood picture of the quality and safety of health care in America and to highlight areas where improvement is needed. We believe the public will best be served by annual reports like this one that will provide people with research-based information about the safety of the Nation's health care system.

Other efforts to communicate with the public about medical errors and patient [safety] will be required to meet this need. Research and demonstration projects that will be conducted by AHRQ can help further inform those efforts. The research and demonstration projects being carried out will help us to understand what kinds of information people would find most useful, and how and when to provide it to them.

Mr. Chairman, in closing let me say that there is a great need for a system with strong peer review protections in place that will shield doctors, nurses, and others from reprisals or other actions against them if they come forward with information about errors and patient safety problems. We also need to take steps to ensure that medical data collected for such purposes will always remain private.

We will make sure useful information that will make a difference in the quality and safety of the health care services Americans receive is disseminated to all Americans and all health care providers.

Finally, I want to reiterate that top quality health care is a hallmark for America, and this Administration is committed to patient safety and a reduction of medical errors. Improving patient safety will require the concerted involvement of all that care about these issues. The keys to moving forward are an emphasis on collaboration, research to develop evidence about how to design and implement safer systems of care, the collection of data that yield the information that we need to improve safety, and the development of reliable information that the public can use.

I look forward to answering any questions that you may have. Thank you.

Source: Excerpted from United States Senate Committee on Health, Education, Labor, and Pensions, Hearings Schedule for the First Session of the 107th Congress—2001; and from Testimony of Tommy G. Thompson, Secretary, Department of Health and Human Services, before the Committee on May 24, 2001.

Problems can also be spotlighted by their widespread applicability to many people (e.g., the high cost of prescription medications to millions of Americans) or by their sharply focused impact on a small but powerful group whose members are directly affected (e.g., the high cost of medical education).

Some problems gain their place on the agenda or have their hold on a place strengthened because they are closely linked to other problems that already occupy secure places on the policy agenda. Efforts by the legislative and executive branches of the federal government to address the nation's budget deficit problem, at least in part through reduced expenditures on the Medicare program, has been a recurring example of the linkage of one problem (cost increases in the Medicare program) to another (growth of the federal deficit). Linking the control of growth in Medicare expenditures to the reduction of the federal deficit significantly strengthened political prospects for the development of legislation intended to curtail Medicare program expenditures, as was demonstrated in the Balanced Budget Act of 1997 (P.L. 105-33). This legislation called for reductions in the growth of Medicare expenditures of $385 billion in the 1998–2007 period.

Problems can also emerge more or less simultaneously along several paths. Such problems occupy places of considerable prominence on the policy agenda. For example, the problem of the high cost of health services, both for the private and the public sectors, has received attention by policymakers over many years. This problem emerged along a number of mutually reinforcing paths. In part, the cost problem has been prominent on the health policy agenda at times because the cost trend data disturbs many people. The data contribute to and reinforce a widespread acknowledgment of the problem of health costs in public poll after public poll and has focused intense attention from some of those who pay directly for health services through the provision of health insurance benefits, especially the politically powerful business community. Finally, the health cost problem, as it relates to public expenditures—for the Medicare and Medicaid programs especially—has been linked at times to another significant item on the nation's policy agenda, the need to control the federal budget.

The *combination* of these circumstances regarding the health cost problem reinforces each circumstance and helps explain why this problem perennially occupies a prominent place in the minds of many policymakers. The fact that this problem persists has more to do with the nature of potential solutions than whether health costs have been identified as a problem.

Possible Solutions

The second variable in agenda setting is the existence of possible solutions to problems. The existence of problems—even serious, fully acknowledged ones with widespread implications, such as high costs and uneven access to needed health services—does not invariably lead to policies that attempt to address or solve them. For this to happen, potential solutions to the problems must also exist. The availability of possible solutions depends on the generation of ideas for solving problems and, usually, on a period of idea testing and refinement.

While the menus of alternative solutions to the problems that face policymakers vary in size and quality, there are almost always alternative possible solutions. Many alternatives, each with its opponents and proponents (as is often the case) can slow advancement through the policymaking process as the relative merits of the competing alternatives are considered. Without at least one solution that is viewed as having the potential to actually solve the problem, however, issues do not advance in the policymaking process except in some spurious effort to create the illusion that a problem is being addressed.

When alternatives exist, typically each with its opponents and proponents, it is necessary to make choices. Decisions must be made about whether various potential solutions under consideration are worth developing into legislative proposals. Frequently, in response to a particular problem, multiple ideas will be considered worthy of such action, resulting in the simultaneous development of several competing proposals, each intended to solve the same problem. This tends to make agenda setting rather chaotic, although rigorous research and analysis can sometimes help provide some clarity about the choices that policymakers face.

The Real World of Health Policy

Health Insurance: Proposals for Expanding Private and Public Coverage

The following material is a portion of the testimony given by William J. Scanlon, Director, Health Care Issues, United States General Accounting Office, to the Committee on Finance, U.S. Senate, on March 15, 2001. The committee was holding hearings on "Living Without Health Insurance: Solutions to the Problem."

Mr. Chairman and Members of the Committee:

I am pleased to be here today as the Committee begins considering options to expand health insurance coverage for the 1 in 6 nonelderly Americans (under 65) who are uninsured. These 42 million people represent a heterogeneous population. As we noted in our testimony before your Committee earlier this week, the majority of the uninsured are working, often for small businesses or in certain industries such as agriculture or construction that are less likely to offer health insurance, or are low-income persons who are ineligible for or not enrolled in public programs. A disproportionate share of young adults, Hispanics, and residents of southern or western states are uninsured. But the uninsured population also includes people employed by larger-sized firms and other industries as well as those of all income levels, ages, races and ethnicities, and geographic locations. Given the heterogeneity of this population, a variety of approaches have been proposed in the Congress and by proponents to increase private or public health insurance coverage in ways that may match the needs of different uninsured persons and maximize the potential impact for expanding coverage.

Several recent congressional efforts represent important steps toward increasing the availability of health insurance for workers and low-income families, including

- improving the availability of private health insurance for individuals changing jobs or with preexisting health conditions,
- increasing the percentage of health insurance premiums that self-employed individuals can deduct from their taxable income,
- giving additional flexibility to states to expand Medicaid eligibility to a larger group of low-income children and their parents, and
- establishing the new federal-state State Children's Health Insurance Program (SCHIP), which had already enrolled more than 3 million low-income children in 2000.

These steps help millions of Americans, and the full effect of some of these actions likely has not yet been realized. Despite these efforts, however, millions of Americans remain uninsured.

To assist the Committee as it considers the variety of proposals offered to expand coverage to the uninsured, my remarks today will provide an overview of potential approaches for increasing private or public coverage and considerations that could impact their effectiveness in reaching significant numbers of the uninsured. Specifically, I will focus on

- proposed additional tax incentives, such as deductions or credits, to encourage individuals to purchase private health insurance or employers to offer coverage;

- proposed expansions to public programs, including expanding Medicaid and SCHIP to additional low-income children and adults, and allowing near-elderly individuals not yet 65 to "buy in" to Medicare; and
- the potential for unintended consequences of private and public coverage expansions on existing private health insurance coverage.

✻ ✻ ✻

The Role of Research in Health Policy Agenda Setting

Biomedical research, as well as that done in the interdisciplinary field of health services research, contributes to improved problem identification and specification and to the development of possible solutions. Thus, research can support establishing the health policy agenda. These contributions can be very important in view of the fact, as noted by Shortell and Reinhardt (1992, 3–4), that the public policymaking process

> inevitably proceeds on the basis of deeply held perceptions that may have been shaped by personal experience, by anecdotes, or by formally structured information from a variety of sources. Sometimes these perceptions may be an accurate reflection of the facts. At other times, however, they will rest on the most casual of empirical bases and border on folklore. Finally, at yet other times these perceptions may be deliberately manipulated through biased information supplied by particular interest groups.

Against this backdrop, biomedical and health services research make their contributions, clarifying both the problems and potential solutions to them, and thus assisting policymakers to understand as fully as possible the facts that might affect their decisions. The breadth of the valuable information the research community can contribute to agenda setting in the health policy domain is a function of the health determinants discussed in chapters 1 and 2: the physical environments in which people live and work, their behaviors and biology, social factors, and health services.

The research community has conducted a constant string of studies, and many more are currently under way regarding each of these determinants. Policymakers value the input of the research community sufficiently to fund much of the work through the National Institutes of Health (NIH) (www.nih.gov), the Agency for Health Care Research and Quality (AHRQ) (www.ahcpr.gov), and other agencies.

Examples of the range of studies that are relevant to health policymaking include the following partial list for one health determinant, health services. Centered on this health determinant, studies seek to clarify and provide policy alternatives in such areas as:

- *Access to health services.* How can an appropriate and affordable set of health services be made available to all citizens?

- *Organization of health services.* How can health services be organized most effectively and efficiently?
- *Financing health services.* How can the funds necessary to operate a health system be collected most effectively and efficiently?
- *Reimbursement of health services.* How can health services providers be paid for their services most effectively and efficiently?
- *Cost of health services.* How can the cost of health services be controlled more effectively and efficiently?
- *Quality of health services.* How can the quality of health services be assessed and ensured most effectively and efficiently?
- *Special populations.* How can the health service needs of special population groups be met most effectively and efficiently?
- *Ethical and legal issues.* What are the ethical and legal issues that need to be addressed in providing access to affordable health services of an appropriate quality in the most effective and efficient manner possible? (Crane, Hersh, and Shortell 1992, 370–71)

Well-conceived and carefully conducted health-related studies, whether in biomedical or health services research, help shape the health policy agenda in two ways: (1) by documenting the existence and nature of health-related problems and (2) by analyzing potential solutions to these problems. Agenda setting, as has been noted, always begins with the existence of problems. Moynihan (1970, 30) has correctly observed that "society cannot act on social problems until it knows it has them, and it often does not know it has them until it can count them."

Research plays an important documentation role by gathering, cataloging, and correlating facts that depict the state of the policymaker's world. For example, researchers have documented and continue to re-document the dangers of tobacco smoke; the presence of HIV and the numbers of people living with AIDS, and with a variety of cancers, heart disease, and other disease; the impact of poverty on health; the existence of large numbers of people who lack health insurance coverage; the existence of disparities in health among population segments; and the dangers imposed by exposure to various toxins in the physical environments, among many other threats to health. The quantification and documentation of health-related problems gives these problems some chance of emerging on the policy agenda.

The Real World of Health Policy

The Agency for Healthcare Research and Quality (AHRQ)

The Agency for Healthcare Research and Quality (AHRQ) (www.ahcpr. gov), formerly the Agency for Health Care Policy and Research (AHCPR), a component of the U.S. Department of Health and Human Services, Public Health Service, is the federal government's focal point for research to enhance the quality, appropriateness, and effectiveness of health services and access to those services. AHRQ has established a broad base of scientific research on the organization, financing, and delivery of health services, and through the promotion of improvements in clinical practice.

AHRQ's research projects examine the availability, quality, and costs of health services; ways to improve the effectiveness and appropriateness of clinical practice, including the prevention of disease; and other areas of health services research, such as services for persons with HIV infection. AHRQ uses mechanisms of grants, cooperative agreements, and contracts to carry out research projects, demonstrations, evaluations, and dissemination activities.

Agency Profile

Mission: To support research designed to improve the outcomes and quality of health care, reduce its costs, address patient safety and medical errors, and broaden access to effective services. The research sponsored, conducted, and disseminated by the Agency for Healthcare Research and Quality (AHRQ) provides information that helps people make better decisions about health care.

Created: December 1989 as the Agency for Health Care Policy and Research (AHCPR), a Public Health Service agency in the Department of Health and Human Services (HHS). Reporting to the HHS Secretary, the Agency was reauthorized on December 6, 1999, as the Agency for Healthcare Research and Quality. Sister agencies include the National Institutes of Health, the Centers for Disease Control and Prevention, the Food and Drug Administration, the Health Care Financing Administration, and the Health Resources and Services Administration.

Budget: $269.9 million. Nearly 80 percent of AHRQ's budget is awarded as grants and contracts to researchers at universities and other research institutions across the country.

Staff: 294

Main functions: AHRQ sponsors and conducts research that provides evidence-based information on health care outcomes; quality; and cost, use, and access. The information helps health care decisionmakers—patients and clinicians, health system leaders, purchasers, and policymakers—make more informed decisions and improve the quality of health care services.

AHRQ's Customers

Clinical decisionmakers: The evidence developed through AHRQ-sponsored research and analysis helps clinicians, consumers, patients, and health care institutions to make informed choices about what treatments work, for whom, when, and at what cost.

Health care system decisionmakers: Health plan and delivery system administrators use the findings and tools developed through AHRQ-sponsored research to make choices on how to improve the health care system's ability to provide access to and deliver high-quality, high-value care. Purchasers use the products of AHRQ-sponsored research to obtain high-quality health care services.

Public policy decisionmakers: Public policymakers use the information produced by AHRQ to expand their capability to monitor and evaluate changes in the health care system and to devise policies designed to improve its performance. Federal, State, and local policymakers as well as private-sector policy advisory groups such as the Institute of Medicine (IOM), professional societies, patient advocacy groups, and health care associations make decisions based on AHRQ information.

AHRQ's Strategic Goals

AHRQ's strategic goals reflect the needs of its customers. These goals are to:

Support improvements in health outcomes. The field of health outcomes research examines the end results of the structure and processes of health care on the health and well-being of patients and populations. A unique characteristic of this research is the incorporation of the patient's perspective in the assessment of effectiveness. Public and private-sector policymakers are also concerned with the end results of their investments in health care, whether at the individual, community, or population level.

Strengthen quality measurement and improvement. Achieving this goal requires developing and testing quality measures and investigating the best ways to collect, compare, and communicate these data so they are useful to decisionmakers. AHRQ's research will also emphasize studies of the most effective ways to implement these measures and strategies in order to improve patient safety and health care quality.

Identify strategies that improve access, foster appropriate use, and reduce unnecessary expenditures. Adequate access and appropriate use of health care services continues to be a challenge for many Americans, particularly the poor, the uninsured, members of minority groups, rural and inner city residents, and other priority populations. The Agency will support studies of access, health care utilization, and expenditures to identify whether particular approaches to health care delivery and payment alter behaviors in ways that promote access and/or economize on health care resource use.

In addition the 1999 reauthorizing legislation directs AHRQ to:

Improve the quality of health care. AHRQ is to coordinate, conduct, and support research, demonstrations, and evaluations related to the measurement and improvement of health care quality. This includes a call for the development of an annual report on national trends in health care quality beginning in fiscal year 2003. AHRQ is also to disseminate scientific findings about what works best and facilitate public access to information on the quality of, and consumer satisfaction with, health care.

Promote patient safety and reduce medical errors. AHRQ is to develop research and building partnerships with health care practitioners and health care systems and establish a permanent program of Centers for Education and Research on Therapeutics. These initiatives will help address concerns raised in a 1999 report by the Institute of Medicine (IOM) [see (Committee on Quality of Health Care in America 1999) for this report; and for a follow-up report, see (Committee on Quality of Health Care in America 2001)] that estimates as many as 98,000 patients die as a result of medical errors in hospitals each year.

Advance the use of information technology for coordinating patient care and conducting quality and outcomes research. AHRQ is to:

- Promote the use of information systems to develop and disseminate performance measures.
- Create effective linkages between health information sources to enhance health care delivery and coordination of evidence-based health care services.
- Promote protection of individually identifiable patient information used in health services research and health care quality improvement.
- Establish an Office of Priority Populations. AHRQ is to ensure that the needs of these populations (low-income groups, minorities, women, children, the elderly, and individuals with special heath care needs) are addressed throughout the Agency's intramural and extramural research portfolio. Beginning in fiscal year 2003, this will include an annual report on prevailing disparities in health care delivery as it relates to these priority populations.

The Health Services Research Pipeline

The Agency achieves its mission through health services research that reflects a pipeline of activities that together build the infrastructure, tools, and knowledge for improvements in the American health care system. The pipeline comprises three critical and interdependent priorities:

1. New knowledge on priority health issues. This is the essential knowledge base that investigators create which enables us to understand the determinants of the outcomes, quality, and costs of care as well as identify instances when care falls short of achieving its intended outcomes. AHRQ recognizes that the future of and vision for health services research come from the scientific community—investigators who are on the front line of the clinical, health system, and health policy problems to be resolved through research. Because the nurturing of novel research approaches, concepts, and directions is essential for

progress within the health services research field, AHRQ actively encourages and supports peer-reviewed, investigator-initiated research.

2. New tools and talent for a new century. These tools apply and translate new knowledge into instruments for measurement, databases, informatics, and other applications that can be used to assess and improve care. In addition, AHRQ works to ensure that the infrastructure for health services research remains strong, including building the supply of talented researchers. The Agency encourages students to enter the field of health services research, sponsors over 20 predoctoral and postdoctoral training programs, nurtures the careers of new investigators, and promotes the careers of established researchers.

3. Translating Research Into Practice. The final step of the pipeline focuses on closing the gap between what we know and what we do. AHRQ funds research and demonstrations to translate the knowledge and tools acquired into measurable improvements in health care. In addition, AHRQ develops partnerships with public and private-sector organizations to disseminate the knowledge and tools for use in the health care system.

Source: Excerpted from descriptive material provided by AHRQ on its web site.

The second way in which research informs, and thus influences, the health policy agenda is through analyses that help determine which policy solutions may work. The fundamental contribution of biomedical research to the development of ever-advancing medical and health technology in the United States is well established. This research has made possible the diagnosis and treatment of previously untreatable diseases. Along different avenues of inquiry, health services research has revealed much of value to policymakers as they propose, consider, and prioritize alternative solutions to problems. Often taking the form of demonstration projects intended to provide a basis in fact for determining the feasibility, efficacy, or basic workability of a possible policy intervention, research-based recommendations to policymakers, or what Brown (1991) calls "prescriptions" for them, can play an important role in policy agenda setting. Potential problem solutions that might lead to public policies—even if the policies themselves are formulated mainly on political grounds—must stand the test of plausibility. Research that supports a particular course of action being contemplated by policymakers or that helps attest to its likelihood of success—or at least to the probability that it will not boomerang or embarrass them—can make a significant contribution to policymaking by helping to shape the policy agenda.

What research cannot do for policymakers, however, is make their decisions for them. Every difficult decision regarding the health policy agenda—indeed, all policy decisions—ultimately rests with policy-makers.

Decision Making Regarding Alternative Possible Solutions

The existence of problems and alternative possible solutions are two prerequisites for use of the classical, rational model of decision making outlined in Figure 4.3. This decision-making model reflects the basic pattern of the organizational decision-making process typically followed in both the private and public sectors in the United States. However, differences in the use of this model in the two sectors typically arise when the *criteria* to be used in evaluating alternative solutions to problems are introduced.

Some of the criteria used in evaluating and comparing alternative solutions in both the private and public sectors are, of course, the same or very similar. For example, the criteria set in both sectors usually includes consideration of whether a particular solution will actually solve the problem; whether it can be implemented within available resources and technologies; its costs and benefits relative to other possible solutions; and the results of an advantage-to-disadvantage analysis of the alternatives.

However, there is one very pervasive difference in the criteria sets used in the two sectors: the variation in the roles played by political

Figure 4.3 The Rational Model of Decision Making

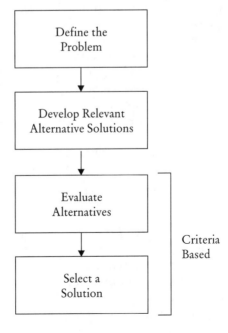

concerns and considerations. Decisions made by policymakers in the public sector must reflect much greater political sensitivity to the public at large as well as to the preferences of relevant individuals, organizations, and interest groups than most decisions made in the private sector. This helps explain the considerable importance of the third variable in agenda setting in the health policymaking process—political circumstances.

Political Circumstances

The existence of a problem that might be solved or lessened by a change in policy, even in combination with a possible solution to that problem, is not of itself sufficient to move the problem/solution combination along in the policymaking process. A political force, or what is sometimes called the political will, is also necessary to advance a problem/potential solution combination.

Thus, the political circumstances surrounding each problem/potential solution in the policymaking process form the crucial third variable in creating a window of opportunity through which problems/potential solutions move toward actual development of legislation. This variable is at least as important as the other two variables in this complex equation. In fact, the establishment of a political thrust forceful enough to move policymakers to attempt to do something substantive about a health-related problem is often the most challenging variable in the problem's emergence from among the set of competing issues vying for places on the policy agenda.

Whether the political circumstances attendant to any particular problem/potential solution combination is sufficient to actually open the window of opportunity for its advancement in the policymaking process depends very much on the nature of other competing entries on the policy agenda. The array of competing problems is always an important variable in agenda setting. When the nation is involved in serious threats to its national security or its civil order, for example, or when a state is in the midst of a sustained recession, health policy will be treated differently than when policymakers are less preoccupied with other, perhaps more urgent, concerns.

The political circumstances surrounding any particular problem/potential solution combination include such factors as the relevant public attitudes, concerns, and opinions; the preferences and relative ability to influence political decisions of various groups interested in the problem or in the way in which it is addressed; and the positions and views of involved key policymakers in the executive and legislative branches of government. Each of these factors can exert a powerful influence on whether a problem is addressed through policy, as well as on the nature of the way the problem is addressed, that is, on the shape and scope of any policy developed to address the problem. Two factors, in particular, are very important: the involved interest groups and the chief executive.

Their roles in the political circumstances aspect of agenda setting are examined in more detail in the next section.

Interest Group Involvement

To appreciate fully the role of interest groups in helping to set the policy agenda, it is useful to first consider the role of individual members of American society in health policy agenda setting. In a representative form of government, such as that of the United States, individual members of society, unless they are among the elected representatives, usually do not have the opportunity to vote directly on policies. They do, however, have opportunities to vote on policymakers. Thus, policymakers are interested in what the individual members of society want, even when what they want is not easy to discern.

However, one of the great myths of a democratic society is that its members, when confronted with tough problems, such as the high cost of health services for everyone, the lack of health insurance for many, or the existence of widespread disparities in health among segments of the society ponder the problems carefully and express their preferences to their elected officials, who then factor these opinions into their decisions about how to address the problems through policy.

Sometimes this does happen, but even when the public expresses its opinions about an issue, the result is clouded by the fact that the American people are heterogeneous in their views. Opinions are invariably mixed on just about all health-related problems and their solutions. Public opinion polls can help sort out conflicting opinions, but polls are not always straightforward undertakings. Complicating their use is the fact that on many issues individuals' opinions are subject to evolutionary change.

Yankelovich (1992) points out that the public's thinking on difficult problems that might be addressed through public policies evolves through predictable stages, beginning with awareness of the problem and ending with judgments about its solution. In between, people explore the problem and alternative solutions, with varying degrees of success. The progress of individuals along this continuum of stages has a great deal to do with their views on both problems and solutions.

The diversity among society, together with the fact that their individual views on important problems and potential solutions to the problems evolve and change over time explains, in large part, the tendency of organizations and interest groups to be more influential than individuals in establishing the policy agenda. Interest groups, in particular, can exert extraordinary power and influence in the political marketplace for health policies, as was discussed in chapter 3.

By organizing and focusing the opinions of their members, whether individuals or organizations, interest groups are able to present a unified position to policymakers on their preferences regarding a particular problem or its solution. A unified position is far easier for policymakers to assess and to respond to than the diverse opinions and preferences of many individuals acting alone. Although individuals tend to be keenly interested in their own health, as well as in the health of those they care about, their interests in specific health policies tends to be rather diffuse. This stands in contrast to the highly concentrated interests of those who earn their livelihoods in this domain or who stand to gain other benefits within the health domain. This phenomenon is not unique to health. Indeed, in general, the interests of those who earn their livelihoods in any industry or economic sector are more concentrated than the interests of those who merely use its outputs; and these interests are far more concentrated than those of individuals who only incidentally or occasionally interact with the domain.

One result of the existence of concentrated interests is the formation of organized interest groups that seek to influence the formulation, implementation, and modification of policies to some advantage for the group's members. Because all interest groups seek policies that favor their members, their own agendas and behaviors, as well as their preferences regarding the larger public policy agenda, are often predictable.

Feldstein (1996) argues, for example, that all interest groups representing health services providers seek through legislation to increase the demand for members' services, to limit competitors, to permit members to charge the highest possible prices for their services, and to lower their members' costs of operating as much as possible. Likewise, an interest group representing a group of health services consumers logically seeks policies that minimize the costs of the services to the members, ease their access to the services, increase the availability of the services, and so on. Essentially, this is human nature at work.

Interest groups frequently play powerful roles in setting the nation's health policy agenda, as they do subsequently in the development of legislation and in the implementation and modification of health policies. These groups sometimes play their role proactively by seeking to stimulate new policies that serve the interests of their members. Alternatively, they sometimes play their role reactively by seeking to block changes in public policies that they do not believe serve their members' best interests.

Opportunities to join interest groups are widely available for those who are interested in the policy agenda. As chapter 3 discussed, individual physicians can join and have some of their interests represented by the American Medical Association. Nurses can join the American Nurses Association (ANA) (www.ana.org). Not only can hospitals join the American Hospital Association, but teaching hospitals can join the Association of American Medical Colleges' (AAMC) (www.aamc.org) Council of Teaching Hospitals and Health Systems; children's hospitals can join the National Association of Children's Hospitals (NACH) (www.childrenshospitals.net/nach); and investor-owned hospitals can join the Federation of American Hospitals (FAHS) (www.fahs.com).

Managed care organizations can join the American Association of Health Plans (AAHP) (www.aahp.org), and health insurance companies can join the Health Insurance Association of America (HIAA) (www.hiaa.org).

Even subsets of the general population can join a group that seeks to serve their health-related interests through interest groups. For example, the American Association of Retired Persons (AARP) (www.aarp.org) is a powerful group representing the interests of many of the nation's older citizens. Other consumer-oriented interest groups include the Alliance for Retired Americans (www.retiredamericans.org), Families U.S.A. (www.familiesusa.org), which describes itself as the "voice of health care consumers," and the Consortium for Citizens with Disabilities (www.c-c-d.org).

Tactics of Interest Groups

As influential participants in public policymaking, interest groups are integral to the process in the United States. And they are especially ubiquitous in the health domain. But how do they exert their influence on agenda setting and at other points in the health policymaking process? The answer to this question involves four tactics that interest groups rely on heavily as their means of influencing the process: lobbying, electioneering, litigation, and, especially more recently, shaping public opinion in order that it might in turn influence the policymaking process to the groups' advantage (Kingdon 1995; Edwards, Wattenberg, and Lineberry 2001). Each of these tactics is described in turn in the following sections.[1]

Lobbying

This widely used influencing tactic has deep roots in American public policymaking. "Lobbying is as old as legislation and pressure groups are as old as politics" (Schriftgeisser 1951, 3). In the minds of many people lobbying conjures a negative image of money exchanging hands for political favors and backroom deals, but ideally it is nothing more than communicating with public policymakers for the purpose of influencing their decisions to be more favorable to, or at least consistent with, the preferences of those doing the lobbying (Buchholz 1994; Milbrath 1976).

Lobbying, as the word for these influencing activities, and *lobbyists*, as the word for people who do this work, arose in reference to the place where such activities first took place. In early Washington, DC, before members of Congress had either offices or telephones, certain people who sought to influence their thinking waited for the legislators and talked to them in the lobbies of the buildings they frequented. The original practitioners of this influencing tactic spent so much time in lobbies that they came, naturally enough, to be called lobbyists, and their work, lobbying.

Like many other groups of people, lobbyists come in a great variety. The vast majority of them operate in an ethical and professional manner, effectively representing the legitimate interests of the groups they serve. The few, however, who behave in a heavy-handed, even illegal, manner, have to some extent tarnished the reputations of all who do this work. Their image is further affected by the fact that their work, if it is properly done, is essentially selfish in nature. Lobbyists seek to persuade others that their position—the position of the interests they represent—is the correct one. Their whole professional purpose is to persuade others to make decisions that are in the best interests of those who employ or retain the lobbyists.

Results of studies as well as opinions on the effectiveness of the lobbying tactic as a means of influencing the public policymaking process are mixed at best (Milbrath 1976; Kingdon 1995). There is no doubt that lobbying has an impact on the policymaking process, but it seems to work best when applied to policymakers who are already committed to, or who are at least sympathetic to, the lobbyist's position on a public policy issue (Edwards, Wattenberg, and Lineberry 2001). Lobbyists certainly played a prominent role in the defeat of President Clinton's 1993 Health Security Act bill. Similarly, they played a significant role in the repeal of the 1988 Medicare Catastrophic Coverage Act (P.L. 100-360). In part, the ambivalence over the role of lobbying in influencing policymaking derives from the difficulty inherent in isolating its effect from some of the other influencing tactics discussed later.

The Real World of Health Policy

E-mail Overload in Congress

The explosion in electronic communications is dramatically changing the way Americans interact with one another, with businesses, and with government. While virtually all institutions are struggling to adapt to the demands of a "paperless environment," the challenges facing Congress are among the most difficult and contentious. Growing numbers of citizens are frustrated by what they perceive to be Congress' lack of responsiveness to e-mail. At the same time, Congress is frustrated by what it perceives to be e-citizens' lack of understanding of how Congress works and the constraints under which it must operate. This growing tension is exacerbated by several factors. First, the volume of e-mail to congressional offices has risen dramatically over the past two years. The number of e-mail messages reaching the House of Representatives, for example, rose from 20 million in 1998 to 48 million in 2000, and it continues to grow by an average of one million messages per month. The heavy e-mail traffic generated by the recent nomination of John Ashcroft as U.S. Attorney General slowed Senate servers to a crawl, causing delays in e-mail delivery that lasted hours—and, in some cases, days. This flood of e-mail has been fueled by the ease and speed of online communications, the electorate's growing interest in national politics, and the grassroots activities of lobbyists and e-businesses that are electronically motivating the public to "make their voices heard in Washington." Unfortunately, these advocacy organizations are also encouraging the public to engage in e-mail practices—like spamming congressional offices—that result in unmanageable demands on Congress.

Second, unlike businesses that have the finances and flexibility to rapidly increase their capacity to handle rising demands, congressional offices face budgetary obstacles that make rapid adaptation difficult. For example, offices have received insufficient budget increases over the past five years to deal with these new demands. And congressional staffing levels have actually declined over the past decade.

Third, most congressional offices have not yet taken advantage of the software to efficiently process constituent e-mail. Most offices continue to treat e-mail like postal mail, replying with stamped letters rather than e-mail. They resist upgrading their e-mail practices, in part due to outdated misconceptions they hold about the drawbacks of e-mail. Most offices are responding [to] the challenge of managing rapidly rising volumes with marginal budget increases by maintaining a communications status quo.

But the status quo is no longer tenable. It fails to meet the needs of citizens who expect greater responsiveness from their elected officials. It also fails to meet the needs of congressional offices that want to better balance their resource limitations with the expectations of the public, but believe that no feasible options exist. Feasible options do exist. Most offices on Capitol Hill could handle e-mail far better by investing in more modern software packages and more training for their Systems Administrators. More importantly, offices could handle e-mail much more efficiently by better using the hardware and software they already own.

Source: Excerpted with permission from Congress Online Project. Kathy Goldschmidt, with assistance from Nicole Folk, Mike Callahan, and Rick Shapiro. "E-mail Overload in Congress: Managing a Communications Crisis." The report can be read in its entirety at www.congressonlineproject.org.

Whatever degree of influence lobbyists do exert on the public policymaking process is made possible by several well-understood sources of their influence with policymakers. Ornstein and Elder (1978) identify five ways that lobbyists can be of direct help to a member of Congress, each of which can be extended to other policymakers.

- Lobbyists are an important source of information for policymakers. Although most policymakers must be concerned with many policy issues simultaneously, most lobbyists can focus and specialize. They can become quite expert, and can draw on the insight of other experts, in the areas they represent.
- Lobbyists can assist policymakers with the development and execution of political strategy. Lobbyists typically are politically savvy and can provide what amounts to free consulting to the policymakers they choose to assist.
- Lobbyists can assist elected policymakers in their reelection efforts. (More is said about this in the next section, on electioneering.) This assistance can take several forms, including campaign contributions, votes, and workers for campaigns.
- Lobbyists can be important sources of innovative ideas for policymakers. Policymakers are judged on the quality of their ideas as well as on their abilities to have those ideas translated into effective policies. For most policymakers, few gifts are as valued as a really good idea, especially when they can turn that idea into a bill that bears their name.
- Finally, lobbyists can be friends with policymakers. Lobbyists often are gregarious and interesting people in their own right. They entertain, sometimes lavishly, and they are socially engaging. Many of them have social and educational backgrounds similar to those of policymakers. In fact, many lobbyists have been policymakers earlier in their careers. It is neither unusual nor surprising for lobbyists and policymakers to become friends.

Electioneering

The effective use of the electioneering tactic in influencing the policymaking process is based on the simple fact that policymakers who are sympathetic to a group's interests are far more likely to be influenced than are policymakers who are not sympathetic. Thus, interest groups seek to help elect to office, and to help keep in office, policymakers whom they view as sympathetic to the interests of the group's members. Electioneering, or using the resources at their disposal to aid candidates for political office, is a common means through which interest groups seek to exert their influence on the policymaking process. Many groups have considerable resources to devote to this tactic.

Interest groups, to varying degrees, have a family of resources that involve electoral advantages or disadvantages for political candidates. "Some groups—because of their geographical dispersion in congressional districts throughout the country; their ability to mobilize their members and sympathizers; and their numbers, status, or wealth—are thought to have an ability to affect election outcomes" (Kingdon 1995, 51).

One of the most visible aspects of the electioneering tactic is the channeling of money into the campaign finances of the interest groups' supporters and sympathizers (their candidates) through political action committees, or PACs. This source of funds now covers about half the costs of congressional elections in the United States (Edwards, Wattenberg, and Lineberry 2001). Health-related interest groups participate heavily in this form of electioneering.

Although PACs are important sources of influence for interest groups, the most influential among groups are those with multiple ways of exerting their influence through lobbying and electioneering activities. The hospital industry is a notable example. The American Hospital Association is a leading campaign contributor through its PAC. In addition, however, it has many other resources at its disposal. As Kingdon (1995) has pointed out, every congressional district has hospitals whose trustees are community leaders and whose managers and physicians are typically articulate and respected in their communities. These spokespersons can be mobilized to support sympathetic candidates or to contact their representatives directly regarding any policy decision.

Referring to the Carter administration's proposed Hospital Cost Containment Act of 1977, one policymaker, quoted in Kingdon (1995, 51–52) challenged the wisdom of the administration's decision to take on this influential group with the following words:

> The whole cost containment thing is a quagmire. I don't know how in the hell the administration got involved with it as their first move [in the healthcare domain]. Here you have thousands of hospitals in this country. More than half of them are community hospitals, and you know what that means. There's a lot of community pride wrapped up in them; they've been financed by bake sales. "It's *our* hospital." Others of them are proprietary hospitals, owned by politically powerful physicians. The rest of them have some religious affiliation and here they are doing the Lord's work. Why would you want to take them on? Dumb, dumb, dumb.

As Ornstein and Elder observe, "The ability of a group to mobilize its membership strength for political action is a highly valuable resource; a small group that is politically active and cohesive can have more political impact than a large, politically apathetic, and unorganized group" (1978, 74). The ability to mobilize people and other resources at the grassroots level helps explain the relative capabilities of various groups to influence policymakers and, through them, the policymaking process. The most influential health interest groups, including the AHA and AMA, have particularly strong grassroots organizations to call into play in the exercise of their lobbying and electioneering tactics.

Litigation

A third tactic available to interest groups in their efforts to influence the policymaking process is litigation. Interest groups, acting on behalf of their members, seek to influence the policy agenda and the larger policymaking process through litigation in which they challenge existing policies, seek to stimulate new policies, or try to alter certain aspects of the implementation of policies. Use of the litigation tactic, in both state and federal courts, is a widespread and increasingly used tactic by interest groups to influence policymaking in the health domain.

Several examples of the role of the courts in health policymaking were described in chapter 3. In one of the cases cited there, a group of commercial insurers and HMOs and New York City challenged the State of New York's practice of adding a surcharge to certain hospital bills to raise money to help fund health services for indigent people (Green 1995). The U.S. Supreme Court heard this case. Because its outcome was of considerable importance to their members, a number of health interest groups filed *amicus curiae* briefs ("friend of the court" briefs) as a means of seeking to influence the Court's decision. Through such written depositions, groups state their collective positions on issues and describe how the decision in the case will affect their members. This practice is widely used by health interest groups as well as by groups in other domains. Through the practice, the Supreme Court has been accessible to these groups who, in expressing their views, have helped determine which cases the Court will hear as well as how it will rule on them (Caldeira and Wright 1990). This practice also is frequently and effectively used by interest groups in lower courts as well to help shape the health policy agenda.

The use of the litigation tactic is not limited to attempts to help shape the policy agenda, however. One particularly effective use of the litigation tactic is to turn to the courts to help fill in specific details of the actual implementation of vague pieces of legislation. This practice provides opportunities for interest groups to exert enormous influence on policymaking overall by influencing the rules, regulations, and administrative practices that guide the implementation of public statutes or laws. More will be said about this in the next chapter, where the discussion turns specifically to rulemaking in the overall public policymaking process. For now, recall from chapter 1 that the rules and regulations established to implement laws and programs are themselves authoritative decisions that fit the definition of public policies.

Shaping Public Opinion

Because policymakers are influenced by the opinions held by the electorate, many interest groups seek to shape public opinion as another tactical means through which they might ultimately influence the policymaking process. This tactic, for example, was used extensively in the congressional debate over national health reform in 1993 and 1994. It is estimated that interest groups spent more than $50 million seeking to shape public opinion on the issues involved in that debate. For example, anyone who followed the debate even peripherally became familiar with the health insurance industry's "Harry and Louise" ads (Hacker 1997). The extensive health reform debate of the early 1990s was not the first use of this public opinion tactic by healthcare interest groups, however.

Intense opposition in some quarters to the legislation, especially by the AMA, fueled the congressional debate over the Medicare legislation in the 1960s. The American public had rarely if ever been exposed to so feverish a campaign to shape opinions as it experienced in the period leading up to enactment of the Medicare legislation in 1965.

Among the many activities undertaken in that campaign to influence public opinion, and through this, policymakers, perhaps none is more entertaining in hindsight—certainly few are more representative of the campaign's tone and intensity—than one action taken by the AMA. As part of its campaign to influence public opinion on Medicare, the AMA sent every physician's spouse a recording, with the advice that they should host their friends and neighbors and play the record for them. The idea was to encourage these people to write letters in opposition to the legislation to their representatives in Congress. Near the end of the recording, these words can be heard:

> Write those letters now; call your friends and tell them to write them. If you don't, this program, I promise you, will pass just as surely as the sun will come up tomorrow. And behind it will come other federal programs that will invade every area of freedom as we have known it in this country. Until one day . . . we will awake to find that we have socialism. And if you don't do this, and I don't do it, one of these days you and I are going to spend our sunset years telling our children and our children's children what it was like in America when men were free. (As quoted in Skidmore 1970, 138)

The words in this quotation are made all the more interesting by the fact that the voice on the recording belongs to Ronald Reagan.

There is no firm evidence of the impact, on either policymakers or policymaking, of the appeals to public opinion made by interest groups (Edwards, Wattenberg, and Lineberry 2001). The extent and persistence of the practice, nevertheless, suggests that interest groups believe that it does make a difference. One variable, as discussed in the beginning of this section, does clearly mitigate the usefulness of the tactic and makes its use by interest groups vastly more difficult: the heterogeneity of the American population.

For example, in the congressional debate over health reform in 1993 and 1994, the majority viewpoint at the beginning of the debate was that health reform was needed. However, at no time during the debate was a public consensus achieved on the nature of the reform that should be undertaken. No feasible alternative for reform ever received majority support in any public opinion poll. During most of the debate, in fact, public opinion was approximately evenly divided among the possible reform options (Brodie and Blendon 1995).

Using lobbying, electioneering, litigation, and their efforts to shape public opinion as tactics, interest groups seek to influence the policy agenda and the larger public policymaking process to the strategic advantage of their members. The degree of success they achieve is highly dependent on the resources at their disposal. Ornstein and Elder (1978) categorize the resources of interest groups into:

- physical resources, especially money and the number of members;
- organizational resources such as the quality of a group's leadership, the degree of unity or cohesion among its members, and the group's ability to mobilize its membership for political purposes;
- political resources such as expertise in the intricacies of the public policymaking process and a political reputation for being able to influence the process ethically and effectively;
- motivational resources such as the strength of ideological conviction among the membership; and
- intangible resources such as the overall status or prestige of a group.

The particular mix of these resources available to an interest group, as well as the effectiveness with which the group uses the resources, helps determine the group's performance in influencing the policy agenda and other aspects of the policymaking process. A particular group's performance, of course, also is affected by its level of resources compared to those of other groups that may be pursuing competing or conflicting outcomes from the policymaking process (Feldstein 1996; Kingdon 1995; Edwards, Wattenberg, and Lineberry 2001). The political marketplace, as discussed in chapter 3, is a place where many people and groups seek to have their policy preferences prevail.

One particularly important group resource is the relative proportion of its potential members who are actual members. Although it seems somewhat counterintuitive, small groups typically perform better than large groups in exerting influence on the policymaking process. This phenomenon exists because small groups tend to have greater proportions of potential members who are actual members. "Part of a group's stock in trade in affecting all phases of policymaking—agendas, decisions, or implementation—is its ability to convince government officials that it speaks with one voice and truly represents the preferences of its members" (Kingdon 1995, 52).

Large numbers of potential members can, of course, work to a group's advantage. Converting many potential members into actual members might result, for example, in more financial resources, or it might result in a membership spread through every congressional district. However, the costs of organizing a large group, especially if their interests are not extremely concordant and focused, can be quite high, higher perhaps than the benefits members might gain from membership.

To gain the cohesive benefit of having a large proportion of potential members of a group actually join the group, the so-called free-rider problem must be overcome (Olson 1965). The larger the group, the more difficult it is to overcome the free-rider problem. All interest groups seek to provide collective goods for their members. In the process, when they succeed, they may also be providing the benefits of the collective goods for nonmembers. A collective good is something of value, the benefits of which cannot be withheld from a group's actual members or from its potential members. Better reimbursement rates for all hospitals under the Medicare program or more generous overall funding for AIDS research are collective goods that can benefit all hospitals or all AIDS researchers. In such situations, it does not matter that some of the beneficiaries do not belong to the interest groups whose efforts secured the benefits.

Large interest groups can certainly be effective. Once they are well organized, in fact, they can be extremely effective. However, it is much more difficult for them to organize in the first place. This means that small, cohesive interest groups frequently have an advantage over larger ones in the competition to influence public policymaking. They gain their advantage primarily because they are more likely to represent a greater proportion of potential members. It is easier for them to speak with one voice for their members than groups that represent only a small fraction of their potential members or that have memberships divided on policy issues.

The Influential Role of Chief Executives in Agenda Setting

A second especially influential participant in setting the policy agenda, including that for policy in the health domain, is the chief executive—the president, governor, or mayor. In cases where these individuals enjoy popularity, they can easily play preeminent roles in agenda setting. Kingdon (1995) attributes the influential role in agenda setting of presidents (and his point also applies to other chief executives) to certain institutional resources inherent in the executive office.

The politically advantageous resources routinely available to chief executives include the ability to present a unified administration position on issues, which stands in stark contrast to the legislative branch where opinions and views tend to be heterogeneous, and the executive's ability to command public attention. Properly managed, this latter ability can stimulate substantial public pressure on legislators in support of the executive's preferences and viewpoints. Chief executives can even rival powerful interest groups in their ability to shape public opinion around the public policy agenda.

Lammers (1997) emphasizes the ability of chief executives to perform "issue-raising activities" as crucial to their ability to influence agenda setting. He notes that the development of legislation is "generally preceded by a variety of actions that first create a widespread sense that a problem exists that needs to be addressed" (1997, 112). Problems and preferred solutions can be emphasized by chief executives in a number of ways, including press conferences, speeches, and addresses. This can be especially potent in such highly visible contexts as State of the Union or State of the State addresses.

The Real World of Health Policy

State of the State Address

The following are excerpts, many of them health-related, from the January 23, 2001 address by Angus S. King, Jr., Maine's 71st Governor. First elected in 1994, he is serving a second four-year term.

Mr. Speaker, Mr. President, Mr. President Pro Tem, Mr. Chief Justice, Members of the 120th Legislature, Citizens of Maine, in each of the past six years, I have come before you at this time to report on the State of the State, to take stock of where we are and, more importantly, where we want to be.

As a direct result of the strength of the Maine economy, we have had the enviable task of coping with wave after wave of revenue surplus—funding long-deferred maintenance on our public infrastructure, cutting taxes by more than $450 million, building up the Rainy Day Fund from $6.4 million to $143 million, embarking upon a visionary land conservation effort, making the largest two-year investment in our schools—both buildings and programs—in the history of the state, and undertaking an historic initiative—linking our University and the private sector—in research and development—that will change the face of Maine.

But all of this progress came from the same place: the growing economy of Maine. Greater prosperity, more people making more money, and, yes, paying taxes is what underlies all the achievements I mentioned.

My commitment to better jobs, better pay, better benefits in Medway and Madison as well as Sanford and Scarborough has not and will not flag, for whatever we want to do for our people—whether in education, health care, domestic violence, environmental protection, or research and development—it all rests on jobs and economic growth.

Tonight, however, I want to talk about the economy through the lens of our children, and in the process focus on two basic ideas—community and opportunity—and, if we can preserve the one and seize the other, we will shape a great future for Maine.

Before turning to community, however, let me at least outline some important initiatives I will bring before you this winter, without details tonight, but with much more discussion to come.

First, I will be offering a set of proposals to make private health insurance more affordable for individuals and small businesses, to contain health care costs, and to empower consumers through information and incentives so that they may play an increased role in determining their own health care future.

Next, we will continue the fight I declared here last year against "Public Enemy #1" by reaffirming zero tolerance towards domestic and sexual abuse. In the past year, a great deal of momentum has developed on this issue, and I welcome the opportunity to work with this Legislature and dedicated organizations across the state to continue the fight against this intolerable plague.

We will pursue policies that encourage and enable the development of affordable housing for all Maine people, and I urge every Maine community to make housing for its lower income families and elderly a moral and economic imperative. When it comes to housing, NIMBY [*Not in My Back Yard*] has no place in Maine.

We will work together to increase the number of college graduates in Maine using earnings from the NEXTGEN college savings program and working with the newly created MELMAC education foundation to provide scholarship dollars to Maine students. This initiative, when coupled with the growing resources allocated to Research and Development proposed in my budget, give us a running start on the goal of "30 and 1,000", 30% of Maine's adults with college degrees and $1,000 in R and D investment behind each Maine worker.

We will continue investments in our highways and bridges, as well as in air, rail, trail and marine, and we'll do so while providing a sustainable funding plan that also results in reduced highway debt.

I have proposed a reliable source of tourism funding which will sustain and support one of our most important industries.

I will propose a pilot program to redefine forest management to focus on results instead of regulations.

We will work with Maine businesses on "Smart Production," an initiative that will start industrial processes on a path toward zero environmental impact while simultaneously increasing our market competitiveness.

I will propose a "Smart Growth" package of initiatives that will preserve our neighborhoods, keep our communities livable, and strengthen the natural resource economy of our rural areas.

I will offer a bill to get mercury out of products in Maine and continue to work with our neighbors so that fish advisories in Maine will finally become be a thing of the past.

And let's finally get the State out of the retail liquor business and save $5 million every year for the taxpayers.

I will offer a proposal to return order to the citizen initiative process and sanctity to our voting places by extending the existing restrictions on polling place politicking to those collecting signatures just as they now apply to those collecting votes.

I will propose some insurance against the next economic slow down by constitutionally protecting the Rainy Day Fund.

We will continue the battle begun last year to insure access to life-giving prescription drugs to our most vulnerable citizens. No one within the sound of my voice should doubt the determination of anyone in this room on this score.

Just last Friday, for example, one of the last acts of Secretary [of the United States Department of Health and Human Services] Donna Shalala was to grant Maine's request to extend the Medicaid discount to prescription drugs to all Mainers who do not have drug insurance and who are at or below 300% of poverty. This means that beginning in July [of 2001], 225,000 Maine people will pay 25% less for medically necessary drugs.

But now, and for the rest of the evening, I want to talk about kids—mine, yours, and all those in Maine. And, as I mentioned earlier, I want to do this in the context of preserving community and seizing opportunity.

Because even in a state renowned for its natural resources, our greatest treasures are not the mountains we ascend, the rivers we canoe, the oceans we sail or even the books we read. It's the children we raise—they are the true measure of our worth, and how we prepare them for their own lives will be the best gauge of our success.

Look at what we've accomplished for our children in just the last few years:

Make no mistake, improving job options and opportunities for parents is one of the best things we can do for their kids. Since the winter of 1995, we have added over 67,000 net new jobs; that's net new jobs—over and above the replacement of job losses in Wilton, Winslow, Westbrook, or anywhere else in Maine. If you do the math, that comes out to 255 new jobs a week, week in and week out for five years. And, this fall, we posted the lowest unemployment rate since 1945.

Six years ago an overwhelmed child protective system in Maine received over 17,000 reports of possible child abuse or neglect; of these, the Department of Human Services was unable to investigate 2,700 cases, leaving the children and families represented by these cases at risk.

Today, with the support of the Legislature and a Herculean effort from the managers and front-line workers at the Department of Human Services, that backlog of almost 3,000 cases has been reduced to 203. That's good news for the kids of Maine.

* * *

And let's talk about the health of our kids. Four years ago, under the leadership of the 118th Legislature, we expanded Medicaid and created Cub Care coverage for children of low-income working families in Maine. But passing the bill and setting up the program was only the start. The folks at DHS then went to work to make it work, creating the nation's best outreach and sign-up process. While many states had long and complicated application forms stretching to ten pages or more, our folks got it all on one, easy-to-read piece of paper.

The result is that we now have the fourth highest rate of insured—that's insured, not uninsured—kids in the country, an astounding 94% of the children in Maine. Because of our success, we are one of only ten states slated to receive additional federal funds that other states failed to allocate. We will be working with you to make sure our kids benefit from this new money.

Also, in the area of children's mental health:

- Case management services to children have increased by 70% just last year;
- In-home supports have been expanded by 700% in the last two years;
- The numbers of children placed in out-of-state treatment has been reduced by 46% over the last two years; and
- We have developed, in partnership with the Judiciary and Corrections Department, an innovative drug court program that intensively treats kids with criminal and substance abuse problems.

Next, four years ago we made a difficult choice to raise the excise tax on cigarettes. Since that time, youth smoking in Maine has declined an amazing 27%. We still have too many kids smoking, though, and if we agree to push this tax up one more notch that figure will continue to fall and we'll be saving lives all over the state.

※ ※ ※

All of this good progress was summed up the summer before last when the Children's Rights Council in Washington looked at these and a bunch of other factors and rated Maine as the number one state in the United States in which to raise a child.

※ ※ ※

Five years ago, we began to work on this idea of preserving community through an unusual kind of government program called Communities for Children—one staff person, practically no budget, but a powerful idea—harness the creativity, energy, and effort that is already out there—from Eastport to Kittery and Bethel to Belfast—and be the catalyst for sharing experiences both successes and failures—so each community doesn't have to reinvent the wheel, or the teen center, in this case.

The results have been wonderful. 220 towns are now involved. Each "partner community" creates a leadership council made up of caring residents that assess the realities facing children and youth in their community. The council develops prevention programs and policies and tracks the results of their work. And they communicate with each other—through Communities For Children—about what works and what doesn't.

* * *

Candidates for the presidency are sometimes quite specific in their campaigns on various health policy issues, sometimes even to the point of endorsing specific legislative proposals (Fishel 1985). Examples include the emphasis given to enactment of the Medicare program by Presidents Kennedy and Johnson in their campaigns, and President Clinton's highly visible commitment to fundamental health reform as a central theme of his 1992 campaign. Another issue-raising mechanism favored by some chief executives is the appointment of special commissions or task forces (Linowes 1998). President Clinton used this tactic in the 1993 appointment of the President's Task Force on Health Care Reform (Johnson and Broder 1996).

Governors can also utilize commissions to elevate issues on the policy agenda. For example, Massachusetts made history when its Gay and Lesbian Student Rights Law was signed by Governor William F. Weld. He established the nation's first Governor's Commission on Gay and Lesbian Youth, which helped lead the state legislature to enact the law. This law prohibits discrimination in public schools on the basis of sexual orientation. Gay students are guaranteed redress if they suffer name-calling, threats of violence, and unfair treatment in school.

Chief executives occupy positions that permit them to be very influential in each phase of the policymaking process. In addition to their issue-raising role in agenda setting, they are well positioned to help focus the legislative branch on the development of legislation, and to prod legislators to continue their legislative work on favored issues even when facing enormous competing demands on their time and attention. In addition, chief executives are central to the implementation of policies by virtue of their positions atop the executive (or implementing) branch of government, as discussed in chapter 6, and they play a crucial role in modifying previously established policies, as discussed in chapter 7.

The Nature of the Health Policy Agenda

The confluence of problems and potential solutions and political circumstances that surround them invariably shape a health policy agenda. This agenda, however, is extraordinarily dynamic, changing quite literally on a day-to-day basis. In addition, the nation's health policy agenda does not exist in a vacuum. Instead, it coexists with policy agendas in other domains such as defense, welfare, education, and communication. This is further complicated by the fact that in a pluralistic society where difficult problems exist and where clear-cut solutions are rare, there are likely to be a number of different "sides" to any particular problem or potential solution to it, each with its supporters and detractors. The number, ratio, and intensity of these supporters and detractors are determined by the impact of the problem and its solution on those who take positions. One consequence of this phenomenon is severely crowding and confounding the health policy agenda. It is impossible, in fact, for anyone to actually describe this agenda in its full form at any point in time.

As policymakers seek to accommodate the needs and preferences of different interests, or "sides," on particular problem/potential solution combinations over time within the health policy agenda, the inevitable result is a set—a very large and diverse set—of policies that are riddled with incompatibilities and inconsistencies. American health policy offers many examples of this result.

The nation's mix of policies regarding the production and consumption of tobacco products, a mix that simultaneously facilitates and discourages tobacco use, provides a good example of the coexistence of public policies at cross-purposes. Sometimes, the result is a set of related policies with a consistent purpose but with different emphases about which people can disagree. The nation's mix of AIDS policies, for example, reflects this phenomenon. Some policies have been developed to support the clinical study of the human immunodeficiency virus (HIV) and its impact on humans. Other policies concurrently support the search for an effective vaccine. President Clinton, on May 18, 1997, in a move reminiscent of President John F. Kennedy's call to put an American on the surface of the moon before the end of the 1960s, proclaimed a national goal of finding a vaccine for AIDS by 2007. In support of this goal, the President announced the creation of a dedicated AIDS vaccine research unit at the National Institutes of Health. Still other AIDS-related policies support education about transmission of the virus and attempt to change human behaviors that help spread the virus. There is significant disagreement within the health policy community about the appropriate mix of these types of policies and the share of available funds that should be allocated to each. This discord exists in spite of the fact that all of these policies share the ultimate purpose of minimizing the suffering and death caused by HIV.

This phenomenon of multiple and conflicting policies, which Foote (1991) has termed "polyintervention," can also be observed in the health policy agenda related to, and in the eventual pattern of public policies related to, medical technology. Policymakers have sought to serve the goal of spreading the benefits of new medical technology and at the same time to serve such goals as protecting the public from unsafe technologies and attempting to slow the growth in overall health costs through controlling the explosive growth of new technologies. The result is a large group of technology-related policies that seek to foster (NIH, National Science Foundation, other biomedical funding, and tax credits for biomedical research in the private sector, for example), to inhibit (state-run certificate-of-need programs that restrain the diffusion of technology), and to control (FDA regulation and product liability laws) the development and use of medical technology in the United States.

There are several reasons for the ambivalence about whether policy should foster or inhibit and control technology. As reflected in the policy agenda and in the pattern of existing policies that pertain to medical technology, these reasons relate to the particular perspectives on medical technology that one or more interest groups hold. It is the diversity of interests that stand to be served by supporting or inhibiting medical technology that largely shape this phenomenon.

The most important aspect of the health policy agenda, however, is that when the existence of a problem is widely acknowledged, when possible solutions have been identified and refined, and when favorable political circumstances exist, a window of opportunity opens, albeit sometimes only briefly. Through this window, problem/potential solution combinations move forward to a new and different set of activities, development of legislation (see Figure 4.1). As described next, in chapter 5, it is through the development of legislation that policymakers seek to convert some of their ideas, hopes, and hypotheses about addressing problems into concrete policies in the form of new public laws or amendments to existing ones.

Summary

The policy formulation phase of policymaking involves agenda setting and the development of legislation, as shown in Figure 4.1. Agenda setting is the central topic of this chapter.

The development of legislation, which is discussed in chapter 5, follows a carefully scored choreography that includes the drafting and introduction of legislative proposals, their referral to appropriate committees and subcommittees, House and Senate floor action on proposed legislation, conference committee action when necessary, and presidential action on legislation enacted by the Congress.

Following the conceptualization of Kingdon (1995), agenda setting in public policymaking is described as a function of the confluence of three "streams" of activities: problems, possible solutions to the problems, and political circumstances. When all three streams flow together in a favorable alignment, a "window of opportunity" opens (see Figure 4.1), allowing a problem/potential solution combination, that might be developed into a new public law or an amendment to an existing one, to advance to the next point in the policymaking process: development of legislation.

Discussion Questions

1. Discuss the formulation phase of policymaking in general terms.
2. Discuss agenda setting as the confluence of three streams of activities. Include the concept of a "window of opportunity" for legislation development in your answer.
3. Describe the nature of problems that drive policy formulation.
4. Discuss the role of research in health policy agenda setting.
5. Contrast decision making in the public and private sectors as it relates to selecting from among alternative solutions to problems.
6. Discuss the involvement of interest groups in the political circumstances that affect agenda setting. Incorporate the specific ways in which they exert their influence on agenda setting in your response.
7. Discuss the role of chief executives in agenda setting at the federal level.
8. Discuss the nature of the health policy agenda that results from agenda setting at the federal level.

Note

1. This discussion of the tactics used by interest groups in influencing the public policymaking process is drawn from pages 125–32 of Longest (1997).

References

Brodie, M., and R. J. Blendon. 1995. "The Public's Contribution to Congressional Gridlock on Health Care Reform." *Journal of Health Politics, Policy and Law* 20 (2): 403–10.

Brown, L. D. 1991. "Knowledge and Power: Health Services Research as a Political Resource." In *Health Services Research: Key to Health Policy*, edited by E. Ginzberg, 20–45. Cambridge, MA: Harvard University Press.

Buchholz, R. A. 1994. *Business Environment and Public Policy: Implications for Management*, 5th ed. Upper Saddle River, NJ: Prentice-Hall.

Caldeira, G. A., and J. R. Wright. 1990. "Amici Curiae Before the Supreme Court: Who Participates, When, and How Much?" *Journal of Politics* 52: 782–804.

Committee on Quality of Health Care in America, Institute of Medicine. 1999. *To Err Is Human: Building a Safer Health System*. Washington, DC: National Academy Press.

———. 2001. *Crossing the Quality Chasm: A New Health System for the 21st Century*. Washington, DC: National Academy Press.

Crane, S. C., A. S. Hersh, and S. M. Shortell. 1992. "Challenges for Health Services Research in the 1990s." In *Improving Health Policy and Management: Nine Critical*

Research Issues for the 1990s, edited by S. M. Shortell and U. E. Reinhardt, 369–84. Chicago: Health Administration Press.

Edwards. G. C., M. P. Wattenberg, and R. L. Lineberry. 2001. *Government in America: People, Politics, and Policy*. White Plains, NY: Longman Publishing Group.

Feldstein, P. J. 1996. *The Politics of Health Legislation: An Economic Perspective*, 2nd ed. Chicago: Health Administration Press.

Fishel, J. 1985. *Presidents and Promises*. Washington, DC: Congressional Quarterly Press.

Foote, S. B. 1991. "The Impact of Public Policy on Medical Device Innovation: A Case of Polyintervention." In *The Changing Economics of Medical Technology*, edited by A. C. Gelijns and E. A. Halm, 69–88. Washington, DC: National Academy Press.

Gormly, W. T., Jr., and C. Boccuti. 2001. "HCFA and the States: Politics and Intergovernmental Leverage." *Journal of Health Politics, Policy and Law* 26 (3): 557–80.

Green, J. 1995. "High-Court Ruling Protects Hospital-Bill Surcharges." *AHA News* 31 (18): 1.

Hacker, J. S. 1997. *The Road to Nowhere*. Princeton, NJ: Princeton University Press.

Johnson, H., and D. S. Broder. 1996. *The System: The American Way of Politics at the Breaking Point*. Boston, MA: Little, Brown and Company.

Kingdon, J. W. 1995. *Agendas, Alternatives, and Public Policies*, 2nd ed. New York: HarperCollins College Publishers.

Lammers, W. W. 1997. "Presidential Leadership and Health Policy." In *Health Politics and Policy*, 3rd ed., edited by T. J. Litman and L. S. Robins, 111–34. Albany, NY: Delmar Publishers Inc.

Linowes, D. F. 1998. *Creating Public Policy: The Chairman's Memoirs of Four Presidential Commissions*. Westport, CT: Praeger Publishers.

Longest, B. B., Jr. 1997. *Seeking Strategic Advantage Through Health Policy Analysis*. Chicago: Health Administration Press.

Lowi, T. 1964. "American Business, Public Policy, Case Studies, and Political Theory." *World Politics* 16 (July): 677–715.

Milbrath, L. W. 1976. *The Washington Lobbyists*. Westport, CT: Greenwood Publishing Group, Inc.

Moynihan, D. P. 1970. *Maximum Feasible Misunderstanding*. New York: Free Press.

Olson, M. 1965. *The Logic of Collective Action*. Cambridge, MA: Harvard University Press.

Ornstein, N. J., and S. Elder. 1978. *Interest Groups, Lobbying and Policymaking*. Washington, DC: Congressional Quarterly Press.

Price, D. 1978. "Policymaking in Congressional Committees: The Impact of 'Environmental' Factors." *American Political Science Review* 72(2): 548–74.

Schriftgeisser, K. 1951. *The Lobbyists*. Boston, MA: Little, Brown and Company.

Shortell, S. M., and U. E. Reinhardt. 1992. "Creating and Executing Health Policy in the 1990s." In *Improving Health Policy and Management: Nine Critical Research Issues for the 1990s*, edited by S. M. Shortell and U. E. Reinhardt, 3–36. Chicago: Health Administration Press.

Skidmore, M. 1970. *Medicare and the American Rhetoric of Reconciliation*. Tuscaloosa, AL: University of Alabama Press.

Yankelovich, D. 1992. "How Public Opinion Really Works." *Fortune* (October 5): 102–8.

5

POLICY FORMULATION:
DEVELOPMENT OF LEGISLATION

AS NOTED in the previous chapter, the formulation phase of health policymaking includes two distinct and sequentially related parts: agenda setting and legislation development. This chapter, which focuses on the development of legislation, is a companion to the previous chapter in which the agenda-setting aspect of policy formulation was the focus. Policy formulation can be fully appreciated only through the combination of the various activities associated with agenda setting and with legislation development.

As in the discussion of agenda setting in chapter 4, this discussion of legislation development is confined almost exclusively to its occurrence at the federal level of government. However, state and local governments develop legislation of their own and in general this is done in a manner similar to the federal approach. The problems that legislation is developed to address differ at each level, as do the contexts, many of the participants, and specific mechanisms and procedures used in developing legislation.

The result of the entire formulation phase of policymaking is public policy in the form of new public laws or amendments to existing laws. New health-related laws or amendments that eventually emerge from the activities associated with the development of legislation originate from the policy agenda. Recall that the policy agenda is established through the interactions of a diverse array of health-related problems; possible solutions to the problems; and dynamic political circumstances that relate both to the problems and to their potential solutions. Combinations of problems, potential solutions, and political circumstances that achieve priority on the policy agenda move on in the overall policymaking process to the next component of policy formulation—legislation development (see the shaded portion of Figure 5.1).

The Choreography of Legislation Development

Development of legislation is the point in policy formulation where specific legislative proposals, which are characterized in the previous chapter as hypothetical or unproved potential solutions to the problems they are intended to address, advance through a series of steps that can end in new or amended public laws. These steps, not unlike those of a dance, are specified or choreographed. Only when all of the steps in the legislation development process are completed (although this happens for only a fraction of the legislative proposals that begin the steps) is the result a change in policy, either in the form of new public laws or statutes or, as far more typically, in the form of amendments to previously enacted laws. The steps that make up legislation development provide the framework for most of the discussion in this chapter.

The pathway formed by the steps through which legislation is developed extends from the origination of ideas for proposed legislation, which actually emerge in the agenda-setting stage, to formal drafting of legislative proposals, and then through several other steps, eventually to the enactment of laws derived from some of the proposals. Remember, however, that only a small fraction of the legislative proposals that are formally introduced in a Congress—the two annual sessions spanning the term of office of members of the House of Representatives—actually are enacted into law. Proposals that are not enacted by the end of the congressional session in which they were introduced die and must be reintroduced in the next Congress if they are to be considered further.

Only a small fraction of the problem/potential solution combinations that might be addressed through legislation are addressed in this way. When they are, the tangible final product is an enacted law, which can be an entirely new law or one or more amendments to previously enacted laws. As the bridge between the policy formulation and implementation phases (shown in Figure 5.1), formal enactment of proposed legislation into law represents a significant transition between these two phases of the overall public policymaking process. The focus in this chapter is on ways in which public laws are developed and enacted in the policymaking process; their implementation is discussed in chapter 6.

It is important to remember, as described in chapter 4, that individuals and health-related organizations, and especially the interest groups to

Figure 5.1 A Model of the Public Policymaking Process in the United States: Policy Formulation Phase

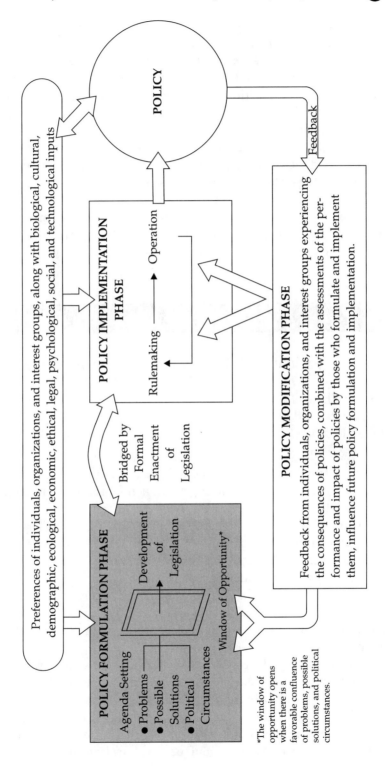

which they belong, are instrumental in the agenda setting that precedes legislation development. They also actively participate in the development of legislation. Once health policy issues achieve a prominent place on the policy agenda and move to the next stage of policy formulation, development of legislation, those with concerns and preferences about policy in a particular area often actively continue to participate in support of its formulation.

Individuals and health-related organizations and interest groups can participate directly in originating ideas for legislation, can help with the actual drafting of legislative proposals, and frequently can participate in the hearings sponsored by legislative committees as they undertake the development of legislation. When there are competing bills seeking to address a problem, those with interests in the problems align themselves with favored legislative solutions and oppose those they do not favor.

The Real World of Health Policy

Patients' Bill Sparks Fierce Lobbying Battle

Sharon Theimer
The Associated Press
June 11, 2001

WASHINGTON—Health maintenance organizations, seeking to prevent patients from gaining new rights to sue them, are putting a new twist on their message, warning that such legislation will damage the economy.

Insurers and businesses are spending millions of dollars on a new campaign to oppose a patients' rights bill, which has become a Senate priority since Democrats took control last week.

The Senate is considering two versions of the legislation. The Kennedy-McCain bill would give consumers broad power to sue managed-care plans; a competing measure sponsored by Sens. Bill Frist, R-Tenn., and John Breaux, D-La., and supported by President Bush would provide a more limited right to sue.

The lobbying effort includes ads warning consumers that the legislation is "bad for the economy. Bad for working people."

Telephone calls offering a similar message will target business owners. E-mails sent to doctors nationwide will link to video of mock newscasts, produced by the HMO industry, warning that patients' rights legislation will empower trial lawyers to pursue frivolous lawsuits.

"We will spend whatever it takes," said Mark Merritt, chief strategist for the American Association of Health Plans.

Groups pressing for improved patients' rights—labor unions, the Association of Trial Lawyers of America and the American Medical Association—plan to focus on grass-roots organizing to influence lawmakers. The doctors' lobby already has held town hall—style meetings across the country.

The competing efforts could reach the level of lobbying that was credited with defeating the Clinton administration's health care plan in 1994. That campaign included pervasive ads about "Harry and Louise," a fictional couple opposed to government-managed health care.

Merritt's group is against both plans introduced in the Senate to give patients more rights to sue insurers over treatment and coverage decisions. The group is planning its own ads and belongs to a coalition that is launching ads this week.

The campaign aimed at businesses and doctors is refined a bit, warning that the bill sponsored by Sens. Ted Kennedy, D-Mass., and John McCain, R-Ariz., would also let patients sue their employers and physicians over health coverage decisions.

Trial lawyers, the AMA and other patients' rights supporters accuse the HMOs of using scare tactics to stop the legislation.

"We think it has very reasonable protections for consumers who are lucky enough to have health insurance," said Judy Waxman of Families USA. "It provides the same floor of protection for everybody; no matter where you live, what state you're in or who you work for."

Source: Reprinted with permission of The Associated Press.

The Result of Legislation Development: Laws and Amendments to Laws

The laws and amendments to existing laws that result from the formulation phase of policymaking are quite tangible, and purposely so. They can be seen and read in a number of places. The U.S. Constitution prohibits the enactment of laws that are not specifically and directly made known to the people who are to be bound by them. In practice, federal laws are published for the citizenry immediately upon enactment. Of course, it is incumbent on persons who might be affected by laws to know of them and to be certain that they understand the impact of those laws. In the world of professionals who are involved in the pursuit of health, a great deal of attention is paid to the task of ascertaining the impact of laws (Longest 1997).

At the federal level, enacted laws are first printed in pamphlet form called *slip law*. Later, laws are published in the *United States Statutes at Large* and eventually incorporated into the *United States Code*. The *Statutes at Large*, published annually, contain the laws enacted during each session of Congress. In effect, they are compilations of all laws enacted in a particular year. The *United States Code* is a complete compilation of all of the nation's laws. New editions of the code are published every six years, with cumulative supplements published annually.

The series of steps through which laws are made and amended, as outlined in this chapter, comprise legislation development that begins with the origination of ideas for legislation and extends through the enactment of some of those ideas into law or the amendment of existing laws. The steps apply equally whether the resulting legislation is completely new or, as is so often the case, it represents the amendment of prior legislation. (Excellent and extensive descriptions of the steps through which federal legislation is developed can be found on the Internet by accessing "How Our Laws Are Made" and "Enactment of a Law" at http://thomas.loc.gov.)

Originating and Drafting Legislative Proposals

The development of legislation begins with the conversion of the ideas, hopes, and hypotheses about how problems might be addressed through changes in policy—ideas that emerge from agenda setting—into concrete legislative proposals called *bills*. Proposed legislation can also be introduced as a resolution. As a practical matter, there is little difference between a bill and a resolution, and they are not differentiated operationally here.

Origins of Ideas for Public Policy

Ideas for public policy in the form of law, which are expressed in bills, originate in many places. They obviously come from the members of Congress, whether from the House of Representatives or the Senate. In fact, many legislators are elected to Congress, at least in part, on the basis of the legislative ideas they expressed in their election campaigns. Promises to introduce certain legislative proposals, made during campaigns specifically to the constituents whom candidates seek to represent, are core aspects of the American form of government and are frequent sources of eventual legislative proposals.

Once in office, legislators are well positioned to become even more aware of and knowledgeable about the need for amendment or repeal of existing laws or for the enactment of entirely new laws through their evolving understanding of the problems and potential solutions that face their constituents or the larger society.

But the source of ideas for laws is not limited to legislators. Individual citizens, health-related organizations, or, far more likely, interest groups representing many individuals or organizations may avail themselves of their right to petition government—a right guaranteed by the First Amendment—and to propose ideas for the development of legislation. In effect, this process results directly from the participation of individuals, organizations, and groups in the agenda-setting aspect of policy formulation. The ideas behind many of the nation's public laws originate in this way because certain individuals, organizations, or interest groups have considerable knowledge of the problem/potential solutions combinations that affect them or their members.

Interest groups tend to be very influential in legislation development, as they are in agenda setting, because of their pooled resources. Well-staffed interest groups, for example, also can draw on the services of legislative draftspersons to help draft the preferred ideas and concepts into appropriate legislative language.

An increasingly important source of ideas for legislative proposals, which also plays a role in agenda setting, is "executive communication" from members of the executive branch to members of the legislative branch. Such communications are usually in the form of a letter from a senior member of the executive branch, such as a member of the President's Cabinet; from the head of an independent agency; or even from the President. Through these communications, the executive branch serves as a direct source of ideas for policy in the form of laws. These communications from the executive branch to the legislative branch typically include comprehensive drafts of proposed bills. They are sent to the Speaker of the House of Representatives and, simultaneously, to the President of the Senate, who can then insert them into the legislation development procedures at appropriate places.

The executive branch as an important source of ideas for policy in the form of laws is based in the Constitution. Although the U.S. Constitution establishes a government characterized by the separation of powers, in Article II, Section 3, it imposes an obligation on the President to report to Congress from time to time on the "State of the Union" and to recommend for consideration such policies in the form of laws as the President considers necessary, useful, or expedient. Many of the executive communications to the Congress follow up on ideas first aired in the President's annual State of the Union Address to Congress.

Executive communications that pertain to proposed legislation are referred by the legislative leaders who receive them to the appropriate standing committee or committees having jurisdiction in the areas incorporated in the executive branch proposals. The chairperson of that standing committee usually introduces the bill promptly either in the form in which it was received or with any changes the chairperson considers necessary or desirable. Only members of the Congress can actually introduce proposed legislation, no matter who originates the idea or drafts the proposal.

The practice of having committee chairpersons introduce legislative proposals that arise through executive communication is followed even when the majority of the House or the Senate and the President are not of the same political party, although there is no constitutional or statutory requirement that a bill be introduced to put the executive branch's recommendations into effect. When the chairperson of the committee with jurisdiction does not introduce a bill that is based on executive communication, the proposed legislation is considered by the committee or one of its subcommittees to determine whether the bill should be introduced.

The most important of the regular executive communications is the one through which the President annually transmits a proposed federal budget to Congress (Oleszek 2001). More is said about the budget process later in this chapter. Here, suffice it to say that the President's budget proposal, together with supportive testimony by officials of the various executive branch departments and agencies, along with testimony from individuals, organizations, and interest groups concerned about the budget—before one of the 13 Subcommittees of the Appropriations Committees of the House and Senate—is the basis of the appropriation bills that are eventually drafted by these committees.

The Real World of Health Policy

Budget of the United States Government, FY 2002

The President submits a proposed annual federal budget to the Congress in spring. The following is the letter by which President Bush transmitted his FY 2002 budget proposal.

To the Congress of the United States:

On February 28, 2001, I submitted *A Blueprint for New Beginnings* [which can be read at www.whitehouse.gov/omb/budget], which provided the Congress with my budget plan to fund America's important priorities, reduce the debt by a historic amount, and provide fair and responsible tax relief for the American people. Today I am sending to the Congress more details on my proposed budget.

A budget is much more than a collection of numbers. A budget is a reflection of a nation's priorities, its needs, and its promise. This budget offers a new vision of governing for our Nation. My budget strengthens and reforms education; preserves and protects Medicare and Social Security; strengthens and modernizes our military; improves health care; and protects our environment. Importantly, this budget creates an unprecedented $1 trillion reserve for additional needs and contingencies.

This budget also retires the maximum amount of debt possible by providing the fastest, largest debt reduction in history, $2 trillion over 10 years. Debt held by the public will be reduced to its lowest share of the economy since World War I.

After funding important priorities and retiring all Government debt possible, my budget uses the remaining portion of the surplus to provide fair and reasonable tax relief to every American who pays income taxes. My budget uses roughly one-fourth of the budget surplus to provide the typical family of four $1,600 in tax relief. The American people have been overcharged for Government, and they deserve a refund.

My budget does all these things, and more. I believe America's best days are yet to come, and I look forward to working with the Congress in a bipartisan fashion to ensure that our Nation reaches its full potential as we begin a new century.

George W. Bush
April 9, 2001

Source: Excerpted from Office of Management and Budget. 2001. *Budget of the United States of America, FY 2002.* Washington, DC: OMB. Available on the Internet at www.whitehouse.gov/omb/budget.

Drafting Legislative Proposals

The drafting of legislative proposals is something of an art in itself, one requiring considerable skill, knowledge, and experience. Any member of the Senate or House of Representatives can draft bills, and these legislators' staffs are usually instrumental in drafting legislation. When issues are especially complex, the Legislative Counsel's Office in the Senate or House of Representatives can be called on for assistance in drafting bills. When bills are drafted in the executive branch, the services of trained legislative counsels are typically involved. These legislative counsels work in several executive branch departments and their work includes the drafting of bills to be forwarded to Congress. Similarly, proposed legislation that arises in the private sector, typically from interest groups, is drafted by people with expertise in the intricate task. No matter who drafts legislation, however, because only members of the Congress can officially sponsor proposed legislation, the legislative sponsors are ultimately responsible for the language in their bills. Commonly, a bill will have multiple sponsors and may have many cosponsors. Once ideas for solving problems through policy are drafted in the form of changes in law, they are ready for the next step, introduction for formal consideration by the Congress.

The Real World of Health Policy

The Clinton Health Reform Proposal of 1993

In late 1993, after many months of feverish drafting by a team including some of the nation's foremost health policy experts, President Clinton presented his proposal for legislation that would fundamentally reform the American healthcare system (Hacker 1997). The document, 1,431 pages in length, outlined the President's vision of the way in which health services should be provided and financed in America. The proposal was in the form of a comprehensive draft of a bill (to be called the Health Security Act) that could be enacted into law. However, the proposal faced a long and difficult path of legislation development to possible enactment. The fate of this proposed legislation is not atypical. It illustrates the destiny that befalls many ideas and hopes for solving problems through public policy as they travel along the pathway of their potential development into legislation. Hacker and Skocpol (1997, 315–16) have described the pathway followed by the Health Security plan:

> The rise and fall of health care reform is the oldest story in American health politics. Time and again in the twentieth century, reformers have unsuccessfully fought for expanded or universal health insurance. Then, in the aftermath of political defeats, private market actors have rapidly transformed patterns of health care financing and delivery. After World War II, this old story gained a new twist with the passage of federal legislation to augment the technological arsenal of American medicine. While proposals for national health insurance languished in Congress, the federal government pumped public funds into the medical industry, subsidizing private health insurance, hospital construction, and medical education and research, and generating new markets, profits, and political resources for major stakeholders in the one-seventh of the American economy now devoted to health care (Jacobs 1995).

Only in 1965, with the passage of Medicare and Medicaid, was the pattern of defeats followed by market transformations and incremental reforms momentarily broken. Yet that rare moment of victory for advocates of extended public financing of health care did not prove to be an entering wedge for universal health insurance through federal funding or mandates, as health reformers back then had hoped. By the 1970s, distrust of government, slow economic growth, and mounting fiscal constraints left reformers without much hope for achieving universal health insurance. Reformers found themselves struggling to protect existing public programs while advocating piecemeal regulations to control health care costs and narrow gaps in the private health insurance market.

The Health Security plan sponsored by President Bill Clinton during 1993 and 1994 aimed to break the political impasse facing post-1960s health reformers. With a "window of opportunity" for government-led reforms finally open (Kingdon 1995; Hacker 1996), President Clinton sought to enact comprehensive federal rules that would, in theory, simultaneously control medical costs and ensure universal insurance coverage. The bold Health Security initiative was meant to give everyone what they wanted, delicately balancing competing ideas and claimants, deftly maneuvering between major factions in Congress, and helping to revive the political prospects of the Democratic Party in the process (Hacker 1997).

But as everyone knows, the Health Security effort failed miserably (Skocpol 1996; Johnson and Broder 1996).

The failure of this legislative proposal to make it successfully through the remaining steps to enactment into law has been characterized as a matter in which "the bold gambit of comprehensive reform had once again succumbed to the power of antagonistic stakeholders, a public paralyzed by the fears of disrupting what it already had, and the challenge of coalition building engendered by the highly decentralized character of American government" (Peterson 1997, 291).

Although the Health Security proposal drafted by the Clinton Administration was not enacted into law, it did make it through the next step in the intricate dance of legislation development, formal introduction.

Introducing and Referring Proposed Legislation to Committees

Members of the Senate or the House of Representatives who have chosen to sponsor or cosponsor legislation introduce their proposals in the form of bills. On occasion, identical bills are introduced in both the Senate and the House for simultaneous consideration. When bills are introduced in either chamber of the Congress, they are assigned a sequential number (e.g., H.R. 1, 2, 3, . . . , n; or S. 1, 2, 3, . . . , n) based on the order of introduction by the presiding officer, and are referred to the appropriate standing committee or committees—that is, to the committees that have jurisdiction in the area of the bill—for further study and consideration.

Legislative Committees and Subcommittees

Both the Senate and the House of Representatives are organized into committees and subcommittees. The committee structure of the Congress is a fundamental feature of the activities involved in the development of legislation and is crucial to the actual development of legislation. Committee and subcommittee deliberations provide the settings for intensive and thorough consideration of legislative proposals.

At present, there are 17 standing committees in the House and 16 in the Senate. Each of the standing committees has jurisdiction over certain areas of legislation, and all bills that pertain to a particular area are referred to its committee. Information about the committees is available on their homepages, which can be accessed readily through the web site maintained by the Library of Congress, http://*thomas.loc.gov*.

Sometimes the content of a bill makes the assignment to more than one committee appropriate; in this case the bill is assigned to more than one committee either jointly or, more commonly, sequentially. For example, the Clinton administration's massive 1993 legislative proposal, the Health Security plan, described in the previous Real World section, was introduced simultaneously in the House and the Senate as H.R. 3600 and S. 1757. Because of its scope and complexity, the bill was then referred, jointly, to ten House Committees and two Senate Committees for consideration and debate.

Membership on the various congressional committees is divided between the two major political parties. The proportion of the members from each party is determined by the majority party, except that one-half of the members on the Committee on Standards of Official Conduct are from the majority party and one-half from the minority party. Legislators typically seek membership on committees that have jurisdiction in areas in which the policymakers have particular interests and expertise. The interests of their constituencies typically exert significant influence on the interests of policymakers. For example, members of the House of Representatives from agricultural districts or financial centers are often influenced by this in their preferences for committee memberships, as are senators in terms of whether they hail from primarily rural or highly urbanized states or from the industrialized northeast or the more agrarian west. The members of a committee rank in seniority in accordance with the order of their appointment to the committee.

The majority party in each chamber also controls the appointment of committee and subcommittee chairpersons. The chairpersons of congressional committees and subcommittees exert great power in the development of legislation because they determine the order and the pace that legislative proposals are considered by the committees or subcommittees they lead.

Each committee has a professional staff to assist with administrative details involved in its consideration of bills. In addition, under certain conditions, a standing committee may appoint consultants on a temporary or intermittent basis to assist the committee in its work. By virtue of expert knowledge, the professional staff serving committees and subcommittees are key participants in legislation development.

Committees with Health Policy Jurisdiction

Although no congressional committee is devoted exclusively to the health policy domain, several committees and subcommittees have jurisdiction in health-related legislation development. In one analysis of the period from 1980 to 1991, it was shown that the distribution of congressional committee hearings on health-related issues was divided among more committees than hearings in any other policy domain. The authors of this analysis concluded that no other policy area is characterized by this degree of jurisdictional fragmentation (Baumgartner and Talbert 1995).

There is, in fact, some overlap in the jurisdictions of the committees with important health-related legislative responsibilities. Most general health bills are referred to the House Committee on Energy and Commerce and to the Senate Committee on Health, Education, Labor and Pensions. However, any bills involving taxes and revenues must be referred to the House Committee on Ways and Means and to the Senate Committee on Finance. This gives these two committees substantial health policy jurisdiction because so much health policy involves taxes as a source of funding. The main health policy interests of these committees, as well as those of the Committee on Appropriations in each chamber of the Congress, are outlined here, beginning with those in the Senate.

- *Committee on Finance (www.senate.gov/~finance), with its Subcommittee on Health Care.* This Senate committee has jurisdiction over all bills that relate to health programs under the Social Security Act and to health programs financed by a specific tax or trust fund. This gives the committee jurisdiction over matters related to Medicare and Medicaid.

- *Committee on Health, Education, Labor, and Pensions (www.senate. gov/~labor), with its Subcommittee on Aging; Subcommittee on Children and Families; and Subcommittee on Public Health.* This Senate committee has jurisdiction over bills that relate to health personnel, the Public Health Service Act, the Federal Food, Drug and Cosmetic Act, and the Developmental Disabilities Assistance and Bill of Rights Act.

- *Committee on Appropriations (www.senate.gov/~appropriations/), with its Subcommittee on Labor, Health and Human Services, and Education; and its Subcommittee on Veterans, Housing and Urban Development.* This Senate committee has jurisdiction over appropriations for the Department of Health and Human Services and the Department of Veterans Affairs.

- *Committee on Ways and Means (waysandmeans.house.gov) with its Subcommittee on Health.* This House committee has jurisdiction over bills that pertain to providing payments from any source for health services, healthcare systems, or health-related research. The jurisdiction of the Subcommittee on Health includes bills related to the healthcare programs of the Social Security Act (including Titles XVIII and XIX, which are the Medicare and Medicaid programs), and tax credit and deduction provisions of the Internal Revenue Code dealing with health insurance premiums and healthcare costs.

- *Committee on Energy and Commerce (www.house.gov/commerce), with its Subcommittee on Health and its Subcommittee on Environment and Hazardous Materials.* This House committee has jurisdiction over all bills related to Medicaid; Medicare Part B; public health; health personnel; mental health and research; biomedical research and development programs; health maintenance organizations; food and drugs; drug abuse; and the Clean Air Act and environmental protection in general, including the Safe Drinking Water Act.

- *Committee on Appropriations (www.house.gov/appropriations), with its Subcommittee on Labor, Health and Human Services, and Education; its Subcommittee on Veterans Affairs, Housing and Urban Development, and Independent Agencies; and its Subcommittee on Agriculture, Rural Development, Food and Drug Administration, and Related Agencies.* This House committee has jurisdiction over appropriations for the Department of Health and Human Services, the Food and Drug Administration, and the Department of Veterans Affairs.

Committee and Subcommittee Operations

Depending on whether the chairperson of a committee has assigned a bill to a subcommittee, either the full committee or the subcommittee can, if they choose, hold hearings on bills. At these public hearings, members of the executive branch, representatives of health-related organizations and interest groups, and other individuals are permitted to present their views and recommendations on the legislation under consideration.

The Real World of Health Policy

Statement of Mary Jane England, M.D.
President, Washington Business Group on Health
Before the
Committee on Health, Education, Labor, and Pensions
United States Senate
March 28, 2001

Good morning Mr. Chairman and members of the committee. It is an honor to be here today to speak with you about the proposed "Health Information for Consumers Act" to establish consumer assistance programs for health care consumers.

The Washington Business Group on Health is a national nonprofit organization devoted to the analysis of health policy and related work site issues. Our members include 165 of the nation's largest and most innovative public and private sector employers that provide health coverage to more than 39 American million workers, retirees and their families. WBGH's mission since 1974 has been to represent employers in promoting market-based, performance-driven health care delivery systems that improve the health and productivity of companies and communities.

Employers are in a unique position to comment on health care services because the health of their business depends on the health of their workforce. If employees' health care needs are not met, their ability to contribute to the company is compromised. In addition, as major payors of health services, WBGH employers have promoted organized systems of care so that employees have access to care that is coordinated, high-quality and accessible.

Employers often play the role of an ombudsman by acting as an intermediary between the health plan and the employee. If an employee is denied a particular health care service, for instance, they often approach the human resources department for assistance, who in turn work with the health plan to resolve the issue. In today's health care environment, such interventions are common and speak to the complex nature of service delivery. Employers are also in a position to deliver information that can help their employees navigate the health care system and educate themselves about health promotion and prevention. Many of our members have developed innovative, cutting edge programs designed to assist employees in becoming responsible and informed consumers. As such, WBGH is excited about the opportunity to speak to not only the need, but also the design of, the proposed ombudsman programs that this legislation would establish.

WBGH applauds the Committee for taking this important step to improve the service delivery of health care for Americans. Given the complex nature of today's health system, quality information is more important than ever. The proposed consumer assistance program will empower and inform consumers, lessening the frustration and hopelessness often felt in the face of a confusing, ever-changing health care system. This is so valuable, important, and sorely needed. In addition to offering consumers a vehicle for navigating the health care system, this program provides the ability to resolve issues before they worsen and become more problematic. This proactive function of an ombudsman is perhaps the most valuable service it provides—because in addition to consumers getting the assistance they need with negotiating a confusing system—costly litigation is avoided. WBGH and its members favor avoiding unnecessary litigation whenever possible, because resources directed at such cases take away from valuable, precious health care dollars.

In addition to being a source of education for the consumer and a resource for resolving issues early, ombudsman programs offer health plans the ability to learn in a safe environment. Because the mode is educational rather than litigious, health plans will be able to use the information garnered from ombudsman programs to meet the needs of the population it serves. In this way, ombudsman programs provide a safe environment where problems are avoided and lessons are easily learned.

There are four issues that my comments will focus on today. WBGH suggests that the legislation include:

- National standards that are broad and flexible enough to promote innovation in the collection and dissemination of information;
- Special attention needed to avoid confusion with regard to ERISA plans;
- Program evaluation requirement to ensure that the services are high quality, meet the needs of the population served, and produce positive outcomes; and
- System of coordination with programs already in existence to avoid unnecessary duplication, both of services and funding.

National Standards

WBGH understands the importance of giving states the ability to establish and administer consumer assistance programs that best suit the unique needs of specific communities and populations. While respecting the importance of this flexibility, WBGH is concerned that state by state differences in program design could present significant challenges for health plans and employers that operate in multiple states. In addition, allowing states complete flexibility will likely result in inconsistencies that could negatively affect the consumer, if needed services are not provided. Given this dilemma of preserving states' flexibility while also maintaining consistency and high quality, WBGH proposes that national standards be used to ensure that each state follows similar principles and goals in establishing and administering consumer assistance programs. In addition to creating a baseline of consistency and quality, this will avoid creating unnecessary burdens on employers and health plans that operate in multiple states. It is also important that the standards be broad enough to encourage innovative practices in the collection and dissemination of information. I would also highly encourage programs to examine the cutting edge practices already in place that might be replicated or used as a blueprint for future programs. Many of WBGH's members may be helpful in this regard.

ERISA Plans

Because many of WBGH employers are self-funded health plans covered by ERISA, I wanted to draw your attention to this special area of concern. As you know, ERISA plans are subject to a set of specific rules different from state laws. Because of this major difference, it will be important for state consumer assistance programs to have a clear understanding about which health plans are in their purview and which are exempt, such as ERISA plans. If such lines are blurred, the goal of the consumer assistance program could be thwarted and more confusion about the health care system will result. In order to avoid such negative consequences, the legislation should reflect the importance of providing information to the consumer assistance program about which health plans are covered, as well as which plans are not. Doing so will prevent the misinterpretation of law and resulting frustration on the part of the employee, or consumer.

In addition, another issue that should be considered is that some self-funded ERISA covered employer health plans contract out specific services, such as pharmacy or mental health benefits, which may be included in the consumer assistance program purview. In other cases, the employer plan may have several options, including an HMO that may be covered in part by ERISA and in part by state law. In these cases, it will be crucial that consumer assistance programs are well informed about which programs, plans and services are covered by ERISA, as well as those covered by state law. Again, this will avoid unnecessary confusion and frustration for the employee. It is important that the consumer assistance

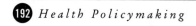

program be regarded as a helpful, knowledge source of information, so these issues ought to be addressed appropriately at the onset.

Evaluation

It is important that consumer assistance programs evaluate their efforts. WBGH suggests that an evaluation process be established that will ensure that quality services are provided, measure the program outcomes, and perhaps most important, set up a mechanism for improving such services. Establishing a process of evaluation will ensure that the services provided meet the needs of the population served, and that they continue to evolve as the health delivery system changes. This is of particular importance given the rapid changes in how health services are structured and administered today.

Coordination with Other Programs

In order to maximize the efficiency and usefulness of the consumer assistance programs established as a result of this legislation, coordination with other programs is a must. Many states already operate some form of consumer assistance program or ombudsman office, and future programs should be coordinated with these established programs. In addition, given the inclusion of Medicaid and Medicare beneficiaries in the legislation, the programs that are developed should be closely coordinated and created in partnership with already developed education and outreach efforts of these two programs. Further, the programs funded by this legislation should also be coordinated with existing consumer education efforts by the Departments of Labor and Health and Human Services and with currently existing private sector ombudsman initiatives. By organizing new programs to work with existing ones, unnecessary duplication of efforts and wasted resources will be avoided.

That concludes my remarks today. Thank you for your time today as you consider this important piece of legislation that will help shape Americans into informed and responsible consumers. I appreciate the opportunity to share the Washington Business Group on Health's perspective on this issue, and as always, I welcome any questions from the committee.

Source: Reprinted with permission of Washington Business Group on Health. Mary Jane England's testimony before the United States Senate Committee on Health, Education, Labor, and Pensions on the Health Information for Consumers Act.

Following such hearings, the members of committees or subcommittees "mark up" the bills they are considering. This term comes from the procedure of going through bills, line by line, and making changes by amending the original bill. Sometimes when similar bills or bills addressing the same issue have been introduced, they are combined in the markup process. In cases of subcommittee involvement, when the subcommittee has completed its markup, and a vote to approve the bill has occurred, the subcommittee reports out the bill to the full committee with jurisdiction. When no subcommittee is involved, or after a full committee has reviewed the work of the subcommittee and the full committee has voted to approve the bill, the full committee reports out the bill for a vote, this time to the floor of the Senate or the House.

If a committee has voted to report a bill favorably, a member of the committee staff, in the name of a committee member, writes the committee report. This is an extremely important document. The committee report describes the purposes and scope of the bill and the reasons why the committee recommends its approval by the entire Senate or House. Committee reports are very useful and informative documents in recording the legislative history of a public law. They are used by courts in considering matters related to particular laws that have been enacted, and by executive branch departments and agencies as guidance for implementing enacted laws. These documents provide a rich source of information regarding legislative proposals that have reached this stage of legislation development for those who are interested in the history, purpose, and meaning of the enacted laws.

Generally, a committee report contains a section-by-section analysis in which the purpose of each section of a bill is described. All changes in existing law that the bill would require are indicated in the report, and the text of laws being repealed by the bill are set out. Committee amendments to a bill as it was originally referred to the committee are described at the beginning of the report, and explanations of the amendments are included. Executive communications pertaining to the bill usually are quoted in full in the report.

The Real World of Health Policy

A State-Level Example of Influencing Legislation Development

An example of input into state legislation development appears in the 1995 session of the Pennsylvania legislature, when that body considered so-called "any willing provider" legislation. As part of legislation development in this area, the Pennsylvania House of Representatives Insurance Committee held a series of hearings during 1995 on the potential legislation, House Bill 630. This bill, which did not pass in the legislature, would have created increased difficulty for managed care plans in excluding providers from their networks. Ability of the plans to contract selectively for the services of providers would be reduced, thus effectively preventing the plans from selecting providers judged acceptable in terms of the plans' criteria for efficiency and quality in professional practice.

A number of individuals and health-related organizations and interest groups had serious concerns about the potential development of any legislation in this area. These concerns became intense at the time of the hearings, both in Pennsylvania and across the nation in other states that were considering such legislation. In fact, the interests grouped their concerns about any willing provider laws with their concerns about mandatory point-of-service laws into a broader set of concerns they referred to as "selective contracting restrictions." The leaders of the nation's managed care plans identified such restrictions as the top item on their public policy agenda for 1995 (Ernst & Young 1995).

At the first of four hearings in a series sponsored by the Insurance Committee of the Pennsylvania House of Representatives, a spokesperson from one of Pennsylvania's larger health services systems, speaking on behalf of the Hospital Association of Pennsylvania, testified that the proposed legislation was anticompetitive in that it would "destroy the gatekeeper concept that is central to managed care, severely limiting a managed care organization's ability to control health care costs and the quality of their networks" (Hospital Association of Pennsylvania 1995, 2).

Representatives from several other health-related organizations and interest groups also testified at this hearing, as a means of directly participating in the development of this legislation. These included representatives of Blue Cross of Northeastern Pennsylvania, the Insurance Federation of Pennsylvania, Pennsylvania Nurses Association, Geisinger Health Plan, and HealthAmerica (an HMO). Views on this legislation by the Patient Advocacy Coalition, several individual physicians, and a pharmacist were also presented at this hearing. In the end, of course, only legislators vote on legislative proposals. Their decisions, however, can and typically do reflect input from many sources.

House or Senate Floor Action on Proposed Legislation

Following approval of a bill by the full committee with jurisdiction, the bill is discharged from the committee along with its bill report. The House or the Senate, depending on where the bill is being considered, receives it from the relevant committee and places it on the legislative calendar for floor action.

Bills can be further amended in debate on the floor of the House or the Senate. However, because such great reliance is placed on the committee process in both chambers, amendments to bills proposed from the floor require considerable support.

Once passed in either the House or the Senate, bills are sent to the other chamber, where the step of referral to a committee with jurisdiction, and perhaps then to a subcommittee, is repeated, and where another round of hearings, markup, and eventual action may take place. If the bill is again reported out of committee, it goes to the involved chamber's floor for a final vote. If passed in the second chamber, any differences in the House and Senate versions of a bill must be resolved before the bill is sent to the White House for action by the President. The Congress uses conference committees to iron out any differences in the versions of bills passed by both House and Senate.

Conference Committee Actions on Proposed Legislation

To resolve differences in a bill that both chambers of the Congress have passed, a conference committee is established (Van Beck 1994). Conferees usually are the ranking members of the committees that reported out the bill in each chamber. If they can reach agreement on resolving the differences, a conference report is written, which is then voted on by both houses of the Congress. If the conferees cannot reach agreement, or if either house does not accept the report, the bill dies; but if both chambers accept the conference report, the bill is sent to the President for action.

Presidential Action on Proposed Legislation

The President has several options regarding proposed legislation that has been approved by both the House and the Senate. The bill can be signed, in which case it immediately becomes law. The President can veto the bill, in which case it must be returned to Congress along with an explanation of the basis for rejection. A two-thirds vote in both houses of the Congress can override a presidential veto. The President's third option is neither to veto the bill nor to sign it. In this case, the bill becomes law in ten days, but the President has made a political statement of disfavor regarding the legislation. Finally, when the President receives proposed legislation near the close of a Congressional session, the bill can be pocket vetoed if the President does nothing about it until the Congress is adjourned. In this case, the bill dies.

Legislation Development for the Federal Budget

Because enactment of legislation related to the federal government's annual budget is so crucial to the performance of government and to the well-being of the American people, special procedures have been developed to guide this process. The Congressional Budget and Impoundment Control Act of 1974 (P.L. 93-344), and its subsequent amendments, provides Congress with the procedures through which it establishes target levels for revenues, expenditures, and the overall deficit for the coming fiscal year. These congressional budget procedures are designed to coordinate decisions on sources and levels of federal revenues and on the objectives and levels of federal expenditures. Such decisions have a substantial impact on other policy decisions, including those that pertain to the health policy domain. Figure 5.2 shows, step by step, the procedures followed in developing legislation for the annual federal budget. The schedule begins when the President submits a proposed budget to Congress. The steps in this rather elaborate process are more fully described in the next section.

Procedures in Establishing the Federal Budget

The procedures through which the federal budget is annually established begin, formally, with the initial decision on the overall size of the budget pie for a given year, as well as the sizes of its various pieces. To accomplish this, Congress annually adopts a *concurrent resolution* that imposes overall constraints on spending, based in part on the size of the anticipated revenue budget for the year, and distributes the overall constraint on spending among groups of programs and activities. Concurrent resolutions are routinely used as a means of expressing legislative agreements that guide the operations of both chambers of the Congress.

In particular, the agreements expressed in a concurrent resolution guide the standing committees in both chambers that have jurisdiction in terms of actions necessary for them to take to meet the budget targets. These actions typically include changes in public laws, either in the form of new laws or of amendments to existing laws.

Figure 5.2 Steps in the Federal Budget Process

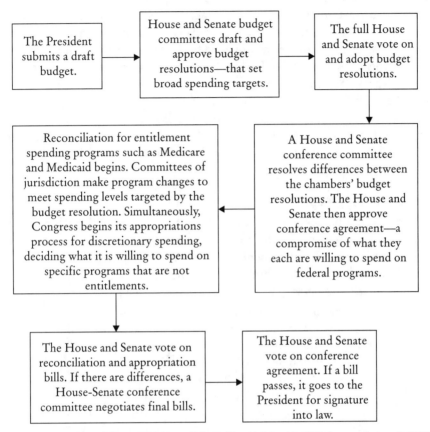

Source: Reprinted from *AHA News*, Vol. 33, No. 19, May 19, 1997, by permission, © 1997, American Hospital Publishing, Inc.

The Real World of Health Policy

How Does the Government Create a Budget?

The President and Congress both play major roles in developing the Federal budget.

The President's Budget

The law specifies that, by the first Monday in February, the President submit to Congress his proposed Federal budget for the next fiscal year, which begins October 1.

In some years, it is not possible for the President to adhere to the normal schedule. The law does not require an outgoing President to transmit a budget, and it is impractical for an incoming President to complete a budget within a few days of taking office. President George W. Bush submitted a summary budget plan, A Blueprint for New Beginning—A Responsible Budget for America's Priorities, to Congress on February 28, 2001.

President Bush's detailed budget—which includes a main book and several accompanying books[1] —covers thousands of pages and provides an abundance of information. These books, which were submitted in April 2001, allow people from all walks of life to examine the budget from many different perspectives.

Action in Congress

Congress first passes a "budget resolution"—a framework within which the Members will make their decisions about spending and taxes. It includes targets for total spending, total revenues, and the surplus or deficit, and allocations within the spending target for the two types of spending—*discretionary* and *mandatory*—explained below.

- *Discretionary spending*, which accounts for one-third of all Federal spending, is what the President and Congress must decide to spend for the next year through the 13 annual appropriations bills. It includes money for such activities as the FBI and the Coast Guard, for housing and education, for space exploration and highway construction, and for defense and foreign aid.

- *Mandatory spending*, which accounts for two-thirds of all spending, is authorized by permanent laws, not by the 13 annual appropriations bills. It includes entitlements—such as Social Security, Medicare, veterans' benefits, and Food Stamps—through which individuals receive benefits because they are eligible based on their age, income, or other criteria. It also includes interest on the national debt, which the Government pays to individuals and institutions that hold Treasury bonds and other Government securities. The President and Congress can change the law in order to change the spending on entitlements and other mandatory programs—but they don't have to.

Think of it this way: For discretionary programs, Congress and the President must act each year to provide spending authority. For mandatory programs, they may act to change the spending that current laws require.

---

1 They are the main budget book, entitled *Budget of the United States Government: Fiscal Year 2002*, as well as *Analytical Perspectives*, *Appendix*, *Historical Tables*, and *A Citizen's Guide to the Federal Budget*, from which this material is excerpted. All of these books can be read at the web site of the Office of Management and Budget (OMB) (www.whitehouse.gov/omb/budget).

Currently, the law imposes limits, or "caps," through 2002 on annual discretionary spending. The budget proposes to revise these caps beginning in 2001 to recognize changing fiscal conditions, and extend the caps at appropriate levels through 2006. Within the cap, however, the President and Congress can, and often do, change the spending levels from year to year for the thousands of individual Federal spending programs.

In addition, the law requires that legislation that would raise mandatory spending or lower revenues—compared to existing law—be offset by spending cuts or revenue increases. This requirement, called "pay-as-you-go," or PAYGO, is designed to prevent new legislation from reducing the surplus or increasing the deficit. The budget also proposes extending the PAYGO system.

Once Congress passes the budget resolution, it turns its attention to passing the 13 annual appropriations bills and, if it chooses, "authorizing" bills to change the laws governing mandatory spending and revenues.

Congress begins by examining the President's budget in detail. Scores of committees and subcommittees hold hearings on proposals under their jurisdiction. The House and Senate Armed Services Authorizing Committees, and the Defense and Military Construction Subcommittees of the Appropriations Committees, for instance, hold hearings on the President's defense plan. To consider the budget's proposed changes in taxes, the House Ways and Means and the Senate Finance Committees will hold hearings. The Budget Director, Cabinet officers, and other Administration officials work with Congress as it accepts some of the President's proposals, rejects others, and changes still others. Congressional rules require that these committees and subcommittees take actions that are consistent with the budget resolution.

If you read through the President's budget, the budget resolution, or the appropriations or authorizing bills that Congress drafts, you will notice that the Government measures spending in two ways—"budget authority" and "outlays."

Budget authority (or BA) is what the law authorizes the Federal Government to spend for certain programs, projects, or activities. What the Government actually spends in a particular year, however, is an outlay. To see the difference, consider what happens when the Government decides to build a space exploration system.

The President and Congress may agree to spend $1 billion for the space system. Congress appropriates $1 billion in BA. But the system may take 10 years to build. Thus, the Government may spend $100 million in outlays in the first year to begin construction and the remaining $900 million over the next nine years as construction continues.

Monitoring the Budget

Once the President and Congress approve spending, the Government monitors the budget through:

- agency program managers and budget officials, including the Inspectors General, or IGs;
- the Office of Management and Budget;
- congressional committees; and
- the General Accounting Office, an auditing arm of Congress.

This oversight is designed to:

- ensure that agencies comply with legal limits on spending, and that they use budget authority only for the purposes intended;
- see that programs are operating consistently with legal requirements and existing policy; and
- ensure that programs are well managed and achieving the intended results.

Prodded by Congress, the Executive Branch has begun to pay more attention to good management of late, starting with the 1993 Government Performance and Results Act. This law is designed to improve Government programs by using better measurements of their results in order to evaluate their effectiveness.

Source: Excerpted from Office of Management and Budget. 2001. *A Citizen's Guide to the Federal Budget.* Washington, DC: OMB. This document can be read at OMB's web site at www.whitehouse.gov/omb/budget.

Using the budget legislation development for FY 1998, which began October 1, 1997, as a prototypical example, the House of Representatives passed its budget resolution on May 21, 1997, and the Senate passed its version on May 23, 1997. With passage in both chambers, this concurrent resolution on the budget became a nonbinding blueprint for the FY 1998 federal budget; the resolution also outlined broad budget targets for the time period to 2002.

Another key element in the development of annual federal budget legislation, the mechanism through which Congress actually implements the constraints on revenue and spending as contained in the concurrent budget resolution, involves two sets of activities that go on more or less simultaneously. Discretionary spending is determined through the *appropriations process.* House and Senate Appropriations Committees, working through 13 subcommittees, develop 13 appropriations bills. Separately, in a process called *budget reconciliation,* existing laws are brought into conformity with the existing concurrent resolution on the budget.

The Real World of Health Policy

Appropriation Testimony
President's Fiscal Year 2002 Budget
Request for the National Cancer Institute

Mr. Chairman and Members of the Subcommittee:

I am Richard Klausner, the Director of the National Cancer Institute (NCI). I am pleased to appear before you to present a brief review of some of the activities supported by the NCI and to present the President's budget proposal for fiscal year 2002. The significant budget increases over the past several years have allowed the NCI to aggressively implement its strategic plans to:

- Support a broad-based portfolio of superb research to increase our knowledge about all aspects of cancer
- Translate basic science to transform all aspects of cancer prevention and care
- Train the next generation of cancer researchers
- Address both the quality of cancer care and the disparate burden of cancer experienced in America across the cancer continuum

Cancer Trends

Four years ago, the NCI initiated an annual report to the Nation on the burden of cancer. This report is developed in collaboration with the American Cancer Society, the Centers for Disease Control and Prevention and its National Center for Health Statistics. This spring, we will report the latest cancer statistics for the country through 1998. Total cancer death rates are falling now by 1.1% per year with black males showing the largest drop of 2% per year. For breast and prostate cancer, death rates are now falling by 3.5% per year. Despite overall progress, incidence and/or death rates for some cancers are rising. These cancers, which include esophageal cancer, liver cancer, non-Hodgkin's lymphoma, acute myelogenous leukemia and melanoma, account for about 13% of the total cancer burden in the U.S. The NCI has convened task forces and directed new research to understand these trends.

* * *

Molecular Targets: A New Era In The Discovery And Development Of Preventive And Therapeutic Agents For Cancer

Revealing the actual molecular machinery of cancer has long promised to bring a new, highly selective approach to both prevention and treatment. Examples of molecularly targeted therapy for cancer are beginning to emerge. For example, chronic myelogenous leukemia (CML) is known to be the result of the breaking and recombination of two chromosomes. The fused chromosomes produce a new gene which tells the cell to produce a protein called bcr-abl whose uncontrolled activity is responsible for the growth of the leukemia cell. A new drug, called STI571, developed as a collaboration between Novartis Pharmaceuticals and NCI-funded investigators, is highly effective at turning off the activity of bcr-abl. In recently published studies, virtually every patient with the chronic phase of CML, the disease expressing the molecular target, has shown a complete correction of their blood abnormalities. This is an oral drug with apparently few and mild side effects. We now know that this same drug has activity against two other distinct molecular machines present in a variety of cancers. As a result, the NCI in collaboration with Novartis is rapidly developing numerous clinical trials to test STI571, alone or in combination with other drugs, in leukemia, gastrointestinal sarcomas (in which dramatic responses have already been seen), brain tumors, lung, prostate, breast, ovary and pediatric cancers.

To expand the discovery, validation and development of more molecular targets in cancer, the NCI has initiated a series of funding programs including:

1. Molecular Targets Drug Discovery (MTDD) grants—four new grant programs to discover and validate molecular targets for cancer for which we have received over 170 applications.
2. Interdisciplinary Research Teams for Molecular Target Assessment (IRT/MTA)—a new approach to the development of clinically useful assays to measure and monitor cancer in patients according to the actual molecular targets where treatment is directed.
3. Chemistry/Biology Centers—we have funded six centers of excellence to bring chemists and biologists together to discover chemicals that report on and can perturb the molecular machinery of cancer.

* * *

The way scientific discovery eventually leads to advances in medical practice is through the clinical trial. Currently, the NCI is actively accruing patients (about 25,000 a year) to over 840 clinical trials including about 700 early phase trials where we can test the safety and possible effectiveness of new agents. In FY 2000, 261 new trials were opened compared to 177 in FY 1999. Our goal is to double the number of new agents entering such clinical testing over the next two years. Over the past year, completed clinical trials have demonstrated new treatment regimens that show a 50% increase in survival for resectable gastric cancer and a 40% increase in survival rates for metastatic renal cancer, to cite just two examples.

Over the past year, we have been implementing our strategic plan to address the pressing question of cancer disparities through our Quality of Cancer Care initiatives, our newly formed Center to Reduce Cancer Health Disparities and our Comprehensive Minority Biomedical Programs. Eighteen Special Population Networks for Cancer Awareness, Research and Training have been launched as have 12 new partnership programs between NCI-funded Cancer Centers and Minority Serving Institutions. These and other activities are aimed at increasing our understanding of cancer disparities, increasing the participation of minority and underserved communities in the cancer research enterprise and finding ways to address the disparities in cancer burden.

I am pleased to present the President's budget request for the National Cancer Institute for FY 2002, a sum of $4,177,203,000, which reflects an increase of $439,275,000 over the comparable Fiscal Year 2001 appropriation.

The NIH budget request includes the performance information required by the Government Performance and Results Act (GPRA) of 1993. Prominent in the performance data is NIH's second annual performance report which compares our FY 2000 results to the goals in our FY 2000 performance plan. As performance trends on research outcomes emerge, the GPRA data will help NIH to identify strategies and objectives to continuously improve its programs.

Source: Excerpted from testimony given by Richard Klausner, MD, Director, National Cancer Institute, to the United States Senate Committee on Appropriations, Subcommittee on Labor, Health and Human Services, Education, May 23, 2001.

The first step in reconciliation involves instructions contained in the concurrent resolution on the budget directing the appropriate standing House and Senate committees to determine and recommend changes in existing laws or bills that will achieve the constraints established in the concurrent resolution on the budget. Although these instructions to the relevant committees specify the amount of spending reductions or revenue increases each committee must attain, the instructions leave to the discretion of the committees the specific changes to laws or bills that must be made to accomplish the budget targets.

Again using as a prototypical example the procedures for developing budget legislation for FY 1998, the committees with jurisdiction—the Committee on Ways and Means and the Committee on Energy and Commerce in the House of Representatives and the Committee on Finance in the Senate—began work in early June 1997 on specific legislative changes that were necessary to meet the spending and revenue targets established in the concurrent budget resolution. The results of the committees' work were voted on by the total membership in the respective chambers of Congress in late June 1997.

The second step in budget reconciliation involves combining the committee recommendations into an *omnibus reconciliation bill* that in effect packages together all legislative changes made in the various standing committees necessitated by reconciling existing law with the budgetary targets established earlier in the concurrent resolution on the budget. This legislative development is the responsibility of the House and Senate Budget Committees. These committees then report their omnibus reconciliation bills to the entire House and Senate. When passed in both chambers and signed by the President, or when a presidential veto is overridden, the federal budget process is completed for the year. Examples of how annual federal budget legislation invariably contains health policy that significantly influences the nation's pursuit of health are given in the next section.

Health Policy in Federal Budget Legislation

A great deal of federal health policy is embedded in the legislation that emerges annually through the federal budgeting process. Although, of course, other health-related legislation is formulated outside the budget process (e.g., P.L. 101-629, the Safe Medical Devices Act of 1990; P.L. 103-43, the National Institutes of Health Revitalization Act of 1990; P.L. 104-191, the Health Insurance Portability and Accountability Act of 1996; P.L. 106-354, the Breast and Cervical Cancer Prevention and Treatment Act of 2000; and P.L. 106-430, the Needlestick Safety and Prevention Act of 2000), much of the nation's health policy, due in large part to its budgetary implications, emerges through the legislation development associated with the annual federal budget. In the 1980s and 1990s, many of these health policies were contained in the massive pieces of legislation known as omnibus budget reconciliation acts (OBRA) or consolidated omnibus budget reconciliation acts (COBRA). While not an exhaustive list, the following examples illustrate the types of health policy, in the form of public laws, that have emerged through the federal budget process since 1980:

- P.L. 96-499, the Omnibus Budget Reconciliation Act of 1980 (OBRA '80) contained, in Title IX of the act, the Medicare and Medicaid Amendments of 1980. These amendments made extensive modifications in the Medicare and Medicaid programs, with 57 separate sections pertaining to one or both of the programs. Many of the changes reflected continuing concern with the growing costs of the programs and were intended to help control these costs.

  Examples of the changes specific to Medicare under Part B of the program included removal of the 100-visits-per-year limitation on home health services and of the requirement that patients pay a deductible for home care visits. These changes were intended to encourage home care over more expensive institutional care. Another provision permitted small rural hospitals to use their beds as "swing beds" (alternating their use as acute care beds or long-term-care beds as needed) and authorized swing-bed demonstration projects for large and urban hospitals. An important change in the Medicaid program required the programs to pay for the services that the states had authorized nurse-midwives to perform.

- P.L. 97-35, the Omnibus Budget Reconciliation Act of 1981 (OBRA '81), in its Title XXI, Subtitles A, B, and C, contained further amendments to the Medicare and Medicaid programs. Just as in 1980, this legislation included extensive changes in the programs, with 46 sections pertaining to them. Enacted in the context of extensive efforts to reduce the growth of the federal budget, many of the provisions hit Medicare and Medicaid especially hard. For example, one provision eliminated the coverage of alcohol detoxification facility services, another removed the use of occupational therapy as a basis for initial entitlement to home health service, and yet another increased the Part B deductible.

  In other provisions, OBRA '81 combined 20 existing categorical public health programs into four block grants. The block grants were: (1) Preventive Health and Health Services, which combined such previously categorical programs as rodent control, fluoridation, hypertension control, and rape crisis centers, among others, into one block grant to be distributed among the states by a formula based on population and other factors; (2) Alcohol Abuse, Drug Abuse, and Mental Health Block Grant, which combined existing programs created under the Community Mental Health Centers Act; the Mental Health Systems Act; the Comprehensive Alcohol Abuse and Alcoholism Prevention, Treatment, and Rehabilitation Act; and the Drug Abuse, Prevention, Treatment, and Rehabilitation Act; (3) Primary Care Block Grant, which consisted of the Community Health Centers; and (4) Maternal and Child Health Block Grant, which consolidated seven previously categorical grant programs from Title V of the Social Security Act and from the Public Health Services Act. These included the maternal and child health and crippled children's programs, genetic disease service, adolescent pregnancy services, sudden infant death syndrome, hemophilia treatment, Supplemental Security Income (SSI) payments to disabled children, and lead-based poisoning prevention.

- P.L. 99-272, the Consolidated Omnibus Budget Reconciliation Act of 1985 (COBRA '85), contained a number of provisions that affected the Medicare program. Hospitals that served a disproportionate share of poor patients received an adjustment in their prospective payment system (PPS) payments; hospice care was made a permanent part of the Medicare program and states were given the ability to provide hospice services under the Medicaid program; FY 1986 PPS payment rates were frozen at 1985 levels through May 1, 1986, and increased 0.5 percent for the remainder of the year; payment to hospitals for the indirect costs of medical education were modified; and a schedule was established to phase out payment of a return on equity to proprietary hospitals.

  This legislation established the Physician Payment Review Commission (PPRC) to advise Congress on physician payment policies for the Medicare program. The legislation also required that the PPRC advise Congress and the Secretary of the DHHS regarding the development of a resource-based relative value scale (RBRVS) for physician services.

  Under another of COBRA's important provisions, employers were required to continue health insurance for employees and their dependents who otherwise would lose their eligibility for the coverage due to reduced work hours or termination of their employment.

- P.L. 99-509, the Omnibus Budget Reconciliation Act of 1986 (OBRA '86), altered the PPS payment rate for hospitals once again and reduced payment amounts for capital-related costs by 3.5 percent for part of FY 1987, by 7 percent for FY 1988, and by 10 percent for FY 1989. In addition, certain adjustments were made in the manner in which "outlier," or atypical, cases were reimbursed.

  The legislation established further limits to balance billing by physicians providing services to Medicare clients by setting "maximum allowable actual charges" (MAACs) for physicians who did not participate in the Medicare Participating Physician and Supplier (PAR) program (see the Deficit Reduction Act of 1984, P.L. 98-369 in the Appendix). In another provision intended to realize savings for the Medicare program, OBRA '86 directed the DHHS to use the concept of "inherent reasonableness" to reduce payments for cataract surgery as well as for anesthesia during the surgery.

- P.L. 100-203, the Omnibus Budget Reconciliation Act of 1987 (OBRA '87), contained a number of provisions with a direct impact on the Medicare program. It required the Secretary of the DHHS to update the wage index used in calculating hospital PPS payments by October 1, 1990, and to do so at least every three years thereafter. It also required the Secretary to study and report to Congress on the criteria being used by the Medicare program to identify referral hospitals. Deepening the reductions established by OBRA '86, one provision of the act reduced payment amounts for capital-related costs by 12 percent for FY 1988 and by 15 percent for 1989.

  Regarding payments to physicians for services provided to Medicare clients, the legislation reduced fees for 12 sets of "overvalued" procedures. It also allowed higher fee increases for primary care than for other physician services and increased the fee differential between participating and nonparticipating physicians (see the 1984 P.L. 98-369 in the Appendix).

  The legislation also contained a number of provisions bearing on the Medicaid program. Key among these: the law provided additional options for children and pregnant women, and required states to cover eligible children up to age six with an option for allowing coverage up to age eight. The distinction between skilled nursing facilities (SNFs) and intermediate care facilities (ICFs) was eliminated. The legislation contained a number of provisions intended to enhance the quality of services provided in nursing homes, including requirements that nursing homes enhance the quality of life of each resident and operate quality assurance programs.

- P.L. 101-239, the Omnibus Budget Reconciliation Act of 1989 (OBRA '89), included provisions for minor, primarily technical, changes in the PPS and a provision to extend coverage for mental health benefits and to add coverage for Pap smears. Small adjustments were made in the disproportionate share regulations, and the 15 percent capital-related payment reduction established in OBRA '87 was continued in OBRA '89. Another provision required the Secretary of DHHS to update the wage index annually in a budget-neutral manner beginning in FY 1993.

  As part of the OBRA '89 legislation, the Health Care Financing Administration (HCFA) was directed to begin implementing an RBRVS for reimbursing physicians under the Medicare program on January 1, 1992. The new system was phased in over a four-year period beginning in 1992.

  Another important provision in this legislation initiated the establishment of the Agency for Health Care Policy and Research (AHCPR). This agency succeeded the National Center for Health Services Research and Technology Assessment (NCHSR). The new agency was created to conduct and to foster the conduct of studies of healthcare quality, effectiveness, and efficiency. In particular, the agency was to conduct and to foster the conduct of studies on the outcomes of medical treatments and to provide technical assistance to groups seeking to develop practice guidelines.

- P.L. 101-508, the Omnibus Budget Reconciliation Act of 1990 (OBRA '90), contained the Patient Self-Determination Act, which required healthcare institutions participating in the Medicare and Medicaid programs to provide all of their patients with written information on policies regarding self-determination and living wills. Under this legislation, the institutions were also required to inquire whether patients had advance medical directives and to document the replies in the patients' medical records.

  The legislation made additional minor changes in the PPS, including further adjustments in the wage index calculation and in the disproportionate share regulations. Regarding the wage index, one provision required the Prospective Payment Assessment Commission (ProPAC), which was established by the 1983 Social Security Amendments (see P.L. 98-21 in the Appendix) to help guide the Congress and the Secretary of DHHS on implementing the PPS to further study the available data on wages by occupational category and to develop recommendations on modifying the wage index to account for occupational mix.

  The legislation also included a provision that continued the 15 percent capital-related payment reduction that was established in OBRA '87 and continued in OBRA '89 and another provision that made permanent the reduced teaching adjustment payment established in OBRA '87. One of its more important provisions provided a five-year deficit reduction plan that was to reduce total Medicare outlays by more than $43 billion between fiscal years 1991 and 1995.

- P.L. 103-66, the Omnibus Budget Reconciliation Act of 1993 (OBRA '93), established an all-time record, five-year cut in Medicare funding and included a number of other changes affecting the Medicare program. For example, the legislation included provisions to end return on equity (ROE) payments for capital to proprietary SNFs and reduced the previously established rate of increase in payment rates for care provided in hospices. In addition, the legislation cut laboratory fees drastically by changing the reimbursement formula and froze payments for durable medical equipment, parenteral and enteral services, and for orthotics and prosthetics in FYs 1994 and 1995.

  OBRA '93 contained the Comprehensive Childhood Immunization Act, which provided $585 million to support the provision of vaccines for children eligible for Medicaid, children who do not have health insurance, and Native American children.

Because Congress was involved so intensively in considering the Clinton administration's Health Security legislative proposal during 1994, relatively little attention was given to health in the budget legislation development during that year. Specifically, President Clinton's attempt to reform the American healthcare system through the Health Security proposal, which was introduced in late 1993 and died with the 1994 Congress (Hacker and Skocpol 1997; Hacker 1997), consumed almost all of the energy expended during 1994 for health-related legislation development.

Following the demise of the Health Security bill, an attempt was made in 1995 to enact unprecedented cutbacks in the Medicare and Medicaid programs as part of a far-reaching budget reconciliation bill that sought a balanced federal budget. President Clinton vetoed the bill. In 1996, the political wrangling over the budget grew even worse. Proposed changes in the Medicare and Medicaid programs, changes that were linked to the development of a plan to balance the federal budget over a seven-year span, would have meant massive cuts in these programs. The differences over these plans between the Republican-controlled Congress and President Clinton, a Democrat, were so fundamental that they led to a complete impasse in the budget negotiations in 1996, which led to a brief shutdown of the federal government in the absence of budget authority to operate.

Stung by public criticism of the harmful budget battle of 1996, Congress again found its negotiating footing in 1997 and developed a suitable concurrent budget resolution in a timely way. On August 5, 1997, President Clinton signed the 1997 federal budget legislation into law.

- P.L. 105-33, the Balanced Budget Act of 1997, contained the most significant changes in the Medicare program since its inception in 1965. Overall, this legislation required a five-year reduction of $115 billion in the Medicare program's expenditure growth and a $13 billion reduction in growth of the Medicaid program. A new "Medicare+Choice" program was created, which gave Medicare beneficiaries the opportunity to choose from a variety of health plan options the plan that best suits their needs and preferences. Significant changes were also made in the traditional Medicare program. Among them, hospital annual inflation updates were reduced as were hospital payments for inpatient capital expenses and for bad debts. Other provisions established a cap on the number of medical residents supported by Medicare graduate medical education payments and provided incentives for reductions in the number of residents.

   An important provision of this act established the State Children's Health Insurance Program (SCHIP) and provided states with $24 billion in federal funds for 1998 until 2002 to increase health insurance for children. Other provisions established two new commissions. The Medicare Payment Review Commission (MedPAC) replaced the Physician Payment Review Commission and the Prospective Payment Review Commission. The new commission was required to submit an annual report to Congress on the status of Medicare reforms and make recommendations on Medicare payment issues. The National Bipartisan Commission on the Future of Medicare was established by this legislation and charged to develop recommendations for Congress on actions necessary to ensure the long-term fiscal health of the Medicare program. This commission was charged to consider several specific issues that were debated in the development of the Balanced Budget Act of 1997, but rejected. These issues included raising the eligibility age for Medicare, increasing the Part B premiums, and developing alternative approaches to financing graduate medical education.

As BBA began to be implemented, health interest groups affected by the law, including the American Hospital Association, mounted an intense lobbying campaign to reverse some of BBA's effects. The campaign was made easier because the nation's budget surplus was growing at an unexpected rate. Two very important health-related laws were enacted within the context of federal budget legislation.

- P.L. 106-113, the Medicare, Medicaid and SCHIP Balanced Budget Refinement Act of 1999 (BBRA), changed the BBA provisions in a number of ways. For example, hospitals treating a disproportionate share (DSH) of low-income Medicare and Medicaid patients receive additional payments from Medicare. BBRA froze DSH adjustments at 3 percent (the FY 2000 level) through FY 2001 and reduced the formula to 4 percent from the BBA-established 5 percent in FY 2002, and then 0 percent for subsequent years. The law increased hospice payment by 0.5 percent for FY 2001 and by 0.75 percent for FY 2002. Medicare reimburses teaching hospitals for their role in providing graduate medical education (GME). Prior to BBA, Medicare's indirect medical education (IME) adjustment payments increased 7.7 percent for each 10 percent increase in a hospital's ratio of interns and residents to beds. BBA decreased the adjustment to 6.5 percent in FY 1999, 6.0 percent in FY 2000, and 5.5 percent in FY 2001 and subsequent years. BBRA froze the IME adjustment at 6.5 percent through FY 2000; reduced it to 6.25 percent in FY 2001, and to 5.5 percent in FY 2002 and subsequent years.

- P.L. 106-554, the Medicare, Medicaid, and SCHIP Benefits Improvement and Protection Act of 2000 (BIPA) was legislation attached as an amendment to the Appropriations Bill and signed into law by President Clinton on December 21, 2000. It effectively changed a number of provisions previously enacted in BBA and BBRA. Among the important changes were:

— an increase of 3.4 percent for Medicare inpatient payments in Fiscal Year 2001, and an estimated 3.5 percent in FY 2002

— an increase of 4.4 percent in Medicare outpatient payments in 2001

— indirect medical education (IME) payments at 6.5 percent in FY 2001 and FY 2002

— elimination of the additional one percent cut in Medicare disproportionate share hospital (DSH) payments in FY 2001 and 2002

— an increase, from 55 to 70 percent, in Medicare payments for bad debt

— an increase for the direct graduate medical education (GME) payment floor to 85 percent of the national average

— elimination of the BBA's FY 2001 and 2002 Medicaid DSH cut

— removal of the 2 percent payment reduction for rehabilitation hospitals in FY 2001

— a 3.2 percent increase in skilled nursing service payments in FY 2001

— a one-year delay of the 15 percent reduction for home health, and the full market basket in FY 2001

— an increase of 3 percent in incentive payments for psychiatric hospitals/units

— expansion of Medicare payment for telehealth services to rural areas

From Formulation to Implementation

When legislatures approve proposed legislation, and the chief executive then signs it, the policymaking process crosses an important threshold. The point at which proposed legislation is formally enacted into law is the point of transition from policy formulation to policy implementation. As shown in Figure 5.1, the formal enactment of legislation serves to bridge the formulation and implementation phases of the policymaking process and triggers the implementation phase of the process. Policy implementation is considered in the next chapter.

Summary

The policy formulation phase of policymaking involves agenda setting and the development of legislation. Agenda setting, discussed in chapter

4, entails the confluence of problems, possible solutions to the problems, and political circumstances that permit certain problem/possible solution combinations to progress along to the point of legislation development.

Legislation development, the other component of policy formulation and the central topic of this chapter, follows a carefully prescribed choreography that includes the drafting and introduction of legislative proposals, their referral to appropriate committees and subcommittees, House and Senate floor action on proposed legislation, conference committee action when necessary, and presidential action on legislation voted on favorably by the legislature. These steps apply whether the legislation is new or, as is so often the case, it is the amendment of prior legislation.

The tangible final products of legislation development are public laws or amendments to existing ones. At the federal level, these are first printed in pamphlet form called *slip law*. Subsequently, laws are published in the *Statutes at Large* and then incorporated into the *United States Code*.

Discussion Questions

1. Discuss the link between agenda setting and the development of legislation.
2. Describe the steps in legislation development.
3. Discuss the various sources of ideas for legislative proposals.
4. What are the most important congressional committees regarding health policy? Briefly describe their roles.
5. Describe the federal budget process. Include the relationship between the federal budget and health policy in your response.

References

Baumgartner, F. R., and J. C. Talbert. 1995. "From Setting a National Agenda on Health Care to Making Decisions in Congress." *Journal of Health Politics, Policy and Law* 20 (2): 437–45.

Ernst & Young LLP. 1995. "Anti-selective Contracting Laws." *CapitolWATCH* 95 (July 5): 2.

Hacker, J. S. 1996. "National Health Care Reform: An Idea Whose Time Came and Went." *Journal of Health Politics, Policy and Law* 21 (4): 647–96.

———. 1997. *The Road to Nowhere*. Princeton, NJ: Princeton University Press.

Hacker, J. S., and T. Skocpol. 1997. "The New Politics of U.S. Health Policy." *Journal of Health Politics, Policy and Law* 22 (2): 315–38.

Hospital Association of Pennsylvania. 1995. "HAP Testifies Any Willing Provider Legislation Can Do More Harm than Good." *Pennsylvania Hospitals Nineties* 6 (10): 1.

Jacobs, L. R. 1995. "Politics of America's Supply State: Health Reform and Technology." *Health Affairs* 14 (2): 143–57.

Johnson, H., and D. S. Broder. 1996. *The System: The American Way of Politics at the Breaking Point.* New York: Little, Brown and Company.

Kingdon, J. W. 1995. *Agendas, Alternatives, and Public Policies,* 2nd ed. New York: HarperCollins College Publishers.

Longest, B. B., Jr. 1997. *Seeking Strategic Advantage Through Health Policy Analysis.* Chicago: Health Administration Press.

Oleszek, W. J. 2001. *Congressional Procedures and Policy Process,* 5th ed. Washington, DC: CQ Press.

Peterson, M. A. 1997. "Introduction: Health Care into the Next Century." *Journal of Health Politics, Policy and Law* 22 (2): 291–313.

Skocpol, T. 1996. *Boomerang: Clinton's Health Security Effort and the Turn Against Government in U.S. Politics.* New York: Norton.

Van Beck, S. D. 1994. *Post-passage Politics: Bicameral Resolution in Congress.* Pittsburgh, PA: University of Pittsburgh Press.

6

POLICY IMPLEMENTATION

POLICY FORMULATION, as a phase of the overall public policy-making process, is described as two sets of interrelated activities—agenda setting and the development of legislation—in chapters 4 and 5. Sometimes these formulation activities lead to policies in the form of new or amended public laws. When they do, enactment of laws demarcates the transition between policy formulation and policy implementation, although the boundary between the two phases of policymaking is very porous. The bridge connecting policy formulation and policy implementation in the center of Figure 6.1 is intentionally shown as a two-way connector between the two phases of policymaking.

Implementing organizations, primarily the departments and agencies in the executive branch of government, are established and maintained, and the people within them employed, to carry out the intent of public laws as enacted by the legislative branch. Legislators rely on the implementers to bring their legislation to life. Thus, the relationship between those who formulate and those who implement policies is highly symbiotic.

In short, health policies in the form of changes in public law must be implemented effectively if they are to exert their intended impact on the determinants of health. Otherwise, policies are only so much paper and rhetoric. When implemented, however, laws can change the physical environment in which people live and work, affect their behavior and even their biology, and influence tremendously the availability and accessibility of health services.

Figure 6.1 A Model of the Public Policymaking Process in the United States: Policy Implementation Phase

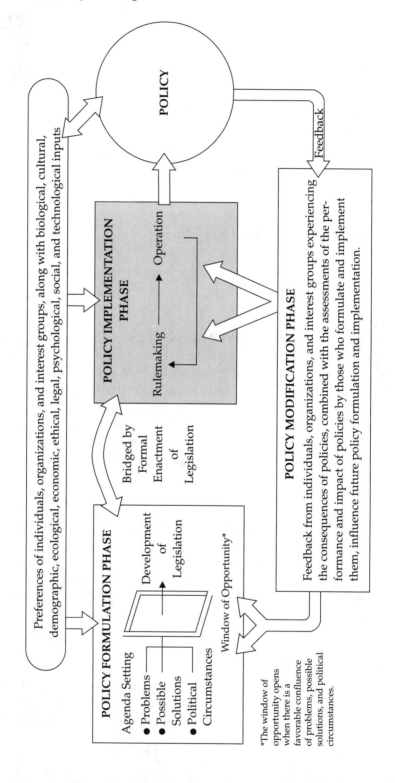

This chapter focuses on the implementation phase of public policy-making—a phase that also involves two interrelated sets of activities. The shaded portion of Figure 6.1 shows that policy implementation begins with *rulemaking*, which is the establishment of the formal rules and regulations necessary to fully operationalize the intent embedded in public laws. The second set of activities in policy implementation is associated with the *operation* of public laws. If a policy in the form of a public law is intended to protect people from exposure to toxic substances in their environments, for example, its operation entails the activities involved in providing such protection. Such activities might include measuring and assessing dangers from substances in the environment or imposing fines as a means to prevent or restrict environmental pollution.

The implementation phase of public policymaking involves managing human, financial, and other resources in ways that make the objectives and goals embodied in enacted legislation achievable by those responsible for its implementation. The most important point in understanding policy implementation, as part of the larger process of policymaking, is that it is primarily a *management* undertaking. That is, policy implementation is in its essence the utilization of human and other resources in pursuing the objectives embedded in public laws.

Depending on the scope of policies being implemented, the managerial tasks involved can be fairly simple and straightforward or they can require massive effort. President Lyndon B. Johnson once observed that the preparations made for implementing the Medicare program represented "the largest managerial effort the nation [had] undertaken since the Normandy invasion" (Iglehart 1992, 1, 468). No matter what the scale, however, the implementation of public laws always includes two separate but interrelated sets of activities—rulemaking and operation.

The Cyclical Relationship Between Rulemaking and Operation

It is important to note the cyclical relationship between rulemaking and the operational activities involved with implementation of a law. As shown in the shaded portion of Figure 6.1, rulemaking precedes operation in the sequence of these activities, but the operational activities feed back into rulemaking. This cyclical relationship is important. It means that experience gained with the operation of policies can influence the modification of rules or regulations used in the implementation phase. In a practical sense, this means that the rules and regulations promulgated to implement policies undergo revision—sometimes extensive and continual revision—and that new rules can be adopted as experience dictates.

This characteristic of policymaking tends to make the process much more dynamic than it would otherwise be.

Another characteristic vital to a comprehensive understanding of policymaking is that some of the implementing decisions made for public laws within the executive branch organizations are themselves policies. For example, rules or regulations promulgated to implement a law are just as much policies as are the laws they support. Similarly, operational decisions made by implementing organizations, to the extent that they require or influence particular behaviors, actions, or decisions by others, are policies. Furthermore, decisions made in the judicial branch regarding the applicability of laws to specific situations or regarding the appropriateness of the actions of implementing organizations are policies. Recall the definition of public policy, given in chapter 1, as authoritative decisions made in the legislative, executive, or judicial branches of government that are intended to direct or influence the actions, behaviors, or decisions of others. By definition, policies are established both within the policy formulation and the policy implementation phases of the policymaking process.

Responsibility for Policy Implementation

In the implementation phase, much, although not all, of the responsibility for policymaking shifts from the legislative branch of government to the executive branch. Implementation responsibility rests heavily with executive branch departments such as the Department of Health and Human Services (DHHS) (www.dhhs.gov) and the Department of Justice (DOJ) (www.usdoj.gov); with subdivisions of such departments; and with a number of independent federal agencies such as the Environmental Protection Agency (EPA) (www.epa.gov); the Consumer Product Safety Commission (CPSC) (www.cpsc.gov); and the Food and Drug Administration (FDA) (*fda.gov*). These and many other executive branch organizations exist to implement the laws formulated by the legislative branch.

The Centers for Medicare & Medicaid Services (CMS) (www.cms.gov), formerly the Health Care Financing Administration (HCFA), is a good example of an implementing organization. CMS is the primary federal implementing agent for the public laws that established and now continue the Medicare and Medicaid programs. A federal agency within the DHHS, it was created in 1977 to administer the Medicare and Medicaid programs. It does this primarily though its role as a purchaser of healthcare services for the Medicare and Medicaid beneficiaries. In addition, the agency seeks to:

- establish effective policies in the form of rules or regulations for the reimbursement of healthcare providers;
- assure that Medicare and Medicaid contractors and state agencies operate appropriately;
- conduct informative research on the effectiveness of various methods of healthcare management, treatment, and financing; and
- assess the quality of healthcare facilities and services used by program beneficiaries.

CMS staff work in its Baltimore, Maryland, headquarters and in ten regional offices nationwide. The regional offices provide a more decentralized presence, which can contribute to customer service and program oversight.

The Real World of Health Policy

CMS at a Glance

The Center for Medicare & Medicaid Services (CMS) is a federal agency within the U.S. Department of Health and Human Services. CMS runs the Medicare and Medicaid programs—two national health care programs that benefit about 75 million Americans. And with the Health Resources and Services Administration (HRSA), CMS runs the Children's Health Insurance Program (SCHIP), which is expected to cover many of the approximately 10 million uninsured children in the United States.

Additional Responsibilities

CMS also regulates all laboratory testing (except research) performed on humans in the United States. Approximately 158,000 laboratory entities fall within CMS's regulatory responsibility. And CMS, with the Departments of Labor and Treasury, helps millions of Americans and small companies get and keep health insurance coverage and helps eliminate discrimination based on health status for people buying health insurance.

Running the Programs

CMS spends over $360 billion a year buying health care services for beneficiaries of Medicare, Medicaid and the SCHIP. CMS:

- assures that the Medicaid, Medicare and Children's Health Insurance programs are properly run by its contractors and state agencies;

- establishes policies for paying health care providers;
- conducts research on the effectiveness of various methods of health care management, treatment, and financing; and
- assesses the quality of health care facilities and services and taking enforcement actions as appropriate.

Source: Excerpted from CMS's web site, under the heading, About CMS.

Legislative Oversight

Although organizations in the executive branch bear most of the responsibility for implementing policies, the legislative branch maintains a very important oversight responsibility in the implementation phase. Oversight of the executive branch's implementation of the policies enacted by the legislative branch is actually mandated in the Legislative Reorganization Act of 1946. Generally, legislative oversight is intended to accomplish the following:

- ensure that implementing organizations adhere to congressional intent;
- improve the efficiency, effectiveness, and economy of government's operations;
- assess the ability of implementing organizations and individuals to manage and accomplish implementation, including investigation of alleged instances of inadequate management, waste, fraud, dishonesty, or arbitrary action; and
- ensure that implementation of policies reflects the public interest.

Effective legislative oversight is accomplished through several means. One powerful oversight technique occurs within the context of the funding appropriations that Congress must make for the continuing implementation of many of the laws it enacts. Although some health policies, such as the Medicare program, are entitlements, many others require annual funding through appropriations acts. Examples include the research programs of the NIH, health activities of the Department of Veterans Affairs (VA), and the activities of the U.S. Public Health Service (USPHS) and the FDA. Review by the appropriations committees of the House and Senate is an important means of overseeing the performance of these and similar organizations in carrying out their implementation responsibilities. Implementation inadequacies—real or perceived—may be reflected in the budgets appropriated by Congress for implementing organizations.

The Real World of Health Policy

Report of Oversight Plans
Pursuant To Clause 2(D)(1) Of Rule X
Approved February 28, 2001

Committee On Appropriations
House of Representatives
(107th Congress)

Letter Of Transmittal

February 28, 2001

Hon. Dan Burton,
Chairman, Committee on Government Reform,
House of Representatives,
Washington, DC.

Hon. Robert W. Ney,
Chairman, Committee on House Administration,
House of Representatives,
Washington, DC.

Dear Mr. Chairmen: On behalf of the Committee on Appropriations, I hereby transmit the Committee's plan for Oversight activities for the 107th Congress. The Committee intends to have an active and productive Congress, reviewing both ongoing governmental activities and analyzing the Budget requests in order to reflect the priorities of the American people.

The Committee looks forward to working with all Members of the House of Representatives in order to fulfill our responsibilities under the Rules.

With best regards,

Sincerely,

C. W. Bill Young, Chairman

107th Congress
1st Session
House Of Representatives
Report Of Oversight Plans Of The
House Committee On Appropriations

Approved February 28, 2001

Mr. Young of Florida, from the Committee on Appropriations, submitted to the Committee on Government Reform and the Committee on House Administration the following

Report
Oversight Plans Of The House Committee On Appropriations

Clause 2(d)(1) of Rule X of the Rules of the House requires each standing committee of the House to adopt oversight plans at the beginning of each Congress. Specifically, the Rule states in part:

"Rule X, clause (2)(d)(1). Not later than February 15 of the first session of a Congress, each standing committee shall, in a meeting that is open to the public and with a quorum present, adopt its oversight plan for that Congress. Such plan shall be submitted simultaneously to the Committee on Government Reform and to the Committee on House Administration"

Jurisdiction Of The Committee On Appropriations

Rule X of the Rules of the House vests in the Committee on Appropriations broad responsibility over the Federal budget. Specifically the Rule defines the Committee's jurisdiction, as follows:

(1) Appropriation of the revenue for the support of the Government.

(2) Rescissions of appropriations contained in appropriations Acts.

(3) Transfers of unexpected balances.

(4) Bills and joint resolutions reported by other committees that provide new entitlement authority as defined in section 3(9) of the Congressional Budget Act of 1974 and referred to the committee under clause 4(a)(2)."

* * *

General Oversight Responsibilities

2. (a) The various standing committees shall have general oversight responsibilities as provided in paragraph (b) in order to assist the House in—

(1) its analysis, appraisal, and evaluation of (A) the application, administration, execution, and effectiveness of Federal laws; and (B) conditions and circumstances that may indicate the necessity or desirability of enacting new or additional legislation; and

(2) its formulation, consideration, and enactment of such changes in Federal laws, and of such additional legislation, as may be necessary or appropriate.

(b)(1) In order to determine whether laws and programs addressing subjects within the jurisdiction of a committee are being implemented and carried out in accordance with the intent of Congress and whether they should be continued, curtailed, or eliminated, each standing committee (other than the Committee on Appropriations) shall review and study on a continuing basis—

(A) the application, administration, execution, and effectiveness of laws and programs addressing subjects within its jurisdiction;

(B) the organization and operation of Federal agencies and entities having responsibilities for the administration and execution of laws and programs addressing subjects within its jurisdiction;

(C) any conditions or circumstances that may indicate the necessity or desirability of enacting new or additional legislation addressing subjects within its jurisdiction (whether or not a bill or resolution has been introduced with respect thereto);

(D) future research and forecasting on subjects within its jurisdiction; and

(E) specific problems with Federal rules, regulations, statutes, and court decisions that are ambiguous, arbitrary, or nonsensical, or that impose severe financial burdens on individuals.

* * *

Special Oversight Functions

3. (a) The Committee on Appropriations shall conduct such studies and examinations of the organization and operation of executive departments and other executive agencies (including any agency the majority of the stock of which is owned by the United States) as it considers necessary to assist it in the determination of matters within its jurisdiction.

* * *

Additional Functions of Committees

4. (a)(1)(A) The Committee on Appropriations shall, within 30 days after the transmittal of the budget to Congress each year, hold hearings on the budget as a whole with particular reference to—

(i) the basic recommendations and budgetary policies of the President in the presentation of the budget; and

(ii) the fiscal, financial, and economic assumptions used as bases in arriving at total estimated expenditures and receipts.

(B) In holding hearings under subdivision (A), the Committee shall receive testimony from the Secretary of the Treasury, the Director of the Office of Management and Budget, the Chairman of the Council of Economic Advisers, and such other persons as the Committee may desire.

(C) A hearing under subdivision (A), or any part thereof, shall be held in open session, except when the committee, in open session and with a quorum present, determines by record vote that the testimony to be taken at that hearing on that day may be related to a matter of national security. The committee may by the same procedure close one subsequent day of hearing. A transcript of all such hearings shall be printed and a copy thereof furnished to each Member, Delegate, and the Resident Commissioner.

(D) A hearing under subdivision (A), or any part thereof, may be held before a joint meeting of the Committee and the Committee on Appropriations of the Senate in accordance with such procedures as the two committees jointly may determine.

(2) Pursuant to section 401(b)(2) of the Congressional Budget Act of 1974, when a committee reports a bill or joint resolution that provides new entitlement authority as defined in section 3(9) of that Act, and enactment of the bill or joint resolution, as reported, would cause a breach of the committee's pertinent allocation of new budget authority under section 302(a) of that Act, the bill or joint resolution may be referred to the Committee on Appropriations with instruction to report it with recommendations (which may include an amendment limiting the total amount of new entitlement authority provided in the bill or joint resolution). If the Committee on Appropriations fails to report a bill or joint resolution so referred within 15 calendar days (not counting any day on which the House is not in session), the committee automatically shall be discharged from consideration of the bill or joint resolution, and the bill or joint resolution shall be placed on the appropriate calendar.

(3) In addition, the Committee on Appropriations shall study on a continuing basis those provisions of law that (on the first day of the first

fiscal year for which the congressional budget process is effective) provide spending authority or permanent budget authority and shall report to the House from time to time its recommendations for terminating or modifying such provisions.

(4) In the manner provided by section 302 of the Congressional Budget Act of 1974, the Committee on Appropriations (after consulting with the Committee on Appropriations of the Senate) shall subdivide any allocations made to it in the joint explanatory statement accompanying the conference report on such concurrent resolution, and promptly report the subdivisions to the House as soon as practicable after a concurrent resolution on the budget for a fiscal year is agreed to.

Rule XIII of the Rules of the House prescribes special reporting requirements of the Committee on Appropriations. Specifically Rule XIII, clause 3(f) states:

* * *

Content of Reports

"(f)(1) A report of the Committee on Appropriations on a general appropriation bill shall include—

(A) a concise statement describing the effect of any provision of the accompanying bill that directly or indirectly changes the application of existing law; and

(B) a list of all appropriations contained in the bill for expenditures not previously authorized by law (except classified intelligence or national security programs, projects, or activities).

(2) Whenever the Committee on Appropriations reports a bill or joint resolution including matter specified in clause 1(b)(2) or (3) of rule X, it shall include—

(A) in the bill or joint resolution, separate headings for 'Rescissions' and 'Transfers of Unexpended Balances'; and

(B) in the report of the committee, a separate section listing such rescissions and transfers."

* * *

Oversight Plan

The Committee on Appropriations takes seriously its responsibility to conduct oversight of Government agencies and programs. This function is carried out by the Committee throughout the year at many levels of investigation and examination. For the 107th Congress the Committee intends to proceed in the following manner:

1. Subcommittee Hearings. The Appropriations Committee has a long tradition of in-depth analysis of the President's pending budget as

well as analysis of the effective use of previously appropriated resources. For example, during the 106th Congress the Committee on Appropriations held 429 days of hearings, took testimony from 4,916 witnesses, and published 169 volumes of hearings totaling 188,907 pages. This level of oversight and investigation will continue during this Congress.

2. Investigations. In addition to formal oversight, the Committee utilizes various investigative agencies to conduct in-depth analysis of specific problem areas. These investigations are conducted by the Committee's own Surveys and Investigations Staff, the General Accounting Office, and the Congressional Research Service. In the previous Congress, the Committee received 56 Surveys and Investigations studies and 143 investigative reports from the GAO.

3. Appropriations Bills. The ultimate exercise of oversight is the "power of the purse" which the Committee takes as its highest responsibility. This allocation of scarce Federal dollars demands strict compliance with all budgetary concepts and strictures. The Committee intends to follow the requirements of the Congressional Budget with regard to the subdivision of budget authority and outlays to the 13 subcommittees. Appropriations bills will be developed in accordance with the results of all the oversight activities in paragraphs 1 and 2, above and brought to the floor for consideration within all relevant budgetary constraints.

Source: Excerpted from the *Report of Oversight Plans for the House Committee on Appropriations*, February 28, 2001. This report can be read on the Committee's web site, www.house.gov/appropriations.

Other oversight techniques include direct contact between members of Congress and their staffs and executive branch personnel who are involved in implementing policies, and the use of oversight agencies specifically created by Congress to help with their oversight task (Nadel 1995), including the Congressional Budget Office (CBO) (www.cbo.gov) and the General Accounting Office (GAO) (www.gao.gov).

Legislative oversight responsibility goes beyond the appropriations procedure. Each standing committee of the House and Senate has certain oversight responsibilities. With a parallel in the Senate, this responsibility is spelled out for the standing committees in the House of Representatives in Clause 2(d)(1) of Rule X of the Rules of the House, which requires "each standing committee of the House to adopt oversight plans at the beginning of each Congress." In Clause 2(b)(1), each standing committee is further required to:

review and study, on a continuing basis, the application, administration, execution, and effectiveness of those laws or parts of laws, the subject matter of which is within the jurisdiction of that committee and the organization and operation of the Federal agencies and entities having responsibilities in or for the administration and execution thereof, in order to determine whether such laws and the programs thereunder are being implemented and carried out in accordance with the intent of the Congress and whether such programs should be continued, curtailed, or eliminated.

There is also a judicial dimension to the implementation of policies. Legislation, as well as the rules made by those responsible for its implementation, can be challenged in the courts. Administrative law judges in the implementing agencies hear the appeals of people or organizations who are dissatisfied with the way the implementation of a policy affects them. For example, the Environmental Protection Agency's Office of Administrative Law Judges (OALJ) (www.epa.gov/oalj) is an independent office in the Office of the Administrator of the EPA. These administrative law judges conduct hearings and render decisions in proceedings between the EPA and people, businesses, government entities, and other organizations that are regulated under environmental laws. Administrative law judges preside in enforcement and permit proceedings under the Administrative Procedure Act and also conduct other proceedings involving alleged violations of environmental laws, including:

- Clean Air Act (CAA);
- Clean Water Act (CWA);
- Comprehensive Environmental Response, Compensation and Liability Act (CERCLA);
- Emergency Planning and Community Right-To-Know Act (EPCRA);
- Federal Insecticide, Fungicide, and Rodenticide Act (FIFRA);
- Marine Protection, Research and Sanctuaries Act (MPRSA);
- Safe Drinking Water Act (SDWA);
- Solid Waste Disposal Act, as amended by the Resource Conservation and Recovery Act (RCRA);
- Toxic Substances Control Act (TSCA); and
- Subchapter II of TSCA, known as the Asbestos Hazard Emergency Response Act (AHERA).

Federal administrative law judges are certified by the Office of Personnel Management and assured decisional independence. Decisions issued by administrative law judges at EPA are subject to review by the Environmental Appeals Board (EAB). The initial decision of these judges—

unless a party appeals to the EAB or the EAB on its own initiative elects to review the initial decision—becomes the EPA's final order.

The Beginning of Implementation: Rulemaking

Enacted laws seldom contain enough explicit language to guide their implementation completely. Rather, they are often vague on implementation details, leaving it to the implementing organizations to specify, publish, and circulate the rules or regulations (remember, these terms have the same meaning in the policy context) subsequently used to guide the law's actual operation. For this reason, implementation typically begins with *rulemaking*.

Usually the link is fairly direct between the enactment of a new or amended law and the promulgation of the rules necessary for its full implementation. The development of rules typically takes place in a timely way so that implementation can proceed smoothly, but this is not always the case. Laws are formulated in the legislative branch and implemented, primarily, in the executive branch, after all, and sometimes this separation has significant implications.

For example, in 1946 Congress enacted the Hospital Survey and Construction Act (P.L. 79-725), also known as the Hill-Burton Act, after its sponsors, Senators Lester Hill and Harold Burton. This law provided grants to build, expand, or modernize hospitals. It contained provisions that required grantees to provide "a reasonable volume of services to those unable to pay" and to make their facilities "available to all persons residing in their service areas." However, it was not until significant court action in the 1970s that the Department of Health, Education and Welfare (DHEW), now the Department of Health and Human Services (DHHS), issued effective rules governing these free-care obligations. For 30 years, those responsible for implementing the law simply avoided issuing final rules that required hospitals to meet these obligations, probably because they wished to avoid anticipated conflict with the hospital industry over the enforcement of these provisions of the law.

Rules that are established by executive departments and agencies through formal rulemaking have legal effect. As authoritative decisions made within government for the purpose of guiding the decisions, actions, and behaviors of others, rules or regulations are by definition policies. These policies are codified in the *Code of Federal Regulations* (CFR) and thus, like public laws, are available to anyone interested in reading them.

Rules of Rulemaking

The promulgation of rules, as a formal part of the implementation phase of policymaking, is itself guided by certain rules and protocols. Key among these is the requirement that implementing agencies publish *proposed* rules. The purpose of a notice of proposed rulemaking (NPRM) is to give those with interests in the issue an opportunity to participate in the rulemaking prior to the adoption of a *final rule*. Proposed and final rules are published in the *Federal Register*, which is a daily publication that provides a uniform system for publishing presidential and federal agency documents. It includes major sections for Presidential Documents, Rules and Regulations, Proposed Rules, and Notices. The CFR and the *Federal Register*, along with numerous other documents, can be read on a web site maintained by the Government Printing Office (GPO) called GPO Access (www.access.gpo.gov/gpoaccess).

Each proposed rule document begins with a heading that includes the name of the issuing agency; the CFR title and part(s) affected; and a brief description of the specific subject of the document, and in some cases an agency docket number, which identifies the document within the agency's internal filing system. A Regulation Identifier Number (RIN) may also be included. Instructions for filing comments and the date by which comments must be filed are also provided. The Proposed Rules section of the *Federal Register* also contains documents relating to previously published proposed rules, extending comment periods, announcing public hearings, making available supplemental information, withdrawing proposed rules, or correcting previously published proposed rules. This section also includes advanced notices of proposed rulemaking. An advanced notice describes a problem or situation and the anticipated regulatory action of the agency and seeks public response concerning the necessity for regulation as well as the adequacy of the agency's anticipated regulatory action.

A proposed rule is effectively a *draft* of a rule or set of rules that will be used to guide the implementation of a law while the final rules are still under development. Rules can be added, deleted, or modified over the life of a public law; thus rulemaking is an ongoing component in the life of any public law. Publication of a proposed rule is an open invitation for all parties with an interest in the rule to react before it becomes final. For example, in 1989, Congress amended the Medicare policy to change the way physicians who treat Medicare patients are paid for their services. This procedure—which used resource-based relative value scales (RBRVS)—sought to base payment on the actual demands of professional work involved in various physician-provided services and to capture for each service the relevant physician practice expenses, liability insurance costs, and regional norms. The net effect of this change in policy was to decrease the amount of payment for many procedure-based services, such as surgery, and to increase payment for many primary care services. Publication in the *Federal Register* of the proposed rules to implement this change quite literally served as an invitation to physicians who would be affected by this change, and their interest groups, to bargain and negotiate the new levels of payment for their services (Moon 1993). As might be expected, many accepted the invitation.

The Real World of Health Policy

Proposed and Final Rules

A Proposed Rule

Department of Health and Human Services
Food and Drug Administration
21 CFR Parts 16 and 807
Docket No. 00N-1625
Medical Devices; Rescission of Substantially Equivalent Decisions and Rescission Appeal Procedures
AGENCY: Food and Drug Administration, HHS.
ACTION: Proposed rule.
SUMMARY: The Food and Drug Administration (FDA) is proposing regulations under which FDA may rescind a decision issued under the Federal Food, Drug, and Cosmetic Act (the act) that a device is substantially equivalent to a legally marketed device, and, therefore, may be marketed. In addition, under this proposal, a premarket notification (commonly known as a "510(k)") holder may request administrative review of a proposed rescission action. This proposed rule is being issued in order to standardize the procedures for considering rescissions.
DATES: Submit written comments by April 16, 2001.
ADDRESS: Submit written comments to the Dockets Management Branch (HFA-305), Food and Drug Administration, rm. 1061, 5630 Fishers Lane, Rockville, MD 20852.
FOR FURTHER INFORMATION CONTACT: Heather S. Rose-crans, Center for Devices and Radiological Health (HFZ-404), Food and Drug Administration, 9200 Corporate Blvd., Rockville, MD 20850, 301-594-1190.

* * *

Source: Excerpted from *Federal Register*, January 16, 2001 (Volume 66, Number 10), Proposed Rules, pages 3523–3526.

A Final Rule

Department of Health and Human Services
Office of the Secretary
45 CFR Parts 160 and 164
Standards for Privacy of Individually Identifiable Health Information; Final Rule
Department of Health and Human Services, Office of the Secretary
45 CFR Parts 160 and 164
Rin: 0991-AB08
Standards for Privacy of Individually Identifiable Health Information
AGENCY: Office of the Assistant Secretary for Planning and Evaluation, DHHS.

ACTION: Final rule.

SUMMARY: This rule includes standards to protect the privacy of individually identifiable health information. The rules below, which apply to health plans, health care clearinghouses, and certain health care providers, present standards with respect to the rights of individuals who are the subjects of this information, procedures for the exercise of those rights, and the authorized and required uses and disclosures of this information. The use of these standards will improve the efficiency and effectiveness of public and private health programs and health care services by providing enhanced protections for individually identifiable health information. These protections will begin to address growing public concerns that advances in electronic technology and evolution in the health care industry are resulting, or may result, in a substantial erosion of the privacy surrounding individually identifiable health information maintained by health care providers, health plans and their administrative contractors. This rule implements the privacy requirements of the Administrative Simplification subtitle of the Health Insurance Portability and Accountability Act of 1996.

DATES: The final rule is effective on February 26, 2001.

* * *

Source: Excerpted from *Federal Register*, December 28, 2000 (Volume 65, Number 250), Rules and Regulations, pages 82461–82510.

Changes in proposed rules often result from the interactions between officials of implementing organizations and those whom the rules will affect directly. In fact, these interactions, triggered by the publication of a proposed rule or a notice of proposed rulemaking, are among the most active points of involvement in the entire policymaking process for individuals, for health-related organizations, and interest groups with a stake in how a particular public law is implemented. The role of interest groups is especially potent at this point in the process.

The Role of Interest Groups in Rulemaking

Implementation of any complex health-related law readily provides examples of what Thompson (1997) calls the "strategic interaction" that occurs during rulemaking between implementing organizations and affected interest groups. For example, among the numerous rules proposed in implementing the 1974 National Health Planning and Resources Development Act (P.L. 93-641) were some that sought to reduce obstetrical capacity in the nation's hospitals. One proposed rule, in 1977, called for hospitals to perform at least 500 deliveries annually or close their obstetrical units. Notice of this proposed rule elicited immediate objections, especially from hospitals in rural areas where compliance would be extremely difficult or impossible. The implementing organization (DHEW, now DHHS) received more than 55,000 written reactions to the proposed rule, almost all of them negative (Zwick 1978). As a result, the final rule was far less restrictive, in fact making no reference at all to a specific number of deliveries necessary to keep rural obstetrics units open.

All policies affect one or more interest groups. Because the individual and organizational members of interest groups are so often the targets of rules established to implement health-related public laws, these groups routinely seek to influence rulemaking. Regulatory policies seek to prescribe and control the actions, behaviors, and decisions of certain individuals or organizations. Allocative policies seek to provide income, services, or other benefits to certain individuals or organizations at the expense of others. Thus, interest groups that represent the individuals and organizations so directly affected by public policies can be expected to be actively interested in all aspects of policymaking, including rulemaking. As the discussion in chapter 3 of interest groups in the political marketplace shows, these groups tend not to be passive about what they want to accomplish on behalf of their members. Many are well organized and aggressive in pursuit of their preferences, seeking to influence both the formulation and the implementation of policies that affect them.

Lobbying and other forms of influence become especially intense when some interest groups strongly support, while others oppose, the formulation of a particular law or the manner in which it is to be implemented. The preferences of particular interest groups may well come in conflict with the preferences of other groups. Policymakers almost always face this dilemma when they confront important choices in the formulation and implementation of policies. As noted in chapter 3, legislators in such situations can be expected to seek to maximize their net political support through their decisions and actions. The same can be said for those responsible for the management of implementing agencies and organizations. This means that rulemaking is often influenced by interest group preferences, with the more politically powerful groups exerting the greatest influence.

The potential of conflicting interests among various groups regarding health policy can be seen in some of the general preferences of several categories of individuals and organizations shown in Figure 6.2. Although some similarities exist among the preferences of the various categories, there are also some important differences. Policymakers generally can anticipate that these individuals and organizations, working through their interest groups to a great extent, will seek to have their preferences reflected in any policies that are enacted and to have their preferences influence the subsequent implementation of such policies as well.

Health policy is replete with examples of the influence of interest groups on rulemaking. One such example can be seen in the rulemaking that stemmed from enactment of the Medicare program. In part to improve its chances for passage, the Medicare legislation (P.L. 89-97) was written so that the Social Security Administration (the original implementing agency, subsequently replaced by the Health Care Financing Administration) would reimburse hospitals and physicians in their customary manner. This meant that they would be paid on a fee-for-service basis, with the fees established by the providers. Each time providers gave services to Medicare program beneficiaries, they were paid their "usual and customary" fees for doing so.

However, unlike the physicians and hospitals, some prepaid providers, such as health maintenance organizations (HMOs), had a different method of charging for their services. Their approach was to charge an annual fee per patient no matter how many times the patient might see a physician or use a hospital. In this situation, the hospitals and fee-for-service physicians had an obvious preference for having the Social Security Administration reimburse them according to their customary payment pattern. But in addition they could see an advantage in not permitting the competing prepaid organizations to be paid in their cus-

Figure 6.2 Typical Policy Preferences of Selected Health-Related Individuals and Organizations

Federal Government
- Deficit reduction/Increased surpluses
- Control over growth of Medicare and Medicaid expenditures
- Fewer uninsured citizens
- Slower growth in healthcare costs

State Government
- Medicaid funding relief
- More Medicaid flexibility
- Fewer uninsured citizens
- More federal funds and slower growth in healthcare costs

Employers
- Slower growth in healthcare costs
- Simplified benefit administration
- Elimination of cost-shifting
- No mandates

Consumers
- Insurance availability
- Access to care (with choices)
- Lower deductibles and copayments

Insurers
- Administrative simplification
- Elimination of cost-shifting
- Slower growth in healthcare costs
- No mandates

Technology Producers
- Continued demand
- Sustained research funding
- Favorable tax treatment

Individual Practitioners
- Income maintenance
- Professional autonomy
- Malpractice reform

Provider Organizations
- Improved financial condition
- Administrative simplification
- Less uncompensated care

Suppliers
- Continued demand
- Sustained profitability
- Favorable tax treatment

Professional Schools
- Continued demand
- Student subsidies

tomary manner—that is, in making them subject to the fee-for-service payment rules. Their preferences, vigorously made known to the Social Security Administration through the powerful American Medical Association and to a somewhat lesser extent through the American Hospital Association, resulted in the prepaid organizations being forced to operate under fee-for-service payment rules until the rules were finally changed in 1985 (Feldstein 1996).

Another example of the influence of interest groups on rulemaking arose in the late 1990s as some hospitals and physicians sought to develop organizations that would permit them to compete with health plans in providing health services to defined populations. These providers, largely through their interest groups, complained to the federal government that extant antitrust policies precluded or inhibited them from undertaking such arrangements (Ginsburg 1997). In response, the Department of Justice and the Federal Trade Commission took the initiative to issue statements serving to guide hospitals and physicians who are contemplating such arrangements on the exact types of joint ventures between hospitals and physicians that would not be challenged under the rules through which antitrust laws are implemented (U.S. Department of Justice and Federal Trade Commission 1996).

Other Interactions Between Rulemakers and Those Affected by the Rules

In certain instances, especially when the development of rules is anticipated to be unusually difficult, or when such development seems likely to attract severe disagreement and conflict—or when rules probably will be subject to continual revision—special provisions may be made regarding their development. For example, after passage of the Health Maintenance Organization Act (P.L. 93-222) in 1973, DHEW (now DHHS) organized a series of task forces, with some members drawn from outside the implementing organization, to help develop the proposed rules for implementing the law. This strategy produced rules that were much more acceptable to those who would be affected by them than might otherwise have been the case.

Another strategy used to support rulemaking is the creation of advisory commissions. For example, following enactment of the 1983 Amendments to the Social Security Act (P.L. 98-21), which established the prospective payment system (PPS) for reimbursing hospitals for the care of Medicare beneficiaries, Congress established the Prospective Payment Assessment Commission (ProPAC) to provide nonbinding advice to HCFA (now CMS) in implementing the reimbursement system. A second commission, the Physician Payment Review Commission (PPRC), was established later to advise Congress and HCFA (now CMS) regarding payment for physicians' services under the Medicare program. These commissions proved useful in helping HCFA (now CMS) make required annual decisions regarding reimbursement rates, fees, and other variables involved in operating the Medicare program. The Balanced Budget Act of 1997 (P.L. 105-33) replaced both commissions with a new commission—the Medicare Payment Review Commission (MedPAC) (www.medpac.gov)—which incorporates and expands the roles of ProPAC and PPRC.

After laws have been enacted, and after initial rules necessary for implementing them have been promulgated, the implementation phase enters an operational stage (see Figure 6.1). At the point of operation, those involved in policy implementation are required to fulfill the mandates inherent in the laws they are responsible for implementing, by following the rules or regulations promulgated to guide the implementation. Ideally, this is exactly what happens as policy implementation unfolds. However, as the next section points out, the possibility always exists that some individuals with implementing responsibilities will disagree with the purposes of the enacted laws and may seek to stall, alter, or even subvert the laws in their implementation phases.

The power of those with implementation responsibilities to affect the final outcomes and consequences of policies should not be underestimated. It is a power similar to that possessed by those in private-sector organizations with operational responsibilities for the achievement of organizational missions and objectives.

The Real World of Health Policy

MedPAC

The Medicare Payment Advisory Commission (MedPAC) is an independent federal body established by the Balanced Budget Act of 1997 (P.L. 105-33) to advise the U.S. Congress on issues affecting the Medicare program. The Commission's statutory mandate is quite broad: In addition to advising the Congress on payments to health plans participating in the Medicare+Choice program and providers in Medicare's traditional fee-for-service program, MedPAC is also tasked with analyzing access to care, quality of care, and other issues affecting Medicare.

The Commission's 17 members bring diverse expertise in the financing and delivery of health care services. Commissioners are appointed to three-year terms (subject to renewal) by the Comptroller General and serve part time. Appointments are staggered; the terms of five or six Commissioners expire each year. The Commission is supported by an executive director and a staff of analysts, who typically have backgrounds in economics, health policy, public health, or medicine.

MedPAC meets publicly to discuss policy issues and formulate its recommendations to the Congress. In the course of these meetings, Commissioners consider the results of staff research, presentations by policy experts, and comments from interested parties. Commission members and staff also seek input on Medicare issues through frequent meetings with individuals interested in the program, including staff from congressional committees and the Health Care Financing Administration, health care researchers, health care providers and beneficiary advocates.

Two reports, issued in March and June each year, are the primary outlet for Commission recommendations. In addition to these reports and additional reports on subjects requested by the Congress, MedPAC advises the Congress through other avenues, including comments on reports and proposed regulations issued by the Secretary of the Department of Health and Human Services, testimony, and briefings for congressional staff.

Source: Excerpted from MedPAC's web site, www.medpac.gov.

Operation

The operation stage of implementation (see Figure 6.1) involves the actual conduct or running of the programs and processes embedded in enacted public laws. This stage is the domain, although not exclusively, of the appointees and civil servants who staff the government. For any policy, two variables are especially important to a successful operational stage: (1) the policy itself in terms of how it is designed; and (2) certain characteristics of the organization(s) charged with a policy's implementation, including the competence of the managers. Each of these variables is examined.

The Impact of a Policy on Its Own Operation

As with any writing intended to influence the actions, behaviors, or decisions of others (e.g., legal contracts or procedure manuals), the language and construction of an individual policy—especially a policy in the form of a public law—plays a crucial role in the course and success of its operational life. The impact of the construction of a public law can be felt both in the rulemaking associated with its implementation and in its operation. The construction or design of a policy includes its objectives, the hypothesis or the causal relationships embedded within it, and the degree of flexibility left to those responsible for its implementation.

Policy Objectives

Well-written laws always include clearly articulated objectives that the law is intended to achieve, although clear objectives are only part of the makeup of a good policy. When those with implementation responsibility for a particular public law know what the law is really intended to accomplish—what its objectives are—then it is easier to operate the programs and procedures embedded within it. In contrast, when the objectives of a policy are not clear or when they are multiple or conflicting, successful operation is made more difficult, if not impossible, to achieve, even before the effort begins.

An example of the problem of multiple, conflicting objectives within a single law can be found in the National Health Planning and Resources Development Act of 1974 (P.L. 93-641). Congress hoped this massive policy would fulfill many of the objectives it had previously attempted to attain through a wide variety of earlier, more focused policies. As outlined in Section 1513 of P.L. 93-641, its multiple objectives included:

- improving the health of people;
- increasing the accessibility (including overcoming geographic, architectural, and transportation barriers), acceptability, continuity, and quality of health services; and
- restraining increases in the cost of providing health services.

As has been noted in regard to the multiple objectives embedded in P.L. 93-641, "the legislation proposed every health system desideratum its authors could imagine" (Morone 1990, 272). This expansive set of inherently contradictory objectives eventually doomed the policy; Congress repealed it in 1986.

Hypothesis of the Policy

Vague or conflicting objectives are not the only potentially serious problems with the construction of policies—problems that can make their operational stages very difficult if not impossible. The procedural paradigm set forth in a public law can also be flawed. Embedded in every policy is a *hypothesis* about the effect of operationalizing the policy: if someone does A, then B will result. As Thompson (1997) has noted, however, only in a perfect world would policymakers always base their laws on entirely plausible hypotheses. As he notes, "Limits to their knowledge and the political dynamics of policy formulation often impede this development" (Thompson 1997, 158).

If the hypothesis underpinning a policy is wrong, the policy cannot be successfully implemented because its operational stage will not solve the problem the policy is intended to address. It will not matter that its objectives are appropriate, or even that they are noble. In formulating the National Health Planning and Resources Development Act (P.L. 93-641), the inherently contradictory objectives noted earlier, for example, Congress patched together an oddly matched pair of strategies: voluntary, community-based planning on the one hand, and heavy-handed regulation, at least of capital expansion in the health sector, on the other. To no one's surprise, at least in hindsight, the combination did not work very well. The core hypothesis of the policy was seriously flawed.

Degree of Flexibility in Implementing the Policy

Another potential difficulty with the construction of policies is the nature and extent of decisions left to the implementing organizations. These decisions arise by virtue of the explicitly directive language in the law, by what is not said in the law, or by confusing or vague language in the law. For example, although a degree of flexibility in developing the rules to be used in policy implementation can be advantageous, vague policy directives can create all sorts of problems for those with implementation responsibilities.

The Occupational Safety and Health Act of 1970 (P.L. 91-596), for example, contained a number of vague directives and phrases that created significant problems for its implementers. In Section 2 of the law, the language stressed the importance of fostering healthful working conditions "so far as possible." This language was in lieu of specific objectives or targets for achieving reductions in occupational injuries or diseases. In Section 6, the statute authorized the Secretary of Labor, in implementing the law, to issue standards dealing with toxic substances in the workplace "to the extent feasible." In attempting to operationalize this complex law, considerable time and energy were expended in attempting to decide if this phrase meant that implementers could take the economic costs of their actions to employers into account in establishing standards dealing with workplace toxic substances. In these instances, effective implementation was impeded by some of the policy's vague and imprecise language.

In contrast, language that is too restrictive can also impede the implementation of a policy. In combination with the very imprecise language noted in the Occupational Safety and Health Act, Congress was precise and extremely restrictive in writing into the law the range of fines that could be assessed against firms that violated standards. For less serious violations, the fine would be $1,000. For serious, willful violations, the fine could be up to $10,000. Most analysts considered the limits of these fines to be far too low to be effective deterrents, especially for large, profitable enterprises. In this instance, effective operation of the law was impeded by some of its very specific language.

The way in which laws are written—that is, the way in which policies are designed—has substantial impact on how they are subsequently implemented. The impact is felt both in rulemaking and in operation. In general, in recent decades, Congress has tended to enact longer and much more detailed laws in attempting to enhance their implementation (Melnick 1994). But no matter how a law is written, its implementation is also directly affected by the organization or agency charged with the task, including the competence of its managers.

The Impact of Implementing Organizations and Their Managers on Implementation

The essence of the implementation phase of policymaking is that one or more organizations or agencies undertakes to operationalize enacted legislation, ideally in a manner that permits realization of the legislative intent behind the legislation. This involves promulgating the rules under which implementation will proceed as well as actually putting the laws into operation.

As noted earlier, one important constant in the dynamic circumstances that are involved in rulemaking and in operationalizing public laws is that the bulk of these implementation responsibilities rests with executive branch organizations. For example, the CMS is primarily responsible for implementing the Medicare program; the FDA is primarily responsible for implementing many of the nation's food and drug policies. State insurance departments are responsible for implementing the states' policies regarding health insurance, and so on. Consideration of the operation of policies thus must include attention to the characteristics and attributes of implementing organizations that contribute to their organizational success at policy implementation, including the roles of their managers in successful implementation. The organizational structure of DHHS, which contains a number of agencies with implementation responsibilities, is shown in Figure 6.3.

As noted earlier, certain characteristics of the organization(s) charged with a policy's implementation, including the competence of the managers, have significant effect on how well policies are implemented. The effect on implementation of the fit between an implementing organization and the objectives of the policies it is responsible for implementing, and the effect of the competence of the organization's managers on implementation are examined in the next two sections.

The Fit Between Implementing Organizations and Objectives of Policies

No characteristic of an implementing organization is more basic to success than a close fit between the organization and the objectives of the policies it must implement. The keys to such a fit include (1) whether or not the organization is sympathetic to the policy's objectives and (2) whether or not the organization has the necessary resources, in the form of authority, money, personnel, status or prestige, information and expertise, technology, and physical facilities and equipment, to implement the policy effectively.

Figure 6.3 Organization Chart of the Department of Health and Human Services

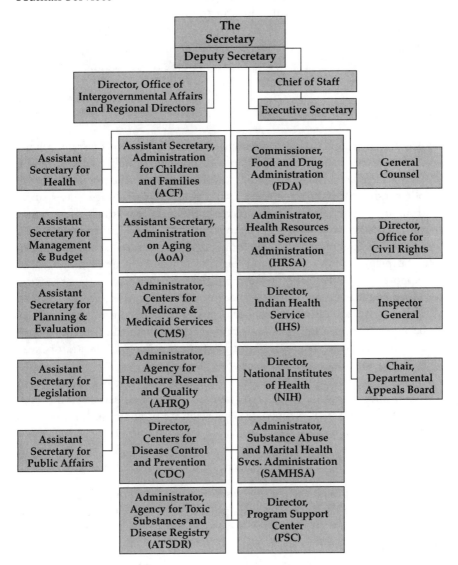

Central to whether a policy-implementing organization is sympathetic to the objectives of the policy is the attitude and perspective of its senior leaders and managers. They are the people most instrumental in ensuring that necessary support for the implementation task is garnered. If an implementing organization's leaders are not sympathetic to the policies they must implement, they are unlikely to protect it from unwarranted amendments or intrusions by nonsupporters, especially by legislators who are hostile to the policy and those who seek to influence those legislators. Strong allies in the legislative branch and among interest groups can be important to this protective task, but much of the responsibility rests with the leaders of the implementing organization.

The connection between any organization's resources and its capacity to fulfill its purposes is quite straightforward. However, in the world of public management, one resource can be especially problematical. As has been noted,

> Among the factors that threaten implementation capacity, none ranks higher in importance than the limited status, or prestige, of public administration [or management] in the United States. Compared to their counterparts in other industrialized democracies, civil servants in the United States suffer from low public esteem. One observer aptly notes that "the ineffectiveness and inefficiency" of the public sector is a belief "so widely and firmly held that one . . . can regard it as a unifying theme of our creed" (Waldo 1980, 17).
>
> Suspicion and mistrust of bureaucracy show up even among liberals who support government action to accomplish health care reform (Jacobs 1993).
>
> Sensing this vulnerability, the media, oversight committees in Congress, and others often caricature the performance of public bureaucracies. They become expert at blaming administrative agencies—at making them "the fall guys of American government"—rather than at helping administrators keep their programs on track (Derthick 1990, 181).
>
> Health agencies with excellent performance records may dodge some of the problems spawned by limited status of public administration. But even they cannot escape it completely. The Medicare program, for instance, has much lower administrative costs per benefits paid than private insurance companies. Yet various political players sporadically toss brickbats at the program, claiming that it is bureaucratic and wasteful (Thompson 1997, 164).

Another important aspect of whether there is a good fit between an implementing organization and the policies it is supposed to implement is the organization's repertoire of technologies for use in carrying out its work. Implementing organizations rely on a variety of methods and technologies to implement policies. Just as policies differ in substantial ways (recall the distinction between allocative and regulatory policies made in chapter 1), the technologies needed to implement them also differ (Thompson 1997).

Regulatory policies require implementation technologies that prescribe and control the behaviors of whoever is being regulated. Such technologies include capacity for rule promulgation, investigatory capacity, and the ability to impose sanctions. Allocative policies, on the other hand, require technologies such as processes through which implementing organizations deliver income, goods, or services. Such technologies include targeting recipients or beneficiaries, determining eligibility for benefits, and managing the supply and quality of goods or services provided through the policy. The Occupational Safety and Health Administration (OSHA), for example, relies heavily on regulatory technologies as it seeks to protect workers from hazards in the workplace. In contrast, CMS relies heavily, although not exclusively, on allocative technologies in implementing the Medicare program.

Only when the leaders of an implementing organization are fully sympathetic to the objectives of a policy and when they have adequate resources for the task, including possession of the appropriate technologies to get the job done, can they fully and effectively carry out their implementation duties. Even then, however, other factors play a part in the degree of success achieved, including notably the contributions made by the organization's managers.

The Competence of Implementing Organizations' Managers

The performance of the managers of implementing organizations, especially those at senior levels, directly affects the performance levels achieved by implementing organizations. The contributions made by managers depend on their management competence, as well as how adeptly they play a trio of interrelated roles: designer, strategist, and leader (Zuckerman and Dowling 1997). These roles are discussed below; then attention is given to the importance of management competence in implementing organizations. Although the roles managers play are discussed here in sequence, in reality they exist as parts of a whole—a mosaic—in which all three are played simultaneously by managers.

The Designer Role.   Designer roles involve managers in establishing intentional patterns of relationships between people and other resources in their organizations. In doing this, managers designate individual positions and aggregate these positions into work groups such as teams, departments, and divisions of organizations. In short, they design the structure of their organizations.

The designer role for managers of implementing organizations is a continual challenge. In their volatile environments, organization design is not something managers in typical implementing organizations can do once, before turning their attention elsewhere. Instead, organizing is ongoing and involves not only initial design, but also routine redesign. For example, these are some of the typical circumstances under which public-sector managers are likely to be involved in making organization design changes:

- A significant change occurs in an implementing organization's external environment that directly influences its operations. Such changes include new or amended public laws for the organization to implement and changes in the rules that affect their operationalizing of public laws. Environmental changes might also include a major reduction in the organization's budget or a reorganization initiative undertaken in the executive branch.

- An organization adapts new technologies in carrying out its work or is given new responsibilities for implementation. An organization design change may be required to infuse necessary resources into the new activities. Conversely, when old technologies are abandoned or when previous responsibilities are shifted elsewhere, new structural arrangements may be necessary to accommodate the changes.

- An organization experiences a change in its management personnel. Leadership changes are a routine matter in the executive branch organizations that carry out policy implementation. People move in and out of public service. Administrations change. Changes at or near the top level of organizations routinely stimulate organizational redesigns. New leadership provides a ripe opportunity to rethink the way in which the affected organization is designed and how it conducts its work. New managers typically view their organization's design from a fresh, and often different, perspective, and may wish to have its design reflect their own ideas and preferences to the extent possible.

- Often, large-scale organization design changes involving substantial reorganizing or restructuring occur in the context of a larger set of changes brought about through total quality management (TQM) or continuous quality improvement (CQI) programs or through so-called reengineering initiatives. Such changes can result from these initiatives within the organizations themselves or as part of larger programs of change initiated by commitments of chief executives.

The Real World of Health Policy

Reforming the Medicare and Medicaid Agency

Among President George W. Bush's earliest cabinet selections, Tommy G. Thompson stepped down as Governor of Wisconsin and was sworn in as Secretary of the Department of Health and Human Services (HHS) on February 2, 2001. Shortly thereafter, Thomas Scully was selected as the

Administrator of HCFA (renamed Centers for Medicare and Medicaid Services, or CMS). Mr. Scully had been President of the Federation of American Hospitals (www.fahs.com). The Federation's members include proprietary or for-profit corporations or other organizations involved in the delivery of health services. On June 14, 2001, the HHS Press Office issued the following press release in which significant organizational changes in this vital implementing agency were announced.

HHS Press Office
For Immediate Release
June 14, 2001

HHS Secretary Tommy G. Thompson today announced the first wave of efforts to reform and strengthen the services and information available to nearly 70 million Medicare and Medicaid beneficiaries and the health care providers who serve them.

As part of that effort, Secretary Thompson unveiled the new name for the federal agency that runs the Medicare and joint federal-state Medicaid programs—the Centers for Medicare & Medicaid Services, currently known as the Health Care Financing Administration. The new name reflects the increased emphasis at the Centers for Medicare & Medicaid Services on responsiveness to beneficiaries and providers, and on improving the quality of care that beneficiaries receive in all parts of Medicare and Medicaid.

To achieve these goals, the Centers for Medicare & Medicaid Services will:

- launch a national media campaign to give seniors and other Medicare beneficiaries more information to help them make decisions about how they want to get their health care;
- instill a new culture of responsiveness at the Centers for Medicare & Medicaid Services in serving beneficiaries, physicians and other health care providers, states and lawmakers;
- enhance 1-800-MEDICARE (1-800-633-4227) to a 24-hour a day, seven days a week service that will provide far more detailed information to help beneficiaries to make Medicare decisions;
- restructure the agency around three centers that reflect the agency's major lines of business;
- reform the contractor process to improve the quality and efficiency of the Medicare claims processing services (Medicare carriers and fiscal intermediaries) that pay nearly a billion fee-for-service Medicare claims each year.

"We're making quality service the number 1 priority in this agency," Secretary Thompson said. "These sweeping reforms will strengthen our programs and enable our dedicated employees to better serve Medicare and Medicaid beneficiaries as well as health care providers. We're going to encourage innovation, better educate consumers about their options and be more responsive to the health care needs of Americans."

Secretary Thompson said the new name better reflects the mission of the agency, as well as a renewed commitment to be more responsive to health care consumers and providers.

"This is only the beginning—more changes are on the way. We're going to keep fine-tuning this department so Americans are receiving the highest quality health care possible. Our commitment to excellence is unwavering."

"We need to make sure that the people who are covered by Medicare know exactly what choices they have for their health care coverage," said Tom Scully, Medicare & Medicaid administrator. "Too many consumers just don't understand Medicare coverage options and the costs associated with them, from their Medigap options to Medicare+Choice to the cost of prescription drugs. We need to get that information to them and their family members, while working closely with the doctors and other health care providers who give them medical care."

The Centers for Medicare & Medicaid Services will launch a $35 million national media campaign in the fall of 2001 to highlight the health care options and information resources available, including (www.medicare.gov) and 1-800-MEDICARE (1-800-633-4227). The Centers for Medicare & Medicaid Services will also expand the capacity of the toll-free phone line with call center experts available 24 hours a day, seven days a week and develop a program with public libraries to train librarians to help Medicare beneficiaries gather information about Medicare at (www.medicare.gov). The toll-free phone line currently works only during business hours.

These outreach initiatives are part of the effort to be more responsive to health care consumers and their needs. The Centers for Medicare & Medicaid Services will focus much of its attention on being responsive, accessible and understandable to beneficiaries, physicians and other health care providers, health plans, states and other stakeholders. The agency will have specific individuals dedicated to work with each state and territory in the United States, and with all organizations that work with the Centers for Medicare & Medicaid Services' stakeholders. More initiatives to improve responsiveness and outreach are in the works and will be announced in the near future.

The three new business centers being created as part of the reforms are the Center for Beneficiary Choices, the Center for Medicare Management, and the Center for Medicaid and State Operations.

The Center for Medicare Management focuses on the management of the traditional fee-for-service Medicare program, including development and implementation of payment policy and management of the Medicare carriers and fiscal intermediaries. The Center for Beneficiary Choices focuses on beneficiary education, providing beneficiaries with the information they need to make their health care decisions. This center also includes management of the Medicare + Choice program, consumer research and demonstrations, and grievance and appeals. The Center for Medicaid and State Operations focuses on programs administered by the states, including Medicaid, the State Children's Health Insurance Program, private insurance, survey and certification and the Clinical Laboratory Improvement Amendments (CLIA).

To manage the Medicare program more effectively and responsively, the Centers for Medicare & Medicaid Services will develop a legislative proposal to be submitted to Congress that would provide for competitive bidding of claims processing services. Medicare contracts with private health insurance companies to process and pay Medicare claims. Collectively, these contractors employ about 22,000 individuals and handle more than 900 million Medicare claims each year.

Currently, these contracts are governed by laws that are more restrictive than general federal contract laws. The Centers for Medicare & Medicaid Services will be working with Congress to develop legislation that will allow the agency to competitively award these contracts by using performance based incentives to improve the level of service to beneficiaries and providers, reduce administrative costs and improve efficiency.

"Contractor reform is an important part of the improvements we will be making over the next few months to serve our beneficiaries more efficiently," said Secretary Thompson. "As we improve the agency's efficiencies we will not only save the Trust Funds for taxpayers now, we will help to strengthen them for our children and grandchildren."

Source: HHS News (www.hhs.gov/news).

The organizational changes stimulated by changes in the environments of many implementing organizations have made the designer roles of their managers increasingly more important and more challenging. But the designer role is only one of the three roles played by these managers. How they play their other roles in carrying out their implementation responsibilities also affects the performance of their organizations.

The Strategist Role.   The strategist role pertains to the efforts of managers to establish suitable organizational purposes and objectives and to develop and implement plans or strategies that are capable of accomplishing those objectives for their organizations. When managers think strategically, they are thinking about how to adapt their organizational domains to the challenges and opportunities presented to them by their environments. Implementing organizations are dynamic, open systems. They exist in the context of often remarkably complex external environments, and frequently have extensive organizational histories.

The managers of an implementing organization routinely engage in ongoing exchanges with others in their organization's external environment and are influenced, sometimes dramatically, by what goes on in that external environment. Imagine, for example, the significance for an implementing organization of being assigned major new responsibilities or of having some of its core responsibilities curtailed. Or envision the operational impact on an implementing organization of a decisive shift in control of the Congress, such as occurred in the 1992 congressional election, or the midterm defection of Senator James Jeffords in 2001 from the Republican Party—a move that shifted overnight the control of the United States Senate from the Republicans to the Democrats because of the closeness of the party split in the Senate at the time.

When managers think and act strategically—when they are performing their strategist roles—they acknowledge the fact that their organization is affected by what goes on outside it, and their decisions and actions reflect this relationship. Thus, a crucial component of their strategist role is expertise in discerning the significant information in their environments.

Effective managers engage in situational analysis as a means of identifying and assessing pertinent environmental information. Contemporary managers of implementing organizations must analyze enormous amounts of information that could potentially affect their organizations. Much of this information pertains to the plans of executive branch administration, but information on the activities occurring in the legislative branch is also relevant. In addition, external biological, cultural, demographic, ecological, economic, ethical, legal, psychological, social, and technological information must also be analyzed for its potential direct impact on the organization.

In conducting comprehensive situational analyses, managers are required to proceed in four interrelated steps: (1) environmental scanning to identify strategic issues (i.e., trends, developments, opportunities, threats, or possible events) that could affect the organization; (2) monitoring the strategic issues identified; (3) forecasting or projecting the future directions of strategic issues; and (4) assessing the implications of the strategic issues for the organization.

Good situational analysis, however, includes more than external discernment. It adds a comprehensive assessment of the internal strengths and weaknesses of the organization and of the values held by those in the organization.

Armed with the external and internal information garnered from a thorough situational analysis, managers can formulate or refine relevant missions and objectives for their organizations, and can more accurately determine the strategies to be used in achieving them. The importance of this role is directly proportional to the nature of the relationship between an organization and its external environment, and to the volatility of both its external and internal environments. Most implementation organizations are highly dependent on their external environments, and both their internal and external environments tend to be very dynamic and fluid.

The Leader Role.   Effective leadership is essential if implementing organizations are to succeed in carrying out their implementation responsibilities. Leadership is necessary in all purposeful organizations because some people determine, initiate, integrate, and oversee the work of others. Some lead, others follow. As leaders, the senior-level managers in implementing organizations are responsible for:

- molding a widely shared internal and external agreement on implementing the organization's purposes and priorities;
- building widespread support for the organization's purposes and priorities among internal and external stakeholders, especially among administrative branch superiors, legislators with oversight responsibility for the organization, and relevant interest groups;
- striking a workable balance among the economic and professional interests of the organization's members, the demands and preferences of its external stakeholders, and the public interest the organization is required to serve; and
- negotiating and maintaining effective relationships with people and organizations, regulated by or otherwise affected by the implementing organization, who supply resources to the implementing organization, and with other organizations with whom the implementing organization must work closely in carrying out its policy implementation responsibilities.

The fulfillment of their leader roles requires that the leaders of implementing organizations engage in *transformational leadership*. Leadership in transforming or revitalizing implementing organizations is accomplished through decisions about organizational mission and structure, resources, priorities, quality and other performance standards, and the acquisition of new technologies. This is different from *transactional leadership* through which leaders summon extra motivation and performance from those they lead through transactions with them. In these transactions, leaders help meet certain needs of the followers if they perform to the leader's expectations (Burns 1978). But such transactions are not the main determinants of the success of those who lead policy-implementing organizations. In this role, the focus must be on leadership of the entire organization, and at that level the responsibility is for transformational leadership.

The essence of transformational leadership is the ability to develop and instill in the participants within an organization a common vision of what the organization is to accomplish and how it is to be accomplished and to stimulate determined and widespread adherence to that vision. Leaders at the organizational level must focus on the various decisions and activities that affect the entire organization, including those intended to ensure its survival and overall health. In effect, their role is to "manage culture" (McLaughlin and Kaluzny 1990). Successful organizational leaders must also establish objectives; inculcate appropriate values in the organization's participants; build intra- and interorganizational coalitions; and interpret and respond to various challenges and opportunities presented to the organization from its external environment.

As in all organizations, the leaders of implementing agencies and organizations can benefit from the histories and experiences of their organizations. Organizational leadership is invariably facilitated in situations in which:

- the existence of long-standing shared values and commonly accepted principles and norms help shape the organization's mission and operating practices and resolve conflicts among competing views;
- a history of success in implementing policies helps legitimize the organization's claims for support from internal and external stakeholders; and
- a history of effective relationships with oversight actors and relevant interest groups, and the availability of adequate financial resources, provide a sense of organizational pride and stability, and an appropriate degree of self-determination and autonomy.

The possession of basic management skills—especially communication and motivation skills—also facilitates organizational leadership. Leaders who can effectively articulate and communicate their views and preferences have a distinct advantage in having them considered and thus in providing guidance for the behaviors of their followers. Similarly, successful organizational leaders are likely able to mobilize widespread commitment among stakeholders to their preferences regarding the organization and to motivate stakeholder contributions to the realization of these preferences.

The capability to successfully play their management roles as designers, strategists, and leaders requires that managers possess certain competencies. A *management competency* can be defined as a cluster or package of knowledge and skill at using the knowledge. The management competencies required of managers in the organizations and agencies that implement policy—if they are to be able to do their work well—parallel to a great extent the classification developed by Katz (1974) of management skills appropriate for work in the private sector: *conceptual*, *technical*, and *interpersonal*. Katz's concept of interpersonal skill is expanded to include competence in collaborating between and among organizations, yielding an *interpersonal/collaborative* competency. Each of these competencies is discussed below.

Conceptual Competency. In all organizational settings, possession of an adequate cluster of conceptual knowledge and skills is a competency that permits managers to envision the places and roles of their organizations or agencies in the larger context within which they exist. This competency also allows managers to visualize the complex interrelationships within their workplaces—relationships among staff and other resources, and among departments or other units of an organization or agency. Adequate conceptual competency allows managers to identify, understand, and interact with their organization's or agency's myriad external and internal stakeholders; that is, with the individuals, groups, organizations, and agencies who have an interest or stake in the decisions and actions of the organization or agency. Conceptual competency also enhances managers' abilities to comprehend organizational cultures and historically developed values, beliefs, and norms and to visualize the futures of their organizations or agencies.

Technical Competency. The cluster of knowledge and associated skills that comprise technical competency pertains to competence in managing—in knowing how to effectively play designer, strategist, and leader roles—*and* in the actual direct work of a particular agency or organization. For example, managers in the FDA must know about managing and about at least some aspects of food or drug safety and efficacy. Managers in the Centers for Disease Control and Prevention (CDC) (www.cdc.gov) must know about managing and about some aspects of developing and applying disease prevention and control, environmental health, or health promotion and education activities designed to help in the pursuit of health.

Interpersonal/Collaborative Competency.　An important ingredient in managerial success in any setting is the cluster of knowledge and related skills about human interactions and relations by which managers direct or lead others in pursuit of objectives. *Interpersonal* competency incorporates knowledge and skills useful in effectively interacting with others. This includes the knowledge and related skills that permit managers to develop and instill a common vision and stimulate a determination to pursue the vision and fulfill objectives related to it. The essence of the interpersonal competency of managers is knowledge of how to motivate people, how to communicate their visions and preferences, how to handle negotiations, and how to manage conflicts.

The core elements of traditional interpersonal competency expand considerably when organizations or agencies are involved in collaboration or cooperative endeavors involving other organizations or agencies. Interpersonal relationships that occur within organizations differ from those that occur among or between collaborating organizations, agencies, or different levels of government. *Collaborative* competency is the ability to partner with other entities. This requires the ability to create and maintain multiparty organizational arrangements; to negotiate complex agreements, perhaps even contracts, that sustain these arrangements; and to produce mutually beneficial outcomes through such arrangements.

A partnering skill crucial to success in establishing and maintaining effective interorganizational or interagency collaborations is the ability of managers to develop shared cultures, or at least to minimize the differences that exist in the cultures of collaborating entities. In this context, culture is the pattern of shared values and beliefs that become ingrained in organizations or agencies over time and that influence the behaviors and decisions of the people in them. Collaborating organizations and agencies frequently have different cultures, which complicates the relationships between or among them.

The Real World of Health Policy

Food Safety

Food-borne illnesses remain a major public health problem. Ensuring the safety of food in the United States is the shared responsibility of a number of organizations at the federal, state, and local levels of government through their implementation of a number of laws. However, there is no single agency that can speak for the government on food safety. From the farm to the consumer's dinner table, food safety responsibilities are widely shared as follows:

- On the farm, food is regulated by state agencies supported principally by the Environmental Protection Agency (EPA), which acts to ensure that pesticides are approved for safe use, by the FDA, which oversees use of drugs and feed in milk- and food-producing animals, and by the Animal and Plant Health Inspection Service (APHIS), a unit of the U.S. Department of Agriculture (USDA), which is concerned with food/animal disease control. Federal responsibility also covers production and harvesting activities that discharge wastewater to surface and ground waters and solid waste to land, all of which could contaminate growing and process waters or grazing land.

- Food processing for foods other than meat, poultry, and egg products (except shell eggs) is regulated by the FDA. Meat, poultry, and all other egg products are regulated by the Food Safety and Inspection Service (FSIS).

- Food being transported for interstate commerce is subject to federal and state regulation, although this area has received little attention in the past. FSIS and FDA have jointly published an advanced notice of proposed rulemaking on whether regulations are needed to govern during transport the handling of meat, poultry, seafood, eggs, and other foods susceptible to harmful bacteria.

- The importation of food from foreign countries is overseen by FSIS for meat, poultry, and most egg products, and by FDA for all other foods. If an imported food is suspect, it can be tested for contamination and its entry into the United States denied.

- Restaurants, supermarkets, and institutional food services (such as schools and hospitals) are generally regulated by state and local health authorities. FDA publishes the *Food Code*, which consists of model recommendations for safeguarding public health when food is offered to the consumer. Recommendations are developed by consensus of state government representatives at the Conference for Food Protection. FSIS and FDA are working with states to update the *Food Code* in light of the changing retail and food service environment and emerging food safety issues, especially with regard to meat, poultry, egg products, and seafood. The Conference for Food Protection serves as one forum for fostering cooperation among federal, state, and local governments in the oversight of food products and of the conditions under which they are produced, processed, transported, stored, and handled through retail sale or food service to the consumer.

- National standards for drinking water are set by EPA and enforced generally by local public water authorities; FDA establishes complementary standards for bottled water.

- Surveillance of food-borne illness is primarily the responsibility of state and local health departments and the Centers for Disease Control and Prevention (CDC), which seek to identify cases of illness, determine their source, and control outbreaks. FDA or FSIS are called in when a link to a regulated food is suspected.

- In the home, consumers also have a responsibility for proper handling and storage of food. Because consumer mishandling contributes to many cases of food-borne illness, FSIS has promulgated safe-handling labels for raw meat and poultry products.

- Other responsibilities related to food safety include research into the cause and transmission of food-borne illnesses, and education on treatment and prevention of these illnesses. These responsibilities are carried out by the USDA, FDA, CDC, EPA, the National Institutes of Health (NIH), other federal components, and the states. Basic biomedical research on pathogenic organisms is conducted at the NIH. The federal government also supports related research in universities. The private sector supports research within its own laboratories and in universities.

A more extensive discussion of the food safety responsibility can be found in Committee to Ensure Safe Food Production from Production to Consumption and National Research Council. 1998. *Ensuring Safe Food: From Production to Consumption*. Washington, DC: National Academy Press. A key recommendation from this study, found on page 97, is that Congress establish by law "a unified and central framework for managing federal food safety programs, one that is headed by a single official and which the responsibility and control of resources for all federal food safety activities, including outbreak management, standard-setting, inspection, monitoring, surveillance, risk assessment, enforcement, research, and education."

Within organizations or agencies, conflict management responsibilities primarily involve managers in issues of intrapersonal conflict (within a person), interpersonal conflict (between or among individuals), intragroup conflict (within a group), or intergroup conflict (between or among groups). In interorganizational or interagency collaborations, managers become involved in managing conflicts between and among the participating organizations or agencies.

When more than one organization or agency is involved in the implementation of a policy, as is frequently the case, the capability of the implementing organizations to work effectively and collaboratively with each other to carry out implementation responsibilities is highly important to success. Rarely is a health policy implemented by a single organization, and never when the policy is large in scope. The responsibility for implementing the Medicaid program, for example, does not rest entirely with a single organization. It involves the federal CMS working with the Medicaid agencies in each state and with such private-sector organizations as hospitals, nursing homes, and health plans. The successful implementation of the Medicaid program depends heavily on the quality of the interactions among these and other organizations. Even more likely to call collaborative capabilities into play are situations in which several different implementing organizations are required to coordinate and integrate their implementation responsibilities for a variety of policies all intended, in one way or another, to address a particular problem. It is not unusual for a chief executive (president or governor) to direct through an Executive Order, two or more agencies to work collaboratively or to establish a mechanism such as a joint task force to facilitate such collaboration.

The Real World of Health Policy

Executive Order
President's Task Force to Improve Health
Care Delivery for Our Nation's Veterans

By the authority vested in me as President by the Constitution and the laws of the United States of America, including the Federal Advisory Committee Act, as amended (5 U.S.C. App.), and in order to provide prompt and efficient access to consistently high quality health care for veterans who have served the Nation, it is hereby ordered as follows:

Section 1. Establishment. There is established the President's Task Force to Improve Health Care Delivery for Our Nation's Veterans (Task Force).

Sec. 2. Membership. The Task Force shall be comprised of 15 members appointed by the President. Two of the 15 members shall serve as cochairs of the Task Force. The Task Force membership shall include health care experts, officials familiar with Department of Veterans Affairs and Department of Defense health care systems, and representatives from veteran and military service organizations.

Sec. 3. Mission. The mission of the Task Force shall be to:

(a) identify ways to improve benefits and services for Department of Veterans Affairs beneficiaries and Department of Defense military retirees who are also eligible for benefits from the Department of Veterans Affairs through better coordination of the activities of the two departments;

(b) review barriers and challenges that impede Department of Veterans Affairs and Department of Defense coordination, including budgeting processes, timely billing, cost accounting, information technology, and reimbursement. Identify opportunities to improve such business practices to ensure high quality and cost effective health care; and

(c) identify opportunities for improved resource utilization through partnership between the Department of Veterans Affairs and the Department of Defense to maximize the use of resources and infrastructure, including: buildings, information technology and data sharing systems, procurement of supplies, equipment and services, and delivery of care.

Sec. 4. Administration.

(a) The Department of Veterans Affairs shall, to the extent permitted by law, provide administrative support and funding for the Task Force.

(b) Members of the Task Force shall serve without any compensation for their work on the Task Force. Members appointed from among private citizens of the United States, however, while engaged in the work of the Task Force, may be allowed travel expenses, including per diem in lieu of subsistence, as authorized by law for persons serving intermittently in Government service (5 U.S.C. 5701–5707), to the extent funds are available.

(c) The co-chairs of the Task Force shall appoint an Executive Director to coordinate administration of the Task Force. To the extent permitted by law, office space, analytical support, and additional staff support for the Commission shall be provided by executive branch departments and agencies as directed by the President.

(d) The heads of the executive branch departments and agencies shall, to the extent permitted by law, provide the Task Force with information as requested by the co-chairs.

(e) At the call of the co-chairs, the Task Force shall meet as necessary to accomplish its mission.

(f) The functions of the President under the Federal Advisory Committee Act, as amended, except for those in section 6 of that Act, that are applicable to the Task Force, shall be performed by the Department of Veterans Affairs, in accordance with the guidelines that have been issued by the Administrator of General Services.

Sec. 5. Reports. The Task Force shall report its findings and recommendations to the President, through the Secretary of Veterans Affairs and Secretary of Defense. The Task Force shall issue an interim report in 9 months from the date of the first meeting of the Task Force. The

Task Force shall issue a final report prior to the end of the second year of operation.

Sec. 6. Termination. The Task Force shall terminate 30 days after submitting its final report, but no later than 2 years from the date of this order.

GEORGE W. BUSH
THE WHITE HOUSE,
May 28, 2001

Source: Excerpted from Executive Order establishing President's Task Force to Improve Health Care Delivery for Our Nation's Veterans, May 28, 2001, Washington, DC: The White House.

The Managerial Challenges of Policy Implementation

Implementing health policies is often quite challenging. The challenge is managerial in nature: to successfully—within the resource constraints imposed on the agency or organization—carry out the intended purpose of the laws being implemented. Whether it is CMS carrying out the legislative intent and objectives embedded in the Medicare and Medicaid laws, FDA managing the implementation of some of the laws that govern the nation's food supply or the laws that govern pharmaceuticals as part of the nation's pursuit of health, or some other executive branch agency at work, the challenges are frequently substantial.

One way to more fully understand these challenges is to imagine yourself as the person in charge of a complex implementing organization—its manager. For this purpose, we utilize a *hypothetical* scenario to illustrate some of the types of managerial challenges inherent in implementing public policies, as has been done by Levin (1993). The scenario involves implementing a national HIV vaccination program at some future time, when an effective vaccine capable of preventing people from becoming infected with the HIV might be discovered. Although the world still awaits such a vaccine [progress in the development of a vaccine can be monitored through the Office of AIDS Research (OAR) of the National Institutes of Health (NIH) at their web site, www.nih.gov/od/oar/], envision a scenario in which a vaccine has been developed in a laboratory in the United States.

In all likelihood, successful development of this vaccine will trigger a federal policy to immunize the American population against HIV infection. This policy might well take the form of a new public law. Following an expedited FDA approval—a pattern already established in the late 1980s when pressure from those demanding rapid access to new drugs potentially effective in treating AIDS caused the FDA to reconsider its lengthy approval process—the scenario calls for the swift enactment of a federal law. In this scenario, the law sets forth a policy of administering the vaccine to every man, woman, and child in the United States, except those for whom medical exceptions must be made and with consideration to those who might oppose the vaccine on religious grounds. (Incidentally, the latter exemption is likely to raise significant debate within the legislation development phase of this new policy.)

Further complications will arise in developing this legislation because HIV/AIDS is an international issue. There will be pressures to recognize that other parts of the world need the vaccine more urgently than does the United States. Even within the context of its being a worldwide issue, however, when a vaccine becomes available, it is very likely that the United States will enact a law to make it available to the American people. Whatever form the hypothetical new HIV vaccination law takes, its enactment will trigger implementation. An agency or agencies with responsibility for implementation will be designated in the law.

Put yourself in the role of the manager of this agency or interagency effort. The first order of business in implementing the policy will be, as quickly as possible, to complete the first round of rulemaking to guide the implementation of the new policy. Rulemaking, which will be extremely urgent, will also be very complicated and contentious. It is likely that those with rulemaking responsibility will rely, in part, on an expert panel or commission for guidance in establishing rules for implementing this policy.

When rulemaking is complete, the scenario will turn to operationalizing the vaccination policy. People will actually be injected with the vaccine. Those with implementation responsibilities may take some valuable lessons from the nation's experiences with planning in 1976 to implement a policy to vaccinate the American population against the swine flu virus (Silverstein 1981). However, the HIV vaccination policy is likely to be far more extensive than any prior efforts to vaccinate the American population, including the polio vaccination program.

Based at least partly on past experience, some of the problems likely to arise in implementation of the hypothetical HIV vaccination policy can be predicted, as can some aspects of the response of the people with implementation responsibility in the face of these problems. For example, it is reasonable to anticipate that even though the FDA will have approved the vaccine for human use, it perhaps will have done so under extreme pressure and without absolute certainty or agreement either among its own scientific staff or within the larger scientific community concerning the vaccine's safety and effectiveness. This will invite continuing speculation about the vaccine's efficacy and about the wisdom of the entire vaccination policy.

Possible side effects of the vaccine will likely be identified and debated in the scientific community; the debates will probably be substantive because such a vaccine is likely to have some potentially serious negative side effects. Professional judgments will be expressed openly in the media and, because they will not be uniform, the general public will frequently be confused and fearful.

It is predictable that the focus of media attention in the early days of the implementation phase will include the scientific controversy over the vaccine's safety and efficacy, and that media attention will probably extend considerably beyond this issue. The media can be counted on to scrutinize the controversies that will surely arise over the plans for actually distributing the vaccine. For example, an important issue likely to be widely treated in the media is the question of who gets the vaccine first. Widespread discussion and disagreement around this issue can be anticipated. People will have differing opinions about many aspects of this question. Should the vaccine go first to those at highest risk even if their own behaviors place them at risk? Should the first available supplies of the vaccine be concentrated in those geographical locations where HIV has had its most devastating impact, even though that is where the heaviest concentrations of already infected people, people for whom a preventive vaccine is ineffective, are located? Whose ethical values or preferences will guide such operational decisions?

Another implementation problem, almost certain to arise, rests on the fact that in the face of lingering uncertainty about the long-term side effects of the vaccine, its manufacturers will demand to be indemnified from suits that might arise from the use or misuse of the vaccine. Perhaps some of the private practitioners who will help administer the vaccine will seek protection from legal actions as well. Insurance companies that sell liability protection to the vaccine's manufacturers and distributors, as well as insurance companies and health plans that may be required under the vaccination policy to pay for the vaccination of their subscribers or members will have strong interests in the policy and preferences about the way in which it is operated. Addressing their interests and preferences will have been important components of the formulation of this policy, and their interests and preferences will continue to demand attention throughout policy implementation.

Ways in which policy implementers manage problems such as those arising from the scientific controversies over the hypothetical HIV vaccine's safety and efficacy, plans for its distribution within the population, and indemnification for those who manufacture, distribute, and administer it will have a great deal to do with the ultimate success or failure of the HIV vaccination policy. Those operating the policy will either be able to manage the problems effectively or not. Their degree of success or failure will bear directly on the policy's impact. Policies, no matter how appropriate or well conceived, unless they are also well implemented, cannot have the desired impact or outcome. Thus, both the care given to policy formulation and implementation have much to do with a policy's eventual impact.

Summary

The implementation phase of the policymaking process includes rulemaking in support of implementation as well as the actual operation of policies. Rulemaking is a necessary part of policymaking because enacted laws seldom contain enough explicit and directive language concerning the steps necessary to guide their implementation adequately.

Implementing organizations routinely promulgate rules or regulations to help guide the operation of enacted laws. The drafting and issuing of rules are themselves guided by certain rules and established procedures. These help to ensure that those who will be affected by the implementation of a policy will have ample opportunity to participate in the rulemaking associated with its implementation.

The second set of implementation activities involves the actual running of the programs embedded in enacted legislation. These operational activities are largely the domain of the appointees and civil servants who staff the executive branch of government.

Two variables are important to the successful operation of policies. First, the clarity of the policy itself, especially in the embedded hypothesis stating the problem, its solution, and the particular actions directed by the policy, and the inherent language expressing its objectives, have a direct impact on its implementation. Related to this, the level of flexibility permitted the implementing organizations by the construction of a policy directly affects the course of implementation and the outcome for any policy. The second variable influential in the implementation experience for any policy consists of the characteristics and attributes of the organizations with implementation responsibilities and the capabilities of the managers of these organizations.

Discussion Questions

1. Describe, in general terms, the implementation phase of the public policymaking process.
2. Who is responsible for policy implementation?
3. Discuss legislative oversight of policy implementation.
4. What does it mean to characterize policy implementation as public management?
5. Discuss rulemaking. Include the role of interest groups in rulemaking in your response.
6. Describe, in general terms, the operation stage of policy implementation.
7. Discuss the impact of a policy on its own implementation.
8. Discuss the impact of implementing organizations on policy implementation.
9. Discuss the food safety initiative as an example of the role of effective interorganizational relationships among implementing organizations in policy implementation.
10. Discuss the problems that could be expected to arise in implementing an HIV vaccination policy in the future.

References

Burns, J. M. 1978. *Leadership*. New York: Harper & Row.

Derthick, M. 1990. *Agency Under Stress*. Washington, DC: The Brookings Institution.

Feldstein, P. J. 1996. *The Politics of Health Legislation: An Economic Perspective*, 2nd ed. Chicago: Health Administration Press.

Ginsburg, P. B. 1997. "The Dynamics of Market-Level Change." *Journal of Health Politics, Policy and Law* 22 (2): 363–82.

Iglehart, J. K. 1992. "The American Health Care System: Medicare." *New England Journal of Medicine* 327 (20): 1467–72.

Jacobs, L. R. 1993. "Health Reform Impasse: The Politics of American Ambivalence Toward Government." *Journal of Health Politics, Policy and Law* 18 (3): 629–56.

Katz, R. L. 1974. "Skills of an Effective Administrator," *Harvard Business Review* 52 (5): 90–102.

Levin, M. A. 1993. "The Day After an AIDS Vaccine Is Discovered: Management Matters." *Journal of Policy Analysis and Management* 12 (3): 438–55.

McLaughlin, C. P., and A. D. Kaluzny. 1990. "Total Quality Management in Health: Making It Work." *Health Care Management Review* 15 (3): 7–14.

Melnick, R. S. 1994. *Between the Lines: Interpreting Welfare Rights*. Washington, DC: The Brookings Institution.

Moon, M. 1993. *Medicare Now and in the Future*. Washington, DC: Urban Institute.

Morone, J. A. 1990. *The Democratic Wish: Popular Participation and the Limits of American Government.* New York: Basic Books.

Nadel, M. 1995. "Congressional Oversight of Health Policy." In *Intensive Care: How Congress Shapes Health Policy,* edited by T. E. Mann and N. J. Ornstein, 127–42. Washington, DC: American Enterprise Institute and The Brookings Institution.

Silverstein, A. M. 1981. *Pure Politics and Impure Science.* Baltimore, MD: The Johns Hopkins University Press.

Thompson, F. J. 1997. "The Evolving Challenge of Health Policy Implementation." In *Health Politics and Policy,* 3rd ed., edited by T. J. Litman and L. S. Robins, 155–75. Albany, NY: Delmar Publishers.

U.S. Department of Justice and the Federal Trade Commission. 1996. *Statements of Antitrust Enforcement Policy in Health Care.* Washington, DC: U.S. DOJ and FTC.

Waldo, D. 1980. *The Enterprise of Public Administration.* Novato, CA: Chandler and Sharp.

Zuckerman, H. S., and W. L. Dowling. 1997. "The Managerial Role." In *Essentials of Health Care Management,* edited by S. M. Shortell and A. D. Kaluzny, 34–62. Albany, NY: Delmar Publishers.

Zwick, D. I. 1978. "Initial Development of Guidelines for Health Planning." *Public Health Reports* 93 (5): 407–20.

7

POLICY MODIFICATION

POLICYMAKING IS not a perfect process. Mistakes of omission and commission are routinely made in both the formulating and implementing phases of public policymaking. The model of the policymaking process described throughout this book comes full cycle because of a third phase of the process, modification. This phase is a necessary part of policymaking because perfection eludes policymakers in the formulation and implementation phases. Even when decisions about policies are correct at the time they are made, things change. Suitable policies made in one era may lose some of their usefulness or become totally inadequate with subsequent changes in biological, cultural, demographic, ecological, economic, ethical, legal, psychological, social, and technological variables.

In a policymaking process without a modification phase, policies would be formulated in their original version, and then implemented, and that would be the end of the process—except, of course, for consequences of the policies. In practice, however, policymaking does not work this way. The consequences of policies, including consequences for those who formulate and implement the policies, as well as for the individuals, organizations, and interest groups outside the process but affected by them, cause people to seek to modify existing policies. This occurs continually in the process.

At a minimum, modification of policies that provide benefits to certain individuals, organizations, or interest groups may be sought because modifications that increase, maintain, or do not decrease, these benefits over time are desirable to beneficiaries. To the contrary, those affected by policies in a negative way will seek to modify them in order to minimize the negative consequences. In addition, when the policymakers who formulate and implement public policies observe them in operation, they may evaluate a particular policy against their objectives for that policy. When preferences and reality do not match, efforts to modify the policy typically ensue.

Almost all policies have histories. They are formulated in their initial version; then evolve and change over time as they are implemented, either through amendments to the original legislation or through new or revised rules and changes in how they are operated. Some policies eventually die—they are repealed by the legislative branch—but most have long and dynamic lives during which they are continually and routinely modified in various ways. This chapter addresses the policy modification phase of public policymaking (see the shaded portion of Figure 7.1), beginning with drawing a distinction between policy initiation and policy modification.

Distinguishing Policy Modification from Policy Initiation

Conceptually, policy *modification* can be differentiated from policy *initiation*, although in reality the two are closely intertwined. Policy initiation—the establishment of an original public law—results when the confluence of problems, possible solutions, and political circumstances lead to the initial development of legislation in the formulation phase (as described in chapters 4 and 5) and, when enacted into public law, then to subsequent first iterations of rulemaking and operation as the law is implemented, as described in chapter 6. In contrast, policy modification results when the consequences of existing policies feed back into the agenda-setting and legislation-development stages of the formulation phase and into the rulemaking and operational stages of the implementation phase and stimulate changes in legislation, rules, or operations. This is shown as the feedback loop in Figure 7.1. Examine the loop closely, noting that it feeds back into the overall process in several places.

The history of American health policy demonstrates clearly that policymakers can, and on occasion do, initiate entirely new policies. For example, in 1798 Congress established the U.S. Marine Hospital Service to provide medical care for sick and disabled seamen. This was the initial policy from which eventually grew the U.S. Public Health Service. In 1921 Congress enacted the initial Maternity and Infancy Act (P.L. 67-97) through which grants were made to states to encourage them to

Figure 7.1 A Model of the Public Policymaking Process in the United States: Policy Modification Phase

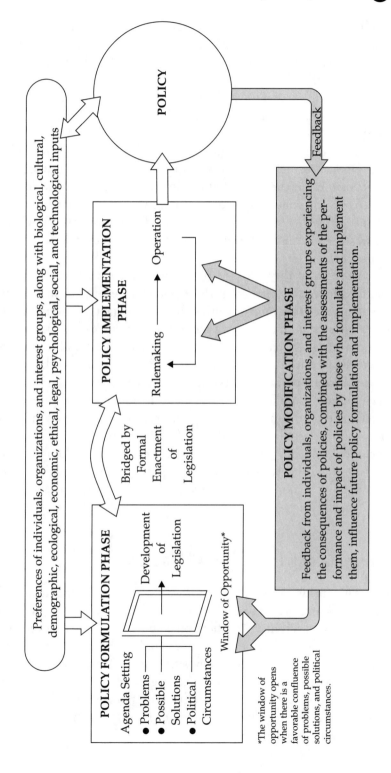

develop health services for mothers and children. This new policy became the prototype for federal grants-in-aid to the states. In 1935 Congress enacted the Social Security Act (P.L. 74-271), which initiated the major entrance of the federal government into the area of social insurance. This policy, through a long life during which it has been modified many times, now encompasses, among many other things, the Medicare and Medicaid programs.

As these examples illustrate, some health policies are indeed formulated and implemented *de novo*. But a very important feature of health policymaking in the United States is that the vast majority of contemporary health policies spring from relatively few earlier initial policies. *Most health policies are the result of modifying prior policies.* This is why understanding the modification phase of the policymaking process is so important.

A review of the chronology of important American health policies, such as the one contained in the Appendix, readily illustrates just how frequently contemporary health policies are in fact amendments of previously enacted public laws, or how frequently they result from changes— often, a string of changes—in the rules and practices that determine how laws are currently being implemented. Few decisions in the policymaking process are permanent. None of the authoritative decisions that have been defined as policies are permanent. Modification of prior policies— whether in the form of decisions representing public laws, implementation rules or regulations, rulings of a court, or operational practices— pervades the entire policymaking process. The likelihood that prior decisions will be revisited and changed is a distinguishing feature of public policymaking in the Untied States. It is the feature that makes policymaking a cyclical process.

Policymaking Is a Cyclical Process

Careful consideration of the modification phase of policymaking is fundamentally important to understanding the process as a continual cycle of interrelated activity. Modification is routinely triggered when the consequences of enacted and implemented policies impact on those affected. Whether the consequences are positive or negative, these consequences will stimulate efforts to modify existing policies. Beneficiaries will seek changes that give them more benefits or that protect existing ones. Those who are affected negatively will seek to modify policies and thus reduce their negative consequences.

The Real World of Health Policy

Testimony
Beatrice Braun, M.D.
American Association of Retired Persons Board Member
Before the
House of Representative Committee on Energy and Commerce
Subcommittee on Health
May 16, 2001
The Need for a Medicare Prescription Drug Benefit

I am Beatrice Braun from Spring Hill, Florida and a member of AARP's Board of Directors. Thank you for the opportunity to discuss with you today the need for a prescription drug benefit in Medicare.

The Medicare program has been, is, and will likely remain the nation's principal source of health benefits and a key source of financial protection for older Americans and those with disabilities. The program also provides financial protection for the families of Medicare beneficiaries, and it further serves younger Americans with its guarantee of future protection as they plan their retirements. In addition, Medicare is a strong and stable underpinning of the financing of our nation's health care system.

As we examine approaches to updating Medicare, it is essential that we modernize the Medicare benefit package. In particular, it is time to add an outpatient prescription drug benefit in recognition of the changing health care technology that has made prescription drugs an increasingly important—now central—component of modern medical care. A prescription drug benefit in Medicare would improve the quality of health care received by millions of older Americans. It could reduce unnecessary hospitalizations and shorten nursing homestays. A well-managed benefit also offers the potential to reduce the risks of drug interactions and polypharmacy by helping to assure that beneficiaries are taking the right medications in the correct dosages. It makes no more sense to have a Medicare program today without prescription drug coverage than it would to have a program that excludes inpatient hospital or physician coverage.

Background

Medicare today—while the centerpiece of health benefits protection for retirees and those with disabilities—covers only about half of the health spending of older Americans. Further, Medicare beneficiaries spend a significant share of their income on health care. In 2000, out-of-pocket costs for older beneficiaries averaged $2,580 or 19 percent of their income. While Social Security and Medicare have done a wonderful job in assuring a floor of income support and financial protection for older Americans, the fact remains that increasing health costs for older individuals coupled with lower incomes in their retirement years often makes the costs of uncovered benefits unaffordable.

* * *

Over the last two decades, the lack of prescription drug coverage has become a critical gap in the Medicare program as modern medicine has turned increasingly to drug treatments. Our nation's long-term investment in biomedical research has yielded enormous scientific progress—and the recent budgetary commitment to doubling the NIH budget highlights our intent to continue that progress. Those investments, coupled with the pharmaceutical industry's spending on research and development, have yielded an array of medications that could not have been even imagined when Medicare was enacted in 1965.

* * *

The coverage gap in Medicare is clear. Medicare is the basic health plan for the population that is most in need of these new tools of modern medicine, but it does not cover prescription drugs. For current and future Medicare beneficiaries a prescription drug benefit would improve the quality of their health care and even their quality of life.

Source: © 2001, AARP. Reprinted with permission.

Those who formulate and implement policies when they think the performance of policies does not measure up will also seek modifications. Although there is typically a very strong affinity for incremental changes in policies, both among those who formulate and implement them and those affected by them, there is nevertheless a relentless pressure for the modification of policies.

As described in this chapter, there are many places in the policymaking process where pressure to modify is exerted. The existence of its modification phase makes the public policymaking process both dynamic and continuously evolving. Decisions within the cycle of the process are always subject to further review and revision. Policy modifications—large and small—emphasize that the separate components of the policymaking process are, in reality, highly interactive and interdependent.

Incrementalism in Policymaking

Not only are most public policies in all domains, including health, modifications of previously established policies, most of the modifications reflect only rather modest changes (Hinckley 1983). The combination of a process that is characterized by continual modification of previous decisions with the fact that these changes tend to be rather modest has led to the very apt characterization of the public policymaking process in the United States as a process of incrementalism (Lindblom 1969, 1992).

The affinity for modest, incremental change in public policy is not in any way restricted to health policy. The operation of the nation's overall political, social, and economic systems reflect preferences for modest rather than fundamental change. As was noted in the discussion of the subject in chapter 3, members of the power elite in America have a very strong preference for incremental changes in public policies. They see incrementalism in policymaking—building on existing policies by modification in small incremental steps—as allowing time for the economic and social systems to adjust without these systems being unduly threatened by change. Incremental policymaking permits a minimum of economic dislocation or disruption and causes minimal alteration in the social system's status quo.

In policymaking that is characterized by incrementalism, significant departures from the existing patterns of policies occur only rarely; instead, most of the time, the impacts and consequences of policies play out relatively slowly and with some degree of predictability. This accounts for the fact that the major participants in the policymaking process—policymakers in all three branches of government; leaders in health-related organizations and interest groups; as well as many individuals who benefit from such policies as the Medicare and Medicaid programs—typically have strong preferences for incrementalism in health policymaking.

The preference rests simply and firmly on the fact that the results and consequences of incrementally made decisions are more predictable and stable than is the case with less incrementally made decisions. Unless a person—whether a policymaker or one affected by policies—is very unhappy with a situation and wishes an immediate and drastic change, the preference for incrementalism will almost always prevail. Furthermore, in a democracy it matters little whose preferences will shape policy if some are in fact very unhappy, so long as the majority is not.

Incrementalism in policymaking also provides a mechanism through which the likelihood of compromises being reached is enhanced among the diverse interests within the political marketplace where policymaking occurs. The potential for compromise is an important feature of a smoothly working policymaking process. When some people hear words like incrementalism and compromise used in the context of public policymaking, they envision compromised principles, inappropriate influence peddling, and corrupt deals made behind closed doors. But, positively, "In a democracy compromise is not merely unavoidable; it is a source of creative invention, sometimes generating solutions that unexpectedly combine seemingly opposed ideas" (Starr and Zelman 1993, 8).

The health policy domain is replete with examples of patterns of incrementally developed policies. For instance, the history of the evolution of the National Institutes of Health (NIH) (www.nih.gov) vividly reflects incremental policymaking over a span of more than 100 years. Beginning in 1887, with the federal government's total expenditures on biomedical research of about $300 and extending into the 1930s when a small federal laboratory conducting biomedical research was initiated, the NIH has experienced extensive elaboration (i.e., the addition of new institutes as biomedical science evolved); growth (i.e., its annual budget was more than $20.3 billion in 2001); and shifts in the emphases of its research agenda (e.g., cancer, AIDS, women's health, and health disparities). Every step in its continuing and incremental evolution has been guided by specific changes in policies, each one an incremental modification intended to have the NIH make carefully measured adjustments in its actions, decisions, and behaviors.

The Mechanics of the Modification Phase

The policymaking process provides abundant opportunities for the consequences that result from the formulation and implementation of public laws to influence the reformulation of future iterations, as well as to change the rules and operational practices that guide their implementation. As the feedback arrows contained in Figure 7.1 illustrate, policies can be modified at four points in the policymaking process: in both the agenda setting and legislation development that occurs in the formulation phase and in the rulemaking and operations that occur in the implementation phase. Modification at each of these points in the overall process is discussed in the following sections.

Modification in the Policy Formulation Phase

Modification of policies in the formulation phase—in effect, the reformulation of existing policies—occurs in both agenda setting and legislation development. Recall from the discussion in chapters 4 and 5 that policy formulation—making the decisions that result in public laws—entails these two distinct and sequentially related sets of activities in which policymakers, and those who would influence their decisions and actions, engage. The result of the formulation phase of policymaking, for initial versions of policies, is policy in the form of new public laws; for subsequent revisions, the result is amendments to existing laws.

Both initial public laws and the subsequent amendments to them that pertain to health stem from the interactions of (1) diverse arrays of health-related problems, (2) possible solutions to the problems, and (3) dynamic political circumstances that relate both to the problems as well as to their potential solutions. The amendment of previously enacted public laws occurs through the process of legislation development just as does the creation of an entirely new legislative proposal. The only significant difference is that the possibility of amendment implies the existence of a particular prior public law that can now be changed through amendments. This previously enacted legislation already has a developmental history and an implementation experience, both of which can influence its amendment.

Modification at Agenda Setting

Remember that agenda setting involves the confluence of problems, possible solutions, and political circumstances. Policy modification routinely begins in this stage of activity as problems already receiving attention become more sharply defined and better understood within the context of the ongoing implementation of existing policies. Possible solutions to problems can be assessed and clarified within the same context, especially when operational experience and the results of demonstrations and evaluations provide concrete evidence of the performance of particular potential solutions under consideration. In addition, the interactions among the branches of government and the health-related organizations and interest groups involved with and affected by ongoing policies become important components of the political circumstances surrounding their reformulation, as well as of the initial formulation of future new policies. People learn from their experiences with policies, and those in positions to do so may act on what they learn.

Leaders in health-related organizations and interest groups, by virtue of their keen interest in certain health policies—interest driven by the fact that they, and their organizations and groups, directly experience the consequences of these policies—may be well positioned to serve as sentinels regarding whether particular policies are having the effects desired by those who formulated and implemented them. Because of their positions, they may be among the first to observe the need to modify a policy, and they can use their experience to help policymakers better define or document problems that led to the original policy. These leaders can gather, catalog, and correlate facts that more accurately depict the actual state of a problem and can then share this information with policymakers.

Similarly, these leaders are well positioned to observe the impact and actual consequences of a hoped-for solution to a problem—a solution in the form of a policy. Possible new solutions or alterations to existing ones can be devised and assessed through the operational experience of the organizations and groups they lead. Finally, their experiences with ongoing policies may become a basis for their attempts to change the political circumstances involved in a particular situation. When the confluence of problems, possible solutions, and political circumstances that led to an original policy are altered, a new window of opportunity may open—this time, permitting the amendment of previously enacted legislation.

Modification at Legislation Development

Health policies in the form of public laws are routinely amended, some of them repeatedly and over a span of many years. Such amendments reflect, among other things, the emergence of new medical technologies, changing federal budgetary conditions, and varying beneficiary demands. These and other stimuli for change often gain the attention of policymakers through the routine activities and reporting mechanisms that occur in the implementation of policies. Pressure to modify policy through changes in existing public laws may also emanate from the leaders of health-related organizations and interest groups—including those that represent individual memberships—who feel the policy consequences. When modifications do occur at the legislation development point in the process, they follow the same set of procedures as the original legislative proposals or bills (steps that were discussed fully in chapter 5).

In some instances, the impetus to modify an existing law arises from changes in another law. For example, policies intended to reduce the federal budget deficit have typically impinged on other policies, often causing their modification. Implementation of the Deficit Reduction Act of 1984 (P.L. 98-369) required a temporary freeze on physicians' fees paid under the Medicare program; and implementation of the Emergency Deficit Reduction and Balanced Budget Act of 1985 (P.L. 99-177), also known as the Gramm-Rudman-Hollins Act, required budget cuts in defense and in certain domestic programs, including a number of health programs.

Modification in the Policy Implementation Phase

Modification of policies in the implementation phase occurs in both rule-making and in the operation of policies. Recall from the discussion in chapter 6 that policy implementation entails these two distinct and sequentially related sets of activities in which policymakers, and those who would influence their decisions and actions, engage. Feedback from the consequences of formulated and implemented policies can also stimulate the modification of policies in the implementation phase, at both the rulemaking point in the process and in the operation of policies, and often at both points concurrently.

Modification at Rulemaking

As noted in chapter 6, rulemaking is a necessary precursor to the operation and full implementation of new public laws because enacted legislation rarely contains enough explicit and directive language to completely guide implementation of the legislation. Newly enacted policies are often vague on implementation details, usually purposely so, leaving it to the implementing organizations to promulgate the rules needed to guide the operation of the policies. Beyond this, one of the most frequently used ways in which existing policies are modified is through changes in the rules or regulations used to guide their implementation.

The practice of using rulemaking to modify policies by updating or changing features of their implementation pervades policymaking. As discussed in chapter 6, rules promulgated by executive branch agencies and departments to guide policy implementation have the force of law. The rules themselves are policies. As implementation occurs, rulemaking becomes a means to modify policies and their implementation over time. In the process, rulemaking creates new policies. Changed rules are modified policies.

Modification in Operation

Policy operation, as discussed in chapter 6, involves the actual running of the programs embedded in public laws. The operational stage of a policy is primarily a responsibility of the appointees and civil servants who staff the government, particularly those who manage the departments and agencies with policy implementation responsibilities. The managers responsible for operating a public law have significant opportunities to modify the policy—especially in terms of its impact on and consequences for those affected by the law—through the manner in which they manage its operation.

Policies implemented by managers who are committed to the objectives of the policies and who have the talent and resources available to vigorously implement them are qualitatively different from policies operated by managers who are not committed to their objectives or who lack adequate talent and resources to achieve full and effective implementation. Modification of policies through changes in the way they are implemented is a routine occurrence in the ongoing policymaking process.

Two principal sources of stimulus for modification exist—one internal and the other external—in the operation of policies. Internally, the managers responsible for operating policies approach the task in ways that are similar to the ways of managers in all settings; that is, they seek to *control* the results of their operations. To accomplish this, they establish standards or operating objectives (e.g., to serve so many clients per day, to process so many reports in a quarter, to distribute benefits to certain categories of beneficiaries, to assess compliance with certain regulations by so many firms); operations ensue; results are monitored; and changes are made in operations, objectives, or both, when results do not measure up to the predetermined standards (Longest 1996). Such routine operational modifications are inherent in the implementation phase of any policy. They are part of the daily work that occurs within organizations that implement health policies.

In addition to the internal pressures to modify policy operation, there are external pressures as well. These pressures for change in the operation of a health policy are exerted by the individuals and especially by health-related organizations and interest groups that experience the consequences of implemented policies. As noted above, all of those who feel the consequences of policies are likely to seek to modify them. One avenue open to them, and one of the key points at which they can exert pressure for the modification of policies in their operational stages, is the opportunity to influence the modification of policies through influencing those who manage their operation.

These opportunities for policy modification arise within the working relationships—sometimes close working relationships—that can be developed between those responsible for implementing public policies and those whom their decisions and activities directly affect. The opportunities to build these relationships are supported by a prominent feature of the careers of bureaucrats: longevity (Kingdon 1995). Elected policymakers come and go, but the bureaucracy endures. Leaders of health-related organizations and interest groups can, and many do, build long-standing working relationships with some of the people responsible for implementing the public policies that are of strategic importance to these organizations and groups.

The most solid base for these working relationships is the exchange of useful information and expertise. The leader of a health-related organization or interest group, speaking from an authoritative position with relevant information based on actual operational experience with the implementation of a policy, can influence the policy's further implementation. If the information supports change, especially if it is buttressed with similar information from others who are experiencing the impact of a particular policy, reasonable implementers may well be influenced to make needed changes. This is especially likely if there is a well-established working relationship, one based on mutual respect for the roles of and the challenges facing each party.

Sometimes the relationships between those who feel the consequences of policies, usually operating through their interest groups, and those responsible for implementing policies important to them, are expanded to include members of the legislative committees or subcommittees with jurisdiction over the policies. This triad of mutual interests forms what has been termed an iron triangle, so called because the interests of the three parts of the triangle "dovetail nicely and because they are alleged to be impenetrable from the outside and uncontrollable by president, political appointees, or legislators not on the committees in question" (Kingdon 1995, 33). As discussed in chapter 3, however, the widely divergent interests of so many organizations and groups, coupled with their increasing presence in the policymaking arena, have made the formation of solid triangles more difficult, and rarer in the health policy domain.

An obvious, and very limiting, problem for those who wish to modify health policies through influencing their operation, as well as the rulemaking that precedes operation, is the sheer enormity of the bureaucracy with which they might need to interact. Consider the enormous number of components of the federal government, with relevance to health policy, that are involved in rulemaking and policy operation. To these components can be added the relevant units of state and local government. Taken all together, the huge challenge of simply keeping track of where working relationships might be useful as a means of modifying policy through influencing policymakers in the implementation phase—to say nothing of actually developing and maintaining the relationships—begins to come into focus. Obviously, selectivity in which of these relationships might be of most strategic importance is necessary.

Modification Through the Cyclical Relationship Between Rulemaking and Operation.

An important aspect of policy modification within the implementation phase of the process is represented by the feedback loop shown between rulemaking and operation in Figure 7.1. As discussed in chapter 6, there is a cyclical relationship between rulemaking and the operational activities involved with a public law's implementation. Although rulemaking precedes operation in the sequence of these activities, the experiences gained in operations feed back into rulemaking.

This cyclical relationship is quite important. It means that experience gained with the operation of policies can influence the modification of rules or regulations subsequently used in their operation. Practically, this means that the rules and regulations promulgated to implement policies undergo revision—sometimes the revision is extensive and continual—and that new rules can be adopted as experience dictates. This feature of policymaking is an important aspect of the continual modification of policy.

The Real World of Health Policy

Implementing the Medicare PPS

The Social Security Amendments of 1983 (P.L. 98-21) initiated the Medicare prospective payment system (PPS) through which hospitals are paid predetermined rates per discharge for diagnosis-related groups (DRGs). Among the provisions of these amendments was one directing the Secretary of DHHS to provide for additional payments to hospitals for certain atypical cases. These so-called "outlier" cases were specified in the legislation to include cases in which the length of stay exceeded the mean for the DRG by a fixed number of days or a fixed number of standard deviations, whichever was fewer; or in which the length-of-stay criterion was not exceeded, but the hospital's adjusted costs for the case exceeded a fixed multiple of the DRG rate, or some other fixed dollar amount, whichever was greater (U.S. Congress 1992).

This change in Medicare policy left the Secretary of DHHS considerable flexibility in establishing exactly what would constitute either a "day" or a "cost" outlier by how the DHHS's administrators wrote these implementing rules. In part, the rules were to reflect the operating experience as the PPS was implemented. The rules promulgated over the years by the DHHS in its implementation of the outlier payment provision of P.L. 98-21 illustrate just how powerful a modifying force rulemaking can be and how the operation of a policy influences and affects rulemaking in a cyclical manner.

The rules established for 1984, the first year of operation for the PPS, defined a day outlier case as one for which the length of stay exceeded the average length of stay for a particular DRG by the lesser of 20 days or 1.94 standard deviations. It defined a cost outlier case to be one in which the hospital's adjusted costs exceeded the greater of 1.5 times the payment amount for the DRG or $12,000. New rules in 1985, reflecting operational realities, modified the outlier thresholds for both day and cost outlier cases. An especially important modification in 1986, based on experience with operating the PPS, pertained to the establishment of rules directing different urban and rural outlier payments. Rule changes in 1988 modified the thresholds again, defining a day outlier as 24 days, or 3 standard deviations above the DRG average, and a cost outlier as $28,000, or 2 times the DRG rate. The rules for 1990 again modified the outlier thresholds, increasing the threshold for day outliers to 28 days, or 3 standard deviations and for cost outliers, to $34,000, or 2 times the DRG rate. The pattern of thresholds being modified through rulemaking that reflects operating experience continues apace. Rules for 1998, established to implement provisions in the Balanced Budget Act of 1997 (P.L. 105-33), called for no further payments for day outliers and set the cost outlier payments very stringently. The rule for 2000, which can be read at www.cms.gov/medicare/ippsmain, the web site maintained to provide rules and proposed rules for PPS, read as follows: "To qualify as a cost outlier in FY 2000, a hospital's charges for a case, adjusted to cost, must exceed the payment rate for the DRG by $14,050. The additional payment amount is equal to 80 percent of the difference between the hospital's entire cost for the stay and the threshold amount."

Policy Modification in Practice

As described in the foregoing sections, modification of previous decisions is possible at many points in the policymaking process. Modification of previous decisions characterizes the process. The modification phenomenon can be vividly seen, for example, in the legislative history of the Medicare program. Policy modification, in both policy formulation and implementation, pervades and is clearly reflected in this program's legislative history. Over the program's life, numerous changes have been made; each change reflecting an instance of policy modification.

Following the feedback loop shown in Figure 7.1, it can be seen that because agenda setting involves the confluence of problems, possible solutions, and political circumstances, policy modification can occur at this stage in a number of ways. As problems become more sharply defined and better understood through the actual experiences of those who feel the consequences of policies, modifications can be triggered.

The individuals and health-related organizations and interest groups that are affected by policies are often the best sources of feedback on their consequences. Similarly, possible new solutions to problems can be conceived and assessed through the operational experiences, especially of the organizations and groups who are affected by particular policies. Their impact and influence is increased when the results of demonstrations and evaluations provide concrete evidence of the performance of particular solutions that are under consideration. Finally, the interactions among the branches of government and those who experience the consequences of ongoing policies become important elements in the political circumstances surrounding the amendment of these policies.

The consequences that flow from the ongoing policymaking process also help modify policies by directly influencing the development of legislation. Actual experience with the impact of the implementation of policies that affect their organizations and groups guide their leaders in routinely identifying needed policy modifications. The inputs of those most affected by the Medicare policy—both as beneficiaries and providers of health services—played a role in each of these amendments to the original legislation, although other influences—most notably, budget considerations—also persistently helped guide these changes.

Those who experience the consequences of policies also have extensive opportunities to influence the modification of policies in their implementation phases, both in the rulemaking and the operational stages. The modification of rules, as well as changes in the operations undertaken to implement policies, often reflect the actual reported or documented experiences of those affected by the rules and operations. Individuals, and especially organizations and interest groups affected by rules, can provide feedback on their impact directly to those with rulemaking or operational responsibilities. They can also take their views on the rules and operational practices that affect them to the courts or the legislative branch. Both can also be pathways to modifications.

The Real World of Health Policy

Modifications in Medicare Policy

Imbedded in the chronology of Medicare-related legislation are many examples of how the modification phase of public policymaking plays out. The chronology of this legislation begins with the enactment of a new policy, the 1935 Social Security Act (P.L. 74-271); but from that point forward the emergence and continuation of the Medicare program is largely a matter of modifying previous policies.

The program emerged on the nation's policy agenda, in large part, through the operation of the Social Security program over a span of three decades, from the mid-1930s to the mid-1960s. President Franklin D. Roosevelt formed a Committee on Economic Security in 1934 and charged its members to develop a program that could ensure the "economic security" of the nation's citizens. The committee considered the inclusion of health insurance as part of the Social Security program from the outset. There was, in fact, strong sentiment for its inclusion among members of the committee (Starr 1982). But in the end they decided not to recommend the inclusion of health insurance because of the tremendous political burdens associated with such a proposal. The AMA, in particular, strongly opposed the concept (Peterson 1993).

As reflected in the original legislation, the objective embedded in the Social Security Act of 1935 was

> . . . to provide for the general welfare by establishing a system of federal old age benefits, and by enabling the several States to make more adequate provision for aged persons, blind persons, dependent and crippled children, maternal and child welfare, public health, and the administration of their unemployment compensation laws. . . .

Although health insurance was not included among the program's original provisions, its addition was considered from time to time in the ensuing years. President Harry S. Truman considered national health insurance a key part of his legislative agenda (Altmeyer 1968). But the AMA's continued powerful opposition and the necessity for the Truman administration to divert its attention to Korea in 1950 meant that President Truman was unable to stimulate the development and enactment of any sort of universal health insurance policy. Faced with dim political prospects for universal health insurance, proponents turned to a much more limited idea—hospital insurance for the aged.

Following a number of rather modest proposals for such insurance, none of which could muster the necessary political support for enactment, two powerful members of the Congress, Senator Robert Kerr (D-Okla.) and Representative Wilbur Mills (D-Ark.), were able to see through to passage a bill that provided federal support for states' programs in welfare medicine. The Amendments to the Social Security Act of 1960 (P.L. 86-778) provided health benefits to the aged, although only to those who were poor. Not until the Democratic margin in Congress was significantly increased in President Lyndon B. Johnson's landslide election in 1964 did anything more expansive have much chance of passing.

With the 1964 election significantly improving Medicare's prospects for passage, it received a very high priority among President Johnson's Great Society programs, and was enacted as part of the Social Security Amendments of 1965 (P.L. 89-97). Medicare did indeed emerge on the nation's policy agenda through a series of attempts to modify the original Social Security Act by expanding the benefits provided to include health insurance. Although these attempts at modifying the original Social Security Act failed more often than not, they set the stage for the eventual modification that resulted in the Medicare program. As Peterson has noted, "The (policy) choices of one period are intimately linked to the choices grasped or missed in a previous era" (1997, 292).

After the original enactment of the legislation establishing the Medicare program, the chronology of related legislation shows a remarkable pattern of the evolutionary, incremental modification of a single, although massive, public policy. In a progression of modifications that continue today, among other changes, services for Medicare beneficiaries have been added and deleted; premiums and copayment provisions have been changed; reimbursement rates and payment mechanisms for service providers have been changed; and features to ensure quality and medical necessity of services have been added, changed, and deleted.

The legislative chronology of the Medicare program reflects significant legislative change from year to year, a pattern likely to continue so long as this complex and expensive [Medicare covers about 38 million people at an annual expenditure in 2001 of about $200 billion (www.cms.gov)] program exists. The pattern of modifications exhibited in the Medicare legislation, chronicled in the next pages, has been heavily influenced by ongoing experience with the implementation of the original legislation and its subsequent modifications. Parts of the legislative chronology presented parallels the list of Medicare-related legislation shown in chapter 5 in the section on "Health Policy in Federal Budget Legislation." The list presented here, however, is much more extensive and encompassing because it captures the full range of Medicare-related legislation from the Social Security program's inception in 1935 through to the present day. As such, this list illustrates how Medicare policy has been modified extensively over the course of the program's life and serves to emphasize the role the modification phase plays in the overall policymaking process.

- *1935: Social Security Act (P.L. 74-271).* This landmark legislation, enacted during the Great Depression, initiated the expansion of the federal government's central role in the domain of social insurance. Importantly, for the future of federal health policy, it included provisions through which the federal government made grants-in-aid to states for the support of programs for the needy elderly, dependent children, and the blind. Over the years, a number of amendments were made to the act, including the amendments of 1960 (P.L. 86-778), known as the Kerr-Mills Act, which established a new program for medical assistance for the aged.

- *1965: Social Security Amendments (P.L. 89-97)*. This legislation provided health insurance for the aged through Title 18 (Medicare) and provided grants to the states for medical assistance programs for the poor through Title 19 (Medicaid).

  Part A of Medicare provided hospital insurance benefits intended to protect beneficiaries against certain costs of hospital and related posthospital services. These benefits were financed by an increase in the Social Security earnings tax (payroll tax). Part B of Medicare provided supplemental medical insurance benefits intended to protect beneficiaries from the costs of certain physician services, laboratory tests, supplies, and equipment, as well as certain home health services. These benefits were financed by voluntary premium payments from those who chose to enroll, matched by payments from general revenues.[1]

- *1967: Social Security Amendments (P.L. 90-248)*. The first modifications, coming two years after the Medicare program's establishment, featured expanded coverage for such things as durable medical equipment for use in the home, podiatrist services for nonroutine foot care, and outpatient physical therapy under Part B, and the addition of a lifetime reserve of 60 days of coverage for inpatient hospital care over and above the original coverage for up to 90 days during any spell of illness.

  In addition, certain payment rules were modified in favor of providers. For example, payment of full reasonable charges for radiologists' and pathologists' services provided to inpatients were authorized under one modification.

- *1972: Social Security Amendments (P.L. 92-603)*. Although, in part, these changes continued the pattern of program expansions started in the 1967 modifications, they marked an important shift to some policy modifications that were intended specifically to help control the growing costs of the Medicare program. Among the most important of the 1972 modifications was the establishment of Professional Standards Review Organizations (PSROs), which were to monitor both the quality of services provided to Medicare beneficiaries as well as the medical necessity for the services.

---

1 Rich histories of the events leading up to the enactment of these amendments have been written by Marmor (1973) and Feder (1977). Such histories document the often rancorous political debates and philosophical differences that preceded the 1965 legislation. This history is not repeated here because the focus is primarily on the pattern of modifications made in the Medicare policy after its enactment as an example of the modification phase of policymaking.

Another modification aimed at cost containment was the addition of a provision to limit payments for capital expenditures by hospitals that had been disapproved by state or local planning agencies. Still another was the authorization of grants and contracts to conduct experiments and demonstrations related to achieving increased economy and efficiency in the provision of health services. Some of the specifically targeted areas of these studies included prospective reimbursement, the requirement that patients spend three days in the hospital prior to admission to a skilled nursing home, the potential benefits of ambulatory surgery centers, payment for the services of physician assistants and nurse practitioners, and the use of clinical psychologists.

At the same time that these and other cost-containment modifications were made in the Medicare policy, a number of cost-increasing changes were also made. Notably, persons who were eligible for cash benefits under the disability provisions of the Social Security Act for at least 24 months were made eligible for medical benefits under the Medicare program. In addition, those who were insured under Social Security, as well as their dependents, who required hemodialysis or renal transplantation for chronic renal disease were defined as disabled for the purpose of having them covered under the Medicare program for the costs of treating their end-stage renal disease (ESRD). The inclusion of coverage for the disabled and ESRD patients in 1972 represented extraordinarily expensive modifications of the Medicare program. In addition, certain less costly but still expensive additional coverages were extended, including chiropractic services and speech pathology services.

- *1976–1977: A major reorganization of the U.S. Department of Health, Education, and Welfare (now the U.S. Department of Health and Human Services).* Although not technically a modification of the Medicare policy, this reorganization resulted in the establishment of the Health Care Financing Administration (HCFA), an agency within DHEW (now DHHS) that assumed primary responsibility for implementation of the Medicare and Medicaid programs. This new agency combined functions that had been located in the Bureau of Health Insurance of the Social Security Administration (Medicare) and in the Medical Services Administration of the Social and Rehabilitation Service (Medicaid), among others.
- *1977: Rural Health Clinic Services Amendments (P.L. 95-210).* This legislation modified the categories of practitioners who could provide reimbursable services to Medicare beneficiaries, at least in rural settings. Under the provisions of this act, rural health clinics that did not routinely have physicians available on site could, if they met certain requirements regarding physician supervision of the clinic and review of services, be reimbursed for services provided by nurse prac-

titioners and physician assistants through the Medicare and Medicaid programs. This act also authorized certain demonstration projects in underserved urban areas for reimbursement of these nonphysician practitioners.

- *1977: Medicare-Medicaid Antifraud and Abuse Amendments (P.L. 95-142)*. These modifications were intended to reduce fraud and abuse in both the Medicare and Medicaid programs and thereby help contain their costs. Specific changes included strengthening criminal and civil penalties for fraud and abuse affecting the programs, modification in the operations of the PSROs, and the promulgation of uniform reporting systems and formats for hospitals and certain other healthcare organizations participating in the Medicare and Medicaid programs.

- *1978: Medicare End-Stage Renal Disease Amendments (P.L. 95-292)*. Since the addition of coverage for ESRD under the Social Security Amendments of 1972 (P.L. 92-603), the costs to the Medicare program had risen steadily and quickly. These amendments sought to help control the program's costs. One modification added incentives to encourage the use of home dialysis and the use of renal transplantation in ESRD. Another modification permitted the use of a variety of reimbursement methods for renal dialysis facilities. Still another modification authorized studies of ESRD itself, especially studies incorporating possible cost reductions in treatment for this disease and authorized the Secretary of DHEW (now DHHS) to establish areawide network coordinating councils to help plan for and review ESRD programs.

- *1980: Omnibus Budget Reconciliation Act, or OBRA '80, (P.L. 96-499)*. Extensive modifications of Medicare and Medicaid policy were made in this legislation. Fifty-seven separate sections pertained to one or both of the programs. Many of the changes reflected continuing concern with the growing costs of the programs and were intended to help control these costs. Examples of the changes that were specific to Medicare included removal of the 100-visits-per-year limitation on home health services and the requirement under Part B that patients pay a deductible for home care visits. These changes were intended to encourage home care rather than more expensive institutional care. Another provision permitted small rural hospitals to use their beds as "swing beds" (alternating their use as acute or long-term care beds as needed) and authorized swing-bed demonstration projects for large and urban hospitals.

- *1981: Omnibus Budget Reconciliation Act, or OBRA '81, (P.L. 97-35)*. Just as in 1980, this legislation included extensive changes in the Medicare and Medicaid programs (46 sections pertained to these programs). Enacted in the context of extensive efforts to make reductions in the federal budget, many of the provisions hit Medicaid especially hard, but others were aimed directly at the Medicare program. For example, one provision eliminated the coverage of alcohol detoxification facility services, another removed the use of occupational therapy as a basis for initial entitlement to home health service, and yet another increased the Part B deductible.

- *1982: Tax Equity and Fiscal Responsibility Act, or TEFRA, (P.L. 97-248).* A number of important changes with significant impact on the Medicare program were contained in this legislation. For example, one provision added coverage for hospice services provided to Medicare beneficiaries. These benefits were extended later and are now an integral part of the Medicare program. However, the most important provisions, in terms of impact on the Medicare program, were those that sought to control the program's costs by setting limits on how much Medicare would reimburse hospitals on a per-case basis and by limiting the annual rate of increase for Medicare's reasonable costs per discharge. These changes in reimbursement methodology represented fundamental changes in the Medicare program and reflected a dramatic shift in the nation's Medicare policy. Another provision of TEFRA pertained to replacing PSROs, which had been established by the Social Security Amendments of 1972 (P.L. 92-603), with a new utilization and quality control program called peer review organizations (PROs). The TEFRA changes regarding the operation of the Medicare program were extensive, but they were only the harbinger of the most sweeping legislative changes in the history of the Medicare program the following year.

- *1983: Social Security Amendments (P.L. 98-21).* This important legislation initiated the Medicare prospective payment system (PPS) and included provisions to base payment for hospital inpatient services on predetermined rates per discharge for diagnosis-related groups (DRGs). PPS was a major departure from the cost-based system of reimbursement that had been used in the Medicare program since its inception in 1965. The dramatic impact of this change on the Medicare is best seen in terms of expenditures. PPS reduced Medicare's hospital expenditures sharply. An analysis by Russell and Manning (1989) showed that 1990 Medicare expenditures for hospital inpatient care were approximately 20 percent lower than would have been the case without implementation of the PPS. In this act, the Congress directed the Reagan administration to study physician payment reform options.

- *1984: Deficit Reduction Act, or DEFRA, (P.L. 98-369).* Among the provisions of this act was one to temporarily freeze physicians' fees paid under the Medicare program. Another placed a specific limitation on the rate of increase in the DRG payment rates that the Secretary of DHHS could permit in the two subsequent years. This act also created two classes of physicians in regard to their relationships to the Medicare program and outlined different reimbursement approaches for them depending on whether they were classified as participating and nonparticipating.

- *1985: Emergency Deficit Reduction and Balanced Budget Act, or the Gramm-Rudman-Hollins Act, (P.L. 99-177).* This legislation established mandatory deficit reduction targets for the five subsequent fiscal years. Under provisions of the law, the required budget cuts would come equally from defense spending and from domestic programs that were not exempted. The Gramm-Rudman-Hollins Act had significant impact on the Medicare program throughout the last half of the 1980s, as well as on other health programs such as community and migrant health centers, veteran and Native American health programs, health professions education, and the NIH (Rhodes 1992). Among other things, this legislation led to substantial cuts in Medicare payments to hospitals and physicians.

- *1985: Consolidated Omnibus Budget Reconciliation Act, or COBRA '85, (P.L. 99-272).* Through a number of provisions of the act that impacted on Medicare, hospitals that served a disproportionate share of poor patients received an adjustment in their PPS payments; hospice care was made a permanent part of the program; FY 1986 PPS payment rates were frozen at 1985 levels through May 1, 1986 and increased 0.5 percent for the remainder of the year; payment to hospitals for the indirect costs of medical education were modified; and a schedule to phase out payment of a return on equity to proprietary hospitals was established.

- *1986: Omnibus Budget Reconciliation Act, or OBRA '86, (P.L. 99-509).* This act altered the PPS payment rate for hospitals once again and reduced payment amounts for capital-related costs by 3.5 percent for part of fiscal year 1987, by 7 percent for fiscal year 1988, and by 10 percent for fiscal year 1989. In addition, certain adjustments were made in the manner in which "outlier" or atypical cases were reimbursed.

- *1987: Omnibus Budget Reconciliation Act, or OBRA '87, (P.L. 100-203).* This legislation required the Secretary of the DHHS to update the wage index used in calculating hospital PPS payments by October 1, 1990, and to do so at least every three years thereafter. It also required the Secretary to study and report to Congress on the criteria being used by the Medicare program to identify referral hospitals. Deepening the reductions established by OBRA 86, one provision of the act reduced payment amounts for capital-related costs by 12 percent for fiscal year 1988 and 15 percent for 1989.

- *1988: Medicare Catastrophic Coverage Act (P.L. 100-360).* This act provided the largest expansion of the benefits covered under the

Medicare program since its establishment in 1965. Among other things, provisions of this act added coverage for outpatient prescription drugs and respite care and placed a cap on out-of-pocket spending by the elderly for copayment costs for covered services. The legislation included provisions that would have the new benefits phased in over a four-year period and paid for by premiums charged to Medicare program enrollees. Thirty-seven percent of the costs were to be covered by a fixed monthly premium paid by all enrollees and the remainder of the costs were to be covered by an income-related supplemental premium that was, in effect, an income-tax surtax that would apply to fewer than half of the enrollees. Under intense pressure from many of their elderly constituents and their interest groups, who objected to having to pay additional premiums or the income-tax surtax, Congress repealed P.L. 100-360 in 1989, without implementing most of its provisions.

- *1989: Omnibus Budget Reconciliation Act, or OBRA '89, (P.L. 101-239).* The act included provisions for minor, primarily technical, changes in the PPS and to extend coverage for mental health benefits and add coverage for Pap smears. Small adjustments were made in the disproportionate share regulations, and the 15 percent capital-related payment reduction established in OBRA '87 was continued in OBRA '89. Another provision required the Secretary of DHHS to update the wage index annually in a budget-neutral manner beginning in fiscal year 1993. The most important provision of OBRA '89 was one through which HCFA was directed to begin implementing a resource-based relative value scale (RBRVS) for reimbursing physicians under the Medicare program on January 1, 1992. The new system was to be phased in over a four-year period beginning in 1992.

- *1990: Omnibus Budget Reconciliation Act, or OBRA '90, (P.L. 101-508).* The act made additional minor changes in the PPS, including further adjustments in the wage index calculation and in the disproportionate share regulations. Regarding the wage index, one provision required the Prospective Payment Assessment Commission (ProPAC), which was established by the 1983 Amendments to the Social Security Act to help guide the Congress and the Secretary of DHHS on implementing the PPS to further study the available data on wages by occupational category and to develop recommendations on modifying the wage index to account for occupational mix. It also included a provision that continued the 15 percent capital-related payment reduction that was established in OBRA '87, and continued in OBRA '89, and another provision that made permanent the reduced teaching adjustment payment established in OBRA '87. One of its more important provisions provided a five-year deficit reduction plan that was to reduce total Medicare outlays by more than $43 billion between fiscal years 1991 and 1995.

- *1993: Omnibus Budget Reconciliation Act, or OBRA '93, (P.L. 103-66).* This legislation established an all-time record five-year cut in Medicare funding and included a number of other changes affecting the Medicare program. For example, the legislation included provisions to end return on equity (ROE) payments for capital to proprietary skilled nursing facilities and reduced the previously established rate of increase in payment rates for care provided in hospices. In addition, the legislation cut laboratory fees drastically by changing the reimbursement formula and froze payments for durable medical equipment, parenteral and enteral services, and for orthotics and prosthetics in fiscal years 1994 and 1995.

It should be noted in this chronology that the period 1993–96 was a unique time in the legislative history of the Medicare program; indeed, for health policy in general. The intense focus on consideration of President Clinton's attempt to reform the American healthcare system through his Health Security Act, which was introduced in late 1993 and died with the 1994 Congress (Hacker and Skocpol 1997; Hacker 1997), meant that little legislative energy was available for other health-related legislation. The hiatus in significant health policy continued following the Health Security bill's demise. Intense efforts in 1995 to enact unprecedented cutbacks in the Medicare and Medicaid programs as part of a far-reaching budget reconciliation bill ended in a veto of the bill by President Clinton.

The budget battle grew even worse in 1996. Proposed changes in the Medicare program, changes that were linked to the development of a plan to balance the federal budget over a seven-year span, would have meant massive cuts in the program. But political and philosophical differences over these plans between the Republican-controlled Congress and President Clinton, a Democrat, were so fundamental that they led to a complete impasse in the budget negotiations in 1996, including a brief shutdown of the federal government in the absence of budget authority to operate. Stung by public criticism of the very disruptive budget battle of 1996, Congress did much better in developing its budget legislation in 1997. The result continued the significant pattern of modification in the Medicare program.

- *1997: Balanced Budget Act of 1997 (BBA) (P.L. 105-33).* This legislation contained the most significant changes in the Medicare program since the program's inception in 1965. Overall, this legislation requires a five-year reduction of $115 billion in the Medicare program's expenditure growth and a $13 billion reduction in growth of the Medicaid program. A new "Medicare + Choice" program was created, which gives Medicare beneficiaries the opportunity to choose from a variety of health plan options the plan that best suits their needs and preferences. Significant changes were also made in the traditional Medicare program. Among them, hospital annual inflation updates were reduced as were hospital payments for inpatient capital expenses and for bad debts. Other provisions established a cap on the number of medical residents supported by Medicare graduate medical education payments and provided incentives for reductions in the number of residents.

An important provision of this act established the State Children's Health Insurance Program (SCHIP) and provided states with $24 billion in federal funds for 1998 until 2002 to increase health insurance for children. Other provisions established two new commissions. The Medicare Payment Review Commission (MedPAC) replaced the Physician Payment Review Commission and the Prospective Payment Review Commission. The new commission was required to submit an annual report to Congress on the status of Medicare reforms and make recommendations on Medicare payment issues. The National Bipartisan Commission on the Future of Medicare was established by this legislation and charged to develop recommendations for Congress on actions necessary to ensure the long-term fiscal health of the Medicare program. This commission was charged to consider several specific issues that were debated in the development of the Balanced Budget Act of 1997, but rejected. These issues included raising the eligibility age for Medicare, increasing the Part B premiums, and developing alternative approaches to financing graduate medical education.

The National Bipartisan Commission on the Future of Medicare concluded its work and released its final report, *Building a Better Medicare for Today and Tomorrow*, on March 16, 1999. The report contained three sets of recommendations: (1) the design of a premium support system for the Medicare program; (2) improvements to the current Medicare program; and (3) financing and solvency of the Medicare program (the report can be read at *thomas.loc.gov/medicare/bbmtt31599.html*. The key recommendations of the commission, however, could not gather the bipartisan support necessary for amending the Medicare policy.

As BBA began to be implemented, health interest groups affected by the law, including the American Hospital Association, mounted an intense lobbying campaign to reverse some of BBA's effects. The campaign was made easier because the nation's budget surplus was growing at an unexpected rate. Two important health-related laws were enacted to modify the BBA.

- *1999: Medicare, Medicaid and SCHIP Balanced Budget Refinement Act of 1999 (BBRA) (P.L. 106-113).* This legislation changed the BBA provisions in a number of ways. For example, hospitals treating a disproportionate share (DSH) of low-income Medicare and Medicaid patients receive additional payments from Medicare. BBRA froze DSH adjustments at 3 percent (the FY 2000 level) through FY 2001 and reduced the formula to 4 percent from the BBA established 5 percent in FY 2002, and then 0 percent for subsequent years. The law increased hospice payment by 0.5 percent for FY 2001 and by 0.75 percent for FY 2002. Medicare reimburses teaching hospitals for their role in providing graduate medical education (GME). Prior to BBA, Medicare's indirect medical education adjustment (IME) payments increased 7.7 percent for each 10 percent increase in a hospital's ratio of interns and residents to beds. BBA decreased the adjustment to 6.5 percent in FY 1999, 6.0 percent in FY 2000, and 5.5 percent in FY 2001 and subsequent years. BBRA froze the IME adjustment at 6.5 percent through FY 2000; reduced it to 6.25 percent in FY 2001, and to 5.5 percent in FY 2002 and subsequent years.

- *2000: Medicare, Medicaid, and SCHIP Benefits Improvement and Protection Act of 2000 (BIPA) (P.L. 106-554).* This legislation was attached as an amendment to the Appropriations Bill and signed into law by President Clinton on December 21, 2000. It effectively changed a number of provisions previously enacted in BBA and BBRA. Among the important changes were:
  — an increase of 3.4 percent for Medicare inpatient payments in Fiscal Year 2001, and an estimated 3.5 percent in FY 2002
  — an increase of 4.4 percent in Medicare outpatient payments in 2001
  — indirect medical education (IME) payments at 6.5 percent in FY 2001 and FY 2002
  — elimination of the additional one percent cut in Medicare disproportionate share hospital (DSH) payments in FY 2001 and 2002
  — an increase, from 55 to 70 percent, in Medicare payments for bad debt
  — an increase for the direct graduate medical education (GME) payment floor to 85 percent of the national average
  — elimination of the BBA's FY 2001 and 2002 Medicaid DSH cut
  — removal of the 2 percent payment reduction for rehabilitation hospitals in FY 2001
  — a 3.2 percent increase in skilled nursing service payments in FY 2001
  — a one-year delay of the 15 percent reduction for home health, and the full market basket in FY 2001
  — an increase of 3 percent in incentive payments for psychiatric hospitals/units

— expansion of Medicare payment for telehealth services to rural areas.

The pattern of extensive modification of policies related to the Medicare Program is likely to continue as long as the program exists. At present, critical, intertwined, issues remain to be resolved. Moon (2001, 928) describes them as follows.

> There are three major issues involving Medicare. First, since the late 1970s, legislators have sought to revise the program in order to improve its management and efficiency and thereby slow the growth in federal expenditures. Second, Medicare's benefit package is inadequate. Many beneficiaries rely on supplemental policies, which results in inefficient delivery of care (Aaron and Reischauer 1995). Medicare does not cover outpatient prescription drugs, and the deductibles and copayments can be very expensive. Thus, about 85 percent of Medicare beneficiaries have some type of supplemental coverage. Even so, Medicare beneficiaries tend to pay more for their health care than do most other Americans—both in absolute dollars and as a share of their total health care expenditures. At present, the average beneficiary pays more than $3,000 out of pocket each year for health care (excluding long-term care) (Maxwell, Moon, and Segal 2001). Third, Medicare has not been as well financed as Social Security, leading to numerous fiscal crises.
>
> These three issues overlap. For example, many of those who want to restructure Medicare also propose that the program provide additional benefits, such as coverage of prescription drugs. There are conflicting views about whether restructuring Medicare will fully resolve the financial problems (Gluck and Moon. 2000), however, and if the basic benefit package is expanded, the costs will increase even more.

In the 107th Congress, Medicare debate centered on the addition of an outpatient prescription drug benefit to the program. The lack of coverage for more than one in four beneficiaries and continued increases in drug expenditures led to several proposals (Henry J. Kaiser Family Foundation 2001). However, even this single issue is complex and controversial. Should drug coverage be provided within Medicare or through private, risk-bearing plans? Should a prescription benefit apply to the poor or to all Medicare beneficiaries? How can the Medicare program control drug costs? How should the new benefit be financed?

Key Structural Features of Policy Modification

Two structural features drive much of the activity in the modification phase of the policymaking process: oversight actors and evaluation. The important roles in policy modification played by these structural features are considered in the next sections.

The Role of Oversight Actors in Policy Modification

Oversight actors in the public policymaking process include participants from each branch of government. Their roles are played differently, but each has important implications for policy modification. In the legislative branch, oversight responsibilities are assigned to committees and subcommittees, which can stimulate modification in policy formulation and implementation. Chief executives (president, governor, or mayor depending on the level of government) and their top appointees monitor implementation and can serve to point out when adjustments and modifications are needed. Courts can determine when modifications are needed, such as when the results of one policy infringe on or even conflict with the desired results of other policies.

Legislative Branch

In the case of Congress, and with parallel arrangements in many state legislatures, committees, and subcommittees have specific oversight responsibilities. The purpose of oversight in this context "is to analyze and evaluate both the execution and effectiveness of laws administered by the executive branch, and to determine if there are areas in which additional legislation (including amendment of existing legislation) is necessary or desirable" (National Health Council, Inc. 1993, 10). While any committee with jurisdiction can hold oversight hearings, the House and Senate Appropriations Committees (www.house.gov/appropriations and www.senate.gov/~appropriations, respectively) have especially important oversight responsibilities inherent in their annual reviews of the budgets of implementing organizations and agencies. Routinely, legislators seeking to influence implementation decisions use the budget review mechanism. In addition, out of oversight hearings often emerge the first or clarifying indications that existing legislation needs to be amended or that new legislation may be needed in a particular area.

Executive Branch

Chief executives play very important oversight roles. In fact, no one else has the power of the chief executive to initiate the modification of policies. In the context of oversight of the implementation of policies, the chief executive role is filled by the president, governor, or mayor, but also includes the staff in the Executive Office as well as the appointees in the various departments and agencies who are responsible to the chief executive.

Judicial Branch

The courts also have a role in modifying health policy. The federal courts play an important oversight role regarding how laws are interpreted and enforced (information on the system of federal courts in the United States can be obtained at The Federal Judiciary Homepage, About the U.S. Courts, at www.uscourts.gov). State courts, as well, are involved in interpreting and enforcing state laws and other policies within their jurisdictions. Anderson (1992) has noted the courts' recent roles in the modification of health policies related to: (1) coverage decisions made by public and private health insurers; (2) states' payment rates for hospitals and nursing homes; and (3) antitrust rulings relating to mergers between healthcare organizations.

These relatively newer areas in which the courts have become significantly involved in policy modification are added to the more traditional areas of their involvement. One of the more important of these, for example, is the exercise of their oversight responsibilities in implementing the nation's environmental protection policies. This traditionally important area has been exemplified in the courts' role in implementing the nation's occupational health and safety laws, which has resulted in numerous modifications of policies in this area.

The Occupational Safety and Health Act (P.L. 91-596) set into motion a massive federal program of standard setting and enforcement that sought to improve safety and health conditions in the nation's workplaces. As Thompson (1981, 24) has noted, "Business and labor leaders . . . have repeatedly appealed decisions by the Occupational Safety and Health Administration (OSHA) to the courts. The development of this program in some respects reads like a legal history." While the courts have their most direct modifying impact on the implementation of policies, especially in ensuring that laws and supporting rules and provisions are appropriately applied, enough adverse judicial decisions growing out of a particular policy can lead to its amendment or even to the stimulation of new legislation.

One of the most complicating aspects of the courts' role in policy modification arises from the fact that the court system in the United States is highly decentralized. Although court autonomy is an important element in the ability of courts to play their roles in the American system of government, one consequence of this autonomy is the possibility of inconsistency in the treatment of policy-relevant issues. As has been noted, "The structure of the judicial system has made it difficult for the courts to provide consistent guidance about what constitutes acceptable behavior" (Anderson 1992, 106). Limitations of the courts aside, they are a vitally important integral structural feature of the policymaking process and play an especially important role in the modification phase of the process.

The Role of Evaluation in Policy Modification

Evaluation is the determination of the value or utility of something for a particular purpose—including health policies—judged according to appropriate criteria (House 1993). To the extent that formal evaluation can guide policy modification, the likelihood of modifications being appropriate is increased. The most efficacious modification of policies is generally based on solid information. The sources of such information include that obtained through evaluations or other analyses of policies.

Continuum of Evaluation Activities

To be most valuable as a source of information to guide policy modification, evaluation must be more than simply an activity that occurs after a policy has been implemented. Effective policy evaluation is part of a continuum of analytical activities that can begin in agenda setting and pervade and support the entire policymaking process. The continuum of these activities can be organized as ex-ante policy analysis, policy maintenance, policy monitoring, and ex-post policy evaluation (Patton and Sawicki 1986).

- *Ex-ante Policy Analysis.* This type of analysis, which is also called "anticipatory," or "prospective," policy analysis, has its utility mainly in influencing agenda setting, whether in the original formulation of a policy or in its subsequent modification. Ex-ante policy analysis helps decision makers clarify the problems they face and identify and assess the various potential solutions to those problems. It may also include analyses of the relative benefits and costs of the various alternatives, thereby providing quantitative information that can help decision makers assess the potential consequences and political implications of their decisions.
- *Policy Maintenance.* This type of analysis is typically undertaken to help ensure that policies are implemented as their formulators designed them and intended them to be implemented. Policy maintenance involves analysis that is part of the exercise of both legislative oversight and managerial control in implementation. As such, it can play a powerful role in identifying when and how to modify a policy, either in reformulating it or by making changes in its implementation.
- *Policy Monitoring.* This type of analysis is the relatively straightforward measuring and recording of the ongoing operation of a policy's implementation. Such monitoring is frequently a necessary precursor

to the conduct of more formal ex-post policy evaluations, providing valuable information for the subsequent ex-post evaluation. Policy monitoring can play a useful role in the exercise of appropriate managerial control and legislative oversight in the implementation phase, pointing out when and where modifications might be needed in rules or regulations, or in operations.

- *Ex-post Policy Evaluation.* This type of analysis, which is also called "retrospective" evaluation, is the process through which the real value of a policy is determined. This sometimes very difficult determination depends on an assessment of the degree to which a policy's objectives are achieved through its implementation.

Policy Evaluation as a Basis for Policy Modification

Evaluation of policies, especially in terms of their impacts and consequences, is a highly technical procedure that can be approached in a variety of ways, although typically one or more of a few basic approaches are used. These include before-and-after comparisons, with-and-without comparisons, actual-versus-planned performance comparisons, experimental and quasi-experimental designs, and cost-oriented policy evaluation approaches (Patton and Sawicki 1986).

Evaluations based on *before-and-after comparisons*, as the name suggests, involve comparing conditions or situations before a policy is implemented and after it has had an opportunity to make an impact on affected individuals, organizations, and groups. This is the most widely used approach to policy evaluation. A variation on this approach, known as *with-and-without comparisons*, involves assessing the consequences for individuals, organizations, or groups with the policy in place and comparing them to situations in which the policy does not exist. In the health policy domain, policy evaluations based on with-and-without comparisons are quite prevalent because the variation in the states across the nation provide something of a natural laboratory for such comparisons.

For example, studies have been made comparing variations in states' use of managed care options for Medicaid populations (Gold 1997). On the point of states as laboratories in which policies can be tried first for their potential as appropriate national policies, Oliver and Paul-Shaheen (1997) have studied policy innovation in states by examining states' enactment of major pieces of health-related legislation in the late 1980s and early 1990s. Their findings cast considerable doubt on the popular proposition that states can invent policies for substantial health system reforms for subsequent use by other states or by the federal government. The authors argue, instead, that it is more appropriate to think of states as "specialized political markets" in which, under certain circumstances, unique solutions to unique problems can be addressed through public policy.

Another useful approach to policy evaluation, *actual-versus-planned performance comparisons*, involves comparing policy objectives (e.g., health status improvements, dollars saved, people inoculated, or tons of solid waste removed) with actual post-implementation results. Neither this, nor the other two approaches to ex-post or retrospective evaluation, however, supports the unassailable assignment of causation to the policies being evaluated. This limitation is a significant weakness of all three approaches to policy evaluation. Nevertheless, these approaches are widely used because they tend to be easily implemented and cost relatively little. The results, however, of any of these comparison approaches to policy evaluation must be interpreted carefully.

To help offset some of the technical limitations and weaknesses of the comparison approaches, two alternative approaches have been developed and are used in some health policy evaluations. These are *experimental* and *quasi-experimental* designs for policy evaluations. Both can permit more meaningful conclusions. In policy evaluations that use experimental designs, individuals are randomly assigned to control or experimental groups so that the actual impact of the policy being evaluated can be better assessed. An excellent example of the power of experimental designs to evaluate policies can be found in the Health Insurance Experiment conducted by the Rand Corporation in the 1970s (Newhouse 1974).

At the time, randomized controlled trials had become the standard approach to clinical research, but the approach had been rarely used in policy evaluation. This important analysis clearly demonstrated the usefulness of the approach for policy evaluation, but the approach is so expensive and difficult to conduct that its impact on policy evaluation remains limited. In view of the expensive nature of true experimental designs, quasi-experimental designs can serve a useful purpose in the conduct of policy evaluations, especially when a true experiment is too expensive or impractical for other reasons. This approach maintains the logic of full experimentation but without some of its restrictions and expenses (Cook and Campbell 1979). Quasi-experimental designs can provide one of the most useful aspects of a policy evaluation: the ability to ascribe causality to a particular policy, although typically this is extremely difficult to do.

A final type of approach to policy evaluation is one based on cost-oriented evaluations. This approach can be especially important in the context of the search for policies that provide value for public dollars. *Cost-benefit analysis* (CBA) and *cost-effectiveness analysis* (CEA) are the two most widely used forms of cost-oriented policy evaluation. In CBA an evaluation is based on the relationship between the benefits and costs of a particular policy where all costs and benefits are expressed in monetary terms. Such analyses can help answer the fundamentally important evaluation question of whether the benefits of a policy are at least worth its costs. Typically, the results of these analyses is a measure of net benefits, which is "the difference between the total monetary input costs of an intervention and the consequences of that intervention, also valued in monetary terms" (Elixhauser et al. 1993, JS2).

In CEA an evaluation is based on the desire to achieve certain policy objectives in the least costly way. This form of analysis compares alternative policies that might be used to achieve the same or very similar objectives. Typically, the results of CEA evaluations are expressed as "the net costs required to produce a certain unit of output measured in terms of health, e.g., lives saved, years of life saved, or quality-adjusted life years" (Elixhauser et al. 1993, JS2–JS3). Much use of these health-related policy evaluation techniques has centered on analyses related to variations in utilization and the relative effectiveness of various medical practices and surgical interventions.

Responsibility for Policy Evaluations

Both the legislative and executive branches of the federal government are involved in policy evaluations and other analyses because they are interested in the performance of the policies they enact and implement. The General Accounting Office (GAO) (www.gao.gov) is the investigative arm of Congress. Its mission permits it to study a very wide range of matters that involve the use of public funds. In carrying out this mission, GAO performs audits and evaluations of a host of programs and activities that arise from the implementation of federal policies. Organizationally, GAO is under the control and direction of the Comptroller General of the United States, who is appointed by the President with the advice and consent of the Senate. The Budget and Accounting Act of 1921 established the organization for the rather limited purpose of independently auditing federal agencies. Over the years, however, Congress has expanded GAO's audit authority, added extensive new responsibilities and duties, and strengthened the organization's ability to perform its work independently.

The majority of its evaluations are made in response to specific congressional requests. GAO is required to perform work requested by committee chairpersons and assigns equal status to requests from ranking minority members of Congressional committees. When possible, GAO also responds to requests for evaluations and audits from individual members of Congress.

Because GAO must maintain the ability to conduct a very wide range of policy evaluations, its staff is drawn from a variety of disciplines, including accounting, law, public and business administration, economics, the social and physical sciences, and others. Their work is organized so that staff members concentrate on specific subject areas, facilitating the development of expertise and in-depth knowledge. When a policy evaluation or audit assignment requires specialized experience not available within GAO, outside experts can be used to assist the permanent staff.

In the executive branch, the Office of Management and Budget (OMB) (www.whitehouse.gov/omb) plays an important analytical role. Its predominant mission is to assist the president in overseeing the preparation of the federal budget and to supervise its administration in executive branch agencies. In helping to formulate the president's spending plans, OMB evaluates the effectiveness of agency programs, policies and procedures, assesses competing funding demands among agencies, and sets funding priorities.

In assisting the Administration in formulating its annual budget plans, OMB evaluates the effectiveness of executive branch organizations' operating decisions and assesses competing funding demands among these organizations. These assessments help establish the Administration's funding priorities, which then guide the development of the budget.

In its role in supervising the various executive branch organizations in their administration of the federal budget, OMB ensures that their reports, rules, testimony, and proposed legislation are consistent with the Administration's preferences. In addition, OMB oversees and coordinates the Administration's procurement, financial management, and information practices and procedures. In each of these areas, OMB's role is to help improve the management of policy implementation, which, as was discussed in Chapter 6, is largely the responsibility of executive branch organizations.

The Congressional Budget Office (CBO) (www.cbo.gov) was created by the Congressional Budget and Impoundment Control Act of 1974. The agency's mission is to provide the Congress with the objective, timely, nonpartisan analyses needed for economic and budget decisions and with the information and estimates required for the Congressional budget process. Compared with the missions of Congress's other support agencies—the Congressional Research Service and the General Accounting Office—CBO's mission is narrow and focused. Even so, given the wide array of activities that the federal budget covers, the agency is involved in wide-ranging health policy activity.

CBO's services can be grouped into four categories: helping the

Congress formulate budget plans, helping it stay within these plans, helping it assess the impact of federal mandates, and helping it consider issues that will affect the federal budget. In the latter role, for example, the analyses cover a variety of federal activities, examining current policies, suggesting alternative approaches, and projecting how the alternatives would affect current programs, the federal budget, and the economy. In line with its nonpartisan mandate, CBO does not offer specific recommendations on policy.

The Real World of Health Policy

CBO's Estimates on the Cost of a Prescription Drug Benefit in the Medicare Program

As pressure mounted for the 107th Congress to add a prescription drug benefit to the Medicare program, CBO's director sent the following letter containing updated estimates of the direct spending effects of four proposals from the 106th Congress for a Medicare prescription drug benefit. The importance of this analysis rested on the fact that Medicare prescription drug plans favored by many Democrats—S 3107, which was co-sponsored by Senator Graham (D-Fla.) and former Senator Robb (D-Va.)—as well as proposals favored by many Republicans, especially the Republican-backed plan passed by the House in 2000 (HR 4680), which would provide drug benefits through private insurers, and S 358, a plan put forth by Senators John Breaux (D-La.) and Bill Frist (R-Tenn.)—cost less or little more than the $300 billion set aside by Congress for adding a prescription drug benefit over ten years in its 2001 budget resolution.

June 11, 2001

Honorable Max Baucus
Committee on Finance
Chairman
United States Senate
Washington, DC 20510

Dear Mr. Chairman:

The Congressional Budget Office (CBO) has prepared the attached updated estimates of the effect on direct spending of four proposals made during the 106th Congress to establish an outpatient prescription drug benefit in Medicare. Those proposals are:

- President Clinton's proposal in the 2000 Mid-Session Review;
- Amendment 3598 to H.R. 4577, as introduced by Senator Robb;
- S. 2807, as introduced by Senators Breaux and Frist and modified in discussions with staff; and
- H.R. 4680, as passed by the House.

The updated estimates reflect CBO's current baseline for spending on outpatient prescription drugs by or for the Medicare population and revisions in CBO's estimating methods. Those revisions are based on updated data and intensive review of our methods to ensure the reasonableness and consistency of the estimates.

The original proposals all would have established a prescription drug benefit in 2003 or earlier. The updated estimates assume that the benefit would begin in 2004.

The original proposals specified dollar amounts for deductibles, benefit caps, and stop-loss thresholds for the first year of the benefit, and occasionally for subsequent years. The updated estimates assume the specified amounts apply beginning in 2004.

Table 1 summarizes the effect of each proposal on direct spending during the 2002–11 period. Tables 2 through 5 [not included here] provide year-by-year estimates and supplemental information for each of the estimates.

If you or your staff have any questions about these estimates, or if you need additional information, we would be happy to be of assistance. The CBO staff contact is Julia Christensen.

I hope this information is helpful to you.

Sincerely,

Dan L. Crippen Director Attachments

cc: Honorable Charles E. Grassley
Ranking Member, Senate Committee on Finance

Honorable Kent Conrad
Chairman, Senate Committee on the Budget

Honorable Pete V. Domenici
Ranking Member, Senate Committee on the Budget

Honorable John B. Breaux
Honorable Bill Frist

Identical letters sent to Honorable W. J. "Billy" Tauzin and Honorable William "Bill" M. Thomas

Table 1. Estimated Effect on Direct Spending of Proposals Introduced During the 106th Congress to Establish a Prescription Drug Benefit in Medicare, Fiscal Years 2004–11 (*in billions*)

Federal Spending on Prescription Drugs for Medicare Enrollees	Clinton	Robb	Breaux-Frist	H.R. 4680
Medicare	417	295	124	101
Spending by Other Federal Programs on Prescription Drugs for Medicare Enrollees	−113	−111	−64	−68
Low-Income Subsidy	100	111	104	108
Subtotal	405	294	164	141
Other Direct Spending	21	24	12	15
Total	425	318	176	157

Source: Congressional Budget Office.

Source: Excerpted from CBO Director's letter of June 11, 2001.

Another organization with important analytical responsibilities is the Agency for Healthcare Research and Quality (AHRQ) (www.ahrq.gov). Formerly the Agency for Health Care Policy and Research (AHCPR), this organization was established by the Omnibus Budget Reconciliation Act of 1989 (P.L. 101-239). The agency was reauthorized by P.L. 106-129 in 1999. This law amended the Public Health Service Act by adding Title IX, known as the Healthcare Research and Quality Act of 1999. The language of this law is instructive about AHRQ's role. Section 901, Mission and Duties, reads as follows:

(a) IN GENERAL—There is established within the Public Health Service an agency to be known as the Agency for Healthcare Research and Quality, which shall be headed by a director appointed by the Secretary [of HHS]. The Secretary shall carry out this title acting through the Director.

(b) MISSION—The purpose of the Agency is to enhance the quality, appropriateness, and effectiveness of health services, and access to such services, through the establishment of a broad base of scientific research and through the promotion of improvements in clinical and health system practices, including the prevention of diseases and other health conditions. The Agency shall promote health care quality improvement by conducting and supporting—

(1) research that develops and presents scientific evidence regarding all aspects of health care, including—

(A) the development and assessment of methods for enhancing patient participation in their own care and for facilitating shared patient-physician decision-making;

(B) the outcomes, effectiveness, and cost-effectiveness of health care practices, including preventive measures and long-term care;

(C) existing and innovative technologies;

(D) the costs and utilization of, and access to health care;

(E) the ways in which health care services are organized, delivered, and financed and the interaction and impact of these factors on the quality of patient care;

(F) methods for measuring quality and strategies for improving quality; and

(G) ways in which patients, consumers, purchasers, and practitioners acquire new information about best practices and health benefits, the determinants and impact of their use of this information;

(2) the synthesis and dissemination of available scientific evidence for use by patients, consumers, practitioners, providers, purchasers, policy makers, and educators; and

(3) initiatives to advance private and public efforts to improve health care quality.

AHRQ's current analytical activities are reflected in its FY 2001 budget request presented by the agency's director during the House and Senate Appropriations hearings. The request was for $250 million, an increase of $46 million from FY 2000. The rationale for the increase was to enable the agency to focus on three new priority areas:

- patient safety and medical errors,
- information technology, and
- worker health.

In addition, the request included funding to support the agency's continuing priorities:

- quality improvement,
- clinical preventive services, and
- building the Nation's capacity for research to improve healthcare.

The Congressional Research Service (CRS) (www.loc.gov/crsinfo) is another analytical resource, especially to members of Congress. The agency was established to provide Congress with information and analysis needed to make more informed decisions. CRS operates in many ways as an extension of, or supplement to, the member's own office staff. As a legislative branch organization within the Library of Congress, CRS's work is performed exclusively for the Congress on a confidential, nonpartisan basis.

The agency's staff includes people with expertise in a wide range of issues and disciplines, including law, economics, foreign affairs, the physical and behavioral sciences, environmental science, public administration, the social sciences, and information science.

CRS analysts support legislators at all stages of the policymaking process by helping identify problems and possible solutions in the formulation of legislative proposals. CRS provides policy analysis and legal research. It is organized into six interdisciplinary research divisions, which are organized around the following broad clusters of public policy issues: American Law; Domestic Social Policy; Foreign Affairs, Defense, and Trade; Government and Finance; Information Research; and Resources, Science, and Industry. Within each division, CRS analysts and specialists are organized into smaller sections, which focus on specific areas of public policy such as education, labor, taxes, and health.

As noted at the beginning of this chapter, policymaking is not a perfect process. The decisions made within this process must be reviewed and changed when necessary. Beyond this operational aspect of the need for policy modification lies the fact that policies have huge consequences for individuals and populations, and for health-related organizations, systems, and interest groups. Because they are so directly affected by the outcomes of the health policymaking process, the leaders of these entities typically devote considerable attention and resources to analyzing this process and the larger public policy environments that face their organizations, systems, or groups. And they seek to influence both. As will be discussed in depth in chapter 8, one pervasive result of this is the ongoing participation of the leaders of health-related organizations, systems, and interest groups in the policy modification phase of the public policymaking process.

When policies have positive consequences (e.g., more services, higher incomes, less pollution, more money for biomedical research), those enjoying the benefits will likely seek to increase them through modification of the existing policies that affect these benefits. Similarly, when policies have negative consequences (e.g., the elimination or reduction of services, lower incomes, more pollution, less money for biomedical research), those experiencing the reductions will likely seek to remedy this through modification of the existing policies that cause the negative consequences. The constant modification of existing policies is indeed an important hallmark of policymaking in the United States.

Summary

The modification phase of the public policymaking process involves the feeding back of the consequences of policies and the actions these consequences stimulate into the other phases of the process. As the feedback loop depicted in Figure 7.1 shows, policy modification occurs in both the agenda setting and legislation development inherent in policy formulation and in the rulemaking and operations that characterize policy implementation.

The modification phase is an extremely important feature of the health policymaking process because most U.S. health policies are the result of modification of prior policies. There are continuing opportunities for the performance of policies and the resulting consequences to stimulate modifications. Changes occur through the influence of policy outcomes on agenda setting or through the amendment of previously enacted public laws. In addition, routinely, the results of policy implementation lead to modifications in both rulemaking and the operation of policies.

In a very real sense, as was pointed out in the overview of the policymaking process presented in chapter 3 and reemphasized in this chapter, the modification phase of policymaking exists because perfection cannot be achieved in the other phases and because policies are established and exist in a dynamic world. Suitable policies made today may become inadequate with biological, cultural, demographic, ecological, economic, ethical, legal, psychological, social, and technological changes in the future.

Discussion Questions

1. Discuss the distinction between policy initiation and policy modification.
2. Discuss the concept of incrementalism in public policymaking.
3. Describe modification in the agenda setting that precedes policy formulation.
4. Discuss how modification occurs at legislation development.
5. Discuss how modification occurs at rulemaking.
6. Discuss how modification occurs at the operational stage of implementing policies.
7. Discuss the cyclical relationship between rulemaking and operation and how this affects modification. Use the implementation of Medicare PPS as an example in your discussion.
8. Discuss the key modifications that have been made in the Medicare policy over its life. Your answer should include some of the reasons for the modifications.
9. Discuss the role of oversight actors in policy modification.
10. Discuss the role of policy evaluation in policy modification.

References

Aaron, H. J., and R. D. Reischauer. 1995. "The Medicare Reform Debate: What Is the Next Step? *Health Affairs* 14 (4): 8–30.

Altmeyer, A. J. 1968. *The Formative Years of Social Security.* Madison, WI: University of Wisconsin Press.

Anderson, G. F. 1992. "The Courts and Health Policy: Strengths and Limitations." *Health Affairs* 11 (4): 95–110.

Cook, T. P., and D. T. Campbell. 1979. *Quasi-Experimentation: Design and Analysis Issues for Field Settings.* Chicago: Rand McNally.

Elixhauser, A., B. R. Luce, W. R. Taylor, and J. Reblando. 1993. "Health Care CBA/CEA: An Update on the Growth and Composition of the Literature." *Medical Care* 31 (7) (Suppl.): JS1–11.

Feder, J. 1977. *Medicare: The Politics of Federal Hospital Insurance.* Lexington, MA: Lexington Books.

Gluck, M., and M. Moon. 2000. *Financing Medicare's Future.* Washington, DC: National Academy of Social Insurance.

Gold, M. 1997. "Markets and Public Programs: Insights from Oregon and Tennessee." *Journal of Health Politics, Policy and Law* 22 (2): 633–66.

Hacker, J. S. 1997. *The Road to Nowhere.* Princeton, NJ: Princeton University Press.

Hacker, J. S., and T. Skocpol. 1997. "The New Politics of U.S. Health Policy." *Journal of Health Politics, Policy and Law* 22 (2): 315–38.

Henry J. Kaiser Family Foundation. 2001. *Medicare and Prescription Drugs.* Menlo Park, CA: The Henry J. Kaiser Family Foundation.

Hinckley, B. 1983. *Stability and Change in Congress,* 3rd ed. New York: Harper & Row.

House, E. R. 1993. *Professional Evaluation: Social Impact and Political Consequences.* Newbury Park, CA: Sage Publications.

Kingdon, J. W. 1995. *Agendas, Alternatives, and Public Policies,* 2nd ed. New York: HarperCollins College Publishing.

Lindblom, C. E. 1969. "The Sciences of 'Muddling Through'." In *Readings in Modern Organizations,* edited by A. Etzioni, 154–65. Englewood Cliffs, NJ: Prentice Hall.

———. 1992. *Inquiry and Change.* New Haven, CT: Yale University Press.

Longest, B. B., Jr. 1996. *Health Professionals in Management.* Stamford, CT: Appleton & Lange.

Marmor, T. R. 1973. *The Politics of Medicare.* Chicago: Aldine.

Maxwell, S., M. Moon, and M. Segal. 2001. *Growth in Medicare and Out-of-Pocket Spending: Impact on Vulnerable Beneficiaries.* New York: Commonwealth Fund.

Moon, M. 2001. "Medicare." *New England Journal of Medicine* 344 (12): 928–31.

National Health Council, Inc. 1993. *Congress and Health: An Introduction to the Legislative Process and Its Key Participants,* 10th ed. Government Relations Handbook Series. Washington, DC: National Health Council, Inc.

Newhouse, J. P. 1974. "A Design for a Health Insurance Experiment" *Inquiry* 11 (1): 5–27.

Oliver, T. R., and P. Paul-Shaheen. 1997. "Translating Ideas into Actions: Entrepreneurial Leadership in State Health Care Reforms." *Journal of Health Politics, Policy and Law* 22 (3): 721–88.

Patton, C. V., and D. Sawicki. 1986. *Basic Methods of Policy Analysis and Planning.* Englewood Cliffs, NJ: Prentice Hall.

Peterson, M. A. 1993. "Political Influence in the 1990s: From Iron Triangles to Policy Networks." *Journal of Health Politics, Policy and Law* 18 (2): 395–438.

———. 1997. "Introduction: Health Care into the Next Century." *Journal of Health Politics, Policy and Law* 22 (2): 291–313.

Rhodes, R. P. 1992. *Health Care Politics, Policy, and Distributive Justice.* Albany, NY: State University of New York Press.

Russell, L. B., and C. L. Manning. 1989. "The Effect of Prospective Payment on Medicare Expenditures." *New England Journal of Medicine* 320 (7): 439–44.

Starr, P. 1982. *The Social Transformation of American Medicine.* New York: Basic Books, Inc., Publishers.

Starr, P., and W. A. Zelman. 1993. "Bridge to Compromise: Competition Under a Budget." *Health Affairs* 12 (Suppl.): 7–23.

Thompson, F. J. 1981. *Health Policy and the Bureaucracy: Politics and Implementation.* Cambridge, MA: The Massachusetts Institute of Technology Press.

U.S. Congress. House Committee on Ways and Means. 1992. *1992 Green Book.* Washington, DC: U.S. Government Printing Office.

8

POLITICAL COMPETENCE

EALTH POLICIES have impact, as was discussed extensively in chapter 2. Individuals and populations, health-related organizations and systems, and health-related interest groups, all of whom feel the effects of health policies, share, to varying degrees depending on the relative importance of the impact of policies on them, two related areas of concern about policies and the process that produces them.

- First, they want to know how policies will affect them and the people and things that they care about or for which they are responsible. In other words, they have a discernment or analytical interest in policymaking and its results. People normally want information about anything that affects them, including health policies, and they prefer to have this information before they feel the impact so they can prepare for it.

- Second, they want to have some ability to influence the policymaking process and thereby the policies that affect them. These effects can, after all, be quite direct and of significant consequence. As a result of specific policies, for instance, certain people gain or lose access to a particular medical procedure or obtain or fail to obtain grants to support research projects. Certain organizations see demand for their services increase or decrease, or see their revenues and expenses rise or fall.

Possession of the dual abilities to effectively *analyze* and *influence* the public policymaking process was termed *political competence* in chapter 1. This chapter describes in more depth the activities necessary to effectively analyze and influence the policymaking process.[1] It is useful to reiterate from chapter 1, that everyone professionally involved in the pursuit of health through any of the determinants of health—physical environment, behavior and biology, social factors, health services—has a vested interest in possessing the political competence necessary to assess the impact of public policies on their domain of interest or responsibility on the one hand, and to exert influence in the public policymaking process on the other hand. Further, from that earlier discussion, it is useful to remember that the single most important factor in political competence—whether the ability to assess impact of public policies or to exert influence in the policymaking process—is to understand the public policymaking process as a *decision-making* process. Public policies, including health policies, are decisions, albeit decisions made in a particular way by particular people. Thus, political competence means understanding the context, participants, and processes of this particular type of decision making. It is the basis on which productive engagement with the policymaking process can occur.

Within the context of the political marketplace, many participants seek to further their objectives by influencing the outcomes of the policymaking process. By understanding the policymaking process, politically competent people know the points at which, and how, they can be involved in the process. They appreciate the fact that they can be involved in setting the policy agenda by helping define the problems that policies might address, by participating in the development of possible solutions to the problems, or by helping to create the political circumstances necessary to turn the ideas for solving problems into actual policies. Politically competent people also know how to effectively participate in the actual drafting of legislative proposals or in providing testimony in the hearings in which legislation is developed and refined, and how to influence health policy by focusing on the rulemaking that helps guide the implementation of legislation enacted into laws. Through effective participation one can exert influence on future health policies and, thus, on the determinants of health and ultimately on health itself. However, there is more to political competence than the ability to exert influence in the policymaking process.

As discussed in chapter 2, health policies impact on the health of people—as individuals and as populations. Policies also have tremendous impact on health-related organizations and systems, and on health-related interest groups and their members. Implicit in political competence is the capability of the leaders of organizations, systems, or groups to accurately analyze the public policy environment of their organization, system, or group. The *policy environment* of a particular entity is the policymaking process, its results, and all the forces that can affect the process that have relevance to the entity.

Such analyses include understanding the strategic consequences of events and forces in the public policy environment. Politically competent leaders are able to assess the impacts, both in terms of opportunities and threats, of public policies on their domains and, because they can do this in advance of the impact, are able to position themselves and their organizations, systems, or groups to make strategic adjustments that reflect planned responses to these impacts.

Consider as an example the strategic importance of policy changes that increase the enrollment of Medicare program beneficiaries in managed care programs. The administrator of the Centers for Medicare & Medicaid Services (CMS) announced in June 2001, that the agency's goal was to double the enrollment of beneficiaries in managed care plans within four years (Pear 2001). At the time of this announcement, only about 5.7 of the 40 million Medicare beneficiaries were enrolled in such plans. This policy shift could have enormous implications for managed care plans serving this population; for physicians, hospitals, and other health services organizations and systems contracting with the plans to provide services; and for beneficiaries and their interest groups, such as the American Association of Retired Persons (AARP) (www.aarp.org). Leaders of these and many other organizations, systems, and groups have vital interests in such a policy shift. The more politically competent among them will be able to respond more effectively.

The Real World of Health Policy

Political Competence and the Distribution of Pennsylvania's Share of the Tobacco Settlement Funds

Tobacco Settlement Could Mean Billions for Pennsylvania

From the November 23, 1998, *Capitol Updates*

Pennsylvania has signed on to an agreement with the tobacco industry that could result in the state receiving $11.2 billion in payments over the next twenty-five years. The $206 billion settlement, negotiated by eight state attorneys general including Pennsylvania, was reached with the country's four largest producing tobacco companies.

If ratified by most of the states, Pennsylvania would receive its initial payment of $138 million no later than June 30, 2000, and another $368 million later that year. The average payment from the tobacco companies to Pennsylvania would average $400 million per year for the next twenty-five years.

Proposals Introduced in Harrisburg (State Capitol) to Spend Tobacco Settlement Funds

From the February 15, 1999, *Capitol Updates*

A number of state legislative leaders have proposed ideas on how to spend anticipated revenues from tobacco manufacturers that were negotiated in the recent tobacco settlement. The House Democratic plan includes the following:

- Improve access to health care by expanding Insurance Coverage for currently uninsured populations;
- Expand public health initiatives such as targeting at-risk youth smokers and matching grants for community based health improvement projects; and
- Increase funding for medical education and research.

The House Democratic Policy Committee will conduct public hearings throughout the state to elicit the views of Pennsylvania citizens on how the funds should be spent.

Representative Robert Godshall (R-Montgomery) has introduced House Bill 226 which would require that 25 percent of all tobacco revenue be spent on cancer research. Representative Dennis O'Brien (R-Philadelphia) is proposing that all proceeds be deposited into the Health Opportunities for Pennsylvania Enhancement Fund (HOPE) to protect the principal and allow interest to accrue. Under the HOPE plan, a board of directors consisting of health care experts would make spending recommendations to the General Assembly.

Governor Ridge and House Republicans are expected to announce their own tobacco settlement proposals soon.

Legislative Briefing on Health Uses of Tobacco Funds

From the April 26, 1999, *Capitol Updates*

Health uses for tobacco funds was the focus of a regional legislative briefing on April 9th sponsored by the Hospital and Health System Association of Pennsylvania (HAP) in Warrendale. Western Pennsylvania state legislators were welcomed by Hospital Council of Western Pennsylvania President Ian Rawson, Ph.D., and briefed by members of the HAP staff, Rosemary Wuenschel and Nancy Heffernan. Government Relations Representatives from UPMC Health System, UPMC Braddock, UPMC McKeesport and the University of Pittsburgh Cancer Institute attended the event.

General Assembly Adjourns
with No Tobacco Settlement Spending Plan

From the December 4, 2000, *Capitol Updates*

The Pennsylvania General Assembly ended the 1999–2000 legislative session without adopting any plan for expenditure of the tobacco settlement funds (an estimated $465 million has been collected so far). There is still disagreement between the General Assembly and Governor Ridge on some issues. For example, there is support in the House for using a portion of the funds to fund prescription drug coverage for seniors, however Senate Republicans and the governor are not in favor of it. There are also questions concerning research, providing health insurance for uninsured low-income adults, and the possible establishment of a reserve fund to guard against a potential decline in settlement revenue. Additional payments from the tobacco industry are expected in January and April, 2001. It is hoped that a tobacco spending plan will be adopted early next year.

Tobacco Settlement Tops Legislative Agenda

From the January 16, 2001, *Capitol Updates*

The General Assembly and Governor Tom Ridge are expected to pass legislation early this year that will determine how Pennsylvania will allocate revenue received from the tobacco manufacturers. The tobacco settlement is projected to add an average of $400 million to the state treasury over the next 25 years. The governor introduced his spending plan early last year but no action was taken by the General Assembly. There is support in the State House for using tobacco settlement dollars to pay for prescription drug services but, at this time, Governor Ridge and Republican leaders in the State Senate do not share that support.

Progress on a Tobacco Settlement Spending Plan

From the May 29, 2001, *Capitol Updates*

Action by the General Assembly may be taken soon on a tobacco settlement spending plan. Two bills have been approved by the Senate and sent to the House for consideration. Senate Bill 504 would create a program for low-income workers with disabilities to purchase health insurance coverage under the Medical Assistance Program. The Department of Public Welfare would administer the program. Senate Bill 507 would create a Community Coordinated Care Program that would approve grants for certain health centers and clinics. The Department of Health would administer the program. The General Assembly has yet to determine the percentage of funding to be used for S.B. 504 and S.B. 507 as well as the other bills related to the tobacco settlement still pending in the legislature. A final tobacco settlement spending plan is expected to be approved by the General Assembly before June 30.

Tobacco Settlement Spending Plan Approved by the Legislature

From the June 25, 2001, *Capitol Updates*

Ongoing conference discussions to negotiate a tobacco settlement spending plan concluded on June 19 with an agreement that was approved by the legislature on June 21. Following is the breakdown of the plan:

30%	providing basic health insurance for the low-income adult uninsured population
19%	grants for medical research
13%	expanded support of home and community-based services
12%	smoking cessation and prevention programs
10%	reimbursements to hospitals for charity care (also called uncompensated care)
8%	expansion of the state's prescription drug benefits for seniors (PACE and PACENET)
8%	an endowment to handle future program costs
100%	

Other initiatives to be funded on a one-time basis include regional biotechnology "greenhouses," venture capital funds for health related start-up companies, education loan programs, and updated medical equipment for eligible facilities.

The Commonwealth could receive up to $425 million annually from the tobacco settlement, depending on the status of cigarette sales and inflation. The full text of the spending plan (H.B. 2) can be found online at http://www.legis.state.pa.us/WU01/LI/BI/billroom.htm.

Tobacco Settlement Spending Plan Is Signed by the Governor

From the July 9, 2001, *Capitol Updates*

The legislation detailing the spending plan for Pennsylvania's share of the tobacco settlement was signed by Governor Tom Ridge on June 26 at the offices of Cellomics, a Harmarville, PA company that provides cell-based analysis for the evaluation of new drugs. The spending plan (H.B. 2), approved by the legislature on June 21, can be found at http://www.legis.state.pa.us/WU01/LI/BI/billroom.htm. Pennsylvania is one of only eight states to dedicate all of its tobacco funds to health care initiatives, including an emphasis on biomedical research.

Tobacco Funds Hit Mark on Biomedical Research

From the July 2, 2001, *The Philadelphia Inquirer*
An Opinion Piece by Elizabeth O'Brien, General Counsel and Associate
Director for Administration, Winstar Institute, Philadelphia

In passing legislation to distribute the Commonwealth's share of proceeds from the tobacco settlement, Gov. Ridge and Pennsylvania's state legislature vaulted to the fore nationally in their support for biomedical research.

Nineteen percent of the settlement proceeds, or roughly $65 million dollars annually, will be used to fund medical research at academic institutions and research centers statewide. Some of these funds will support a new research-grant program administered by the Department of Health, while the lion's share will flow directly to research institutions to enhance infrastructure and expand scientific staff and programs.

Research institutions across the Commonwealth are applauding this important legislation, as are many in the biotechnology business community. This is a period of immense and rapid growth in our understanding of life's genetic building blocks, as marked by the completion of the sequencing of the human genome last year. But much of this new genetic information has yet to be processed, and the task of interpreting it and using it to inform our development of new disease treatments or therapies will require unprecedented commitments of money and technical skill.

Until now, academic research institutions in Pennsylvania have had to rely on the National Institutes of Health and private foundations to fund most of their work in this area. These sources seldom provide all of the funding needed for new equipment, recruitment of talented young investigators, or new research initiatives, preferring to support well-established research programs instead. As a consequence, many research institutions in the state have lacked the resources to move with alacrity into the next era of biomedical research.

All of this should change in the near future. Nearly every academic research institution in the state will soon receive funding under the tobacco settlement legislation to enhance its medical research programs. The largest amounts of funding will go to those institutions that already have the biggest NIH-supported research programs, with the goal of concentrating resources where a strong research foundation already exists.

Proportionally smaller allocations will be made to institutions with fewer federal grant dollars, but even there, the new funding should open doors to new research opportunities.

Perhaps most significantly, the academic research institutions will have considerable latitude to decide how best to use these dollars. Many should now find it possible to improve the quality of their research facilities, and to attract the best and brightest young scientists to work in their laboratories.

For Pennsylvania, the benefits from this far-sighted investment in medical research will be numerous. With the new state support, academic research institutions will be able to compete more successfully for federal grant dollars. Pharmaceutical and biotechnology companies will grow, adding high quality new jobs to their rolls, as they reap the benefits of the new inventions and discoveries issuing forth from the academic laboratories.

But most significantly, the residents of Pennsylvania will have improved access to the newest, most effective treatments for heart disease, cancer, emphysema, and the many other serious diseases linked to tobacco use.

Source: Capitol Updates, © Government Relations, UPMC Health System. Reprinted with permission. *Philadelphia Inquirer,* © Philadelphia Newspapers Inc. Reprinted with permission.

Political Competence and the Advantage of Lead Time

The ability to develop effective responses to the strategic consequences of policy changes—whether new policies or modifications of existing ones—is greatly enhanced by lead time. Political competence can provide the luxury of more lead time. When the leaders of organizations, systems, or groups are able to *anticipate* policy changes months—or better still, years—ahead of when they actually occur, their responses can be more thoughtful and usually more effective or appropriate.

Beyond giving themselves the advantages of longer lead times to prepare for policy shifts and changes, those who understand the emergence of particular policy changes, even before the policy debate over the specific nature of the changes begins, can be positioned to exert influence on emerging policies to the advantage of their organizations. They foresee both the emergence and impact of relevant public policies on their domains of responsibility. This foresight—derived from political competence—enables them to begin to help shape the nature and scope of policies that will affect their organizations, systems, or groups—much to their strategic advantage.

But how is such prescience to be achieved? The answer lies in how the analysis component of political competence is approached. Leaders who look beyond specific decisions reflected in public policies to the environments from which policies derive have a great advantage over those who merely wait until a policy is determined, and then react to it. Wayne Gretzky, a hockey star, when asked what the secret to his success was, replied: "Most players skate to the puck. I skate to where the puck will be. This has made all the difference in my success." Leaders benefit when they focus not only on the policies that affect their domains, but much greater advantage can be gained when they also focus on why and how these policies emerge. Leaders who broadly focus on the public policy environments of their domains, increase their chances of anticipating policy changes in advance of when the changes actually occur.

This anticipatory focus—thinking about where the puck is going, not simply where it is—also facilitates the effective exertion of influence on the factors that lead, ultimately, to policies. It provides an opportunity to actually influence policies in their emergent states. Leaders of entities who understand the public policy environments, with all their complex interplay of actors, actions, inactions, and other variables, are better equipped to both anticipate and influence policies than their less informed—or less politically competent—counterparts. They are prepared to ask more anticipatory, "what if" questions. There is always a vast difference between leading an entity based on solid predictions of *future* policies versus reacting to announced changes, or even to soon to be announced changes. Proactive preparation and the opportunity to exert influence on the ultimate shape of policies are possible with enough foreknowledge. After policy changes occur, only reaction is possible, typically with inadequate time for thoughtful responses if caught by surprise.

Equipped with a better understanding of their analysis and influence responsibilities regarding the public policy environment that faces their domains, leaders can be more politically competent. The most important techniques and tactics that leaders of health-related organizations, systems, and interest groups utilize to analyze and influence their public policy environments are discussed in the next two sections.

Analyzing Public Policy Environments

A number of concrete benefits derive from the effective analysis by leaders of any organization, system, or interest group of its public policy environment. Such analysis of an entity's public policy environment helps its leaders:

- classify and organize complex information about the public policy-making process and about forces and pressures that affect the process;

- identify and assess *current* public policies that do or will affect their entity;
- identify and assess the formulation of *emerging* public policies—including new laws, amendments, and changes in rules—that might eventually affect their entity;
- speculate in a systematic way about potential future relevant public policies; and
- link information about public policies to the objectives and strategies of their organization, system, or group and, thus, to its performance.

These potential benefits to the leaders of organizations, systems, and interest groups are substantial. However, they are somewhat offset by several limitations inherent in any attempt to analyze the complex public policy environments of most entities. These inherent limitations in the ability of individuals, no matter how talented or how well supported their endeavors may be, include some truths about people:

- No one can foretell the future through analyses of public policy environments; at best only informed opinions and guesses about the future can be made.
- People cannot possibly see every aspect of the policymaking process, nor can they even be aware, generally, of every detail of the public policies that will have an impact on their organizations, systems, or interest groups.
- Leaders may effectively discern relevant public policies or emergent ones but be unable to interpret correctly the impact of the policies on their organizations, systems, or groups.
- Leaders may effectively discern and interpret the impact of relevant policies or emergent ones, but find their organizations, systems, or groups unable to respond appropriately.

Although there are limitations to what can be expected from efforts to analyze the public policy environments of health-related organizations, systems, and interest groups, their leaders derive enough benefits from doing so to justify committing substantial resources to carry out the analyses. The most important of these resources is the commitment of senior-level leaders to ensuring that effective analysis occurs.

If effective environmental analyses are to be carried out, the senior-level leaders, those at what Mintzberg (1983) calls the "strategic apex" of their entity, must bear responsibility, although they typically rely on the help of others to carry out the functions and specific activities involved in the analysis. These functions extend beyond the obvious one of discerning important information. They also include organizing the information in useful ways and evaluating the information to plot the issues that are likely to have significant impacts on their organization, system, or group.

Organization Designs for Environmental Analysis

Entities, at least those with sufficient resources, typically build into their structures some formal means of accomplishing effective environmental analyses, although the approach of any organization, system, or interest group may be idiosyncratic to its situation. Management literature is replete with recommendations to create specialized administrative units in organizations for the purpose of conducting environmental analyses (Ginter, Duncan, and Swayne 2002; Sanchez and Heene 2001). These recommendations typically consider the analyses of public policy environments to be conducted as part of larger sets of overall environmental analysis responsibilities of such units. Furthermore, these recommendations often include having the environmental analysis units or activities embedded in departments or units with larger planning, marketing, or public affairs responsibilities.

In an important study of this subject, Lenz and Engledow (1986) focused on a set of ten organizations, inquiring into how they organized themselves for environmental analysis activities. The organizations chosen for the study were in different industries and were selected for the study specifically because they were considered to be at the leading edge of environmental analysis practices. These organizations exhibited considerable variation regarding where within their organization designs the environmental analysis activities were housed, with no apparent contingent relationships between the designs and such factors as the organizations' sizes, their basic strategies, or other aspects of their organization designs.

No matter how entities choose to organize themselves to carry out analyses of their public policy environments, the procedure used to conduct the analyses is well defined and, as will be seen in the next section, is essentially similar across all types of organizational settings.

The Procedure of Analyzing Public Policy Environments

The analysis of the public policy environment of an organization, system, or interest group is part of the larger external environmental analysis through which its leaders seek to determine the externally imposed opportunities and threats facing their organization or system, or, in the case of interest groups, their members. The relevant variables in their external environments include, but are not limited to, the public policy environment. In fact, the external environments of entities include *all* the factors outside their boundaries that can influence their performance. Public policies are certainly among the factors; however, as noted above, biological, cultural, demographic, ecological, economic, ethical, legal, psychological, social, and technological factors are also relevant and must be routinely analyzed if they are to be taken into account in an entity's efforts to perform well.

An effective analysis of a public policy environment may be conducted using a variety of tools and techniques. Some of the more common ones include trend identification and extrapolation; expert opinion gathered through the Delphi technique or focus groups; and scenario development. No matter which technique is used, it is most productively applied within the framework of a five-step set of activities that is useful in analyzing any entity's external environment, including its public policy environment. Four of the steps are routinely considered in the general strategic management literature (Fahey and Narayanan 1986) and have been adapted for use specifically in health-related organizations by Ginter, Duncan, and Swayne (2002). A fifth step is added to their list below. The interrelated steps in conducting analyses of public policy environments are:

- *scanning* the environment to identify strategic public policy issues—that is, issues that may be specific public policies or problems, possible solutions to the problems, and political circumstances that might eventually lead to policies—that are relevant and important to the organization, system, or interest group;
- *monitoring* the strategic public policy issues identified;
- *forecasting* or projecting the future direction of strategic public policy issues;
- *assessing* importance of the strategic public policy issues for the entity; and
- *diffusing* results of the analysis of public policy environments among those in the organization, system, or interest group who can help formulate and implement its response to these issues.

Each of these steps in analyzing public policy environments is examined in turn in the following sections. A more extensive discussion of these steps can be found in Longest (1997, chapter 4).

Scanning the Environment to Identify Strategic Public Policy Issues

Effective environmental scanning acquires and organizes strategically important information from an entity's external environment. This step properly begins with careful consideration by the leaders of what they believe to be strategic public policy issues. In guiding the focus of scanning, it is useful to remember the definition of public policies given earlier: they are authoritative decisions—made in the legislative, executive, or judicial branches of government—that are intended to direct or influence the actions, behaviors, or decisions of others. When these decisions influence in any way the strategic actions, behaviors, or decisions of an entity's leaders, then they can be thought of as relevant strategic public policies.

The set of strategic public policies for any entity constitutes a very large set of decisions. Remember that some of these decisions are codified in the statutory language of specific public laws. Others are the rules or regulations established in order to implement public laws or to operate government and its various programs. Still others are the judicial branch's relevant decisions.

The large set of public policies that are of strategic importance to health-related organizations, systems, or interest groups, however, represents only part of what must be considered strategic public policy *issues*. The problems, potential solutions, and political circumstances that might eventually align to lead to strategic policies must also be considered important strategic public policy issues. These, too, must be taken into account in complete analyses of public policy environments. Thus, effective scanning of the public policy environment involves identifying specific strategic policies *and* identifying emerging problems, possible solutions, and the political circumstances that surround them, which could eventually lead to policies of strategic importance. Together, these form the set of strategic *public policy issues* that should be scanned.

Consideration within any entity about what issues are in fact of strategic importance is largely judgmental, speculative, or conjectural (Klein and Linneman 1984). Obviously, this makes the quality of the judgments, speculations, and conjectures quite important. For this reason, it is useful to have more than one person decide which of the scanned issues are of strategic significance. One widely used approach in making these judgments is to rely on an ad hoc task force or a committee of people from within the organization, system, or interest group to render their collective opinions.

Another popular approach is to use outside consultants who can provide expert opinions and judgments as to what is strategically important in the environments of health-related organizations and interest groups. It is also possible to utilize any of several more formal expert-based techniques. The most useful among these are the Delphi technique, the nominal group technique, brainstorming, focus groups, and dialectic inquiry (Ginter, Duncan, and Swayne 2002; Webster, Reif, and Bracker 1989; Jain 1984; Terry 1977; Delbecq, Van de Ven, and Gustafson 1974). The starting point in any scanning activity, no matter who is doing it or which techniques might be employed, is the question of who or what to scan.

Who or What Should Be Scanned?   Universally, policymakers in federal, state, and local levels of government and those who can influence their decisions—whether through helping shape conceptualization of problems and their potential solutions or through impact on the political circumstances that help drive the policymaking process—are the appropriate focus of scanning activities. The focus can be refined for particular situations by limiting it to strategically important policies and the problems, potential solutions, and political circumstances that might eventually lead to policies that affect the specific organization, system, or interest group.

Another way of identifying who or what should be scanned in a public policy environment is to think of the suppliers of relevant public policies, and those who can influence them, as forming the appropriate focus. As discussed in chapter 3, members of each branch of government play roles as suppliers of policies in the political market, although the roles are very different. Each should receive attention in the scanning activity. Because policies are made in all three branches of government, the list of potential suppliers of public policies—the policymakers—is lengthy, and adding those who can influence the suppliers makes the list even longer.

Effectively scanning an entity's public policy environment identifies specific public policies that are of strategic importance. *Very* effective scanning also identifies the *emerging* problems, possible solutions to them, and the political circumstances that surround them that could eventually lead to strategically important policies. But scanning, even when very effectively done, is only the first step in the overall set of interrelated activities involved in analyzing a public policy environment.

The Real World of Health Policy

Accounting for the Mind-Sets of Policymakers

The upper boundary of what society can and is willing to spend in its pursuit of health is, of course, unknown. This matter has puzzled some very thoughtful people for decades. What is known, however, is that all economic resources, including those used in the pursuit of health, have alternative uses, and people do have a variety of preferences about how the resources should be used. Fuchs (1974, 7), with elegance and prescience, warned about three decades ago of the ultimate necessity of making some difficult choices about health: "We cannot have all the health or all the medical care that we would like to have." Others have echoed and extended this warning (Aaron and Schwartz 1984; Callahan 1987; Reinhardt 1990).

However, the fact that no society or government, not even in a country as rich as the United States, has sufficient resources to provide all the support that people want in their pursuit of health, at least not if their other wants are to be simultaneously met as well, is not well reflected in society's attitudes about health or in public policymaking regarding it.

There is no reason to think that the wants people have regarding their health will abate in the future, nor is there any reason to anticipate that some large new pool of resources will be found to pay exclusively for them. Large federal budget surpluses in recent years have triggered consideration of increased health spending, such as adding a prescription drug benefit to the Medicare program. However, the first use of these additional federal resources was the enactment of the Economic Growth and Tax Relief Reconciliation Act of 2001 (P.L. 107-16), containing plans for a $1.35 trillion reduction in federal income taxes over a decade.

Until the present, the nation's health policy history has shown that ignoring or downplaying the reality of economic constraints or limits—or at least postponing concerns about them—has permitted policymakers to ignore the necessity to make difficult, even painful, choices about the long-run allocation of its available, but ultimately limited resources. Even so, many of the important questions regarding this issue are known. Among the most familiar ones: Are available resources better utilized at the beginning or the end of life? Is prevention better than cure? Are 25,000 vaccinations better than a single organ transplant? Is society better served by more physicians or by more teachers? Or engineers? Or musicians? Is it better served by more museums, art galleries, playgrounds, or stock car racing tracks than by more health-related organizations, systems, and programs? Is it better to improve air quality dramatically or to find better ways of treating asthma and lung cancer? Is it better to spend money on smoking cessation or prevention among teenagers or on cancer research? The answers to such questions are unknown; even the criteria that would appropriately be used in answering the questions have not been addressed. Are the criteria to be ethical or economic? Should they be both? In what mix? Who establishes the criteria?

The precise time at which future health policymakers will, of necessity, turn their attention to such questions is unpredictable. The only certainty is that sooner or later they must address them in the context of the nation's health policy. But four quite different mind-sets or what might be called "world views" among policymakers seem to be impeding their ability to do so.

The True Romantics

One group of policymakers, who can be labeled *true romantics*, includes people who apparently do not recognize—or at least are not affected in any visible way by—the concept of economic limits. Such policymakers simply do not include in their decision making any appreciable consideration of the notion that society's resources are actually limited and that this should be reflected in health policy.

The Pseudo Romantics

Another group, different from the true romantics because they do understand the relevance of considering economic limits as an important component of policymaking, nevertheless behave like true romantics in their decision making. These *pseudo romantics* understand limits, but their willingness to take the limits into account is tempered or even overridden by other concerns or objectives. Because these concerns, if acted on, might interfere with achieving some desirable end, they are simply ignored. Such people, in order to have their way, deny the importance of limits, often relying on the possibility that someone else will give up something so that their preferences can be realized, or that new resources will suddenly be found. People in this group tend to be policymakers with strong convictions about serving the public interest, but appear to be unconvinced or unwilling to acknowledge that all benefits must eventually be paid for.

The Truly Self-Serving

A third mind-set that makes it very difficult for policymakers to fully incorporate consideration of economic limits in decision making can be found in a group that can be labeled, derogatorily, the *truly self-serving*. Policymakers of this mind-set may know very well about the appropriateness of making policy that reflects the reality of economic limits, but are so intent on making certain that their own interests are well served in the policymaking process that they completely ignore the notion of limits. The truly self-serving are so intent on ensuring that their own interests are served that other issues become secondary. The larger picture dictated by a concern about the reality of economic constraints and limits does not matter very much to people with a truly self-serving mind-set. In their ability to ignore limits, the truly self-serving are not unlike the pseudo romantics. However, pseudo romantics do not let limits factor into their decisions because this may serve some larger public-interest purpose; for the truly self-serving the reasons for ignoring limits are altogether selfish.

The Proscrastinators

A fourth mind-set, very well represented in policymaking, that also impedes progress toward fully integrating the reality of economic limits into the nation's health policy can be labeled the *procrastinators*. This very large group includes policymakers who accept the ultimate reality of economic limits and even accept the idea that limits will impose difficult allocation choices, but who also believe that the fateful day when these limits must actually guide decisions can be postponed still further. Procrastinators accept the fact that economic limits ultimately will exert a very heavy influence on health policy. But in their view, the United States can continue to postpone these difficult decisions. For the procrastinators, the difficult decisions about resource allocation for the pursuit of health can be left to future policymakers and the consequences to future generations.

Thus far, the procrastinators have been right. It has indeed been possible to postpone effectively incorporating the reality of economic limits into the nation's health policy. To verify this, one need only look at Figure 1.2 to be reminded of the persisting pattern of steady growth in the economic resources devoted to the pursuit of health. But how far into the future can continuing growth be sustained? Stubborn procrastination in the face of economic limits and the impact of these limits on health policy does indeed have a finite life. The inability, or unwillingness, of health policymakers, heretofore, to take into fuller account the economic limits of the nation's pursuit of health will certainly continue to influence health policy in the future. But eventually health policy will of necessity more fully reflect the implications of wider acceptance among policymakers of economic limits.

Monitoring Strategic Public Policy Issues

Monitoring is more than scanning. It is the tracking, or following, of strategically important public policy issues over time. Public policy issues are monitored because the leaders of organizations, systems, or interest groups, or their support staffs who may be doing the actual monitoring, believe the issues are of strategic importance. Monitoring them, especially when the issues are not well structured or are ambiguous as to strategic importance, permits more information to be assembled so that issues can be clarified and the degree to which they are, or the rate at which they are becoming, strategically important can be determined (Fahey and Narayanan 1986; Thomas and McDaniel 1990).

The monitoring step has a much narrower focus than scanning (Ginter, Duncan, and Swayne 2002). This is because the purpose in monitoring is to build a base of data and information around the set of strategically important public policy issues that are identified through scanning or verified through earlier monitoring. Fewer, usually far fewer, issues will be monitored than will be scanned as part of analyzing public policy environments.

Monitoring is extremely important because it is so often difficult to determine whether public policy issues are strategically important. Under conditions of certainty, the leaders of entities analyzing their environments would fully understand strategic issues and all consequential implications for their decisions and actions. However, uncertainty characterizes much about the strategically important issues faced by most health-related organizations, systems, and groups. Monitoring will not remove uncertainty, but it will likely reduce it significantly as more detailed and sustained information is acquired. As with scanning, techniques that feature the acquisition of multiple perspectives and expert opinions can help the leaders determine what should be monitored; experts in the form of consultants can also be utilized for the actual monitoring if this is beyond the capacity of the entity's regular staff.

Monitoring the strategic public policy issues for most organizations, systems, and interest groups in the health domain will affirm for their leaders that the vast majority of contemporary policies spring from a relatively few earlier policies. This point was emphasized in chapter 7 in the discussion of policy modification. However, the strategically important public policies for most organizations, systems, and interest groups result from the modification of prior policies, not from a constant stream of new policies. For example, the Government Relations Department of the UPMC Health System tracks legislation of interest to the system and notes on its web site that "many of the health-related issues to look for in 2001 have already been under discussion for some time: prescription drug coverage for seniors, a patients' bill of rights/managed care reform, help for uninsured Americans, and Medicare reform" (www.upmc.edu/govrel).

Monitoring reveals that public policies have histories and, in fact, are frequently "living" history. Many of them continually, although incrementally, evolve through the modification phase of policymaking, as discussed in chapter 7. As people monitor these changes, they tend to become intimately familiar with the evolutionary paths of the public policies they monitor. Such knowledge can be very valuable as a background for the next step in analyzing public policy environments, forecasting changes.

Forecasting Changes in Strategic Public Policy Issues

Effective scanning and monitoring cannot, by themselves, provide all the information about the strategic public policy issues in an entity's environment that its leaders would like. Often, if the response to strategic issues is to be made effectively, reliable forecasts of future conditions or states is necessary. That is, information about issues and their effects before they occur is needed. This may give them time to formulate and implement successful responses to the issues.

Scanning and monitoring the public policy environment involves searching this environment for signals, sometimes distant and faint signals, that may be the forerunners of strategically important issues. Forecasting involves extending the issues and their impacts beyond their current states. For some public policy issues (e.g., the impact on patient demand of a change in public policy that redefines the eligibility requirements in the Medicaid program), adequate forecasts can be made by extending past trends or by applying a formula. In other situations, forecasting must rely upon conjecture, speculation, and judgment, although these can be systematically compiled through such means as Delphi panels or focus groups. Sometimes, even sophisticated simulations can be conducted to forecast the future.

However, some degree of uncertainty characterizes the results of all of these forecasting techniques. It is especially difficult to incorporate in the utilization of any of them the fact that strategically important public policy issues never exist in a vacuum, and typically involve many issues at work simultaneously. No forecasting existing techniques or models fully account for this condition.

Trend Extrapolation.   The most widely used technique for forecasting changes in public policy issues is trend extrapolation (Klein and Linneman 1984). This technique, when properly used, can be remarkably effective and is relatively simple to use. Trend extrapolation is nothing more than tracking a particular issue, and then using the information to predict future changes. Public policies do not emerge *de novo*. Instead, they result from linked trains of activities that can and typically do span many years. This feature of the policymaking process makes its results more predictable than some might believe (Molitar 1977).

Even so, trend extrapolation as a technique in environmental analysis must be handled very carefully. It works best under highly stable conditions; under all other conditions it has significant limitations. When used to forecast changes in public policy, it usually permits the prediction of some general trend—such as directional trends in the number of people served by a program or in funding streams—rather than quantification of the trend with great specificity.

Significant policy changes, as well as changes in technology, demographics, or other variables, can render the extrapolation of a trend meaningless or misleading. In spite of this, however, predictions about trends through extrapolation can be quite useful to the leaders of organizations, systems, and interest groups as they seek to predict the paths of their strategically important policy issues. For those who exercise caution in its use and who factor in the effect of changes such as the introduction of a new or modified policy, trend extrapolation can be a very useful technique in forecasting certain aspects of the public policy environments of their health-related organizations, systems, or interest groups.

Scenario Development.   Another technique for forecasting the public policy environment is the development, usually in writing, of scenarios of the future (Leemhuis 1985). A scenario is simply a plausible story about the future. This technique is especially appropriate for analyzing environments that include many uncertainties and imponderables. Such features generally characterize the public policy environments of health-related organizations and interest groups.

The essence of scenario development is to define several alternative future scenarios, or states of affairs. These can be used as the basis for developing contingent responses to the predictions; alternatively, the set of scenarios can be used to select what the organization, system, or interest group leaders consider the most likely future, the one to which they will prepare to respond (Schwartz 1991).

Scenarios of the future can pertain to a single policy issue (e.g., the federal government's policy regarding approval procedures for new medical technology) or to broader-based sets of policy issues (e.g., the federal government's policies regarding regulation of health plans, funding for medical education or research, or a preventive approach to improved health). Scenarios can and, in practice, do vary considerably in scope and depth (Venable et al. 1994).

As a general rule, when using the scenario development technique in forecasting public policy environments, it is useful to develop several scenarios. Multiple scenarios permit the breadth of future possibilities to be explored. After the full range of possibilities has been reflected in a set of scenarios, one can be chosen as the most likely scenario. However, the most common mistake made in using scenario development is to envision too early in the process one particular scenario as "the one true picture of the future" (Fahey and Narayanan 1986). The leaders who think they know which scenario will prevail and who prepare only for the one they select may find that the price of guessing incorrectly can be very high indeed.

Assessing the Strategic Importance of Public Policy Issues

Scanning and monitoring strategic public policy issues, and forecasting future changes in them, are important steps in a good environmental analysis. However, the leaders of organizations, systems, and interest groups must also concern themselves about the specific and relative strategic importance of the issues they are analyzing. That is, they must be concerned with an assessment or interpretation of the strategic importance and implications of public policy issues for their entities.

Frequently, this involves characterizing issues as opportunities for or threats to their entity (see Figure 2.1). However, such assessments are far from an exact science. It may well be that sound human judgment is the best technique for making these determinations, although there are several bases on which the strategic importance of public policy issues can be considered. Experience with similar issues is frequently a useful basis for assessing the strategic importance of a public policy issue. The experience may have been acquired firsthand within the particular organization or interest group where an assessment is being made, or it may come from contact with colleagues in other organizations or groups that have experienced similar public policy issues and who are willing to share their experiences. Great variety exists among the states regarding their public policies that affect the pursuit of health; this variety can be instructive. Similarly, the experiences in other countries with various public policies affecting health and its pursuit can be drawn on for insight. Other bases for assessments include intuition or best guesses about what particular public policy issues might mean to an entity, as well as advice from well-informed and experienced others. When possible, quantification, modeling, and simulation of the potential impacts of public policy issues being assessed can be useful.

Making the appropriate determination is rarely a simple task, even when all the bases suggested above are considered. Aside from the difficulties encountered in collecting and properly analyzing enough information to inform the assessment fully, there sometimes are problems that derive from the influence of the personal prejudices and biases of those conducting the environmental assessment. Such problems can force assessments that fit some preconceived notions about what is strategically important rather than reflecting the realities of a particular situation (Thomas and McDaniel 1990).

Diffusing the Results of Environmental Analysis into Organizations, Systems, and Interest Groups

The final step in analyzing public policy environments is the sometimes very difficult one of diffusing or spreading the results of the effort to all those in the entity who need the information to carry out their own responsibilities. This step is frequently undervalued and may even be overlooked in some situations. Unless this step is effectively carried out, however, it really does not matter how well the other steps in environmental analysis are performed.

There are three basic ways that relevant information about the public policy environment of an entity can be diffused throughout the organization or system, or to the members served by an interest group by the leaders. Those who wish to spread the information can:

- use the leader's *power* to dictate diffusion and use of the information (this approach works best in entities whose leaders can, if they choose, use coercion or sanctions to see that the information is diffused, and even used, in all the appropriate places);
- use *reason* to persuade all those who are affected by the information to use it (this works as well as or better than relying on the leader's power, if the leaders are persuasive); or
- perhaps best of all in most situations, use *education* of participants in the entity to emphasize and convince those who need to be convinced of the importance and usefulness of the information as a way of improving the chances that the information will be properly used.

However it is done, diffusion of strategically important information about public policy issues among the relevant participants in organizations, systems, or interest groups brings the steps in analyzing public policy environments to completion. Given the vital link between entities and the public policies that affect them, no contemporary health-related organization, system, or interest group can expect to succeed in the absence of a reasonably effective set of activities through which its leaders discern and, ultimately, respond to strategically important public policy issues. However, this is only half of the task facing these contemporary leaders regarding their public policy environments. They are also responsible for influencing these environments to the strategic advantage of their organization or system, or to the members of their interest group. This complex task is explored in the next section.

Influencing Public Policy Environments

Not only do the leaders of health-related organizations, systems, and interest groups typically make commitments to discerning and utilizing relevant information from their public policy environments, they also typically develop strong operational commitments to devising ways to exert influence in them. Remember, political competence encompasses the dual responsibilities to analyze and influence the policymaking process to advantage. There is nothing innately wrong with a leader establishing an operational objective of being influential in the entity's public policy environment. However, it goes almost without saying that activities directed to this objective can easily be tainted by overzealous attempts to influence the policymaking process for self-serving purposes. This is an area of activity where adherence to the ethical principles of respect for the autonomy of other people, justice, beneficence, and nonmaleficence are especially important. (It may be useful to review the discussion on "Ethics in the Political Marketplace" in chapter 3.)

As with analyzing public policy environments, the responsibility for seeking to influence events and outcomes in public policy environments rests predominantly with those at the strategic apex of each organization, system, or group; that is, with their senior-level managers and governing board members. These leaders, especially in large entities, may be assisted by specialized staff in fulfilling their responsibilities.

When influencing its public policy environment is a major commitment and endeavor for an entity, it typically establishes a specialized department or unit, usually called the public affairs department or government (sometimes called governmental) affairs (or relations) department, to do much of the actual work involved. Some very large organizations, systems, or interest groups even divide government relations into separate departments, one for the federal government and another for state government. The directors of such departments almost invariably report to the chief executive officer (CEO), because CEOs play vital roles in influencing public policy environments, normally acting as the spokesperson for their organization, system, or group with all outside stakeholders, including those in the public policy environment. Departments or units devoted to governmental affairs mainly serve to enhance the ability of the entity's senior-level managers, especially its CEO, to succeed in influencing the public policy environment to advantage.

The Real World of Health Policy

Organizing to Support Political Competence

Information taken from the web sites of the governmental affairs departments of three representative interest groups and from the director of federal government relations at a large academic health system provides examples of the structures and objectives of these units:

- *American Academy of Pediatrics* (www.aap.org). The Academy's Department of Federal Affairs has been its link to federal legislative activities in Washington, DC, for more than 25 years. Pediatricians who wish to make a difference in child and adolescent health through Congress and/or federal agencies are given the information and tools necessary to become effective child advocates. This office helps them prepare to offer testimony in legislation development or to meet with representatives or senators. AAP's policy agenda includes access to healthcare for all children, immunizations, services for children with disabilities, injury prevention, and Medicaid. It is interested in policy affecting legislation and regulations involving the education of new physicians, the ethics of medical practice, biomedical research, and clinical laboratory testing, for example. The Department of Federal Affairs has three functions:
  - — to ensure that policymakers in both Congress and federal agencies are apprised of Academy policies;
  - — to design, implement, and negotiate successful strategies to attain desired legislative outcomes; and
  - — to represent the Academy with relevant interest groups.
- *Wisconsin Medical Society* (www.wismed.org). The Society's mission is "to advance the science and art of medicine for the people of Wisconsin; ensure physicians are equipped to deal effectively with the economic and political aspects of practice; and serve as the patient and physician advocate to government and other relevant publics." Its Advocacy and Policy Department is responsible for the combined activities of legislative affairs (lobbying), policy research and development, and WISMedPAC, the Society's political action committee. Members of the lobbying team represent the Society before the state and federal governments. On the state level, this includes the legislature and a variety of government agencies. The policy staff assists the lobbyists in seeking to impact legislation and rule changes. The Society regularly submits testimony to the state legislature. The Department staff collaborates with a variety of patient advocacy organizations to strengthen mutual political agendas. In addition, staff communicates with other medical societies, the AMA and both state and national specialty societies in order to learn from related legislative activities in other states.
- *Council on Governmental Relations (COGR)* (www.cogr.edu). The Council is an association of 135 leading research-intensive universities that are recipients of a significant share of the federal funds available to higher education through contracts and grants for research and scholarship. COGR concerns itself with the influence of

government regulations, policies, and practices on the performance of research conducted at colleges and universities. COGR's primary function is to help develop policies and practices that fairly reflect the mutual interest and separate obligations of federal agencies and universities in federal research and training. COGR deals mainly with policies and technical issues involved in the administration of federally sponsored programs at universities. The Council concerns itself with the influence of government regulations, policies and practices on the performance of research conducted at colleges and universities. As part of this process, COGR provides advice and information to its membership, and makes certain that federal agencies understand academic operations and the burden their proposed regulations might impose on colleges and universities.

- *University of Pittsburgh Medical Center Health System (UPMC Health System)* (www.upmc.edu). The organizational structure of this academic health system includes a vice president for government relations, who has overall responsibility for analyzing and influencing the system's public policy environment at the local, state, and federal levels and reports to the system's president. The director of federal government relations reports to the vice president and is responsible for keeping the senior managers "informed up to the minute" on relevant federal policies, including legislative and regulatory matters. This director performs the following specific functions:
  — identifies and analyzes relevant legislative and regulatory matters;
  — recommends appropriate responses to legislative and regulatory matters of interest;
  — carries out the responses, including facilitating the participation of others in the responses; and
  — advocates proactively in specific policy areas, including Medicare reimbursement, biomedical research funding, and transplantation issues.

No matter how an organization, system, or group is designed internally to carry out the tasks associated with influencing its public policy environment, the bottom line of exerting influence in public policy environments is that influence actually must eventually be exerted. As discussed extensively in the Power and Influence in Political Markets section in chapter 3, the exertion of influence in public policy environments is "simply the process by which people successfully persuade others to follow their advice, suggestion, or order" (Keys and Case 1990, 38). But how?

Influence: A Matter of Power and Focus

The effective exercise of influence in the public policy environments of organizations, systems, or interest groups, or by them working in collaboration, depends on having a basis for their influence and on knowing where and when to focus their efforts. Power is the basis of influence in a public policy environment. Power is the potential to exert influence. Much like the sources of interpersonal power discussed in Chapter 3, the power that entities utilize to exert influence in their public policy environments derives from three sources:

- *Positional power* is based on an entity's place or role in the larger society. Organizations, systems, and groups have certain power, or potential to exert influence, simply because they exist and are recognized as legitimate participants in the marketplace for policies. Policymakers entertain the opinions and consider the preferences of the leaders of health-related organizations such as Baxter International Inc. (www.baxter.com), a global medical products and services company, or health-related interest groups such as the American Association of Health Plans (www.aahp.org), which represents more than 1,000 HMOs, PPOs, and other network-based plans, in part, simply because they recognize these people, as leaders of important organizations or groups, as legitimate participants in the policymaking arena. An important aspect of positional power is the recognition given by courts to organizations and interest groups to bring legal actions as part of their efforts to exert influence. Positional power, alone, may gain a hearing for particular views or preferences. The exertion of influence, however, usually requires more and different power.

- *Reward* or *coercive power* is based on the entity's capacity to reward compliance or to punish noncompliance with its preferred decisions, actions, and behaviors by policymakers. The rewards that can be provided or withheld by organizations, systems, and groups include money in the form of campaign contributions, as well as other forms of political support by participants in organizations and groups. Political support includes votes, but it also includes the ability to organize and mobilize grassroots activities designed to persuade other people on particular issues.

- *Expert power* is based on an entity's possession of expertise or information that is valued by others. When seeking to exert influence in public policy environments, useful information and expertise may pertain to the definition or clarification of problems or to the development of solutions. It might also be expertise in the intricacies of the public policymaking process.

Organizations, systems, and interest groups that can marshal these bases of power, especially when they can be integrated, can be very influential indeed. The degree of influence, of course, varies from one entity to another. The relative amount of power each has is important in determining relative influence, but so too are reputations for being able to exert influence ethically and effectively and the strength of ideological convictions held by those who seek to influence. Whatever its bases, however, power is only one part of the complex equation that determines influence.

Leaders of organizations, systems, and interest groups must also be concerned about the *focus* of their efforts to influence their public policy environments. Typically, they are guided in focusing by the identification of policies that are of strategic importance to their entity in the scanning efforts described above, as well as by identification of problems, potential solutions, and political circumstances that might eventually lead to such policies. By focusing in this way, they will seek to influence strategically relevant policymakers in all three branches and in federal, state, and local levels of government. Furthermore, they will extend their efforts to influence to those who have influence with these policymakers.

If leaders of entities are to influence the policymaking process effectively, in addition to influencing policymakers directly, they must also concern themselves with helping to shape the conceptualizations of problems, the development of potential solutions to the problems, as well as the political circumstances that help drive the policymaking process. The suppliers of relevant public policies, and those who can influence them, form the appropriate focus for organizations, systems, and groups seeking to influence their public policy environments to greatest advantage.

A "Map" Can Sharpen Focus

The model of the policymaking process shown in Figure 3.2 can serve as a "map" to where influencing efforts can be most usefully directed. Depending on the circumstances of a particular situation, the proper focus may be one or more of the various component phases, or stages within them, of the policymaking process as shown in Figure 8.1.

Using the map to determine where to exert influence in their public policy environments, leaders of organizations, systems, and groups may focus on those areas where the health policy agenda is shaped by the interaction of problems, possible solutions to the problems, and political circumstances. They can exert influence on policymaking by helping to define the problems that eventually become the focus of public policymaking, by participating in the design of possible solutions to these problems, and by helping to create the political circumstances necessary to convert potential solutions into actual policies. In short, influencing the factors that establish the policy agenda itself can influence policies.

Figure 8.1 Places to Influence Policymaking

Influencing Policy Formulation
    At Agenda Setting
        By defining and documenting problems
            developing and evaluating solutions
            shaping political circumstances through lobbying and the courts
    At Legislation Development
        By participating in drafting legislation
          testifying at legislative hearings
Influencing Policy Implementation
    At Rulemaking
        By providing formal comments on draft rules
          serving on and providing input to rulemaking advisory bodies
    At Policy Operation
        By interactions with policy implementers
Influencing Policy Modification
        By documenting the case for modification through operational
          experience and formal evaluations

Once issues achieve prominent places on the policy agenda, they can, but do not always, proceed to the next stage of the policy formulation phase, development of legislation. At this stage, as discussed extensively in chapter 5, specific legislative proposals go through a process involving a carefully prescribed set of steps that can, but do not always, lead to policies in the form of new legislation, or, as is more often the case, amendments to previously enacted legislation.

Although the path for legislation is long and arduous, it is replete with opportunities for leaders of organizations, systems, or groups to influence legislation development. Both as individuals and through the interest groups to which they belong, leaders of health-related organizations and systems participate directly in the actual drafting of legislative proposals and frequently participate in the hearings associated with the development of legislation.

As discussed in chapter 6, enacted legislation rarely contains the explicit language to fully guide its implementation. Rather, laws are often vague on implementation details, leaving to the implementing agencies and organizations the establishment of the rules needed to fully operationalize the legislation.

The promulgation of rules, as a formal part of the implementation phase of policymaking, because it invites those affected by the rules to comment on *proposed* rules, is one of the most active points of involvement for the leaders of entities and others who have a stake in a particular policy in the entire policymaking process. The exertion of influence at this point of involvement can produce significant results.

In addition to exerting influence directly by commenting on the rules that will guide the implementation of policies, leaders can also exert influence indirectly. This opportunity to exert influence in rulemaking is occasioned by the fact that when the development of rules is anticipated to be unusually difficult or contentious, or when rules are anticipated to be subject to continual revision, special provisions may be made. In particular, advisory bodies or commissions may be established to help shape the development of rules.

The Medicare Payment Advisory Commission (MedPAC) (www. medpac.gov) is one such body. Operationally, MedPAC meets publicly to discuss policy issues and formulate its recommendations to the Congress. In the course of these meetings, commissioners consider the results of staff research, presentations by policy experts, and comments from interested parties such as staff from congressional committees and the Centers for Medicare & Medicaid Services (formerly the Health Care Financing Administration) health services researchers, health services providers, and beneficiary advocates.

Although the opportunities for direct service on such commissions are limited to a very few people, others can influence their thinking. However, leaders of health-related organizations, systems, and interest groups can and do influence the thinking of commission members, and thus the advice commission members ultimately provide about formulating and implementing Medicare policy.

As discussed more fully in chapter 6, influence can be exerted in the operation of policies. The policy operation stage of implementing policies involves the actual running of programs and activities embedded in or stimulated by enacted legislation. Operation is the domain of the appointees and civil servants who staff the government. These people influence policies by their operational decisions and actions. Thus, policies can be influenced by interactions with those who have operational responsibility. This form of influence arises from the working relationships—sometimes close working relationships—that can develop between those responsible for implementing policies and those on whom their decisions and activities impact directly, such as health-related organizations, systems, and groups.

The opportunities to build these relationships are supported by a prominent feature of the careers of bureaucrats: longevity (Kingdon 1995). Elected policymakers come and go, but the bureaucracy endures. Leaders of entities can, and many of them do, build long-standing working relationships with some of the people responsible for implementing the public policies that are of strategic importance to their organizations, systems, or groups.

The most solid base for these working relationships is the exchange of useful information and expertise. A leader, speaking from an authoritative position based on actual operational experience with the implementation of a policy, can influence the policy's further implementation with relevant information. If the information supports change, especially if it buttressed with similar information from others who are experiencing the impact of a particular policy, reasonable implementers may well be influenced to make needed changes. This is especially likely if there is a well-established working relationship, one based on mutual respect for the roles of and the challenges facing each party.

An obvious, and very limiting, problem for those wishing to influence the policymaking process though influencing either the rulemaking or policy operation stages of policy implementation is the enormity of the bureaucracy with which they might need to interact. Consider how many components of the federal government are involved in rulemaking and policy operation that is directly relevant to health-related organizations, systems, and groups. Add to this the relevant units of state and local government and the challenge of keeping track of where working relationships might be useful as a means of influencing policymaking—to say nothing of actually developing and maintaining the relationships—begins to come into focus. Obviously, selectivity in which of these relationships might be of most strategic importance is required.

Although some health policies are developed *de novo*, as has been noted a number of times, the vast majority of them result from the modification of existing policies in rather modest, incremental steps. Policy modification occurs when the outcomes, perceptions, and consequences of existing policies feed back into the agenda-setting and legislation-development stages of the formulation phase, and into the rulemaking and policy-operation stages of the implementation phase and stimulate changes in legislation, rules, or operations (see the feedback loop running along the bottom of Figure 3.2). There are continuing opportunities to influence policies as their outcomes and consequences trigger policy modification. Those who would influence policies have an opportunity to do so in the initial iteration of the policymaking process in regard to any particular policy, but they also get additional opportunities to exert their influence through the subsequent modification of existing policies.

Following the feedback loop in Figure 3.2, it can be seen that because agenda setting involves the confluence of problems, possible solutions, and political circumstances, leaders of health-related entities can be influential in policy modification by making certain that problems become more sharply defined and better understood through the actual experiences of those who are impacted by the policies. Leaders of organizations, systems, or groups are often the best sources of feedback on the consequences of policies, including the effects of policies on the individuals and populations they serve. Similarly, possible new solutions to problems can be conceived and assessed through the operational experiences that entities have with particular policies, especially when the results of demonstrations and evaluations provide concrete evidence of their performance and impact. Finally, leaders—guided by their experiences and interactions with ongoing policies—become important components of the political circumstances surrounding the amendment of these policies.

The experiences with policies of leaders of entities also helps them to modify policies by directly influencing the development of legislation. Actual experience with the impact of the implementation of policies that affect their entity help leaders to routinely identify needed modifications. The history of the Medicare program is a good example of this phenomenon. Over the program's life, services have been added and deleted; premiums and copayment provisions have been changed; reimbursement mechanisms have been changed; features to ensure quality and medical necessity of services have been added, changed, and deleted; and so on. The inputs from entities directly affected by these changes played a role in each of these amendments to the original legislation, although other influences also helped guide these changes.

Leaders of health-related entities also have extensive opportunities to influence the modification of policies in their implementation phases, in both the rulemaking and policy-operation stages. The modification of rules, as well as changes in the operations undertaken to implement policies, often reflect the actual reported or documented experiences of those affected by the rules and operations. Leaders can provide this feedback directly to those with rulemaking or operational responsibilities. They can also take their views on the rules and operational practices that affect their organizations, systems, and groups to the courts or to the legislative branch. Both can also be pathways to modifications.

The Real World of Health Policy

Influencing the Policy Environment of an Academic Medical Center

As discussed in this chapter, health-related organizations, systems, and interest groups have three bases of power available to them in their influencing efforts (i.e., positional, capacity to reward or coerce, and expertise), and they have a number of places in the policymaking process to focus their efforts. Some of the experiences of the leaders of Academic Medical Center (AMC), a part of a state university system, but whose identity is otherwise disguised, richly illustrate the variety of opportunities typically available to the leaders of health-related entities who wish to influence their public policy environments.

The leaders of Academic Medical Center (AMC) can and do approach the challenges of influencing AMC's public policy environment in a variety of ways. The cells in the grid shown in Exhibit 1, each identified by an alpha character, represent the specific combinations of focus and power available to AMC's leaders.

In cell a, for example, the leaders focus on the ways their *positional power* could be used to help *define and document problems* that could be addressed through public policy. For example, as leaders of AMC they are positioned to help policymakers understand the magnitude of the problem of the lack of health insurance among the state's citizens. These leaders are in a position to document the extent and some of the implications of the problems for policymakers. They may use their membership in the Council of Teaching Hospitals (COTH) to help with examples from across the nation.

Furthermore, their positions as leaders of a major primary provider organization permit them to call on others for assistance in this effort.

Exhibit 1 Opportunities to Exert Influence in Public Policy Environments

	Problem Definition	Solutions Identification	Political Circumstances	Legislation Development	Rule-making	Operation
Power Based on Position	cell (a)	(b)	(c)	(d)	(e)	(f)
Power to Reward/ Coerce	(g)	(h)	(i)	(j)	(k)	(l)
Power Based on Expertise	(m)	(n)	(o)	(p)	(q)	(r)

Obviously, they can call on other members of the staff at AMC. They can also solicit the help of their counterparts in other healthcare delivery organizations in the state to buttress their documentation of the problem. In addition, they can utilize interest groups to which they belong, such as the State Hospital Association, to help in this process.

In cell j, AMC's leaders focus on the ways in which their ability to *reward* or to *coerce* policymakers could be used to exert influence in the *development of legislation* that would be to the center's strategic advantage. Legislation to support a major expansion of the center's research facilities, for example, might be sponsored and championed by a legislator who receives campaign support from the center's leaders. This legislative champion of AMC's preferred policy on the issue of support for the new research facility could also be supported in a more intangible form by the leaders working with the legislator to accomplish something of importance to the legislator's district, in terms of its economy and its healthcare services, by opening an ambulatory AMC-staffed primary care center in the district.

In cell n, the center's leaders focus on their opportunities to use the power to exert influence that derives from *expertise* to help *identify and implement policy solutions to problems*. For example, when the state legislature granted $25 million to AMC in 2001 to establish and operate the state's only program in tissue engineering, it did so in response to the AMC's development of a proposal for the initiative as an important advance in the state's medical care and in its economic base. The proposal reflected the center's considerable expertise in tissue engineering.

In cell q, AMC's leaders focus on their opportunities to use *expertise* within the center's staff to influence the final wording on *rules or regulations* that affect the center's organizational performance. For example, there is expertise within the center's staff that would be relevant to the promulgation of federal rules pertaining to funding and operation of graduate medical education programs such as the family practice residency; Medicare reimbursement formulae and practices; and the award of National Institutes of Health research grants, as well as in many other areas. It is routine for leaders at AMC to use their expertise as a mechanism through which to influence the formulation and implementation of rules that affect their organization.

In cell c, AMC's leaders think of ways in which their power to influence based on *position* could be used to change the *political circumstances* surrounding an issue. For example, the members of the State Board of Regents, who are part of AMC's strategic apex, by virtue of their board positions, can and do exert influence on the members of the state legislature. This influence helps determine the state's funding for the state university system, including AMC's state funding.

The examples given above are not exhaustive. Each of the cells discussed contains many other examples of the nexus of focus and power that permit influence to be exerted in AMC's public policy environment. The examples are intended only to stimulate thinking about the range of possibilities to exert influence in public policy environments illustrated in this grid. It should be noted, in this regard, that the real world is not fully captured by this model. In particular, any suggestion that the cells formed by combinations of source of power and focus in the grid in Exhibit 1 can be considered one at the time or in isolation from each other is an obvious oversimplification of reality. More realistically, the leaders of organizations, systems, and interest groups operate in several cells simultaneously even when they are trying to influence single issues in their policy environments. Moreover, they typically focus on many issues at any point in time. This complicates things considerably.

However, the grid does illustrate a very important point for those who would influence an entity's public policy environment. They have many places in the policymaking process where their influence can be legitimately and effectively focused, and they have more than one base of power upon which to seek to exert influence in each of these places.

The Concept of Good Corporate Citizenship

Political competence—the effective analysis and exertion of influence in the public policy environments of health-related organizations, systems, and groups—is enhanced by the practice of good corporate citizenship by these entities. Political competence and corporate citizenship is not the same thing, but they are related. Politically competent organizations, systems, and interest groups also tend to pay attention to their citizenship roles. Entities attuned to their citizenship roles tend to be more politically competent. Thus, it is useful to include discussion of corporate citizenship in the context of political competence.

Many organizations—including health-related organizations, systems, and groups—seek to be good corporate citizens, and society benefits when they are. Entities often state their citizenship aspirations explicitly in corporate mission or vision statements. For example, Alcoa, the world's largest aluminum producer, is headquartered in Pittsburgh but operates globally in numerous local communities. The company acknowledges " . . . acceptance in these communities depends on our living up to high standards of corporate citizenship . . ." (www.alcoa.com). Similarly, Hewlett Packard, widely noted for its corporate citizenship, lists among its corporate objectives one devoted to citizenship: "To honor our obligations to society by being an economic, intellectual and social asset to each nation and each community in which we operate" (www.hp.com).

Aspiring to good corporate citizenship, however, is not the exclusive province of private business organizations. Increasingly, health-related organizations, systems, and groups also exhibit this trait. For example, the vision statement of the UPMC Health System (www.upmc.edu), also headquartered in Pittsburgh but with hospitals and other facilities throughout western Pennsylvania, expresses the system's desire "to be a responsible corporate citizen and an integral part of the western Pennsylvania community."

In many communities in the United States it is increasingly important that health-related organizations and systems assume greater obligations of corporate citizenship—obligations that have traditionally been assumed by private business firms. This is true because these entities are assuming more prominent economic roles in their communities. In the Pittsburgh region, for example, UPMC Health System and Western Pennsylvania Allegheny Health System are respectively the region's largest and fifth-largest employers. Furthermore, the economic roles of health-related organizations and systems extend well beyond the economic ripples that paychecks spread across communities. Their roles in establishing and maintaining the quality of life in communities help entice other businesses to locate in the community (Longest, 1998).

Even beyond their vital health-enhancing roles and their economic contributions, however, health-related organizations and systems can play even larger roles in their communities—roles of good corporate citizenship. By fully developing good citizenship agendas, and by pursuing them vigorously and effectively, these entities join the ranks of their community's most valuable corporate citizens. In the process they enhance their political competence, especially their ability to be influential in the policymaking process.

What Is Good Corporate Citizenship?

There is no universally accepted definition of good corporate citizenship, although the concept is widely viewed in the context of organizations fulfilling their corporate social responsibilities. Similarly, there is also no universally accepted definition of corporate social responsibility. Definitions of corporate social responsibility abound; while varying, they share common elements. For example, one definition states that an organization practices social responsibility when it treats "a mix of stakeholders [which the authors say include employees, customers, stockholders, and the community] well" (Waddock, Graves, and Kelly 2000, 17). A group of Canadian businesses have committed themselves to advancing socially responsible policies and practices. Canadian Business for Social Responsibility (CBSR) defines social responsibility in terms of an entity's "commitment to operate in an economically and environmentally sustainable manner, while acknowledging the interests of a variety of stakeholders" (http://www.cbsr.bc.ca). Business for Social Responsibility (BSR) suggests a socially responsible entity operates "in a manner that meets or exceeds the ethical, legal, commercial and public expectations that society has of business" (http://www.bsr.org).

Organization Behaviors Consistent with Good Corporate Citizenship

More useful than simple definitions, which may be of little value in helping organizations, systems, or interest groups develop or assess citizenship performance, are efforts to specify the organization behaviors associated with being a good corporate citizen or with being socially responsible. One such effort identified three key behaviors associated with an entity fulfilling its social responsibilities (Davenport 2000):

- ethical business behavior—the entity is guided by rigorous ethical standards in all of its business dealings;
- stakeholder commitment—the entity is managed for the benefit of all stakeholders; and
- environmental commitment—the entity moderates its overall environmental impact through programs such as recycling, waste and emission abatement, and the conduct of environmental audits.

Another study considers socially responsible workforce-related organization behaviors (Greening and Turban 2000). Examples of such behaviors include employee relations (including such variables as union relations, employee ownership, and employee participation in management decision making) and an entity's treatment of women and minorities (including such variables as fair hiring policies and opportunities for promotion).

A more extensive listing of the categories of organization behaviors related to good corporate citizenship has been developed by CBSR. It includes the areas of community development, diversity, employee relations, environment, international relationships, market practices, fiscal responsibility, and accountability. Similarly, BSR has developed a list of socially responsible organization behaviors that includes the following areas: business ethics; community involvement; community economic development; environment; governance and accountability; human rights; marketplace; mission, vision, values; and workplace.

A Model of Good Citizenship Organization Behaviors

The various lists of socially responsible organization behaviors can be combined to yield a comprehensive model of the good citizenship behaviors of any organizational entity—including health-related organizations, systems, or interest groups. The model is shown in Figure 8.2.

As Figure 8.3 illustrates, the existence of the range of citizenship-related organization behaviors raises the possibility—unless all organizations practice all the behaviors all the time—that there is likely to be a continuum of levels of citizenship activity from lower to higher among organizations, systems, and groups. The location of an entity on the continuum permits consideration of the present status of its citizenship activity, and of how and where the activity might be adjusted in the future.

Conceptually, the leaders of an entity at Level 1 on the continuum (see Figure 8.3) would not be motivated to pursue citizenship activities, and their entity would exhibit none of the organization behaviors associated with being good corporate citizens in any of the areas listed in Figure 8.2. Level 1 on the continuum is, of course, hypothetical and used to simply establish the lower end of the continuum. If such an entity existed, its leaders, if asked their views on corporate citizenship, might say "We don't know what corporate citizenship has to do with an entity like ours; we try to help people improve their health."

Figure 8.2 Model of Corporate Citizenship Organization Behaviors

- Balancing multiple stakeholder interests
- Community development commitments
- Diversity commitments
- Employer role and workforce development commitments
- Environmental commitments
- Ethical decisions and actions
- Governance excellence and full accountability commitments
- Legal compliance
- Market practices that are fair and legal

(*Components are listed alphabetically.*)

Figure 8.3   Continuum of Levels of Corporate Citizenship Activity

Lower 1 2 3 4 5 Higher

Illustrations

When asked their views on their entity's citizenship activities, leaders in health-related organizations, systems, or groups at different levels on the continuum might respond as follows:

Level 1—*"We don't know what corporate citizenship has to do with an entity like ours; we try to help people improve their health."*

Level 2—*"We know what good corporate citizenship is. It's what we do to justify our tax exemption."*

Level 3—*"We believe in and support corporate citizenship, but we have to focus the resources we devote to it."*

Level 4—*"We fulfill our citizenship responsibilities, although we could better coordinate and synergize our diverse citizenship-related activities."*

Level 5—*"We are a fully realized corporate citizen of the communities we serve."*

Level 2 (which is not hypothetical) entities' leaders are somewhat committed to good citizenship, but make very limited resource allocations to citizenship-related activities. The limited allocations might be based on real resource constraints or on the fact that other priorities (e.g., growth in market share, quality enhancement, technological advances) take precedence. Such entities—if they were nonprofit health services providers, for example—would likely equate the fulfillment of their community benefit obligations that are undertaken to maintain their tax-exempt status with corporate citizenship. In an entity at this level of citizenship activity, organization behaviors that reflect corporate social responsibility (CSR) would often be a side effect of activity driven by other purposes. For example, it might be involved in diversity programs *only* because they provide a means to achieve necessary human resources for the entity in its labor market. When asked their views on corporate citizenship, the leaders of these entities might say, "We know what good corporate citizenship is. It's what we do to justify our tax exemption."

An organization or system at Level 3 has leaders who are committed to good citizenship, at least as they understand it, and who have made significant, focused resource investments in support of citizenship-related activities. Leaders of such entities, however, have limited perspective on the full range of organization behaviors through which they can express and practice good citizenship. Their resource investments in some aspects of citizenship might be substantial, but simultaneously they might have made no investment in other aspects. For example, a Level 3 entity might exhibit significant citizenship-related organization behaviors in such areas as:

- diversity
- employer role and workforce development
- environmental commitment
- governance and accountability
- legal compliance

while concurrently making little if any investment in such areas as:

- balancing multiple stakeholder interests
- community development
- ethical decisions and actions, and
- market practices.

Decisions about where to focus citizenship-related activities in a Level 3 entity are driven by combinations of attention to community benefit obligations, political correctness, market advantage, and desire to be a good corporate citizen. When asked their views on corporate citizenship, the leaders of these entities might say, "We believe in and support corporate citizenship, but we have to focus the resources we devote to it."

Level 4 entities' leaders are committed to good corporate citizenship, both as a matter of principle and for reasons of business-related self-interest; they understand corporate citizenship broadly, and have made substantial and widespread resource commitments to it across a broad front of activities. The leaders of these entities have recognized the business case for citizenship behaviors and have positioned their entities to realize the benefits of these organization behaviors. Not atypically, however, entities at Level 4 on the continuum do not actively coordinate or seek synergies available within their corporate citizenship activities. In fact, many of their activities are ongoing throughout the entity with little or no sharing of information about them across units or among those involved.

The second way in which Level 4 health-related organizations, systems, and groups fall short of Level 5 is in their failure to recognize and capitalize on the synergies that exist between their core health-enhancing missions and their citizenship-related activities. As noted in the section on motives for corporate citizenship, there can be congruence between an entity's citizenship-related activities and its core health-enhancing mission. At Level 4, these potential synergies are unrecognized. When asked their views on corporate citizenship, the leaders of entities at Level 4 on the continuum might accurately say, "We fulfill our citizenship responsibilities, although we could better coordinate and synergize our diverse citizenship-related activities." What they would not likely think to say is how much congruence exists between their citizenship activities and their success at enhancing the health of the people they serve.

Like Level 1 on the continuum in Figure 8.3, Level 5 is also hypothetical. It is a goal toward which some health-related organizations, systems, and groups are perhaps moving, but a goal none have fully realized to date. In a Level 5 entity, its leaders would be strongly motivated toward corporate citizenship and would devote extensive resources to activities across the entire range of possible organization behaviors with potential to help fulfill the entity's citizenship objectives. Coordinated and integrated activities would be ongoing in all of the areas listed in Figure 8.2.

The motives for Level 5 citizenship organization behaviors would be a combination of the business advantages of practicing good corporate citizenship *and* the crucial realization that citizenship-related organization behaviors—along with diagnostic and clinical services—are a means to fulfilling the core health-enhancing mission of a health-related organization, system, or group. When asked their views on corporate citizenship, the leaders of entities at Level 5 on the continuum might accurately say, "We are a fully realized corporate citizen of the communities we serve."

The Motives for Good Corporate Citizenship

Why should health-related organizations, systems, or interest groups make commitments to corporate citizenship? What value are such commitments, and the resulting decisions and activities, to the entities? What value are the commitments to the individuals and communities they serve? Importantly—for health-related organizations, systems, and groups—the value of citizenship commitments and activities can be considered both in economic terms and in terms of impact on the pursuit of health. Values in both areas help explain why good corporate citizenship and political competence are related.

Economics: The Business Case for Good Corporate Citizenship

There is economic value in good corporate citizenship both for the health-related organizations and systems that practice it and for the communities they serve. The economic value to an entity inherent in its practice of good citizenship is substantial, and reason enough for its involvement in citizenship organization behaviors. Tracing this value is complex, but important. Because entities, like people, often act in their self-interest, it is useful to understand how an entity's self-interest is served by its citizenship activities.

In a landmark study conducted by Environics International Ltd. (www.environicsinternational.com), in cooperation with The Prince of Wales Business Leaders Forum (www.pwblf.org) and The Conference Board (www.conference-board.org), samples of 1,000 citizens in each of 23 countries on 6 continents were interviewed on the subject of corporate social responsibility or citizenship behaviors. The results help explain why all types of organizations—including health-related organizations, systems, and groups—should be committed to good corporate citizenship. Among the key findings in this poll were (Environics International Ltd., The Prince of Wales Business Leaders Forum, and The Conference Board, 1999):

- 90 percent of people surveyed want companies to focus on more than profitability
- 60 percent of respondents said that they form an impression of a company based on its citizenship behavior (defined as regard for people, communities, and the environment)
- 40 percent responded negatively to, or said they talked negatively about, companies that they perceived as not being socially responsible
- 17 percent of respondents reported that they had actually avoided the products of companies they perceived as not being good corporate citizens.

Leaders of entities perceive value to their entities in citizenship commitments. Cone, Inc. (www.coneinc.com), a strategic cause marketing company that produces the only longitudinal analysis of rapidly evolving cause marketing trends in the United States, concludes in *The 1999 Cone/Roper Cause Related Trends Report* that leaders of companies see benefits to their reputations, images, and bottom lines when they support causes and socially responsible positions that are important to people (Cone, Inc., 1999).

Bottom-line benefits of corporate citizenship have been demonstrated in numerous ways. BSR (www.bsr.org), summarizing the results of several recent studies, reports that companies experience a range of bottom-line benefits from strong citizenship commitments:

- Companies that made a public commitment to rely on their ethics codes outperformed (as measured by market value added) by two to three times companies that did not do so.

- Companies with a defined corporate commitment to ethical principles did better financially (as measured by annual sales/revenues) than companies that did not have such defined commitments. Conversely, companies that experienced publicity about unethical corporate behavior typically experienced lower stock prices for a minimum of six months following the negative exposure.
- Companies that were "stakeholder-balanced" showed four times the growth rate and eight times the employment growth when compared to companies that were shareholder-only focused.

Although the studies noted above pertain to businesses in general, they are relevant to health-related organizations, systems, and groups. Such studies reflect economic and marketplace advantages for the organizations that make strong commitments to citizenship. These advantages result from a number of factors that apply to all types of entities. For example, citizenship activities related to environmental concerns or to workplace improvements can reduce operating costs by cutting waste and improving productivity. Activities intended to reduce emissions of gases that contribute to global climate change reflect citizenship commitments, but they may also increase energy efficiency, reducing utility bills. Some recycling initiatives also cut waste-disposal costs and generate income through the sale of recycled materials.

Similarly, citizenship-driven workplace improvements reduce absenteeism and increase retention of employees, resulting in savings generated through increased productivity and reduced hiring and training costs. Citizenship activities that enhance an entity's reputation with the public can yield customers and an enhanced reputation within the business community that can make it easier to attract capital or to engage in partnership and collaborative activities with other organizations. Good citizenship also enhances the entity's reputation in its public policy environment.

Another aspect of the economic or business case for corporate citizenship activities lies in the reduced or relaxed regulatory oversight that results from organization behaviors that reflect strong citizenship commitments. Entities that can document the ways in which they exceed regulatory compliance requirements are sometimes given less scrutiny by federal, state, and local government entities. For example, federal and state agencies overseeing environmental and workplace regulations have implemented formal programs that recognize and reward entities that have taken proactive measures to reduce adverse environmental, health, and safety impacts. In many cases, such entities are subject to fewer inspections and paperwork and may be given preference or "fast-track" treatment when applying for operating permits, zoning variances or other forms of governmental permission.

In addition to the economic value of good corporate citizenship to the entities that practice it, there is economic value to their communities. Some of these entities make significant—in some cases extraordinarily significant—economic contributions to their communities. As noted above, in many communities health-related organizations and systems are among the largest and most stable employers. But the economic contributions that health-related organizations and systems can make to their communities go well beyond their role as employers and the economic ripples that paychecks spread across communities.

Economically sound health-related entities—practicing good corporate citizenship—can share the burden of community infrastructure, whether through the taxes paid if they operate as for-profit entities or by payments in lieu of taxes that help support municipal services paid by not-for-profit organizations and systems. Important community contributions are also made when health-related organizations and systems provide *value* in their economic exchanges within the community. Value, when the concept is applied to healthcare services, means quality divided by price. More value in healthcare services is a direct benefit to communities. Health services of good value may even help attract other businesses into a community. Finally, entities can make important economic contributions in their communities by preserving and enhancing the assets that accrue to and are entrusted to them by their communities. Whether such assets accumulate in the form of philanthropic contributions to the organizations or through exemption from taxes, when the assets are utilized wisely for the good of their communities—present and future— they indeed make critically important and long-lasting contributions to the development of and quality of life in their communities.

Health: The Mission Case for Good Corporate Citizenship

Citizenship activities and behaviors of health-related entities can also contribute a great deal to society's pursuit of health. This impact results from the congruence between citizenship-related activities and an entity's core health-enhancing mission and is felt by individuals and by populations, such as at the level of communities or regions.

The fundamental role of health-related organizations and systems is enhancement of health. Mission-related, health-enhancing activities take many forms and can be pursued with varying levels of intensity. At their most intensive level, these activities reflect the fact that health in human beings is a function of numerous determinants, as discussed extensively in chapters 1 and 2. Recall from that discussion that health in individuals and populations is affected by genetics and exposures to biological mechanisms of disease and injury, by lifestyles and behaviors, and by access to appropriate health services. But there is more to health. Health is also affected by the physical environments in which people live and work; by their economic conditions; and by a number of social factors including socioeconomic position, income distribution, discrimination related to race/ethnicity or gender, social networks/social supports, and community cohesion.

The variety of health determinants yields an expansive array of possible targets for intervention in the pursuit of enhanced health: A health-related organization's or system's core mission of enhancing health is supported when its citizenship commitments lead it into behaviors that enhance the quality of work life and community life. Citizenship-related activities that improve employment opportunity, housing, physical and social environments, economic conditions and many other factors that ultimately affect human health, also contribute to fulfillment of the missions of health-related entities. This important synergy is a significant reason for health-related organizations and systems to develop strong corporate citizenship commitments and to act on them. In short, by helping the communities they serve develop in ways that maximize quality of life for their citizens, health-related organizations and systems contribute to the pursuit of health.

Organizations and systems that are good corporate citizens in their communities play several interrelated roles—all contributing to the development of communities and to enhancing the quality of life in them. The most obvious role is a function of the core, health-enhancing missions of these organizations and systems. By successfully pursuing its mission, an entity provides important packages of health services (prevention, care, restoration, rehabilitation, palliation) to its community. As a byproduct of the ways, and for whom, an entity pursues its core mission, it makes other vital community contributions. Health-related organizations and systems are uniquely positioned and may choose to make health-enhancing services available on a charitable basis to certain members of the community, or to subsidize costly but unprofitable services such as burn units or primary care clinics in neighborhoods with high poverty rates.

The most fundamental contribution any health-related organization or system can make to good corporate citizenship within its community is to fulfill the health-enhancing purpose for which it was established. Even in this core activity, however, citizenship can be practiced to different degrees. Health-enhancing activities can take many forms and can be pursued with varying levels of intensity. At their most intensive level, these contributions to quality of life in a community are based on acknowledgment of the fact that health in human beings is a function of numerous determinants. The variety of these determinants, whether for individuals or entire communities, yields an expansive array of possible targets for intervention in the pursuit of enhanced health. And many of them can be supported by citizenship-related activities.

Health-related organizations and systems seeking to make the best possible contributions to quality of life in their communities through their health-enhancing initiatives acquire and act on epidemiological data on the demographic characteristics, harmful environmental exposures, social and economic conditions, quality of life indicators, and patterns of domestic violence in their communities. These organizations and systems also utilize risk status data on such variables as the prevalence of tobacco use, alcohol and substance abuse, nutrition and unsafe sexual practices within their community, and information on the availability in the community of such preventive services as immunizations, genetic screening, behavioral counseling, and injury prevention programs.

Armed with such community-based data and information, entities that seek to maximize their health-enhancing contributions to the quality of life in their communities can undertake broadly based initiatives and programs, including health promotion and disease prevention services where appropriate. They can also make important community contributions by aggressively supporting public policies that enhance health by stimulating improvements across all the health determinants—behavior and biology, physical environment, social factors, and health services—that affect their communities.

Thus, the practice of good corporate citizenship by health-related organizations and systems has economic value to the entities and to the communities they serve. Citizenship-related organization behaviors also can contribute to fulfillment of these entities' core missions—enhanced health. In the process, the entities strengthen and improve their political competence.

Summary

Health policies, once formulated and implemented, have consequences for individuals and populations, as well as for health-related organizations, systems, and interest groups. Those who are affected by policies—those who feel the positive or negative effects of policies—share two fundamental concerns about the policymaking process. They are concerned about analyzing their public policy environments so that they can discern, in advance, the potential impact of policies on themselves, and they are concerned about influencing the formulation and implementation of these public policies.

Effective analysis of public policy environments and, even more so, the capacity to exert influence in these environments are enhanced by the pooling of resources that can be devoted to the tasks by organizations and, especially, by interest groups. The leaders of groups and organizations can best analyze their public policy environments through five steps: scanning, monitoring, forecasting, assessing, and diffusing information about their public policy environments into the organization or group.

Health-related organizations, systems, and interest groups seek to exert influence in their public policy environments so that the consequences for them will be more favorable—or, at least, less unfavorable. Success at influencing these environments is a function of *power* bases on which to mount the efforts and the *focus* of the efforts.

Political competence and corporate citizenship are different things. However, they are related in that politically competent organizations, systems, and interest groups also tend to pay attention to their larger citizenship roles. Entities attuned to their corporate citizenship roles tend to be more politically competent.

Discussion Questions

1. What two major areas of concern do individuals, as well as health-related organizations, systems, and interest groups, share regarding policies and the process through which they are produced? Why are these concerns more easily considered in regard to organizations and groups than in regard to individuals?
2. Discuss the benefits and limitations facing organizations, systems, and interest groups that undertake to analyze their public policy environments.
3. Who is responsible for the analysis of the public policy environment of an organization, system, or interest group? Who helps in the process?
4. Discuss the recommended steps in conducting an effective analysis of the public policy environment of an organization, system, or group.
5. Who is responsible for efforts to exert influence in an organization's, system's, or interest group's public policy environment on behalf of the organization, system, or group? Who helps in the process?
6. Discuss the fact that influence in public policy environments is a matter of power and focus.

7. What is corporate citizenship? Describe a model of the organization behaviors consistent with good corporate citizenship.
8. Discuss the economic case and the health case for a health-related organization or system practicing corporate citizenship.

Note

1. The discussion of the components of political competence in this chapter draws heavily on the author's book, *Seeking Strategic Advantage Through Health Policy Analysis*. Chicago: Health Administration Press, 1996.

References

Aaron, H. J., and W. B. Schwartz. 1984. *The Painful Prescription: Rationing Hospital Care.* Washington, DC: The Brookings Institution.

Callahan, D. 1987. *Setting Limits: Medical Goals in an Aging Society.* New York: Simon and Schuster.

Cone, Inc. 1999. *The 1999 Cone/Roper Cause Related Trends Report.* New York: Cone, Inc.

Davenport, K. 2000. "Corporate Citizenship: A Stakeholder Approach for Defining Corporate Social Performance and Identifying Measures for Assessing It." *Business & Society* 39 (2): 216.

Delbecq, A. L., A. H. Van de Ven, and D. H. Gustafson. 1974. *Group Decision Making Techniques in Program Planning.* Glenview, IL: Scott Foresman.

Environics International Ltd., The Prince of Wales Business Leaders Forum, and The Conference Board. 1999. *The Millennium Poll on Corporate Social Responsibility.* Toronto: Environics International Ltd.

Fahey, L., and V. K. Narayanan. 1986. *Macroenvironmental Analysis for Strategic Management.* St. Paul, MN: West Publishing Company.

Fuchs, V. R. 1974. *Who Shall Live?* New York: Basic Books.

Ginter, P. M., W. J. Duncan, and L. E. Swayne. 2002. *Strategic Management of Health Care Organizations*, 4th ed. Malden, MA: Blackwell Publishers.

Greening, D. W., and D. B. Turban. 2000. "Corporate Social Performance as a Competitive Advantage in Attracting a Quality Workforce." *Business & Society* 39 (3): 262–63.

Jain, S. C. 1984. "Environmental Scanning in U. S. Corporations." *Long Range Planning* 17 (2): 117–28.

Keys, B., and T. Case. 1990. "How to Become an Influential Manager." *The Executive* 4 (November): 38–51.

Kingdon, J. W. 1995. *Agendas, Alternatives, and Public Policies*, 2nd ed. New York: HarperCollins College Publishers.

Klein, H. E., and R. E. Linneman. 1984. "Environmental Assessment: An International Study of Corporate Practices." *Journal of Business Strategy* 5: 66–77.

Leemhuis, J. P. 1985. "Using Scenarios to Develop Strategies." *Long Range Planning* 18: 30–37.

Lenz, R. T., and J. L. Engledow. 1986. "Environmental Analysis Units and Strategic Decision-Making: A Field Study of Selected 'Leading Edge' Corporations." *Strategic Management Journal* 7 (1): 69–89.

Longest, B. B., Jr. 1997. *Seeking Strategic Advantage Through Health Policy Analysis.* Chicago: Health Administration Press.

———. 1998. "The Civic Roles of Healthcare Organizations." *Healthcare Forum Journal* 41 (5): 40–42.

Mintzberg, H. 1983. *Structure in Fives: Designing Effective Organizations.* Englewood Cliffs, NJ: Prentice Hall.

Molitar, G. T. T. 1977. "How to Anticipate Public Policy Changes." *Society for the Advancement of Management: Advanced Management Journal* 42: 4–13.

Pear, R. June 15, 2001. "Medicare Agency Changes Name in an Effort to Emphasize Service." *The New York Times,* National Desk.

Reinhardt, U. E. 1990. "Could Health Care Swallow Us All?" *Business and Health* 8 (2): 47–48.

Sanchez, R., and A. Heene. 2001. *The New Strategic Management: Organizations, Competition, and Cooperation.* New York: John Wiley & Sons, Inc.

Schwartz, P. 1991. *The Art of the Long View.* New York: Doubleday/Currency.

Terry, P. T. 1977. "Mechanisms for Environmental Scanning." *Long Range Planning* 10 (3): 2–9.

Thomas, J. B., and R. R. McDaniel, Jr. 1990. "Interpreting Strategic Issues: Effects of Strategy and the Information-Processing Structure of Top Management Teams." *Academy of Management Journal* 33 (2): 288–98.

Venable, J. M., Q. Li, P. M. Ginter, and W. J. Duncan. 1994. "The Use of Scenario Analysis in Local Public Health Departments: Alternative Futures of Strategic Planning." *Public Health Reports* 108 (6): 701–10.

Waddock, S., S. Graves, and M. Kelly. 2000. "On the Trail of the Best Corporate Citizens." *Business Ethics* 14 (2): 1–14.

Webster, J. L., W. E. Reif, and J. S. Bracker. 1989. "The Manager's Guide to Strategic Planning Tools and Techniques." *Planning Review* 17 (6): 4–13.

APPENDIX

Briefly Annotated Chronological List of Selected U.S. Federal Laws Pertaining to Health[1]

1798

An act of July 16, 1798, passed by the Fifth Congress of the United States, taxed the employers of merchant seamen to fund arrangements for their healthcare through the Marine Hospital Service. In the language of the act, "the master or owner of every ship or vessel of the United States arriving from a foreign port into any port in the United States shall . . . render to the collector a true account of the number of seamen that shall have been employed on board such vessel . . . and shall pay to the said collector, at the rate of twenty cents per month, for every seaman so employed. . . ." The act stipulated in Section 2 that "the President of the United States is hereby authorized, out of the same, to provide for the temporary relief and maintenance of sick or disabled seamen in the hospitals, or other proper institutions now established in the several ports. . . ."

1882

An act of August 3, 1882, was the nation's first general immigration law and included the first federal medical excludability provisions affecting those who wished to immigrate to the United States. The act authorized state officials to board arriving ships to examine the condition of passengers. In the language of the act, "if on such examination, there shall be found among such passengers any convict, lunatic, idiot, or any person unable to take care of himself or herself without becoming a public charge, . . . such persons shall not be permitted to land."

1891

An act of March 3, 1891, added the phrase, "persons suffering from a loathsome or a contagious disease" to the list of medical excludability criteria for people seeking to immigrate to the United States.

1902

P.L. 57-244[2] the *Biologics Control Act*, was the first federal law regulating the interstate and foreign sale of biologics (viruses, serums, toxins, and analogous products). The law established a national board and gave its members authority to establish regulations for licensing producers of biologics.

1906

P.L. 59-384, the *Pure Food and Drug Act* (also known as the Wiley Act), defined adulterated and mislabeled foods and drugs and prohibited their transport in interstate commerce. Passage of this legislation followed several years of intense campaigning by reformers and extensive newspaper coverage of examples of unwholesome and adulterated foods and of the widespread use of ineffective patent medicines.

1920

P.L. 66-141, the *Snyder Act*, was the first federal legislation pertaining to healthcare for Native Americans. Prior to the passage of this legislation, there were some health-related provisions in treaties between the government and the Native Americans, but this was the first formal legislation on the subject. The act provided for general assistance, directing "the Bureau of Indian Affairs, under the supervision of the Secretary of the Interior to direct, supervise, and expend such monies as Congress may from time to time appropriate, for the benefit, care, and assistance of the Indians throughout the United States. . . ."

1921

P.L. 67-97, the *Maternity and Infancy Act* (also known as the Sheppard-Towner Act), provided grants to states to help them develop health services for mothers and their children. The law was allowed to lapse in 1929, although it has served as a prototype for federal grants-in-aid to the states.

1935

P.L. 74-271, the *Social Security Act*, a landmark law developed and passed during the Great Depression, established the Social Security program of old-age benefits. The legislation also included provisions for other benefits such as federal financial assistance to the states for their public assistance programs for the needy elderly, dependent children, and the blind. This legislation also provided incentives for the establishment of state unemployment funds and provided financial assistance for maternal and child health and child welfare services and significantly increased federal assistance for state and local public health programs.

1936

P.L. 74-846, the *Walsh-Healy Act*, authorized federal regulation of industrial safety in companies doing business with the U.S. government.

1937

P.L. 75-244, the *National Cancer Institute Act*, established the first categorical institute within the National Institute of Health, which had been created in 1930 to serve as the administrative home for the research conducted by the U.S. Public Health Service.

1938

P.L. 75-540, the *LaFollette-Bulwinkle Act*, provided grants-in-aid to the states to support their investigation and control of venereal disease.

P.L. 75-717, the *Food, Drug and Cosmetic Act*, extended federal authority to ban new drugs from the market until they were approved by the Food and Drug Administration (FDA). This law also gave the federal government more extensive power in dealing with adulterated or mislabeled food, drugs, and cosmetic products.

1939

P.L. 76-19, the *Reorganization Act*, transferred the Public Health Service from the Treasury Department to the new Federal Security Agency (FSA). In 1953 the FSA was transformed into the U.S. Department of Health, Education and Welfare (DHEW) that, with the subsequent establishment of a new cabinet level Department of Education in 1980,

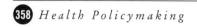

was itself transformed into the U.S. Department of Health and Human Services (DHHS).

1941

P.L. 77-146, the *Nurse Training Act*, provided schools of nursing with support to permit them to increase enrollments and improve their physical facilities.

1944

P.L. 78-410, the *Public Health Service Act*, revised and consolidated in one place all existing legislation pertaining to the U.S. Public Health Service. The legislation provided for the organization, staffing, and functions and activities of the Public Health Service. This law has subsequently been used as a vehicle, through amendments to the legislation, for a number of important federal grant-in-aid programs.

1945

P.L. 79-15, the *McCarran-Ferguson Act*, expressly exempted the "business of insurance" from federal antitrust legislation (the Sherman Antitrust Act of 1890, the Clayton Act of 1914, and the Federal Trade Commission Act of 1914) to the extent that insurance was regulated by state law and did not involve "acts of boycott, coercion, or intimidation." A significant part of the underlying reasoning Congress used in exempting insurance, including health insurance, was the view that the determination of underwriting risks would require the cooperation and sharing of information among competing insurance companies.

1946

P.L. 79-487, the *National Mental Health Act*, authorized extensive federal support for mental health research and treatment programs and established grants-in-aid to the states for their mental health activities. The legislation also transformed the Public Health Services's Division of Mental Health into the National Institute of Mental Health.

P.L. 79-725, the *Hospital Survey and Construction Act* (also known as the Hill-Burton Act), was "An Act to amend the Public Health Service Act (see the 1944 P.L. 78-410 above) to authorize grants to the States for surveying their hospital and public health centers and for planning construction of additional facilities, and to authorize grants to assist in such construction." The legislation was enacted because Congress recognized a widespread shortage of hospital facilities (few were built during the Great Depression and World War II). Under provisions of the act, the states were required to submit a state plan for the construction of hospital facilities based on a survey of need to receive federal funds, which could be dispersed for projects within states.

1948

P.L. 80-655, the *National Health Act*, pluralized the NIH by establishing a second categorical institute, the National Heart Institute. Hereafter, the NIH became the National Institutes of Health.

P.L. 80-845, the *Water Pollution Control Act*, was enacted, in part, "in consequence of the benefits to the public health and welfare by the abatement of stream pollution. . . ." The act left the primary responsibility for water pollution control with the states.

1952

P.L. 82-414, the *Immigration and Nationality Act* (also known as the McCarran-Walter Act), followed an extensive study by the Congress of immigration policy and practice. Among the law's provisions were a number of modifications in the medical excludability scheme affecting people wishing to immigrate to the United States. The act contained extensive provisions for observation and examination of aliens for the purpose of determining if they should be excluded for any of a number of specified "diseases or mental or physical defects or disabilities."

1954

P.L. 83-482, the *Medical Facilities Survey and Construction Act*, amended the Hill-Burton Act (see the 1946 P.L. 79-725) to greatly expand the Hill-Burton program's scope. The legislation authorized grants for surveys and construction of diagnostic and treatment centers (including hospital outpatient departments), chronic disease hospitals, rehabilitation facilities, and nursing homes.

P.L. 83-703, the *Atomic Energy Act*, established the Atomic Energy Commission and authorized it to license the use of atomic material in medical care.

1955

P.L. 84-159, the *Air Pollution Control Act*, provided for a program of research and technical assistance related to air pollution control. The law was enacted, in part, "in recognition of the dangers to the public health and welfare . . . from air pollution. . . ."

P.L. 84-377, the *Polio Vaccination Assistance Act*, provided for federal assistance to states for the operation of their polio vaccination programs.

1956

P.L. 84-569, the *Dependents Medical Care Act*, established the Civilian Health and Medical Program of the Uniformed Services (CHAMPUS) for the dependents of military personnel.

P.L. 84-652, the *National Health Survey Act*, provided for the first system of regularly collected health-related data by the Public Health Service. This continuing process is called the Health Interview Survey and provides a national U.S. household interview study of illness, disability, and health services utilization.

P.L. 84-660, the *Water Pollution Control Act Amendments of 1956*, amended the Water Pollution Control Act (see the 1948 P.L. 80-845) and provided for federal technical services and financial aid to the states and to municipalities in their efforts to prevent and control water pollution.

P.L. 84-911, the *Health Amendments Act*, amended the Public Health Service Act (see the 1944 P.L. 78-410) by initiating federal assistance for the education and training of health personnel. Specifically, the law authorized traineeships for public health personnel and for advanced training for nurses. This support has been gradually broadened and extended by subsequent legislation to many categories of health personnel.

1958

P.L. 85-544, *Grants-in-Aid to Schools of Public Health*, established a program of formula grants to the nation's schools of public health.

P.L. 85-929, the *Food Additive Amendment*, amended the Food, Drug and Cosmetic Act (see the 1938 P.L. 75-717) to require premarketing clearance from the FDA for new food additives. The so-called Delaney Clause, after Representative James Delaney who sponsored the provision, stated that "no additive shall be deemed to be safe if it is found to induce cancer when ingested by man or animal. . . ."

1959

P.L. 86-121, the *Indian Sanitation Facilities Act*, provided for the Surgeon General to "construct, improve, extend, or otherwise provide and maintain, by contract or otherwise, essential sanitation facilities for Indian homes, communities, and lands. . . ."

P.L. 86-352, the *Federal Employees Health Benefits Act*, permitted Blue Cross to negotiate a contract with the Civil Service Commission to provide health insurance coverage for federal employees. The contract served as a prototype for Blue Cross' subsequent involvement in the Medicare and Medicaid programs as a fiscal intermediary.

1960

P.L. 86-778, *the Social Security Amendments* (also known as the Kerr-Mills Act), amended the Social Security Act (see the 1935 P.L. 74-271) to establish a new program of medical assistance for the aged. Through this program, the federal government provided aid to the states for payments for medical care for "medically indigent" persons who were 65 years of age or older. The Kerr-Mills program, as it was called, was the forerunner of the Medicaid program established in 1965 (see P.L. 89-97).

1962

P.L. 87-692, the *Health Services for Agricultural Migratory Workers Act*, authorized federal grants to clinics serving migrant farm workers and their families.

P.L. 87-781, the *Drug Amendments* (also known as the Kefauver-Harris amendments), amended the Food, Drug and Cosmetic Act (see the 1938 P.L. 75-717) to significantly strengthen the provisions related to the regulation of therapeutic drugs. The changes required improved manufacturing practices and procedures and evidence that new drugs proposed for marketing be effective as well as safe. These amendments followed widespread adverse publicity about the serious negative side effects of the drug thalidomide.

1963

P.L. 88-129, the *Health Professions Educational Assistance Act*, inaugurated construction grants for teaching facilities that trained physicians, dentists, pharmacists, podiatrists, nurses, or professional public health personnel. The grants were made contingent on schools increasing their first-year enrollments. The legislation also provided for student loans and scholarships.

P.L. 88-156, the *Maternal and Child Health and Mental Retardation Planning Amendments*, amended the Social Security Act (see the 1935 P.L. 74-271). The changes were intended "to assist states and communities in preventing and combating mental retardation through expansion and improvement of the maternal and child health and crippled children's programs, through provision of prenatal, maternity, and infant care for individuals with conditions associated with childbearing that may lead to mental retardation, and through planning for comprehensive action to combat mental retardation."

P.L. 88-164, the *Mental Retardation Facilities and Community Mental Health Centers Construction Act*, was intended "to provide assistance in combating mental retardation through grants for construction of research centers and grants for facilities for the mentally retarded and assistance in improving mental health through grants for construction of community mental health centers, and for other purposes."

P.L. 88-206, the *Clean Air Act*, authorized direct grants to states and local governments to assist in their air pollution control efforts. The law also established federal enforcement of interstate air pollution restrictions.

1964

P.L. 88-443, the *Hospital and Medical Facilities Amendments*, amended the Hill-Burton Act (see the 1946 P.L. 79-725) to specifically earmark grants for modernizing or replacing existing hospitals.

P.L. 88-452, the *Economic Opportunity Act*, sometimes referred to as the Antipoverty Program, was intended to "mobilize the human and financial resources of the nation to combat poverty in the United States." This broad legislation affected health in a number of ways as it sought to improve the economic and social conditions under which many people lived.

P.L. 88-581, the *Nurse Training Act*, added a new title, Title VIII, to the Public Health Service Act (see the 1944 P.L. 78-410). The legislation authorized separate funding for construction grants to schools of nursing, including associate degree and diploma schools. The law also provided for project grants whereby schools of nursing could strengthen their academic programs and provided for the establishment of student loan funds at these schools.

1965

P.L. 89-4, the *Appalachian Redevelopment Act*, sought to promote the economic, physical, and social development of the Appalachian region. Provisions in the law facilitated a number of steps to achieve this purpose including the establishment of community health centers and training programs for health personnel.

P.L. 89-73, the *Older Americans Act*, established an Administration on Aging to administer, through state agencies on aging, programs for the elderly. The agenda for the joint efforts of the federal agency and the state agencies was detailed in ten specific objectives for the nation's older citizens, including several that were related to their health.

P.L. 89-92, the *Federal Cigarette Labeling and Advertising Act*, required that all cigarette packages sold in the United States bear the label, "Caution: Cigarette Smoking May be Hazardous to Your Health."

P.L. 89-97, the *Social Security Amendments*, a landmark in the nation's health policy, established two new titles to the Social Security Act (see the 1935 P.L. 74-271): (1) Title XVIII, Health Insurance for the Aged, or Medicare; and (2) Title XIX, Grants to the States for Medical Assistance Programs, or Medicaid. Enactment of these amendments followed many years of often acrimonious congressional debate about government's role and responsibility regarding ensuring access to health services for the citizenry. This legislation was made possible by the landslide dimensions of Lyndon B. Johnson's 1964 election to the presidency and by the accompanying largest Democratic majority in Congress since 1934.

In addition to establishing Titles XVIII and XIX, the Social Security Act Amendments of 1965 also amended Title V to authorize grant funds for maternal and child health and crippled children's services. These amendments also authorized grants for training professional personnel for the care of crippled children.

P.L. 89-239, the *Heart Disease, Cancer and Stroke Amendments,* amended the Public Health Act (see the 1944 P.L. 78-410) to establish a nationwide network of Regional Medical Programs. This legislation was intended to "assist in combating heart disease, cancer, stroke, and related diseases." Through its provisions, regional cooperative programs were established among medical schools, hospitals, and research institutions to foster research, training, continuing education, and demonstrations of patient care practices related to heart disease, cancer, and stroke.

P.L. 89-272, the *Clean Air Act Amendments*, amended the original Clean Air Act (see the 1963 P.L. 88-206) to provide for federal regulation of motor vehicle exhaust and to establish a program of federal research support and grants-in-aid in the area of solid waste disposal.

P.L. 89-290, the *Health Professions Educational Assistance Amendments*, amended the original act (see the 1963 P.L. 88-129) to provide further support "to improve the quality of schools of medicine, dentistry, osteopathy, optometry, and podiatry." The law expanded the availability of student loans and introduced a provision whereby 50 percent of a professional's student loan could be forgiven in exchange for practice in a designated shortage area.

1966

P.L. 89-564, the *Highway Safety Act*, sought to improve the nation's system of highways to make them safer for users.

P.L. 89-642, the *Child Nutrition Act*, established a federal program of support, including research, for child nutrition. A key component of the legislation was its authorization of the school breakfast program.

P.L. 89-749, the *Comprehensive Health Planning Act* (also known as the Partnership for Health Act), which amended the Public Health Service Act (see the 1944 P.L. 78-410), was intended "to promote and assist in the extension and improvement of comprehensive health planning and public health services, [and] to provide for a more effective use of available Federal funds for such planning and services. . . ." This legislation sought to promote comprehensive planning for health facilities, services, and personnel within the framework of a federal/state/local partnership. It also gave states greater flexibility in the use of their grants-in-aid for public health services through block grants.

The law, in Section 314a, authorized grants to states for the development of comprehensive state health planning; and, in Section 314b, authorized grants to public or nonprofit organizations "for developing comprehensive regional, metropolitan area or other local area plans for coordination of existing and planned health services." State planning agencies created or designated under this legislation became known as "A" agencies or as "314a" agencies. Within states, the other planning agencies created or designated under this legislation became known as "B," "areawide," or "314b" agencies.

P.L. 89-751, the *Allied Health Professions Personnel Training Act*, provided grant support for the training of allied health professionals. The legislation was patterned after the 1963 Health Professions Education Assistance Act (see P.L. 88-129).

P.L. 89-794, the *Economic Opportunity Act Amendments*, amended the Economic Opportunity Act (see the 1964 P.L. 88-452) to establish Office of Economic Opportunity neighborhood health centers. Located especially in impoverished sections of cities and rural areas, these centers provided poor people a comprehensive range of ambulatory health services. By the early 1970s approximately 100 centers were to have been established under this program.

1967

P.L. 90-31, the *Mental Health Amendments*, amended the Mental Retardation Facilities and Community Mental Health Centers Construction Act (see the 1963 P.L. 88-164) to extend the program of construction grants for community mental health centers. The legislation also amended the term construction so that it covered acquisition of existing buildings.

P.L. 90-148, the *Air Quality Act*, amended the Clean Air Act (see the

1963 P.L. 88-206) "to authorize planning grants to air pollution control agencies; expand research provisions relating to fuels and vehicles; provide for interstate air pollution control agencies or commissions; authorize the establishment of air quality standards; and for other purposes." The act provided for each state to establish air quality standards depending on local conditions, but a minimum air quality was to be ensured through federal review of the states' standards.

P.L. 90-170, the *Mental Retardation Amendments*, amended the Mental Retardation Facilities and Community Mental Health Centers Construction Act (see the 1963 P.L. 88-164) to extend the program of construction grants for university-affiliated and community-based facilities for the mentally retarded. The legislation also authorized a new program of grants for the education of physical educators and recreation workers who work with mentally retarded and other handicapped children and for research in these areas.

P.L. 90-174, the *Clinical Laboratory Improvement Act*, amended the Public Health Service Act (see the 1944 P.L. 78-410) to provide for the regulation of laboratories in interstate commerce by the Centers for Disease Control through processes of licensure, standards setting, and proficiency testing.

P.L. 90-189, the *Flammable Fabrics Act*, was part of government's early efforts to rid the environment of hazards to human health. The legislation sought to regulate the manufacture and marketing of flammable fabrics.

P.L. 90-248, the *Social Security Amendments*, represented the first of many modifications to the Medicare and Medicaid programs, which were established by the Social Security Amendments of 1965 (see the P.L. 89-97). Coming two years after their establishment, this legislation provided expanded coverage for such things as durable medical equipment for use in the home, podiatrist services for nonroutine foot care, outpatient physical therapy, and the addition of a lifetime reserve of 60 days of coverage for inpatient hospital care over and above the original coverage for up to 90 days during any spell of illness. In addition, certain payment rules were modified in favor of providers. For example, payment of full reasonable charges for radiologist and pathologist services provided to inpatients were authorized under one modification.

This law also sought to raise the quality of care provided in nursing homes by establishing a number of conditions that had to be met by nursing homes wanting to participate in the Medicare and Medicaid programs. There was also a provision for limiting the federal participation in medical assistance payments to families whose income did not exceed 133 percent of the income limit for Aid to Families with Dependent Children (AFDC) payments in any state.

1968

P.L. 90-490, the *Health Manpower Act*, extended previous programs of support for the training of health professionals (see the 1963 P.L. 88-129 and the 1964 P.L. 88-581), in effect authorizing formula institutional grants for training all health professionals.

1969

P.L. 91-173, the *Federal Coal Mine Health and Safety Act*, was intended to help secure and improve the health and safety of coal miners.

P.L. 91-190, the *National Environmental Policy Act*, was enacted "To declare a national policy which will encourage productive and enjoyable harmony between man and his environment; to promote efforts which will prevent or eliminate damage to the environment and biosphere and stimulate the health and welfare of man. . . ." This law established the Council on Environmental Quality to advise the President on environmental matters. The legislation required that environmental impact statements be prepared prior to the initiation of major federal actions.

1970

P.L. 91-222, the *Public Health Cigarette Smoking Act*, banned cigarette advertising from radio and television.

P.L. 91-224, the *Water Quality Improvement Act*, a very comprehensive water pollution law, included among its numerous provisions those relating to oil pollution by vessels and on- and offshore oil wells, hazardous polluting substances other than oil, pollution from sewage from vessels, and for training people to work in the operation and maintenance of water treatment facilities. Perhaps its most important provisions pertain to the procedures whereby all federal agencies must deal with water pollution, including requirements for cooperation among the various agencies.

P.L. 91-296, the *Medical Facilities Construction and Modernization Amendments*, amended the Hill-Burton Act (see the 1946 P.L. 79-725) by extending the program and by initiating a new program of project grants for emergency rooms, communications networks, and medical transportation systems.

P.L. 91-464, the *Communicable Disease Control Amendments*, amended the Public Health Service Act (see the 1944 P.L. 78-410), which had established the Communicable Disease Center (CDC), by renaming the CDC the Centers for Disease Control. The legislation also broadened the functions of the CDC beyond its traditional focus on communicable or infectious diseases (e.g., tuberculosis, venereal disease, rubella, measles, Rh disease, poliomyelitis, diphtheria, tetanus, and whooping cough) to include other preventable conditions, including malnutrition.

P.L. 91-513, the *Comprehensive Drug Abuse Prevention and Control Act*, provided for special project grants for drug abuse and drug dependence treatment programs and grants for programs and activities related to drug education.

P.L. 91-572, the *Family Planning Services and Population Research Act*, established the Office of Population Affairs and added Title X, Population Research and Voluntary Family Planning Programs, to the Public Health Service Act (see the 1944 P.L. 78-410). The legislation authorized a range of projects, formulas, training, and research grants and contracts to support family planning programs and services, except for abortion.

P.L. 91-596, the *Occupational Safety and Health Act*, established an extensive federal program of standard-setting and enforcement activities that were intended to ensure healthful and safe workplaces.

P.L. 91-601, the *Poison Prevention Packaging Act*, required that most drugs be dispensed in containers designed to be difficult for children to open.

P.L. 91-604, the *Clean Air Amendments*, was enacted because Congress became dissatisfied with progress toward control and abatement of air pollution under the Air Quality Act of 1967 (see the 1967 P.L. 90-148). This law took away the power of the states to establish different air quality standards in different air quality control regions. Instead, this legislation required states to achieve national air quality standards within each of their regions.

P.L. 91-616, the *Comprehensive Alcohol Abuse and Alcoholism Prevention, Treatment, and Rehabilitation Act*, established the National Institute of Alcohol Abuse and Alcoholism. The law provided a separate statutory base for programs and activities related to alcohol abuse and alcoholism. The legislation also provided a comprehensive program of aid to states and localities in their efforts addressed to combating alcohol abuse and alcoholism.

P.L. 91-623, the *Emergency Health Personnel Act*, amended the Public Health Service Act (see the 1944 P.L. 78-410) to permit the Secretary of DHEW (now DHHS) to assign commissioned officers and other health personnel of the U.S. Public Health Service to areas of the country experiencing critical shortages of health personnel. This legislation also established the National Health Service Corps.

P.L. 91-695, the *Lead-Based Paint Poisoning Prevention Act*, represented a specific attempt to address the problem of lead-based paint poisoning through a program of grants to the states to aid them in their efforts to combat this problem.

1971

P.L. 92-157, the *Comprehensive Health Manpower Training Act*, was, at the time of its enactment, the most comprehensive health personnel legislation yet enacted. The legislation replaced institutional formula grants with a new system of capitation grants through which health professions schools received fixed sums of money for each of their students (contingent on increasing first-year enrollments). Loan provisions were broadened so that health professionals who practiced in designated personnel shortage areas could cancel 85 percent of education loans. The legislation also established the National Health Manpower Clearinghouse and the Secretary of DHEW (now DHHS) was directed to make every effort to provide to counties without physicians at least one National Health Service Corps physician.

1972

P.L. 92-294, the *National Sickle Cell Anemia Control Act*, authorized grants and contracts to support screening, treatment, counseling, information and education programs, and research related to sickle-cell anemia.

P.L. 92-303, the *Federal Coal Mine Health and Safety Amendments*, amended the earlier Federal Coal Mine Health and Safety Act (see the 1969 P.L. 91-173) to provide financial benefits and other assistance to coal miners who were afflicted with black lung disease.

P.L. 92-426, the *Uniformed Services Health Professions Revitalization Act*, established the Uniformed Services University of the Health Sciences. The legislation provided for this educational institution to be operated under the auspices of the U.S. Department of Defense in Bethesda, Maryland. The legislation also created the Armed Forces Health Professions Scholarship Program.

P.L. 92-433, the *National School Lunch and Child Nutrition Amendments*, amended the Child Nutrition Act (see the 1966 P.L. 89-642) to add support for the provision of nutritious diets for pregnant and lactating women and for infants and children (the WIC program).

P.L. 92-573, the *Consumer Product Safety Act*, established the Consumer Product Safety Commission to develop safety standards and regulations for consumer products. Under provisions of the legislation, the administration of existing related legislation, including the Flammable

Fabrics Act, the Hazardous Substances Act, and the Poison Prevention Packaging Act, was transferred to the commission.

P.L. 92-574, the *Noise Control Act*, much like the earlier Clean Air Act (see the 1963 P.L. 88-206) and the Flammable Fabrics Act (see the 1967 P.L. 90-189), continued government's efforts to rid the environment of harmful influences on human health.

P.L. 92-603, the *Social Security Amendments*, amended the Social Security Act (see the 1935 P.L. 74-271) to make several significant changes in the Medicare program. These amendments marked an important shift in the operation of the Medicare program as efforts were undertaken to help control its growing costs. Over the bitter opposition of organized medicine, the legislation established Professional Standards Review Organizations (PSROs) that were to monitor both the quality of services provided to Medicare beneficiaries as well as the medical necessity for the services.

One provision limited payments for capital expenditures by hospitals that had been disapproved by state or local planning agencies. Another provision authorized a program of grants and contracts to conduct experiments and demonstrations related to achieving increased economy and efficiency in the provision of health services. Some of the specifically targeted areas of these studies were to be prospective reimbursement, the requirement that patients spend three days in the hospital prior to admission to a skilled nursing home, the potential benefits of ambulatory surgery centers, payment for the services of physician assistants and nurse practitioners, and the use of clinical psychologists.

Coincident with these and other cost-containment amendments, several cost-increasing changes were also made in the Medicare program by this legislation. Notably, persons who were eligible for cash benefits under the disability provisions of the Social Security Act for at least 24 months were made eligible for medical benefits under the program. In addition, persons who were insured under Social Security, as well as their dependents, who required hemodialysis or renal transplantation for chronic renal disease were defined as disabled for the purpose of having them covered under the Medicare program for the costs of treating their end-stage renal disease (ESRD). The inclusion of coverage for the disabled and ESRD patients in 1972 was an extraordinarily expensive change in the Medicare program. In addition, certain less costly but still expensive additional coverages were extended, including chiropractic services and speech pathology services.

P.L. 92-714, the *National Cooley's Anemia Control Act*, authorized grants and contracts to support screening, treatment, counseling, information and education programs, and research related to Cooley's Anemia.

1973

P.L. 93-29, the *Older Americans Act*, established the National Clearinghouse for Information on Aging and created the Federal Council on Aging. The legislation also authorized funds to establish gerontology centers and provided grants for training and research related to the field of aging.

P.L. 93-154, the *Emergency Medical Services Systems Act*, provided aid to states and localities to assist them in developing coordinated Emergency Medical Service (EMS) Systems.

P.L. 93-222, the *Health Maintenance Organization Act*, amended the Public Health Service Act (see the 1944 P.L. 78-410) to "provide assistance and encouragement for the establishment and expansion of health maintenance organizations. . . ." The legislation, which added a new title, Title XIII, Health Maintenance Organizations (HMOs), to the Public Health Service Act, authorized a program of grants, loans, and loan guarantees to support the conduct of feasibility and development studies and initial operations for new HMOs.

1974

P.L. 93-247, the *Child Abuse Prevention and Treatment Act*, created the National Center on Child Abuse and Neglect. The legislation authorized grants for research and demonstrations related to child abuse and neglect.

P.L. 93-270, the *Sudden Infant Death Syndrome Act*, added Part C, Sudden Infant Death Syndrome, to Title XI of the Public Health Service Act (see the 1944 P.L. 78-410). The legislation provided for the development of informational programs related to this syndrome for both public and professional audiences.

P.L. 93-296, *Research in Aging Act*, established the National Institute on Aging within the National Institutes of Health (NIH).

P.L. 93-344, the *Congressional Budget and Impoundment Control Act*, and its subsequent amendments, provided Congress with the procedures through which it establishes target levels for revenues, expenditures, and the overall deficit for the coming fiscal year. The Congressional budget procedures are designed to coordinate decisions on sources and levels of federal revenues and on the objectives and levels of federal expenditures. These decisions have substantial impact on health policy. The procedures formally begin each year with the initial decision as to the overall size of the budget pie for a given year, as well as the sizes of its various pieces. To accomplish this, each year the Congress adopts a concurrent resolution that imposes overall constraints on spending, based in part on the size of the anticipated revenue budget for the year, and distributes the overall constraint on spending among groups of programs and activities. These constraints are implemented through the reconciliation process. The result of this process is the annual omnibus reconciliation bill, which is, in effect, a packaging together of all legislative changes made in the various standing committees necessitated by reconciling existing law with the budgetary targets established earlier in the concurrent resolution on the budget.

This act also established the U.S. Congressional Budget Office (CBO). The nonpartisan CBO conducts studies and analyses of the fiscal and budget implications of various decisions facing Congress, including those related to health.

P.L. 93-360, the *Nonprofit Hospital Amendments*, amended the 1947 Labor-Management Relations Act (or the Taft-Hartley Act) to end the exclusion of nongovernmental nonprofit hospitals from the provisions of this act as well as from the earlier National Labor Relations Act of 1935 (or the Wagner Act). Both of these acts pertain to fair labor practices and collective bargaining.

P.L. 93-406, the *Employee Retirement Income Security Act* (also known as ERISA), provided for the regulation of almost all pension and benefit plans for employees, including pensions, medical or hospital benefits, disability, and death benefits. The legislation provides for the regulation of many features of these benefit plans.

P.L. 93-523, the *Safe Drinking Water Act*, required the Environmental Protection Agency (EPA) to establish national drinking water standards and to aid states and localities in the enforcement of these standards.

P.L. 93-641, the *National Health Planning and Resources Development Act*, amended the Public Health Service Act (see the 1944 P.L. 78-410) in an attempt "to assure the development of a national health policy and of effective state and area health planning and resource development programs, and for other purposes." The legislation added two new titles, XV and XVI, to the Public Health Service Act. These titles superseded and significantly modified the programs established under Sections 314a and 314b of Title III of the 1966 P.L. 89-749, the Comprehensive Health Planning Act (or the Partnership for Health Act) as well as the programs established under the Hill-Burton Act (see the 1946 P.L. 79-725).

The legislation essentially folded existing health planning activities into a new framework created by the legislation. The Secretary of DHEW (now DHHS) was to enter into an agreement with each state's governor for the designation of a State Health Planning and Development Agency

(SHPDA). The states were to also establish State Health Coordinating Councils (SHCCs) to serve as advisors in setting overall state policy.

A network of local Health Systems Agencies (HSAs) covering the entire nation was established by the legislation. The HSAs were to: (1) improve the health of area residents; (2) increase the accessibility, acceptability, continuity, and quality of health services; and (3) restrain healthcare cost increases and prevent duplication of healthcare services and facilities. An important feature of the planning framework created by P.L. 93-641 was a provision that permitted the HSAs in states that had established certificate-of-need (CON) programs to conduct CON reviews and to make recommendations developed at the local level to the SHPDA.

Congress repealed this law in 1986 (effective January 1, 1987), leaving responsibility for the certificate-of-need programs entirely in the hands of the states.

P.L. 93-647, the *Social Security Amendments* (also known as the Social Services Amendments), amended the Social Security Act (see the 1935 P.L. 74-271) to consolidate existing federal-state social service programs into a block grant program that would permit a ceiling on federal matching funds while providing more flexibility to the states in providing certain social services. The legislation added a new title, Title XX, Grants to the States for Services, to the Social Security Act.

The goals of the legislation pertained to the prevention and remedy of neglect, abuse, or exploitation of children or adults, the preservation of families, and the avoidance of inappropriate institutional care by substituting community-based programs and services. Social services covered under this law included child-care service; protective, foster, and day-care services for children and adults; counseling; family planning services; homemaker services; and home-delivered meals.

1976

P.L. 94-295, the *Medical Devices Amendments*, amended the Food, Drug and Cosmetic Act (see the 1938 P.L. 75-717) to strengthen the regulation of medical devices. This legislation was passed, after previous attempts had failed, amidst growing public concern with the adverse effects of such medical devices as the Dalcon Shield intrauterine device.

P.L. 94-317, the *National Consumer Health Information and Health Promotion Act*, amended the Public Health Service Act (see the 1944 P.L. 78-410) to add Title XVII, Health Information and Promotion. The legislation authorized grants and contracts for research and community programs related to health information, health promotion, preventive health services, and education of the public in the appropriate use of healthcare services.

P.L. 94-437, the *Indian Health Care Improvement Act*, an extensive piece of legislation, was intended to fill existing gaps in the delivery of healthcare services to Native Americans.

P.L. 94-460, the *Health Maintenance Organization Amendments*, amended the Health Maintenance Organization Act (see the 1973 P.L. 93-222) to ease somewhat the requirements that had to be met for an HMO to become federally qualified. One provision, however, required that HMOs must be federally qualified if they were to receive reimbursement from the Medicare or Medicaid programs.

P.L. 94-469, the *Toxic Substances Control Act* (TSCA), sought to regulate chemical substances used in various production processes. The legislation defined chemical substances very broadly. The purpose of TSCA was to identify potentially harmful chemical substances before they were produced and entered the marketplace and, subsequently, the environment.

P.L. 94-484, the *Health Professions Educational Assistance Act*, extended the program of capitation grants to professional schools that had been established under the Comprehensive Health Manpower Training Act (see the 1971 P.L. 92-157). However, this legislation dropped the requirement that schools increase their first-year enrollments as a condition for receiving grants. Under this legislation, medical schools were required to have 50 percent of their graduates to enter residency programs in primary care by 1980. They were also required to reserve positions in their third-year classes for U.S. citizens who were studying medicine in foreign medical schools. However, under intense protest from medical schools, this provision was repealed in 1975.

1977

P.L. 95-142, the *Medicare-Medicaid Antifraud and Abuse Amendments*, amended the legislation governing the Medicare and Medicaid programs (see the 1965 P.L. 89-97) in an attempt to reduce fraud and abuse in the programs as a means to help contain their costs. Specific changes included strengthening criminal and civil penalties for fraud and abuse affecting the programs, modification in the operations of the PSROs, and the promulgation of uniform reporting systems and formats for hospitals and certain other healthcare organizations participating in the Medicare and Medicaid programs.

P.L. 95-210, the *Rural Health Clinic Services Amendments*, amended the legislation governing the Medicare and Medicaid programs (see the

1965 P.L. 89-97) to modify the categories of practitioners who could provide reimbursable services to Medicare and Medicaid beneficiaries, at least in rural settings. Under the provisions of this act, rural health clinics that did not routinely have physicians available on site could, if they met certain requirements regarding physician supervision of the clinic and review of services, be reimbursed for services provided by nurse practitioners and physician assistants through the Medicare and Medicaid programs. This act also authorized certain demonstration projects in underserved urban areas for reimbursement of these nonphysician practitioners.

1978

P.L. 95-292, the *Medicare End-Stage Renal Disease Amendments*, further amended the legislation governing the Medicare program (see the 1965 P.L. 89-97) in an attempt to help control the program's costs. Since the addition of coverage for ESRD under the Social Security Amendments of 1972 (P.L. 92-603), the costs to the Medicare program had risen steadily and quickly. This legislation added incentives to encourage the use of home dialysis and of renal transplantation in ESRD.

The legislation also permitted the use of a variety of reimbursement methods for renal dialysis facilities. And it authorized funding for the conduct of studies of end-stage renal disease itself, especially studies incorporating possible cost reductions in treatment for this disease. It also directed the Secretary of DHEW (now DHHS) to establish areawide network coordinating councils to help plan for and review ESRD programs.

P.L. 95-559, the *Health Maintenance Organization Amendments*, further amended the Health Maintenance Organization Act (see the 1973 P.L. 93-222) to add a new program of loans and loan guarantees to support the acquisition of ambulatory care facilities and related equipment. The legislation also provided for support for a program of training for HMO administrators and medical directors and for providing technical assistance to HMOs in their developmental efforts.

1979

P.L. 96-79, the *Health Planning and Resources Development Amendments*, amended the National Health Planning and Resources Development Act (see the 1974 P.L. 93-641) to add provisions intended to foster competition within the health sector, to address the need to integrate mental health and alcoholism and drug abuse resources into health system plans, and to make several revisions in the certificate-of-need (CON) requirements.

1980

P.L. 96-398, the *Mental Health Systems Act*, extensively amended the Community Mental Health Centers program (see the 1970 P.L. 91-211) including provisions for the development and support of comprehensive state mental health systems. Subsequently, however, this legislation was almost completely superseded by the block grants to the states for mental health and alcohol and drug abuse that were provided under the Omnibus Budget Reconciliation Act of 1981 (see P.L. 97-35).

P.L. 96-499, the *Omnibus Budget Reconciliation Act* (OBRA '80), contained in Title IX of the Medicare and Medicaid Amendments of 1980. These amendments made extensive modifications in the Medicare and Medicaid programs, with 57 separate sections pertaining to one or both of the programs. Many of the changes reflected continuing concern with the growing costs of the programs and were intended to help control these costs.

Examples of the changes that were specific to Medicare included removal of the 100 visits/year limitation on home health services and the requirement that patients pay a deductible for home care visits under Part B of the program. These changes were intended to encourage home care over more expensive institutional care. Another provision permitted small rural hospitals to use their beds as "swing beds" (alternating their use as acute or long-term care beds as needed) and authorized swing-bed demonstration projects for large and urban hospitals. An important change in the Medicaid program required the programs to pay for the services that the states had authorized nurse-midwives to perform.

P.L. 96-510, the *Comprehensive Environmental Response, Compensation and Liability Act* (CERCLA), established the Superfund program that intended to provide resources for the cleanup of inactive hazardous waste dumps. The legislation assigned retroactive liability for the costs of cleaning up the dumps to their owners and operators as well as to the waste generators and transporters who had used the dump sites.

1981

P.L. 97-35, the *Omnibus Budget Reconciliation Act* (OBRA '81), in its Title XXI, Subtitles A, B, and C, contained further amendments to the Medicare and Medicaid programs. Just as in 1980, this legislation included extensive changes in the programs, with 46 sections pertaining to them. Enacted in the context of extensive efforts to reduce the federal budget, many of the provisions hit Medicare and Medicaid especially hard. For example, one provision eliminated the coverage of alcohol detoxification facility services, another removed the use of occupational therapy as a basis for initial entitlement to home health service, and yet another increased the Part B deductible.

In other provisions, OBRA '81 combined 20 existing categorical public health programs into four block grants. The block grants were: (1) Preventive Health and Health Services, which combined such previously categorical programs as rodent control, fluoridation, hypertension control, and rape crisis centers among others into one block grant to be distributed among the states by a formula based on population and other factors; (2) Alcohol Abuse, Drug Abuse, and Mental Health Block Grant, which combined existing programs created under the Community Mental Health Centers Act, the Mental Health Systems Act, the Comprehensive Alcohol Abuse and Alcoholism Prevention, Treatment, and Rehabilitation Act, and the Drug Abuse, Prevention, Treatment, and Rehabilitation Act; (3) Primary Care Block Grant, which consisted of the Community Health Centers; and (4) Maternal and Child Health Block Grant, which consolidated seven previously categorical grant programs from Title V of the Social Security Act and from the Public Health Services Act, including the maternal and child health and crippled children's programs, genetic disease service, adolescent pregnancy services, sudden infant death syndrome, hemophilia treatment, Supplemental Security Income (SSI) payments to disabled children, and lead-based poisoning prevention.

1982

P.L. 97-248, the *Tax Equity and Fiscal Responsibility Act* (TEFRA), made a number of important changes in the Medicare program. One provision added coverage for hospice services provided to Medicare beneficiaries. These benefits were extended later and are now an integral part of the Medicare program. However, the most important provisions, in terms of impact on the Medicare program, were those that sought to control the program's costs by setting limits on how much Medicare would reimburse hospitals on a per-case basis and by limiting the annual rate of increase for Medicare's reasonable costs per discharge. These changes in reimbursement methodology represented fundamental changes in the Medicare program and reflected a dramatic shift in the nation's Medicare policy.

Another provision of TEFRA replaced PSROs, which had been established by the Social Security Amendments of 1972 (see the P.L. 92-603), with a new utilization and quality control program called peer review organizations (PROs). The TEFRA changes regarding the operation of the Medicare program were extensive, but they were only the harbinger of the most sweeping legislative changes in the history of the Medicare program the following year.

P.L. 97-414, the *Orphan Drug Act* (ODA), provided financial incentives for the development and marketing of orphan drugs, defined by the legislation to be drugs for the treatment of diseases or conditions affecting so few people that revenues from sales of the drugs would not cover their development costs.

1983

P.L. 98-21, the *Social Security Amendments*, another landmark in the evolution of the Medicare program, amended the legislation governing the program (see the 1965 P.L. 89-97) to initiate the Medicare prospective payment system (PPS). The legislation included provisions to base payment for hospital inpatient services on predetermined rates per discharge for diagnosis-related groups (DRGs). PPS was a major departure from the cost-based system of reimbursement that had been used in the Medicare program since its inception in 1965. The legislation also directed the administration to study physician payment reform options, a feature that was to later have significant impact (see the 1989 P.L. 101-239).

1984

P.L. 98-369, the *Deficit Reduction Act* (DEFRA), among many provisions, temporarily froze increases in physicians' fees paid under the Medicare program. Another provision in the legislation placed a specific limitation on the rate of increase in the DRG payment rates that the Secretary of DHHS could permit in the two subsequent years.

The legislation also established the Medicare Participating Physician and Supplier (PAR) program and created two classes of physicians in regard to their relationships to the Medicare program and outlined different reimbursement approaches for them depending on whether they were classified as "participating" or "nonparticipating." As part of this legislation, Congress mandated that the Office of Technology Assessment study alternative methods of paying for physician services so that the information could guide the reform of the Medicare program.

P.L. 98-417, the *Drug Price Competition and Patent Term Restoration Act*, provided brand-name pharmaceutical manufacturers with patent term extensions. These extensions significantly increased manufacturers' opportunities for earning profits during the longer effective patent life (EPL) of their affected products.

P.L. 98-457, the *Child Abuse Amendments*, amended the Child Abuse Prevention and Treatment Act (see the 1974 P.L. 93-247) to involve

Infant Care Review Committees in the medical decisions regarding the treatment of handicapped newborns, at least in hospitals with tertiary-level neonatal care units.

The legislation established treatment and reporting guidelines for severely disabled newborns, making it illegal to withhold "medically indicated treatment" from newborns except when "in the treating physician's reasonable medical judgment, i) the infant is chronically and irreversibly comatose; ii) the provision of such treatment would merely prolong dying, not be effective in ameliorating or correcting all of the infant's life-threatening conditions, or otherwise be futile in terms of survival of the infant; or iii) the provision of such treatment would be virtually futile in terms of the survival of the infant and the treatment itself under such circumstances would be inhumane."

P.L. 98-507, the *National Organ Transplant Act*, made it illegal "to knowingly acquire, receive or otherwise transfer any human organ for valuable consideration for use in human transplantation if the transfer affects interstate commerce."

1985

P.L. 99-177, the *Emergency Deficit Reduction and Balanced Budget Act* (also known as the Gramm-Rudman-Hollins Act), established mandatory deficit reduction targets for the five subsequent fiscal years. Under provisions of the legislation, the required budget cuts would come equally from defense spending and from domestic programs that were not exempted. The Gramm-Rudman-Hollins Act had significant impact on the Medicare program throughout the last half of the 1980s, as well as on other health programs such as community and migrant health centers, veteran and Native American health, health professions education, and the National Institutes of Health. Among other things, this legislation led to substantial cuts in Medicare payments to hospitals and physicians.

P.L. 99-272, the *Consolidated Omnibus Budget Reconciliation Act* (COBRA '85), contained a number of provisions that impacted on the Medicare program. Hospitals that served a disproportionate share of poor patients received an adjustment in their PPS payments; hospice care was made a permanent part of the Medicare program and states were given the ability to provide hospice services under the Medicaid program; fiscal year 1986 PPS payment rates were frozen at 1985 levels through May 1, 1986 and increased 0.5 percent for the remainder of the year; payment to hospitals for the indirect costs of medical education was modified; and a schedule to phase out payment of a return on equity to proprietary hospitals was established.

This legislation established the Physician Payment Review Commission (PPRC) to advise Congress on physician payment policies for the Medicare program. The legislation also required that the PPRC advise Congress and the Secretary of the DHHS regarding the development of a resource-based relative value scale for physician services.

Under another of COBRA's important provisions, employers were required to continue health insurance for employees and their dependents who would otherwise lose their eligibility for the coverage due to reduced hours of work or termination of their employment.

1986

P.L. 99-509, the *Omnibus Budget Reconciliation Act* (OBRA '86), altered the PPS payment rate for hospitals once again and reduced payment amounts for capital-related costs by 3.5 percent for part of fiscal year 1987, by 7 percent for fiscal year 1988, and by 10 percent for fiscal year 1989. In addition, certain adjustments were made in the manner in which "outlier" or atypical cases were reimbursed.

The legislation established further limits to balance billing by physicians providing services to Medicare clients by setting "maximum allowable actual charges" (MAACs) for physicians who did not participate in the PAR program (see the Deficit Reduction Act of 1984, P.L. 98-369). In another provision intended to realize savings for the Medicare program, OBRA '86 directed the DHHS to use the concept of "inherent reasonableness" to reduce payments for cataract surgery as well as for anesthesia during the surgery.

P.L. 99-660, the *Omnibus Health Act*, contained provisions to significantly liberalize coverage under the Medicaid program. Using family income up to the federal poverty line as a criterion, this change permitted states to offer coverage to all pregnant women, infants up to one year of age, and by using a phase-in schedule, children up to five years of age.

One part of this omnibus health legislation was the *National Childhood Vaccine Injury Act*. This law established a federal vaccine injury compensation system. Under provisions of the legislation, parties injured by vaccines would be limited to awards of income losses plus $250,000 for pain and suffering or death.

Another important part of the omnibus health legislation of 1986 was the *Health Care Quality Improvement Act*. This law provided immunity from private damage lawsuits under federal or state law for "any professional review action" so long as that action followed standards set out in the legislation. This afforded members of peer review committees protection from most damage suits filed by physicians whom they disciplined. The law also mandated creation of a national data bank through which information on physician licensure actions, sanctions by boards of medical examiners, malpractice claims paid, and professional review actions that adversely affect the clinical privileges of physicians could be provided to authorized persons and organizations.

1987

P.L. 100-177, the *National Health Service Corps Amendments*, reauthorized the National Health Service Corps (NHSC), which had been created under a provision of the Emergency Health Personnel Act of 1970 (see P.L. 91-623).

P.L. 100-203, the *Omnibus Budget Reconciliation Act* (OBRA '87), contained a number of provisions that directly affected on the Medicare program. It required the Secretary of the DHHS to update the wage index used in calculating hospital PPS payments by October 1, 1990, and to do so at least every three years thereafter. It also required the Secretary to study and report to Congress on the criteria being used by the Medicare program to identify referral hospitals. Deepening the reductions established by OBRA '86, one provision of the act reduced payment amounts for capital-related costs by 12 percent for fiscal year 1988 and by 15 percent for 1989.

Regarding payments to physicians for services provided to Medicare clients, the legislation reduced fees for 12 sets of "overvalued" procedures. It also allowed higher fee increases for primary care than for other physician services and increased the fee differential between participating and nonparticipating physicians (see the 1984 P.L. 98-369).

The legislation also contained a number of provisions that affected the Medicaid program. Key among these, the law provided additional options for children and pregnant women, and required states to cover eligible children up to age six with an option for allowing coverage up to age eight. The distinction between skilled nursing facilities (SNFs) and intermediate care facilities (ICFs) was eliminated. The legislation contained a number of provisions intended to enhance the quality of services provided in nursing homes, including requirements that nursing homes enhance the quality of life of each resident and operate quality assurance programs.

1988

P.L. 100-360, the *Medicare Catastrophic Coverage Act*, provided the largest expansion of the benefits covered under the Medicare program since its establishment in 1965 (see P.L. 89-97). Among other things, provisions of this legislation added coverage for outpatient prescription drugs and respite care and placed a cap on out-of-pocket spending by the elderly for copayment costs for covered services.

The legislation included provisions that would have the new benefits phased in over a four-year period and paid for by premiums charged to Medicare program enrollees. Thirty-seven percent of the costs were to be covered by a fixed monthly premium paid by all enrollees and the remainder of the costs were to be covered by an income-related supplemental premium that was, in effect, an income-tax surtax that would apply to fewer than half of the enrollees. Under intense pressure from many of their elderly constituents and their interest groups who objected to having to pay additional premiums or the income-tax surtax, Congress repealed P.L. 100-360 in 1989 without implementing most of its provisions.

P.L. 100-578, the *Clinical Laboratory Improvement Amendments*, amended the Clinical Laboratory Improvement Act (see the 1967 P.L. 90-174) to extend and modify government's ability to regulate clinical laboratories.

P.L. 100-582, the *Medical Waste Tracking Act*, was enacted in response to the highly publicized incidents of used and discarded syringes and needles washing up on the shores of a number of states in the eastern United States in the summer of 1988. The legislation itself was rather limited in that it focused on the tracking of medical wastes from their origin to their disposal rather than broader regulation of transportation and disposal of these wastes.

P.L. 100-607, the *National Organ Transplant Amendments*, amended the National Organ Transplant Act (see the 1986 P.L. 98-507) to extend the prohibition against the sale of human organs to the organs and other body parts of human fetuses.

P.L. 100-647, the *Technical and Miscellaneous Revenue Act*, directed the Physician Payment Review Commission (see the 1985 P.L. 99-272) to consider policies for moderating the rate of increase in expenditures for physician services in the Medicare program and for reducing the utilization of these services.

1989

P.L. 101-239, the *Omnibus Budget Reconciliation Act* (OBRA '89), included provisions for minor, primarily technical, changes in the PPS and a provision to extend coverage for mental health benefits and add coverage for Pap smears. Small adjustments were made in the disproportionate share regulations, and the 15 percent capital-related payment reduction established in OBRA '87 was continued in OBRA '89. Another provision required the Secretary of DHHS to update the wage index annually in a budget-neutral manner beginning in fiscal year 1993.

As part of the OBRA '89 legislation, the Health Care Financing Administration (HCFA) was directed to begin implementing a resource-based relative value scale (RBRVS) for reimbursing physicians under the Medicare program on January 1, 1992. The new system was to be phased in over a four-year period beginning in 1992.

Another important provision in this legislation initiated the establishment of the Agency for Health Care Policy and Research (AHCPR). This agency succeeded the National Center for Health Services Research and Technology Assessment (NCHSR). The new agency was created to conduct or foster the conduct of studies of healthcare quality, effectiveness, and efficiency. In particular, the agency was to conduct or foster the conduct of studies on the outcomes of medical treatments and provide technical assistance to groups seeking to develop practice guidelines. AHCPR's web site address is www.ahcpr.gov.

1990

P.L. 101-336, the *Americans with Disabilities Act* (ADA), provided a broad range of protections for the disabled, in effect combining protections contained in the Civil Rights Act of 1964, the Rehabilitation Act of 1973, and the Civil Rights Restoration Act of 1988. The central goal of the legislation was independence for the disabled, in effect to assist them in being self-supporting and able to lead independent lives.

P.L. 101-381, the *Ryan White Comprehensive AIDS Resources Emergency Act* (CARE), provided resources to 16 epicenters, including San Francisco and New York City, and to states hardest hit by AIDS to assist them in coping with the skyrocketing cost of care and treatment.

P.L. 101-508, the *Omnibus Budget Reconciliation Act* (OBRA '90), contained the Patient Self-Determination Act, which required healthcare institutions participating in the Medicare and Medicaid programs to provide all their patients with written information on policies regarding self-determination and living wills. The institutions were also required under this legislation to inquire whether patients had advance medical directives and to document the replies in the patients' medical records.

The legislation made additional minor changes in the PPS, including further adjustments in the wage index calculation and in the disproportionate share regulations. Regarding the wage index, one provision required the Prospective Payment Assessment Commission (ProPAC), which was established by the 1983 Social Security Amendments (see

P.L. 98-21) to help guide the Congress and the Secretary of DHHS on implementing the PPS to further study the available data on wages by occupational category and to develop recommendations on modifying the wage index to account for occupational mix.

The legislation also included a provision that continued the 15 percent capital-related payment reduction that was established in OBRA '87 and continued in OBRA '89 and another provision that made the reduced teaching adjustment payment established in OBRA '87 permanent. One of its more important provisions provided a five-year deficit reduction plan that was to reduce total Medicare outlays by more than $43 billion between fiscal years 1991 and 1995.

P.L. 101-629, the *Safe Medical Devices Act*, further amended the Federal Food, Drug and Cosmetic Act (see the 1938 P.L. 75-717) and the subsequent Medical Devices Amendments of 1976 (see the P.L. 94-295) to require institutions that use medical devices to report device-related problems to the manufacturers and/or to the FDA. Reportable problems include any incident in which any medical device may have caused or contributed to any person's death, serious illness, or serious injury.

P.L. 101-649, the *Immigration and Nationality Act of 1990*, restructured with minor modifications the medical exclusion scheme for screening people who desired to immigrate to the United States that had been in use since the enactment of the Immigration and Nationality Act of 1952 (see P.L. 82-414).

1992

P.L. 102-585, the *Veterans Health Care Act*, required the Department of Veterans Affairs to establish in each of its hospitals suitable indoor and outdoor smoking areas. This law ran counter to the Department's 1991 internal policy of running its hospitals on a smoke-free basis and was out of step with the private-sector movement to smoke-free hospitals.

1993

P.L. 103-43, the *National Institutes of Health Revitalization Act*, contained provisions for a number of structural and budgetary changes in the operation of the NIH. It also set forth guidelines for the conduct of research on transplantation of human fetal tissue and added HIV infection to the list of excludable conditions covered by the Immigration and Nationality Act (see the 1990 P.L. 101-649).

P.L. 103-66, the *Omnibus Budget Reconciliation Act* (OBRA '93), established an all-time record, five-year cut in Medicare funding and included a number of other changes affecting the Medicare program. For example, the legislation included provisions to end return on equity (ROE) payments for capital to proprietary SNFs and reduced the previously established rate of increase in payment rates for care provided in hospices. In addition, the legislation cut laboratory fees drastically by changing the reimbursement formula and froze payments for durable medical equipment, parenteral and enteral services, and for orthotics and prosthetics in fiscal years 1994 and 1995.

OBRA '93 contained the *Comprehensive Childhood Immunization Act*, which provided $585 million to support the provision of vaccines for children eligible for Medicaid, children who do not have health insurance, and for Native American children.

Note on 1994 and 1995

Chronologies of American health policy will always show these years as a period in which health policymaking appeared dormant because almost no important new federal laws pertaining to health, nor amendments to existing laws, were enacted. This apparent dearth of health policy, however, is misleading. This was a period of extraordinary consideration of health legislation, although very little was enacted. President Clinton attempted a fundamental reform of the American healthcare system through introducing his Health Security proposal in late 1993. The proposed legislation died with the 1994 Congress. The debate consumed almost all of the health-related legislation development energy expended during 1994. Then, following this bill's demise, the 1995 attempt to enact unprecedented cutbacks in the Medicare and Medicaid programs as part of a far-reaching budget reconciliation bill that sought a balanced federal budget ended in the bill being vetoed by President Clinton. The political wrangling over the budget grew even worse in 1996. Proposed changes in the Medicare and Medicaid programs, changes that were linked to the development of a plan to balance the federal budget over a seven-year span, would have meant massive cuts in these programs. The differences over these plans between the Republican-controlled Congress and President Clinton, a Democrat, were so fundamental that they led to a complete impasse in the budget negotiations in 1996, including a brief shutdown of the federal government in the absence of budget authority to operate.

1995

P.L. 104-65, the *Lobbying Disclosure Act*, contained provisions requiring registration with the Secretary of the Senate and the Clerk of the House of

Representatives by any individual lobbyist (or the individual's employer if it employs one or more lobbyists) within 45 days after the individual first makes, or is employed or retained to make, a lobbying contact with either the President, the Vice President, a member of Congress, or any of a number of specified federal officers. This law defines a lobbyist as any individual employed or retained by a client for financial or other compensation for services that include more than one lobbying contact, unless the individual's lobbying activities constitute less than 20 percent of the time engaged in the services provided to that client over a six-month period.

1996

P.L. 104-134, the *Departments of Veterans Affairs, Housing and Urban Development, and Independent Agencies Appropriations Act,* contained several provisions that offered certain protections for enrollees in managed care plans. One provision prohibited plans from restricting hospital stays for mothers and newborns to less than 48 hours for vaginal deliveries and 96 hours following a cesarean section. Another provision required that group health plans that offer both medical and surgical benefits and mental health benefits not impose a more restrictive lifetime or annual limit on mental health benefits than is imposed on medical or surgical benefits.

P.L. 104-191, the *Health Insurance Portability and Accountability Act* (HIPAA) (also known as the Kassebaum-Kennedy Act), provided employees who work for companies that offer health insurance to their employees with guaranteed access to health insurance in the event that they change jobs or become unemployed. In addition, the legislation guaranteed renewability of health insurance coverage so long as premiums are paid. It also provided for increased tax deductions for the self-employed who purchase health insurance and allowed tax deductions for medical expenses related to long-term-care insurance coverage. The legislation also established a limited "Medical Savings Accounts" demonstration project.

P.L. 104-193, the *Personal Responsibility and Work Opportunity Reconciliation Act* (also known as the Welfare Reform Act), made significant changes in the nation's welfare policy with implications for such health determinants as the social and economic environments faced by affected people and affected eligibility for the Medicaid program in a fundamental way. Since the establishment of the Medicaid program in 1965 (see P.L. 89-97), eligibility for a key welfare benefit, Aid to Families with Dependent Children (AFDC), and eligibility for Medicaid benefits have been linked.

Families receiving AFDC have been automatically eligible for Medicaid and enrolled in the Medicaid program. The Personal Responsibility and Work Opportunity Reconciliation Act, however, replaced AFDC with the Temporary Assistance to Needy Families (TANF) block grant. Under the provisions of the TANF block grant, states are given broad flexibility to design income support and work programs for low-income families with children and are required to impose federally mandated restrictions, such as time limits, on federally funded assistance. The welfare reform law does provide that children and parents who would have qualified for Medicaid based on their eligibility for AFDC continue to be eligible for Medicaid, but, in the absence of AFDC, states must utilize different mechanisms to identify and enroll former AFDC recipients in their Medicaid programs.

1997

P.L. 105-33, the *Balanced Budget Act of 1997* (BBA), contained the most significant changes in the Medicare program since the program's inception in 1965. Overall, this legislation required a five-year reduction of $115 billion in the Medicare program's expenditure growth and a $13 billion reduction in growth of the Medicaid program. A new "Medicare+Choice" program was created, which gives Medicare beneficiaries the opportunity to choose from a variety of health plan options the plan that best suits their needs and preferences. Significant changes were also made in the traditional Medicare program. Among them, hospital annual inflation updates were reduced as were hospital payments for inpatient capital expenses and for bad debts. Other provisions established a cap on the number of medical residents supported by Medicare graduate medical education payments and provided incentives for reductions in the number of residents.

An important provision of this act established the State Children's Health Insurance Program (SCHIP) and provided states with $24 billion in federal funds for 1998 until 2002 to increase health insurance for children.

Other provisions established two new commissions. The Medicare Payment Review Commission (MedPAC) replaced the Physician Payment Review Commission and the Prospective Payment Review Commission. The new commission was required to submit an annual report to Congress on the status of Medicare reforms, and to make recommendations on Medicare payment issues. The National Bipartisan Commission on the Future of Medicare was established by this legislation and charged to develop recommendations for Congress on actions necessary to ensure the long-term fiscal health of the Medicare program. This commission was to consider several specific issues that were debated in the development of the Balanced Budget Act of 1997, but rejected. These issues included raising the eligibility age for Medicare, increasing the Part B premiums, and developing alternative approaches to financing graduate medical education.

P.L. 105-115, the *Food and Drug Administration Modernization and Accountability Act*, directs the Secretary of DHHS, at the request of a new drug's sponsor, to identify the drug as a "fast track product" and to facilitate development and expedite review if the new drug is intended for serious conditions and demonstrates the potential to address unmet medical needs for those conditions. The law also mandates development, prioritization, publication, and annual updating of a list of approved drugs for which additional pediatric information may produce health benefits in the pediatric population. It also mandates development of guidance on the inclusion of women and minorities in clinical trials. Among numerous other provisions, the law also authorizes the Secretary of DHHS to permit the shipment of investigational drugs or investigational devices for the diagnosis, monitoring, or treatment of a serious disease or condition in emergency situations. It permits any person, through a licensed physician, to request, and any manufacturer or distributor to provide to the physician, such a drug or device if specified requirements are met.

1998

P.L. 105-357, the *Controlled Substances Trafficking Prohibition Act*, amends the Controlled Substances Import and Export Act to prohibit U.S. residents from importing into the United States a non-schedule I controlled substance exceeding 50 dosage units if they: (1) enter the United States through an international land border; and (2) do not possess a valid prescription or documentation verifying such a prescription. This law has a provision that declares that the federal requirements under the law do not limit states from imposing additional requirements.

P.L. 105-369, the *Ricky Ray Hemophilia Relief Fund Act*, establishes in the U. S. Treasury the Ricky Ray Hemophilia Relief Fund. The law mandates a single payment of $100,000 from the Fund to any individual infected with the human immunodeficiency virus (HIV) if the individual has any blood-clotting disorder and was treated with blood-clotting agents between July 1, 1982, and December 31, 1987, is the lawful current or former spouse of such an individual, or acquired the HIV infection from a parent who is such an individual. The law declares that it does not create or admit any claim of the individual against the United States or its agents regarding HIV and antihemophilic factor treatment; and that acceptance of a payment under this Act is in full satisfaction of all such claims of the individual.

1999

P.L. 106-113, the *Medicare, Medicaid and SCHIP Balanced Budget Refinement Act of 1999* (BBRA). This legislation changed the provisions in the Balanced Budget Act of 1997 in a number of ways. One change, for example, pertained to the way that hospitals treating a disproportionate share (DSH) of low-income Medicare and Medicaid patients receive additional payments from Medicare. BBRA froze DSH adjustments at 3 percent (the FY 2000 level) through FY 2001 and reduced the formula to 4 percent from the BBA established 5 percent in FY 2002, and then 0 percent for subsequent years. The law increased hospice payment by 0.5 percent for FY 2001 and by 0.75 percent for FY 2002. Medicare reimburses teaching hospitals for their role in providing graduate medical education (GME). Prior to BBA, Medicare's indirect medical education adjustment (IME) payments increased 7.7 percent for each 10 percent increase in a hospital's ratio of interns and residents to beds. BBA decreased the adjustment to 6.5 percent in FY 1999, 6.0 percent in FY 2000, and 5.5 percent in FY 2001 and subsequent years. BBRA froze the IME adjustment at 6.5 percent through FY 2000; reduced it to 6.25 percent in FY 2001, and to 5.5 percent in FY 2002 and subsequent years.

P.L. 106-117, the *Veterans Millennium Health Care and Benefits Act*, directs the Secretary of Veterans Affairs, through December 31, 2003, to provide nursing home care to any veteran in need of such care: (1) for a service-connected disability; or (2) who has a service-connected disability rated at 70 percent or more. The law prohibits a veteran receiving such care from being transferred from the providing facility without the consent of the veteran or his or her representative. It also directs the Secretary to operate and maintain a program to provide the following extended care services to eligible veterans: (1) geriatric evaluation; (2) nursing home care, either in facilities of the Department of Veterans Affairs or in community-based facilities; (3) domiciliary services; (4) adult day health care; (5) noninstitutional alternatives to nursing home care; and (6) respite care. The law has a provision that prohibits the Secretary from furnishing such services for a non-service-connected disability unless the veteran agrees to make a copayment for services of more than 21 days in a year and requires the Secretary to establish a methodology for establishing the copayment amount.

2000

P.L. 106-354, the *Breast and Cervical Cancer Prevention and Treatment Act*, amends title XIX (Medicaid) of the Social Security Act to give states the option of making medical assistance for breast and cervical cancer-related treatment services available during a presumptive eligibility period to certain low-income women who have already been screened for such cancers under the Centers for Disease Control and Prevention breast and cervical cancer early detection program. The law also provides for an enhanced match of federal funds to help states pay for these treatment services through their Medicaid programs.

P.L. 106-430, the *Needlestick Safety and Prevention Act*, revised the bloodborne pathogens standard in effect under the Occupational Safety and Health Act of 1970 to include safer medical devices, such as sharps with engineered sharps injury protections and needleless systems, as examples of engineering controls designed to eliminate or minimize occupational exposure to bloodborne pathogens through needlestick injuries. Other provisions require certain employers to: (1) review and update exposure control plans to reflect changes in technology that eliminate or reduce such exposure, and document their consideration and implementation of appropriate commercially available and effective safer medical devices for such purpose; (2) maintain a sharps injury log, noting the type and brand of device used, where the injury occurred, and an explanation of the incident (exempting employers who are not required to maintain specified OSHA logs); and (3) seek input on such engineering and work practice controls from the affected healthcare workers.

P.L. 106-525, the *Minority Health and Health Disparities Research and Education Act*, amends the Public Health Service Act to establish within the National Institutes of Health (NIH) the National Center on Minority and Health Disparities to conduct and support research, training, dissemination of information, and other programs with respect to minority health conditions and other populations with health disparities. This law requires the Center Director, in expending funds, to give priority to conducting and supporting minority health disparities research (research on minority health conditions, including research to prevent, diagnose, and treat such conditions). It also requires coordination of Center research with other health disparities research conducted or supported by the NIH, and requires the Center Director, the NIH Director, and the directors of all other agencies of the NIH to, among other things, establish a comprehensive plan and budget for the conduct and support of all minority health and other health disparities research activities of the agencies of the NIH. The law also has a provision requiring the directors to work together to carry out provisions of the Act relating to participation by minority groups in clinical research.

P.L. 106-554, the *Medicare, Medicaid, and SCHIP Benefits Improvement and Protection Act of 2000 (BIPA)*. This legislation changed numerous provisions previously enacted in BBA and BBRA. Among the important changes were:

- an increase of 3.4 percent for Medicare inpatient payments in Fiscal Year 2001, and an estimated 3.5 percent in FY 2002
- an increase of 4.4 percent in Medicare outpatient payments in 2001
- indirect medical education (IME) payments at 6.5 percent in FY 2001 and FY 2002
- elimination of the additional one percent cut in Medicare disproportionate share hospital (DSH) payments in FY 2001 and 2002
- an increase, from 55 to 70 percent, in Medicare payments for bad debt
- an increase for the direct graduate medical education (GME) payment floor to 85 percent of the national average
- elimination of the BBA's FY 2001 and 2002 Medicaid DSH cut
- removal of the 2 percent payment reduction for rehabilitation hospitals in FY 2001
- a 3.2 percent increase in skilled nursing service payments in FY 2001
- a one-year delay of the 15 percent reduction for home health, and the full market basket in FY 2001
- an increase of 2 percent in incentive payments for psychiatric hospitals/units
- expansion of Medicare payment for telehealth services to rural areas

P.L. 106-580, the *National Institute of Biomedical Imaging and Bioengineering Establishment Act*, amends the Public Health Service Act to provide for the establishment of the National Institute of Biomedical Imaging and Bioengineering. The law requires the Director of the Institute to establish a National Biomedical Imaging and Bioengineering Program which includes research and related technology assessments and development in biomedical imaging and bioengineering. It also requires the Director to prepare and transmit to the Secretary of DHHS and the Director of the National Institutes of Health (NIH) a plan to initiate, expand, intensify, and coordinate Institute biomedical imaging and bioengineering activities. It requires: (1) the consolidation and coordination of Institute biomedical imaging and bioengineering research and related activities with those of the NIH and other federal agencies; and (2) the establishment of an Institute advisory council.

2001

P.L. 107-9, the *Animal Disease Risk Assessment, Prevention, and Control Act*, directs the Secretary of Agriculture to submit a preliminary report to specified congressional committees concerning: (1) interagency measures to assess, prevent, and control the spread of foot and mouth disease and bovine spongiform encephalopathy ("mad cow disease") in the United States; (2) related federal information sources available to the public; and (3) the need for any additional legislative authority or product bans. The law directs the Secretary, in consultation with governmental and private-sector parties, to submit a final report to such committees that discusses such diseases' economic impacts, public and animal health risks, and related legislative, federal agency, and product recommendations.

P.L. 107–38, the *Emergency Supplemental Appropriations Act for Recovery from and Response to Terrorist Attacks on the United States*, makes emergency supplemental appropriations for FY 2001 for emergency expenses to respond to the terrorist attacks on the United States on September 11, 2001, to provide assistance to the victims, and to deal with other consequences of the attacks. The law makes $40 billion available to the Executive Office of the President and Funds Appropriated to the President for the Emergency Response Fund for such expenses as (1) providing federal, state, and local preparedness for mitigating and responding to the attacks; (2) providing support to counter, investigate, or prosecute domestic or international terrorism; (3) providing increased transportation security; (4) repairing damaged public facilities and transportation systems; and (5) supporting national security.

Notes

1. The Library of Congress maintains a web site (thomas.loc.gov), on which extensive information on federal legislation is provided. This is an excellent source of additional information on public laws that pertain to health. Information about public laws can also be accessed through (www.firstgov.gov), the official United States Government web site, or through (www.access.gpo.gov), a site maintained by the Government Printing Office.

2. Reflecting the convention adopted by the Congress, acts began to be referred to by their public law numbers. These numbers reflect both the number of the enacting Congress and the sequence in which the laws are enacted. For example, Public Law (P.L.) 57-244 means the 244th law passed by the 57th Congress. Hereafter, the public law numbers of health-related federal laws in this chronology are provided.

INDEX

ABOUT THE AUTHOR

Beaufort B. Longest, Jr., is the M. Allen Pond Professor of Health Policy & Management in the Graduate School of Public Health and the founding director of the Health Policy Institute at the University of Pittsburgh. Previously, he was on the faculties of Georgia State University and the Kellogg Graduate School of Management at Northwestern University.

He received an undergraduate education at Davidson College and received the Master of Health Administration (MHA) and Ph.D. degrees from Georgia State University. He is a Fellow of the American College of Healthcare Executives and holds memberships in the Academy of Management, Academy for Health Services Research and Health Policy, American Public Health Association, and the Association for Public Policy Analysis and Management. He has the unusual distinction of having been elected to membership in the Beta Gamma Sigma Honor Society in Business as well as in the Delta Omega Honor Society in Public Health.

His research on issues of health policy and management has generated substantial grant support and has led to the publication of numerous peer-reviewed articles. In addition, he has authored or coauthored nine books and 22 chapters in other books. He is coauthor of *Managing Health Services Organizations and Systems*, one of the most widely used textbooks in graduate health policy and management programs. He consults with healthcare organizations and systems, universities, associations, and government agencies on health policy and management issues.